Your Personal
HOROSCOPE
—2010—

Your Personal
HOROSCOPE
—— 2010 ——

*The only one-volume horoscope
you'll ever need*

Joseph Polansky

The author is grateful to the people
of STAR ★ DATA, who truly fathered
this book and without whom it
could not have been written.

HarperElement
An Imprint of HarperCollins*Publishers*
77–85 Fulham Palace Road,
Hammersmith, London W6 8JB
www.harpercollins.co.uk

and *HarperElement* are trademarks of
HarperCollins*Publishers* Ltd

Published by HarperElement 2010

3

© Star ★ Data, Inc. 2010

Star ★ Data assert the moral right to
be identified as the authors of this work

A catalogue record for this book is
available from the British Library

ISBN 978-0-00-728147-3

Printed and bound in Great Britain by
Clays Ltd, St Ives plc

Mixed Sources
Product group from well-managed
forests and other controlled sources
www.fsc.org Cert no. SW-COC-1806
© 1996 Forest Stewardship Council

FSC is a non-profit international organisation established to promote the
responsible management of the world's forests. Products carrying the FSC
label are independently certified to assure consumers that they come
from forests that are managed to meet the social, economic and
ecological needs of present or future generations.

Find out more about HarperCollins and the environment at
www.harpercollins.co.uk/green

Contents

Introduction

Welcome to the fascinating and intricate world of astrology!

For thousands of years the movements of the planets and other heavenly bodies have intrigued the best minds of every generation. Life holds no greater challenge or joy than this: knowledge of ourselves and the universe we live in. Astrology is one of the keys to this knowledge.

Your Personal Horoscope 2010 gives you the fruits of astrological wisdom. In addition to general guidance on your character and the basic trends of your life, it shows you how to take advantage of planetary influences so you can make the most of the year ahead.

The section on each sign includes a Personality Profile, a look at general trends for 2010, and in-depth month-by-month forecasts. The Glossary (*page 3*) explains some of the astrological terms you may be unfamiliar with.

One of the many helpful features of this book is the 'Best' and 'Most Stressful' days listed at the beginning of each monthly forecast. Read these sections to learn which days in each month will be good overall, good for money, and good for love. Mark them on your calendar – these will be your best days. Similarly, make a note of the days that will be most stressful for you. It is best to avoid taking important meetings or major decisions on these days, as well as on those days when important planets in your horoscope are retrograde (moving backwards through the zodiac).

The Major Trends section for your sign lists those days when your vitality is strong or weak, or when relationships with your co-workers or loved ones may need a bit more effort on your part. If you are going through a difficult time, take a look at the colour, metal, gem and scent listed in the 'At a Glance' section of your Personality Profile. Wearing a piece of jewellery that contains your metal and/or gem will strengthen your vitality; just as wearing clothes or decorating your room or office in the colour ruled by your sign, drinking teas made from the herbs ruled by your sign or wearing the scents associated with your sign will sustain you.

Another important virtue of this book is that it will help you to know not only yourself but those around you: your friends, co-workers, partners and/or children. Reading the Personality Profile and forecasts for their signs will provide you with an insight into their behaviour that you won't get anywhere else. You will know when to be more tolerant of them and when they are liable to be difficult or irritable.

In this edition we have included foot reflexology charts as part of the health section. So many health problems could perhaps be avoided or alleviated if we understood which organs were most vulnerable and what we could do to protect them. Though there are many natural and drug-free ways to strengthen vulnerable organs, these charts show a valid way to proceed. The vulnerable organs for the year ahead are clearly marked in the chart. It's very good to massage the whole foot on a regular basis, as the feet contain reflexes to the entire body. Try to pay special attention to the specific areas marked in the chart. If this is done diligently, health problems can be avoided. And even if they can't be completely avoided, their impact can be softened considerably.

I consider you – the reader – my personal client. By studying your Solar Horoscope I gain an awareness of what is going on in your life – what you are feeling and striving for and the challenges you face. I then do my best to address these concerns. Consider this book the next best thing to having your own personal astrologer!

It is my sincere hope that *Your Personal Horoscope 2010* will enhance the quality of your life, make things easier, illuminate the way forward, banish obscurities and make you more aware of your personal connection to the universe. Understood properly and used wisely, astrology is a great guide to knowing yourself, the people around you and the events in your life – but remember that what you do with these insights – the final result – is up to you.

Glossary of Astrological Terms

Ascendant

We experience day and night because the Earth rotates on its axis once every 24 hours. It is because of this rotation that the Sun, Moon and planets seem to rise and set. The zodiac is a fixed belt (imaginary, but very real in spiritual terms) around the Earth. As the Earth rotates, the different signs of the zodiac seem to the observer to rise on the horizon. During a 24-hour period every sign of the zodiac will pass this horizon point at some time or another. The sign that is at the horizon point at any given time is called the Ascendant, or rising sign. The Ascendant is the sign denoting a person's self-image, body and self-concept – the personal ego, as opposed to the spiritual ego indicated by a person's Sun sign.

Aspects

Aspects are the angular relationships between planets, the way in which one planet stimulates or influences another. If a planet makes a harmonious aspect (connection) to another, it tends to stimulate that planet in a positive and helpful way. If it makes a stressful aspect to another planet, this disrupts the planet's normal influence.

Astrological Qualities

There are three astrological qualities: *cardinal*, *fixed* and *mutable*. Each of the 12 signs of the zodiac falls into one of these three categories.

Cardinal Signs	Aries, Cancer, Libra and Capricorn The cardinal quality is the active, initiating principle. Those born under these four Signs are good at starting new projects.
Fixed Signs	Taurus, Leo, Scorpio and Aquarius Fixed qualities include stability, persistence, endurance and perfectionism. People born under these four Signs are good at seeing things through.
Mutable Signs	Gemini, Virgo, Sagittarius and Pisces Mutable qualities are adaptability, changeability and balance. Those born under these four Signs are creative, if not always practical.

Direct Motion

When the planets move forward through the zodiac – as they normally do – they are said to be going 'direct'.

Grand Trine

A Grand Trine differs from a normal Trine (where two planets are 120 degrees apart) in that three or more planets are involved. When you look at this pattern in a chart, it takes the form of a complete triangle – a Grand Trine. Usually (but not always) it occurs in one of the four elements: Fire, Earth, Air or Water. Thus the particular element in which it occurs will be highlighted. A Grand Trine in Water is not the same as a Grand Trine in Air or Fire, etc. This is a very fortunate and happy aspect, and quite rare.

Grand Square

A Grand Square differs from a normal Square (usually two planets separated by 90 degrees) in that four or more planets are involved. When you look at the pattern in a chart you will see a whole and complete square. This, though stressful, usually denotes a new manifestation in the life. There is much work and balancing involved in the manifestation.

Houses

There are 12 signs of the zodiac and 12 houses of experience. The 12 signs are personality types and ways in which a given planet expresses itself; the 12 houses show 'where' in your life this expression takes place. Each house has a different area of interest. A house can become potent and important – a House of Power – in different ways: if it contains the Sun, the Moon or the 'ruler' of your chart, if it contains more than one planet, or if the ruler of that house is receiving unusual stimulation from other planets.

1st House	Personal Image and Sensual Delights
2nd House	Money/Finance
3rd House	Communication and Intellectual Interests
4th House	Home and Family
5th House	Children, Fun, Games, Creativity, Speculations and Love Affairs
6th House	Health and Work
7th House	Love, Marriage and Social Activities
8th House	Transformation and Regeneration
9th House	Religion, Foreign Travel, Higher Education and Philosophy
10th House	Career
11th House	Friends, Group Activities and Fondest Wishes
12th House	Spirituality

Karma

Karma is the law of cause and effect which governs all phenomena. We are all where we find ourselves because of karma – because of actions we have performed in the past. The universe is such a balanced instrument that any act immediately sets corrective forces into motion – karma.

Long-term Planets

The planets that take a long time to move through a sign show the long-term trends in a given area of life. They are important for forecasting the prolonged view of things. Because these planets stay in one sign for so long, there are periods in the year when the faster-moving (short-term) planets will join them, further activating and enhancing the importance of a given house.

Jupiter	stays in a Sign for about 1 year
Saturn	2½ years
Uranus	7 years
Neptune	14 years
Pluto	15 to 30 years

Lunar

Relating to the Moon. See also 'Phases of the Moon', page 8.

Natal

Literally means 'birth'. In astrology this term is used to distinguish between planetary positions that occurred at the time of a person's birth (natal) and those that are current (transiting). For example, Natal Sun refers to where the Sun was when you were born; transiting Sun refers to where the Sun's position is currently at any given moment – which usually doesn't coincide with your birth, or Natal, Sun.

Out of Bounds

The planets move through the zodiac at various angles relative to the celestial equator (if you were to draw an imaginary extension of the Earth's equator out into the universe, you would have an illustration of this celestial equator). The Sun – being the most dominant and powerful influence in the Solar system – is the measure astrologers use as a standard. The Sun never goes more than approximately 23 degrees north or south of the celestial equator. At the winter solstice the Sun reaches its maximum southern angle of orbit (declination); at the summer solstice it reaches its maximum northern angle. Any time a planet exceeds this Solar boundary – and occasionally planets do – it is said to be 'out of bounds'. This means that the planet exceeds or trespasses into strange territory – beyond the limits allowed by the Sun, the Ruler of the Solar system. The planet in this condition becomes more emphasized and exceeds its authority, becoming an important influence in the forecast.

Phases of the Moon

After the full Moon, the Moon seems to shrink in size (as perceived from the Earth), gradually growing smaller until it is virtually invisible to the naked eye – at the time of the next new Moon. This is called the waning Moon phase, or the waning Moon.

After the new Moon, the Moon gradually gets bigger in size (as perceived from the Earth) until it reaches its maximum size at the time of the full Moon. This period is called the waxing Moon phase, or waxing Moon.

Retrogrades

The planets move around the Sun at different speeds. Mercury and Venus move much faster than the Earth, while Mars, Jupiter, Saturn, Uranus, Neptune and Pluto move more slowly. Thus there are times when, relative to the Earth, the planets appear to be going backwards. In reality they are always going forward, but relative to our vantage point on Earth they seem to go backwards through the zodiac for a period of time. This is called 'retrograde' motion and tends to weaken the normal influence of a given planet.

Short-term Planets

The fast-moving planets move so quickly through a sign that their effects are generally of a short-term nature. They reflect the immediate, day-to-day trends in a horoscope.

Moon	stays in a Sign for only 2½ days
Mercury	20 to 30 days
Sun	30 days
Venus	approximately 1 month
Mars	approximately 2 months

T-square

A T-square differs from a Grand Square in that it is not a complete square. If you look at the pattern in a chart it appears as 'half a complete square', resembling the T-square tools used by architects and designers. If you cut a complete square in half, diagonally, you have a T-square. Many astrologers consider this more stressful than a Grand Square, as it creates tension that is difficult to resolve. T-squares bring learning experiences.

Transits

This refers to the movements or motions of the planets at any given time. Astrologers use the word 'transit' to make the distinction between a birth or Natal planet (see 'Natal', page 7) and the planet's current movement in the heavens. For example, if at your birth Saturn was in the sign of Cancer in your 8th house, but is now moving through your 3rd house, it is said to be 'transiting' your 3rd house. Transits are one of the main tools with which astrologers forecast trends.

Aries

♈

Personality Profile

ARIES AT A GLANCE

Element – Fire

Ruling Planet – Mars
  Career Planet – Saturn
  Love Planet – Venus
  Money Planet – Venus
  *Planet of Fun, Entertainment, Creativity and
    Speculations* – Sun
  Planet of Health and Work – Mercury
  Planet of Home and Family Life – Moon
  Planet of Spirituality – Neptune
  *Planet of Travel, Education, Religion and
    Philosophy* – Jupiter

Colours – carmine, red, scarlet

*Colours that promote love, romance and social
  harmony* – green, jade green

Colour that promotes earning power – green

Gem – amethyst

Metals – iron, steel

Scent – honeysuckle

Quality – cardinal (= activity)

Quality most needed for balance – caution

Strongest virtues – abundant physical energy, courage, honesty, independence, self-reliance

Deepest need – action

Characteristics to avoid – haste, impetuousness, over-aggression, rashness

Signs of greatest overall compatibility – Leo, Sagittarius

Signs of greatest overall incompatibility – Cancer, Libra, Capricorn

Sign most helpful to career – Capricorn

Sign most helpful for emotional support – Cancer

Sign most helpful financially – Taurus

Sign best for marriage and/or partnerships – Libra

Sign most helpful for creative projects – Leo

Best Sign to have fun with – Leo

Signs most helpful in spiritual matters – Sagittarius, Pisces

Best day of the week – Tuesday

Understanding an Aries

Aries is the activist *par excellence* of the zodiac. The Aries need for action is almost an addiction, and those who do not really understand the Aries personality would probably use this hard word to describe it. In reality 'action' is the essence of the Aries psychology – the more direct, blunt and to-the-point the action, the better. When you think about it, this is the ideal psychological makeup for the warrior, the pioneer, the athlete or the manager.

Aries likes to get things done, and in their passion and zeal often lose sight of the consequences for themselves and others. Yes, they often try to be diplomatic and tactful, but it is hard for them. When they do so they feel that they are being dishonest and phony. It is hard for them even to understand the mindset of the diplomat, the consensus builder, the front office executive. These people are involved in endless meetings, discussions, talks and negotiations – all of which seem a great waste of time when there is so much work to be done, so many real achievements to be gained. An Aries can understand, once it is explained, that talks and negotiations – the social graces – lead ultimately to better, more effective actions. The interesting thing is that an Aries is rarely malicious or spiteful – even when waging war. Aries people fight without hate for their opponents. To them it is all good-natured fun, a grand adventure, a game.

When confronted with a problem many people will say 'Well, let's think about it, let's analyse the situation.' But not an Aries. An Aries will think 'Something must be done. Let's get on with it.' Of course neither response is the total answer. Sometimes action is called for, sometimes cool thought. But an Aries tends to err on the side of action.

Action and thought are radically different principles. Physical activity is the use of brute force. Thinking and deliberating require one not to use force – to be still. It is not good for the athlete to be deliberating the next move; this will only slow down his or her reaction time. The athlete must act instinctively and instantly. This is how Aries people tend to behave in life. They are quick, instinctive decision-makers and their decisions tend to be translated into action almost immediately. When their intuition is sharp and well tuned, their actions are powerful and successful. When their intuition is off, their actions can be disastrous.

Do not think this will scare an Aries. Just as a good warrior knows that in the course of combat he or she might acquire a few wounds, so too does an Aries realize – somewhere deep down – that in the course of being true to yourself you might get embroiled in a disaster or two. It is all part of the game. An Aries feels strong enough to weather any storm.

There are many Aries people who are intellectual. They make powerful and creative thinkers. But even in this realm they tend to be pioneers – outspoken and blunt. These types of Aries tend to elevate (or sublimate) their desire for physical combat in favour of intellectual, mental combat. And they are indeed powerful.

In general, Aries people have a faith in themselves that others could learn from. This basic, rock-bottom faith carries them through the most tumultuous situations of life. Their courage and self-confidence make them natural leaders. Their leadership is more by way of example than by actually controlling others.

Finance

Aries people often excel as builders or estate agents. Money in and of itself is not as important as are other things – action, adventure, sport, etc. They are motivated by the need to support and be well-thought-of by their partners. Money as a way of attaining pleasure is another important motivation. An Aries functions best in their own businesses or as manager of their own departments within a large business or corporation. The fewer orders they have to take from higher up, the better. They also function better out in the field rather than behind a desk.

Aries people are hard workers with a lot of endurance; they can earn large sums of money due to the strength of their sheer physical energy.

Venus is their money planet, which means that Aries need to develop more of the social graces in order to realize their full earning potential. Just getting the job done – which is what an Aries excels at – is not enough to create financial success. The co-operation of others needs to be attained. Customers, clients and co-workers need to be made to feel comfortable; many people need to be treated properly in order for success to happen. When Aries people develop these abilities – or hire someone to do this for them – their financial potential is unlimited.

Career and Public Image

One would think that a pioneering type would want to break with the social and political conventions of society. But this is not so with the Aries-born. They are pioneers within conventional limits, in the sense that they like to start their own businesses within an established industry.

Capricorn is on the 10th house (career) cusp of Aries' solar horoscope. Saturn is the planet that rules their life's work and professional aspirations. This tells us some interesting things about the Aries character. First off, it shows that, in order for Aries people to reach their full career potential, they need to develop some qualities that are a bit alien to their basic nature: They need to become better administrators and organizers; they need to be able to handle details better and to take a long-range view of their projects and their careers in general. No one can beat an Aries when it comes to achieving short-range objectives, but a career is long term, built over time. You cannot take a 'quickie' approach to it.

Some Aries people find it difficult to stick with a project until the end. Since they get bored quickly and are in constant pursuit of new adventures, they prefer to pass an old project or task on to somebody else in order to start something new. Those Aries who learn how to put off the search for something new until the old is completed will achieve great success in their careers and professional lives.

In general, Aries people like society to judge them on their own merits, on their real and actual achievements. A reputation acquired by 'hype' feels false to them.

Love and Relationships

In marriage and partnerships Aries like those who are more passive, gentle, tactful and diplomatic – people who have the social grace and skills they sometimes lack. Our partners always represent a hidden part of ourselves – a self that we cannot express personally.

An Aries tends to go after what he or she likes aggressively. The tendency is to jump into relationships and marriages. This is especially true if Venus is in Aries as well as the Sun. If an Aries likes you, he or she will have a hard time taking no for an answer; many attempts will be made to sweep you off your feet.

Though Aries can be exasperating in relationships – especially if they are not understood by their partners – they are never consciously or wilfully cruel or malicious. It is just that they are so independent and sure of themselves that they find it almost impossible to see somebody else's viewpoint or position. This is why an Aries needs as a partner someone with lots of social grace.

On the plus side, an Aries is honest, someone you can lean on, someone with whom you will always know where you stand. What he or she lacks in diplomacy is made up for in integrity.

Home and Domestic Life

An Aries is of course the ruler at home – the Boss. The male will tend to delegate domestic matters to the female. The female Aries will want to rule the roost. Both tend to be handy round the house. Both like large families and both believe in the sanctity and importance of the family. An Aries is a good family person, although he or she does not especially like being at home a lot, preferring instead to be roaming about.

Considering that they are by nature so combative and wilful, Aries people can be surprisingly soft, gentle and even vulnerable with their children and partners. The sign of Cancer, ruled by the Moon, is on the cusp of their solar 4th house (home and family). When the Moon is well aspected – under favourable influences – in the birth chart an Aries will be tender towards the family and want a family life that is nurturing and supportive. Aries likes to come home after a hard day on the battlefield of life to the understanding arms of their partner and the unconditional love and support of their family. An Aries feels that there is enough 'war' out in the world – and he or she enjoys participating in that. But when Aries comes home, comfort and nurturing are what's needed.

Horoscope for 2010

Major Trends

In 2009 two major long-term planets – Saturn and Pluto – moved into a stressful alignment with you. This should not be taken lightly, as these planets are formidable and will test your mettle for the next 2 years. (It will be a lot easier for you in 2 years' time.) You are in a period of character building. A period for gaining strength and for building up your spiritual and mental muscles. Rest assured, the cosmos – which is always loving and just – will not give you more than you can bear. It might push you to the edge, but never over the edge.

Yes, you will be working harder. Yes, your overall energy will not be up to its usual standards (we will discuss this further in the Health section, page 19). Yes, you will feel like you are walking uphill with the wind blowing in your face. But if you don't give up, if you reach into your inner reservoirs of strength, many blessings will come. You will learn the art of alchemy – the art of taking negatives and transforming them into positives. You will develop endurance and courage. You will learn to perform well under pressure. And when the difficult period ends, you will be oh-so-much stronger and more confident.

Last year was a strong social year – but more in the nature of friendships. This area is still strong, but not as much as last year. Romance and marriages were getting tested last year, and this trend continues in the year ahead. The cosmos is going to put your social life into the 'right order' and sometimes it uses dramatic means. More on this later.

Spirituality was important last year, and this year it will become even more important – as Jupiter will move through your 12th house of spirituality in the year ahead.

Both Jupiter and Uranus will move into your sign for brief periods in the year ahead – this is a major headline. These are slow-moving planets. The last time Uranus was in Aries was approximately 88 years ago (most of you have never experienced this energy in this lifetime). The last time Jupiter was in Aries was 12 years ago. While these movements are not the 'full-blown' transit (this will happen in 2011), they are announcements of things to come – and they are good announcements. You are getting ready for tremendous freedom and financial abundance – and it can happen very suddenly. The very pressures on you, which seem so onerous and burdensome, will lead you to a greater freedom. (Those of you born early in the sign of Aries – between March 20th and 24th – will feel this transit most keenly.)

Last year Pluto moved into your 10th house of career for good (in 2008 he merely flirted with your 10th house). Pluto is now there for at least another 15 years. So your career is being 'detoxed' – purified of effete attitudes and mis-thinking. More on this later.

Your areas of greatest interest in 2010 are spirituality, children, creativity and fun (until June 7th), health and work (from April 8th to July 22nd), love and marriage (from January 1st to April 8th and from July 22nd onwards), career, and friendships and group activities.

Your paths of greatest fulfilment are spirituality and career.

Health

(Please note that this is an astrological perspective on health and not a medical one. In days gone by there was no difference; these perspectives were identical. But nowadays there can be quite a difference. For the medical perspective, please consult your doctor or health practitioner.)

Health definitely needs watching this year, Aries. As mentioned, two strong planets are in stressful alignment with you most of the year (you do get a little break from April 8th to July 22nd). So, you need to watch your energy. This is the most important thing. Avoid burning the candle at both ends. Rest when tired. Work rhythmically and alternate activities. Wear the gems, metals and aromas of your sign. Try to organize your day so that more gets done with less energy. Delegate tasks where possible. Keep your focus on the essential things in your life and let lesser things go. (This will involve tough choices, but you will have to make them.)

Take a business-like approach to your energy. It is precious. You want to invest it where it will give you the maximum return. You certainly don't want to waste it on frivolities.

When our health is stressed, it doesn't mean that sickness has to happen. It only means that more time, energy and attention need to be devoted to health. The danger this year (especially until April 8th and from July 22nd onwards) is that you will ignore things. Your 6th house of health is not strong for most of the year. You will have to motivate yourself – force yourself – to pay more attention to your health even when you don't feel like it.

The good news is that there is much you can do to enhance your health and prevent problems from developing.

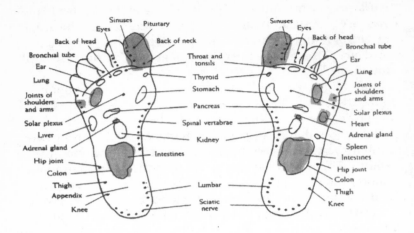

Reflexology

Try to massage the whole foot on a regular basis, but pay extra attention to the points highlighted on the chart. When you massage, be aware of 'sore spots', as these need special attention. It's also a good idea to massage the ankles and top side (as well as the soles) of the feet.

Pay more attention to your heart, arms, shoulders, head, and small intestine. There are many, many natural ways to strengthen these; I'm sure you know about them. However, some of you might want to work with the reflexology chart above.

Arms and shoulders should be regularly massaged. A scalp and face massage is generally very powerful for you, as the sign of Aries rules the head and the face. Therapies such as cranial sacral therapy, which deals with the alignment of the skull bones (ruled by Aries) are also favoured.

Saturn, which rules the back, spine, knees, teeth, bones, gallbladder and overall skeletal alignment, will be in your 6th house of health from April 8th to July 22nd. During this period, pay more attention to these parts of the body. Give more support to your knees when exercising. Regular visits to a chiropractor might be a good idea. Regular back massage would be powerful then, too.

There are certain periods this year where your health is even more stressed than usual – these are from January 1st to 20th, June 21st to July 23rd, September 23rd to October 23rd, and December 7th to 31st. These are periods to slow down and spend more time focusing on your health.

Kali phosphate and Kali sulphate are powerful homoeopathic remedies. The Ram, the Dog and the Pigeon are healing power animals – their medicine is beneficial.

Since your health planet, Mercury, is a fast-moving planet, there will be many short-term trends affecting your health. These will be discussed in the month-by-month reports.

If you mind your energy and follow the guidelines given, you should go through the year ahead with flying colours.

Home and Family

Your 4th house of home and family is not a House of Power this year. Thus you have more freedom and latitude to shape this area of life as you wish. The cosmos is not pushing you one way or the other. Generally, though, this alignment tends to indicate a status-quo kind of year.

However, this year there are two eclipses in your 4th house. This spells change. Also keep in mind that the Moon, your family planet, will get eclipsed twice this year as well. This needn't mean a move. Often it just shows that hidden flaws in the home (and in the family and domestic relationship) are revealed so that they can be corrected.

Those of you born early in the sign of Aries (March 20th–23rd) can easily experience house moves – perhaps a few of them. This is because Uranus makes a brief visit to your sign from May 28th to August 14th. This is a rare transit. Most of you have never experienced anything like this – the last time it happened was 85–88 years ago! I wouldn't be surprised if you move (or live) in a foreign country during this period. In many cases it will indicate a 'vagabond' kind of existence – living in different places for various periods of time – even though you still have an 'official' address. Those of you born later in the sign will merely feel the 'urge' to wander. But this transit is an announcement of things to come in 2011 and beyond.

Parents or parent figures are contemplating moves – but there are many delays involved. Children of appropriate age are having a status quo domestic year. Siblings probably should not move – though they are sorely tempted. They are better off making better use of the space that they have presently. Also, the cosmos is pushing them to reorganize and re-order their present domestic life.

Grandchildren are likely to move this year (especially for those of you born early in the sign of Aries).

Your spouse, partner or current love wants to make major renovations in the home, but you seem cool about it. If you are looking to beautify your home – i.e. repaint, redecorate, buy art objects and the like – May 20th to June 14th is a good time.

Parents or parent figures are contemplating cosmetic-type surgeries. What they really want is to 'transform' and 'reinvent' their body and image, and there are various non-surgical ways to do this. Many of them will opt for these ways, too. Children are also contemplating surgery – but not the cosmetic kind. Siblings need to mind their health more. Your spouse or partner benefits from alternative, experimental therapies – they have good luck with these things. But most importantly, they need to watch their energy – keep energy levels high – and avoid depression.

Finance and Career

Your 2nd house of finance is not a House of Power this year. Thus, most of you seem satisfied with things as they are and have no need to make major changes. Your financial life doesn't need special attention. It's a status-quo kind of a year.

For those of you born early in the sign of Aries (March 20th–23rd) it is a different story. Two powerful planets – Uranus and Jupiter – visit you briefly this year. Uranus will come into your sign from May 28th to August 14th; Jupiter will be in your sign from June 6th to September 10th. A very exciting period – and prosperous, too. The heavens are opening up to you and revealing riches and possibilities beyond your imagination. Your limitations get broken. A new freedom allows for new riches. While this is not the full-blown transit of these planets – these are announcements of things to come. You are being prepared for new freedom and new riches in 2011 and beyond (and this is true for all of you Aries). Your whole financial picture will change with the speed of lightning. You can be wallowing in problems or feel that you are stuck in a rut – and bam! – you are out. A friend, an acquaintance, an opportunity in a foreign land or events in foreign lands change the picture and produce opportunities.

Jupiter and Uranus travelling together is read by astrologers as 'sudden wealth' – and this will happen for those of you born early in the sign. Those of you born later in the sign will experience this in coming years. Sudden wealth is a wonderful thing, but needs to be handled just so – for it tends to be unstable. One should set aside earnings into stable investments. When we say 'sudden wealth' we don't mean that all of you will become millionaires (though many of you will, and some will even become billionaires). We mean that you attain your own 'standard' of wealth suddenly. For some this might mean a pay rise of X amount. For others a specified sum. For others a certain kind of lifestyle. But your net worth will increase 'suddenly'.

There are lessons to be learned from poverty, and lessons to be gleaned from wealth. It is said in various scriptures that one needs to know how to live with both. Now – and in 2011 – you will be learning the lessons of wealth.

Venus is your financial planet and she is a fast-moving planet. During the year she will move through all the signs and houses of your horoscope. Thus money and financial opportunities will come to you in a variety of ways and through a variety of people and conditions. These short-term trends are best dealt with in the month-by-month reports.

There are career changes happening this year – especially for those of you born early in the sign. Those of you born later, after March 26th, will experience these changes in future years – but all is being prepared. Your whole corporate hierarchy (and industry) is undergoing deep and fundamental change and this will open up opportunities for you. The barriers to advancement are being blown away. Your own attitudes to career and success are also getting purified. Non-helpful attitudes (perhaps unconscious) will go, and this will be very helpful to you. Many of you are doing deep re-thinking about your entire career path.

Your career planet shifts between two signs this year (like last year). It begins the year in the sign of Libra, then it moves into Virgo (where it has been for the past 2 years) from April 8th to July 22nd, and then moves back into Libra after July 22nd and for the next 2 years or so. While your career planet is in Libra (January 1st to April 8th and July 22nd to December 31st) you advance your career by 'soft' methods – through social means, through attending or hosting the right parties and gatherings, through making friends in the right places and, in some cases, through marriages, alliances and joint ventures. While Saturn is in Virgo you advance your career the old-fashioned way: through sheer hard work.

Your career planet shifting signs also shows that bosses and superiors value different things this year. Sometimes they value the work ethic – that becomes for them the paramount virtue. But other times they value 'likeability' – social grace, the ability to get on with others – more than merely 'hard work'. You need to be prepared for this shift.

Love and Social Life

When Saturn first moved into Libra (October 29th, 2009) it signalled a testing of current love relationships – marriages and partnerships. This doesn't mean that they had to fail – though many have failed. It only means that great stress was put on these relationships – in the same way a car manufacturer puts unusual stress on a new design – to ferret out weaknesses and flaws and to determine how much stress and rough handling the vehicle can take. For basically sound relationships – where the fundamentals are good – these testings can be very valuable and lead to a more enduring and deeper relationship. For we never really know the depth of our love for or commitment to someone when 'times are good' – when the sun is shining and the roses are blooming. It is during the tough times – the storms of life – that we learn of our love. Does he or she really love me? How much? How deeply? These are the questions that are getting answered now.

For relationships that were not fundamentally sound – that only survived because of fair weather or convenience – this transit signals the end. It is doubtful whether they can survive the tests.

Either way, the end result is good. It is good that a fundamentally flawed relationship ends – this leaves both parties free to find a more perfect relationship.

This testing process continues in the year ahead. There is a brief respite from April 8th to July 22nd (as Saturn moves out of the 7th house and back into the 6th) but then it resumes again from July 22nd onwards.

Last year was a great social year – especially in regard to friendships. This year, those friendships will also get tested.

But Saturn moving through your house of love and marriage also gives us other messages. It shows that you are mixing with people – socially and romantically – who are above you in status, the high and the mighty, people of power, prestige and position. For singles this is a classic aspect of the 'office romance' – romance with the boss or a superior.

Love attitudes this year are practical. Singles are looking for the good provider, the settled and stable relationship, the person who can boost their career. In many cultures this aspect would indicate an arranged marriage. Our common notions of 'romance' are not shared by many cultures – they see it as an illusion and delusion. And many of you are feeling this way these days. Never mind passion – marriage or a relationship is a job, a career move, like any other. One can learn to love anyone, so one might as well learn to love the person who can help in practical ways.

Often these aspects show a marriage of convenience – this is especially so for singles. Those already married are in danger of keeping their relationship going strictly for the sake of it.

Another problem in relationships – and this pertains to those of your born early in the sign (March 20th–23rd) – is Uranus' move into your sign. This is not a great aspect for committed kinds of relationships. It creates a desire for personal freedom – of wanting no obligations whatsoever – and this is the very antithesis of relationship. Those of you involved romantically with an Aries should understand this. Give your Aries mate as much space as possible this year (so long as it isn't destructive). Try doing unconventional things together as a couple – e.g. whitewater rafting, journeys to exotic places, hiking the Grand Canyon or visiting the wildernesses of Greenland – things of that nature will satisfy the Aries' longing for change.

Everything we have been saying pertains to those in or working towards their first marriage. Those in or working towards their second marriage are having a status-quo kind of year – marrieds will tend to stay married and singles will tend to stay single. Those working towards their third marriage had fabulous aspects in 2009 – and still have good aspects in January of this year. Many of you remarried or had serious relationships. Those who didn't still have beautiful opportunity from May 28th to August 14th.

With fast-moving Venus as your love planet, there are many short-term trends in love. These will be discussed in the month-by-month reports.

Self-improvement

Spirituality has been important in your life for many years now. Uranus has been moving through your 12th house of spirituality since 2002. This year spirituality becomes even more important as Jupiter moves into this house on January 18th and stays there for most of the year ahead (there is a brief interlude from June 6th to September 18th where it leaves the 12th house – but mostly it will be in your 12th house.)

So this is a year of spiritual growth and expansion. More so than in previous years. Those of you already on the path will experience more success here – your practices will yield greater results. There will be much interior spiritual revelation happening. You will actually 'enjoy' your spiritual practice – it will not be boring or tedious or done out only through an exertion of will. It will be a joy. You will actually look forward to your periods of meditation and prayer. They will be the highlights of your day.

Those of you not yet on a spiritual path will probably embark on one this year. The 'great invisible' has been calling to you for many years, and this year is likely to succeed.

Jupiter is your planet of religion, higher education and foreign travel. So his presence in your 12th house is giving us many messages. First off, you will be exploring the mystical traditions of your own native religion. No need to embrace other paths or other cultures – your own has everything you need if you could but penetrate it. What we call 'organized' or 'exoteric' religion is really the end result of the mystical experiences of its founders – it is based on mystical experience. If you can tap into this, you will have a newfound respect for your own culture and tradition.

But there are other messages here, too. This is a year for taking a religious pilgrimage. A year for taking spiritually-orientated retreats. A year for having personal experiences with the supernatural or paranormal.

The 'great invisible' has many ways of letting you know that it is around. Your dream life will become more active – and probably prophetic in many cases. In other cases it will just 'dramatize' a conundrum or problem you are having and thus reveal a solution. Often it shows the 'why' of a certain problem. Your intuition will be much sharper. There will be all kinds of synchronistic experiences – strange coincidences that can't be explained logically. You think of someone and that person calls you. You wish for something and it happens. You need a parking spot in a busy area and it magically opens up. You are driving and an interior voice tells you to slow down, and right behind you is a police car.

This interior expansion is preparing the way for your greater freedom and prosperity in coming years. For as you 'break through' on the inner, the outer breakthroughs just naturally happen. You are seeing the intimate connection between your inner and outer life very starkly these days.

Month-by-month Forecasts

January

Best Days Overall: 2, 3, 11, 12, 21, 22, 30
Most Stressful Days Overall: 1, 6, 7, 13, 14, 28
Best Days for Love: 4, 5, 6, 7, 13, 14, 15, 25, 26
Best Days for Money: 4, 5, 6, 7, 13, 14, 15, 16, 17, 18, 23, 24, 25, 26, 27
Best Days for Career: 6, 13, 14, 15, 16, 25

An interesting month, Aries, with many changes in store. You are in the midst of a yearly career peak right now that lasts until the 20th. There is much progress happening there. Also a solar eclipse occurs in your 10th house on the 15th. You should take a reduced schedule during this period – this eclipse seems strong on you – a few days before and after the eclipse. I read this eclipse as a positive from a career perspective. Yes, there are changes and upheavals in your career, but these seem to favour you. Keep a cool head until the dust settles. There are also upheavals in your company and corporate hierarchy and this will change the rules of the game. Parents or parent figures are experiencing dramatic events. There are dramas in the lives of children as well.

Mars, your ruling planet, is retrograde all month. Mercury, your work planet, is retrograde until the 15th. Thus you should not rush into a new job or promotion opportunity these days – these kinds of things will wait for you. Study them more. Ask more questions. Resolve all doubts. Things are not what they seem.

Overall energy is not what it should be, either. Be sure to rest and relax more. Overall health is good, but this is not one of your best months healthwise. You can enhance your health by paying more attention to your spine, knees, bones, teeth, gallbladder and overall skeletal alignment. More visits to a chiropractor might be a good idea. It's important that your spine and overall posture be in the correct alignment. Give more support to your knees when exercising. Health and energy will improve after the 20th. Don't rush into dramatic changes in your health regime until the 15th – these too need more study. After the 15th your judgement will be much better.

Personally, you want to have fun – Mars is in your 5th house – but career responsibilities prevent this. Yes, be ambitious and go after your dreams, but make sure to have some fun, too.

Love is good this month. Those of you who are married are giving priority to the marriage. You seem to hold your lover or partner in high esteem – you have them on a pedestal. Singles have love opportunities at work or with bosses or authority figures. There are opportunities for the classic office romance. You are more practical in love this month. Bottom-line issues seem very important. The passion of love takes a back seat to security issues. But this will change after the 18th, when you seem more idealistic about love. Singles find love opportunities as they pursue their career goals or with people involved in their career.

February

Best Days Overall: 7, 8, 17, 18, 26, 27
Most Stressful Days Overall: 2, 3, 9, 10, 11, 24, 25
Best Days for Love: 2, 3, 14, 15, 24, 25
Best Days for Money: 2, 3, 4, 5, 14, 15, 19, 20, 21, 24, 25
Best Days for Career: 2, 9, 10, 11, 12, 22

Last month, on the 18th, Jupiter made a major move into your 12th house and you are now in a very powerful spiritual period – for many months into the future. This is a great time (but especially after the 18th) to get on the spiritual path or (for those of you already on it) to spend more time cultivating these things. Good for meditation seminars, spiritual studies, spiritual retreats, charitable and altruistic kinds of activities. Also good for going on that religious pilgrimage.

This is the kind of month where you will have many supernatural kinds of experiences – things that can't be explained by logic. Those of you on the spiritual path will understand what is happening and actually rejoice in it, but for newcomers it can be scary. As Franklin Roosevelt said, 'there is nothing to fear but fear itself.' Observe what is happening – your dreams, the strange coincidences, the synchronicities, the intuitions and the hunches – but don't judge. Simple observation will reveal what is happening – there is much more to life than what you experience with your senses.

Health is much improved over last month. To enhance your health even further pay more attention to your spine, knees, bones, teeth, gallbladder and skeletal alignment (like last month) until the 10th. After the 10th pay more attention to your calves and ankles. Massage them regularly and give your ankles more support when exercising. Avoid thinking too much or talking too much – you will have the tendency to do both this month! This will keep your life energy where it belongs: within you. There will be more available for cell repair and healing. (Also for the achievement of your fondest hopes and wishes.)

Your 11th and 12th houses are powerful this month. Thus the tone of the month is social and spiritual. A great period (but especially until the 18th) to get involved with groups and organizations (especially if these are of a spiritual nature).

Career is still powerful. Saturn, your career planet, is receiving wonderful aspect these days – especially early in the month. (It had great aspects last month, too.) But as mentioned, study all career opportunities more carefully.

Though marriage is not likely this month, it is still a happy love and financial month. Until the 11th, love and financial opportunities come through friends and through involvement with groups and organizations. Be sure to keep up to date with the latest technology, and don't be afraid to upgrade your existing equipment. After the 11th love and financial opportunities come in spiritual ways – through intuition and hunches, through involvement in charities and through consciously accessing the spiritual supply. This is a period where you make progress in understanding the spiritual laws of supply.

February 12th to 16th is an amazing period for both love and money. If you feel lucky, go to the casino or buy a lottery ticket. But your good can come in other ways as well. Looks like a happy windfall or opportunity. Singles will meet someone significant during this period. There is also luck in speculations from the 26th to the 28th.

March

Best Days Overall: 6, 7, 16, 17, 25, 26
Most Stressful Days Overall: 2, 3, 9, 10, 23, 24, 29, 30
Best Days for Love: 2, 3, 5, 6, 16, 17, 25, 26, 29, 30
Best Days for Money: 4, 5, 6, 14, 15, 16, 17, 19, 20, 23, 24, 25, 26, 31
Best Days for Career: 2, 8, 9, 10, 11, 21, 29

Mars, your ruling planet, has been retrograde since the beginning of the year. On the 10th he starts moving forward again – and will be in forward motion for the rest of the year. This shows that you have now found your own voice and your own centre. You have direction. You are clear. You are confident. You will start to make more rapid progress towards your goals.

The tone of the month – but especially until the 20th – is spiritual. Read our discussion of this last month. Intuition is guiding you in love and financial affairs.

On the 20th the Sun moves into your own sign and into your 1st house. Thus you enter a yearly personal pleasure peak. Spirituality is still important, but it doesn't preclude having fun or enjoying the delights of the senses – probably you will do these things in a more conscious way. Health and energy will be wonderful. Those of you who have had health problems these past few months will suddenly and miraculously start to feel better. Perhaps some doctor or therapist will get the credit (and they deserve some) but the truth is that the planets have aligned themselves more harmoniously to you – they are giving you more energy. With energy, diseases flee. Life-force is the strongest medicine there is.

You are in the mood for fun and it comes to you. Love and financial opportunities seek you out (instead of the reverse) on the 5th to the 8th (but this will happen all month). You can afford to have fun. The money is there.

Singles don't have to do much to have love – it seeks them out. You are having love (and most other things in life) on your own terms. You are not adapting to the world, the world is adapting to you. Job-seekers have wonderful opportunities all month but especially from the 7th to the 9th and the 15th to the 20th. Job opportunities seek you out, rather than vice versa. Although it is always good to use common sense when looking for a job, during this period poring through the classifieds seems like a waste of time.

Finances are also good. You are earning more and spending more – especially on yourself. Reckless spending seems the major danger.

Avoid speculation on the 11th, 12th, 25th and 26th. Be more careful driving on the 20th. Emotions run high in the family from the 14th to the 16th – be more patient with them. A new car or communication equipment comes to you from the 7th to the 9th.

April

Best Days Overall: 3, 4, 13, 14, 22, 23, 30
Most Stressful Days Overall: 5, 6, 19, 20, 26, 27
Best Days for Love: 5, 15, 16, 25, 26, 27
Best Days for Money: 1, 5, 10, 11, 15, 16, 19, 20, 25, 28, 29
Best Days for Career: 5, 6, 7, 16, 25

The planetary power makes an important shift to the bottom half (the night side) of your horoscope after the 3rd. Thus you are in the 'night-time' of your year. Family, domestic and emotional issues are important – more important than career or outward ambition. This doesn't mean that you abandon your career, only that you start paying more attention to your family and emotional harmony. When this is right – when your home base is stable – your career will improve almost on its own.

You are still very much into your yearly personal pleasure peak until the 20th. The party continues. Enjoy. On the 20th, as the Sun moves into Taurus, your money house, you begin a yearly financial peak. This is one of the most prosperous periods of your year. You are successful mostly because you are more focused on finances – and intense interest is 90 per cent of success. A business partnership or joint venture seems likely until the 25th. Your social contacts and social grace play their roles in your financial life. Your spouse or partner (or current love) is supportive financially. You earn money in happy ways. There is a joy in the financial life – happy experiences. You spend on leisure and entertainment (and also on your children if you have them) – more than usual. There is luck in speculations (though you should avoid them from the 14th to the 16th). If you need to attract outside investors or borrow money, the

4th to the 6th seems like a good time. (There is more sexual activity during this period, too – depending on your age and stage in life.)

Singles find love opportunities as they pursue their normal financial goals and with people involved in their financial life. Love is, once again, practical. Wealth and material gifts are turn-ons. Singles are going for gold. The danger here is relationships of convenience rather than relationships based on love. But by the 25th your love interests change. Communication and mental compatibility become important. There is a joy in sharing one's thoughts with another in an open way. Love is shown through communication. Money is not enough for you; you need to love the other's mind as well.

Health continues to be good. You can make it better by paying more attention to your neck, throat and jaw. Regular neck massage is very powerful this month. There are reflexes between your neck and shoulders that relieve neck tension – you should massage these areas. Your health planet goes retrograde on the 18th, so avoid making dramatic changes to your health regime from the 18th onwards. Saturn retrogrades back into your 6th house of health on the 3rd, so pay more attention to your spine, knees, bones, gallbladder and overall skeletal alignment. Get back into your disciplined health regimes of the past.

May

Best Days Overall: 1, 10, 11, 19, 20, 27, 28
Most Stressful Days Overall: 2, 3, 4, 17, 18, 23, 24, 30, 31
Best Days for Love: 5, 6, 15, 16, 23, 24, 25, 26
Best Days for Money: 5, 6, 8, 9, 12, 13, 15, 16, 18, 25, 26
Best Days for Career: 2, 3, 4, 14, 22, 30, 31

Jupiter and Uranus make a very rare (once every 12 years or so) conjunction in your 12th house this month. A very happy – but dramatic – kind of aspect. Often this brings big financial windfalls. But in your case it is most likely to bring spiritual or religious kinds of breakthroughs. These things tend to change one's whole life and whole attitude to life. A sudden insight into a perplexing problem changes everything. It also shows a sudden journey to a foreign land. Perhaps of a religious nature. There is a dramatic change in a legal issue you are involved with – a happy change. Students hear unexpected good news from universities or graduate schools.

On the 28th, as we have written, Uranus makes a rare move into your own sign – Aries. Thus you are ready for change – you feel it coming on. It might not be here yet (for many of you this will happen in future years) but you are feeling its call and getting yourself ready. You are creating a new 'you' – and when the 'you' is different, everything is different.

Love has been challenging this year – serious love, that is. And now perhaps more so. You want your freedom and independence, and this generally doesn't go well with serious relationships. Existing relationships will be tested by this as well.

The tone of the month ahead is financial (especially until the 20th) and intellectual. You are still in the midst of your yearly financial peak until the 20th. There is still, like last month, luck in speculations. You are spending more than usual on your children (if you have them) and on leisure activities – but can also earn from these fields. Mercury is still retrograde (until the 11th) in your money house, which suggests a need to be more careful in how you communicate about finance or with people involved in your financial life. Sales and marketing are unusually important this month – you should be planning these things until the 11th and then releasing the mailings or advertising blitzes afterwards.

Health is good this month but can be enhanced in the ways discussed last month.

When your 3rd house becomes powerful after the 21st it is a good time to expand your mind and pursue your intellectual interests. This is a time to catch up on all those letters, phone calls and e-mails. Your intellectual refinement will also attract love to you, until the 20th. The mind is as much a sexual organ as any other – perhaps more so. This period is also good for taking courses in subjects that interest you, for teaching and for giving speeches.

June

Best Days Overall: 6, 7, 15, 16, 24, 25
Most Stressful Days Overall: 13, 14, 19, 20, 26, 27
Best Days for Love: 4, 5, 13, 14, 19, 20, 24, 25
Best Days for Money: 4, 5, 6, 9, 10, 13, 14, 15, 24, 25
Best Days for Career: 10, 18, 26, 27

Last month, Uranus moved into your sign. This month, on the 6th, Jupiter joins him and these two very powerful planets are travelling together most of the month – they are conjunct. Many of the trends we wrote of last month are still very much in effect – perhaps even stronger. There are still sudden and unexpected journeys to faraway places, happy financial surprises, sudden lucky experiences, a religious pilgrimage, good luck for students seeking entrance to university or graduate school, good fortune in legal matters.

With Jupiter in your own sign now, Lady Luck is smiling on you. You are living the good life – eating the best foods and going to the best places. There is luck in speculations. There is a need to watch your weight now. Women of child-bearing age are more fertile these days. The urge for personal freedom is even stronger than last month and, again, this tests existing relationships. Singles are more interested in love affairs than in serious romance – and perhaps this is the right way to be right now.

Until the 14th love is close to home and comes through family members or family connections. (Financial opportunities likewise.) Emotional closeness – intimacy – is the way to your heart, and to the heart of a current love. But after the 14th love is about fun – non-serious, just good times, another form of entertainment. The person who shows you the best time is the one who appeals to you.

There is a lunar eclipse on the 26th in your 10th house and this suggests career change. This is not a surprise. You are in the mood for more freedom and will want a career that allows for that. There can be near-death type experiences in the lives of family members or parent figures. Perhaps surgery. As with every lunar eclipse, if there are problems in the home they will be revealed so that you can correct them. Be more patient with family members during the period of the eclipse. Also take a reduced schedule.

Though overall health is good, take a more reduced schedule from the 21st onwards. Do what needs to be done, but focus on what's most essential.

Enhance your health in the ways mentioned last month, until the 10th. After that enhance your health by paying more attention to your lungs, small intestine, arms and shoulders. Watch your speech and your thoughts – keep them positive and constructive. Avoid talking or thinking too much.

Venus re-stimulates an eclipse point from the 9th to the 11th and this can bring upheavals (generally temporary) in love and finance. Be more patient. Let the dust settle. The solutions will be there.

July

Best Days Overall: 4, 5, 13, 21, 22, 31
Most Stressful Days Overall: 10, 11, 17, 23, 24, 25
Best Days for Love: 5, 14, 16, 17, 18, 23, 24
Best Days for Money: 3, 5, 6, 7, 12, 14, 21, 23, 24, 31
Best Days for Career: 7, 16, 23, 24, 25, 26

This month we see phenomena that we haven't seen in a few years. There is a lot of fire in the horoscope. Some 30 per cent and sometimes 50 per cent of the planets will be in fire signs for most of the month. On a world level we will hear more talk of global warming. (This talk will vanish in a few months as the fire element weakens.) There will be more fires and the like. But for you, Aries, this is comfortable. You are fiery by nature and so you revel in this kind of energy. Health is good. You feel optimistic. You have the energy and enthusiasm to achieve any goal. Goals are achieved quickly. The pace of life quickens (only keep in mind that 30 per cent of the planets are retrograde and, after the 23rd, 40 per cent will be retrograde – make haste but with mindfulness and awareness.) The only problem here is too much of a good thing. You can be more rash and impulsive than usual. Your innate optimism might be unrealistic at times and you may try to bite off more than you can chew. Haste is probably the leading cause of accidents, so be especially mindful now – especially from the 28th to the 31st as Mars opposes Uranus.

There is a solar eclipse on the 11th that is strong on you, Aries, so be sure to take a reduced schedule for a few days before and after. Do what you need to do, but spend more quiet time at home and avoid risky activities.

This eclipse occurs in your 4th house and once again has an impact on the family, family members, children and people who are like family to you. There are dramatic experiences in their lives. They will tend to be temperamental. The family unit itself can be in crisis – threatened in some way. Be more patient with family members and parent figures (they are also involved here). Often during these kinds of eclipses (sometimes a week before or after) you discover problems in the physical home and these will need your attention. But these problems have been there for a long time and it is good that they are revealed – this way they can get corrected.

A love affair (not a marriage) gets tested now.

In spite of all the muss and fuss of the eclipse, life is basically good overall. As mentioned, health is good – though you need to rest and relax more until the 23rd. You can enhance your health by paying more attention to your stomach and chest until the 9th and to the heart afterwards. With Jupiter and Uranus in your own sign you are experiencing freedom and prosperity. Love is more difficult, and existing relationships are more stressed. You will have to force yourself to show more love and warmth to others –

you might be unconsciously projecting coldness and criticism, and being judgemental.

August

Best Days Overall: 1, 9, 10, 17, 18, 27, 28
Most Stressful Days Overall: 7, 8, 13, 14, 20, 21
Best Days for Love: 3, 4, 13, 14, 22, 23
Best Days for Money: 2, 3, 9, 17, 27, 30, 31
Best Days for Career: 4, 13, 19, 20, 21, 22

Last month, on the 23rd, you entered another yearly
personal pleasure peak and it is continuing this month as
well (until the 23rd). A party period. You will be working
hard as well – working hard and playing hard. On the 23rd,
as the Sun enters your 6th house, you are more serious
about things and focusing on health and work issues. The
party is still happening but is more subdued – you are taking
a work break.

The power in the fire element is dying down this month
and levels will be more 'normal' (the way they have been
for a few years) after the 23rd. The pace of events is slowing
down. Add the fact that 40 per cent of the planets are in
retrograde motion (and, after the 20th, 50 per cent) and the
slow-down is even stronger. A good month for a holiday as
nothing much is happening in the world anyway. Also good
for learning patience – a general weakness in the Aries
personality.

With so much retrograde activity, the cosmos is calling
you to avoid shortcuts. Be slower but more perfect in what
you do. Pay attention to the little details and get them right.

Health is more stressed this month as three planets in
Libra are stressing you out. Happily you are more focused on
health – making it a priority – and this is a help. Rest and
relax more and pay more attention to your heart and small
intestine. Earth-orientated therapies such as mud packs,
mud baths and healing crystals are good now. If you feel
under the weather, spend more time in the mountains or old

forests or caves – places where the earth energy is strong – and you will feel much better.

The planetary power is now mostly in the Western, social sector of the chart (the sunset period of your year). Sunset is the time for lovers. You are more social now, but love – serious love – seems very complicated. You are no shrinking violet these days. You go after the person you want. You are popular – as you go out of your way for others and for your beloved – yet Saturn in your 7th house seems to deny romance. You have opportunities but feel blocked – inhibited. Perhaps there is some fear about love – some innate pessimism that needs to be looked at.

Mars, your ruling planet, travels with Saturn, your career planet, early in the month – this suggests romantic opportunities with older people, or people of high status and prestige. You are more involved with a parent or parent figure, too.

Love opportunities are there, but go slow and steady. No need to rush into anything.

A business partnership or joint venture seems in the making after the 7th.

September

Best Days Overall: 5, 6, 13, 14, 15, 23, 24, 25
Most Stressful Days Overall: 3, 4, 9, 10, 16, 17
Best Days for Love: 2, 9, 10, 11, 21
Best Days for Money: 2, 5, 11, 12, 21, 22, 26, 27
Best Days for Career: 1, 9, 16, 17, 18, 28

Last month Uranus left your sign and this month, on the 10th, Jupiter follows. After the 10th there is almost no fire in the horoscope (only when the Moon moves through a fire sign temporarily). No more talk of global warming. The earth is colder now. It is at times like these that the world needs people like you, Aries – it needs your fire, your flame of passion and enthusiasm, your optimism and can-do attitude. Your natural leadership qualities get more respect. Yes, it is great to have good ideas and communication skills. Great to have a pragmatic attitude, but without the verve and energy of fire these things ring hollow. Without people like you to motivate others – to light a fire under them – they will just 'go through the motions'.

Health still needs more watching – especially after the 23rd. Like last month, enhance your health by resting and relaxing more and working to a rhythm. Try to alternate your activities. Pay more attention to your heart and small intestine. Be more mindful on the 1st and drive defensively. Avoid risk-taking activities. Mind your temper.

Job-seekers had many opportunities last month and this trend continues in the month ahead. But last month your work planet went retrograde on the 20th and will be retrograde until the 12th of this month. Job opportunities need more study. Job changes as well. After the 12th judgement should be clearer about these things.

With Saturn camping out on an eclipse point all month there are changes in your career. Upheavals happening. There are shakeups in your corporate hierarchy and in your industry. Parents and parent figures are experiencing personal dramas, too. But these shakeups are helping you – opening doors for you. Be alert.

This month the planetary power shifts – and in a dramatic way – from the lower to the upper half of the horoscope. In fact, by the 23rd 90 per cent of the planets will be in the upper half – a huge percentage. This is the time to pursue your career goals. By now your family situation should be more stable, and you can serve them best by being successful in the world.

On the 23rd, as the Sun enters Libra, you enter a yearly social peak. For singles there are many love opportunities – more dating, parties and going out. Those already in a relationship are having their relationships tested. The best way to save a current marriage is to make it your number-one priority – almost your mission in life. Anything less will not do it.

October

Best Days Overall: 3, 4, 11, 12, 21, 22, 30, 31
Most Stressful Days Overall: 1, 2, 7, 8, 13, 14, 28, 29
Best Days for Love: 1, 7, 8, 9, 18, 19, 28
Best Days for Money: 1, 2, 9, 10, 18, 19, 23, 24, 28, 29
Best Days for Career: 7, 16, 13, 14, 26

You are still in a yearly social peak until the 23rd. There is a romantic opportunity with someone older or a boss on the 1st and 2nd. A child of appropriate age has a wonderful career opportunity or has some career success at his or her present job.

There is still a need to make your marriage, current relationship and social life your main mission in life. This will bring social success.

Venus makes a rare retrograde on the 8th. Thus, this is a good period to review your love and social life and see where improvements can be made. As mentioned, this is not a time (from the 8th onwards) to make important love decisions. Often we meet seemingly exciting people under this retrograde, but don't get swept off your feet – go slow and steady in love. There is no rush.

Finances should be reviewed as well. This is no time to make important financial decisions, major purchases or investments. Of course, you continue with your normal expenditures – you don't stop buying groceries or necessities – but you are more careful with the big things.

Health needs watching until the 23rd, but the problems are only temporary. As mentioned, strive to maintain high energy levels. Pay more attention to your heart all month, to your small intestine (until the 3rd), kidneys and hips (from the 3rd to the 21st), and colon, bladder and sexual organs (from the 23rd onwards). Detox regimes are powerful from the 22nd onwards.

Your 8th house was powerful last month and will get even stronger in the month ahead. Whatever your age or stage in life there is a strong libido and more sexual activity.

Your spouse, partner or current love is having a banner financial month (he or she is now in a yearly financial peak). There is better spousal support and generosity now.

This is an excellent period to get rid of the excess and effete from your life – whether possessions, effete material in the body or old, outworn mental and emotional patterns.

For those on the spiritual path, this a period for going more deeply into the mysteries of resurrection and transformation. Both these things depend on getting rid of excess.

On a more mundane level, this is a good time for paying off debt, attracting outside investors to your projects (or dealing with existing investors) or borrowing money. Prosper this month by helping others to prosper – by putting their financial interests ahead of your own.

November

Best Days Overall: 7, 8, 17, 18, 26, 27
Most Stressful Days Overall: 3, 4, 10, 11, 24, 25
Best Days for Love: 3, 4, 5, 13, 23
Best Days for Money: 5, 6, 13, 15, 16, 19, 20, 21, 23, 25
Best Days for Career: 3, 4, 10, 11, 12, 13, 22

Many of the trends that we wrote of last month are still in effect now. Venus, your love and financial planet, is still retrograde – so finances and love are in a period of review and study. Some 90 per cent, and sometimes 100 per cent, of the planets are still in the upper half of the horoscope – ambitions are strong and much career progress is being made. You can continue to de-emphasize emotional and family issues and focus more on outer success. Saturn is still in your house of marriage, testing and reorganizing your love life, marriage and friendships. Proceed slowly in love. Allow time – whether you are planning a marriage or divorce.

Like last month, your 8th house is powerful until the 22nd. Review our discussion of last month.

This month your 9th house is powerful, too. It started to get strong on the 28th of last month and will get even stronger this month. Thus foreign lands are calling to you and there will be happy opportunities for foreign travel, too. Your travel planet, Jupiter, will start to move forward on the 18th, so try to schedule your travel after that. There are also many other happy things going on. There are happy educational opportunities. Students, on the university or graduate school level, seem successful. Applicants likewise. Those of you involved in legal issues should see improvement in the month ahead. There are religious and philosophical breakthroughs for those who want them – and when these things happen there is great joy. The mental horizons get expanded. The Hindu religion considers the 9th house to be the most fortunate of all the houses – so this is a happy month.

Health is much improved this month – especially after the 22nd. Still, with Saturn having an impact on you, pay due attention – especially to your heart (all month), your colon, bladder and sexual organs (until the 9th), and your liver and thighs (from the 9th onwards). Detox is still powerful until the 9th. Regular thigh massage is powerful after the 9th.

Job-seekers should look in foreign lands or with foreign companies. There are also opportunities at universities, religious institutions, travel agencies and publishers.

December

   Best Days Overall: 5, 6, 14, 15, 16, 23, 24
   Most Stressful Days Overall: 1, 7, 8, 21, 22, 28, 29
   Best Days for Love: 1, 2, 12, 22, 28, 29, 31
   Best Days for Money: 1, 2, 4, 12, 13, 17, 18, 22, 23, 31
   Best Days for Career: 1, 7, 8, 10, 20, 28

The planetary momentum is overwhelmingly forward this month. Some 90 per cent are moving forward, and from the 6th to the 10th (and from the 30th onwards) 100 per cent are forward. So this is a month of rapid forward motion – just the way you like things.

Your 10th house of career becomes powerful after the 8th. On the 21st, as the Sun crosses the Midheaven, you enter a yearly career peak. Keep in mind that 90 per cent (and sometimes 100 per cent) of the planets are still in the upper half of the horoscope. So this is a banner career month. You are on top – elevated – respected – honoured and appreciated. There are pay rises and promotions. You are honoured for your professional achievements but also for who you are. Push forward boldly to your goals. Reach for the Sun, Moon and stars.

Health becomes more delicate after the 21st – probably due to the focus on your career and the demands of success. As always, try to rest and relax more. Pay more attention to your heart (all month), your liver and thighs (on the 1st and from the 19th to the 31st), and your spine, knees, teeth, bones, gallbladder and skeletal alignment (from the 2nd to the 19th).

Mercury goes retrograde right in the heart of the Christmas shopping season – from the 10th to the 30th. Probably a good idea to do your shopping early.

With your financial planet (Venus) now moving forward, the financial picture is more clear. Your financial judgement is sound. If you have done your review in the past few months, your goals are clear and you are ready to implement your improvements. Venus is receiving wonderful aspects from Jupiter, so this is a prosperous month. But, as mentioned earlier, you need to be aware of the financial interests of others and put them first. Good to pay off debt. Your spouse or partner seems very generous and is prospering. There are opportunities with troubled properties or troubled companies. You need to keep taxes in mind when making important financial decisions. Inheritance can happen for many of you. Others are planning their estates now.

Love is still delicate. You still need to make your marriage or relationship your number-one priority (a rival to your career). Singles seem most interested in the sexual chemistry. There are many opportunities this month. Marriage seems unlikely, though. A happy sex life will cover many sins in a troubled marriage – but your relationship needs more than that.

Taurus

♉

THE BULL
Birthdays from
21st April to
20th May

Personality Profile

TAURUS AT A GLANCE

Element – Earth

Ruling Planet – Venus
  Career Planet – Uranus
  Love Planet – Pluto
  Money Planet – Mercury
  Planet of Health and Work – Venus
  Planet of Home and Family Life – Sun
  Planet of Spirituality – Mars
  Planet of Travel, Education, Religion and
    Philosophy – Saturn

Colours – earth tones, green, orange, yellow

Colours that promote love, romance and social
  harmony – red–violet, violet

Colours that promote earning power – yellow,
  yellow–orange

Gems – coral, emerald

Metal – copper

Scents – bitter almond, rose, vanilla, violet

Quality – fixed (= stability)

Quality most needed for balance – flexibility

Strongest virtues – endurance, loyalty, patience, stability, a harmonious disposition

Deepest needs – comfort, material ease, wealth

Characteristics to avoid – rigidity, stubbornness, tendency to be overly possessive and materialistic

Signs of greatest overall compatibility – Virgo, Capricorn

Signs of greatest overall incompatibility – Leo, Scorpio, Aquarius

Sign most helpful to career – Aquarius

Sign most helpful for emotional support – Leo

Sign most helpful financially – Gemini

Sign best for marriage and/or partnerships – Scorpio

Sign most helpful for creative projects – Virgo

Best Sign to have fun with – Virgo

Signs most helpful in spiritual matters – Aries, Capricorn

Best day of the week – Friday

Understanding a Taurus

Taurus is the most earthy of all the Earth signs. If you understand that Earth is more than just a physical element, that it is a psychological attitude as well, you will get a better understanding of the Taurus personality.

A Taurus has all the power of action that an Aries has. But Taurus is not satisfied with action for its own sake. Their actions must be productive, practical and wealth-producing. If Taurus cannot see a practical value in an action they will not bother taking it.

Taurus' forte lies in their power to make real their own or other people's ideas. They are generally not very inventive but they can take another's invention and perfect it, making it more practical and useful. The same is true for all projects. Taurus is not especially keen on starting new projects, but once they get involved they bring things to completion. Taurus carries everything through. They're finishers and will go the distance so long as no unavoidable calamity intervenes.

Many people find Taurus too stubborn, conservative, fixed and immovable. This is understandable, because Taurus dislikes change – in the environment or in the routine. They even dislike changing their minds! On the other hand, this is their virtue. It is not good for a wheel's axle to waver. The axle must be fixed, stable and unmovable. Taurus is the axle of society and the heavens. Without their stability and so-called stubbornness, the wheels of the world (and especially the wheels of commerce) would not turn.

Taurus loves routine. A routine, if it is good, has many virtues. It is a fixed – and, ideally, perfect – way of taking care of things. Mistakes can happen when spontaneity comes into the equation, and mistakes cause discomfort and uneasiness – something almost unacceptable to a Taurus. Meddling with Taurus' comfort and security is a sure way to irritate and anger them.

While an Aries loves speed, a Taurus likes things slow. They are slow thinkers – but do not make the mistake of assuming they lack intelligence. On the contrary, Taurus people are very intelligent. It is just that they like to chew on ideas, to deliberate and weigh them up. Only after due deliberation is an idea accepted or a decision taken. Taurus is slow to anger – but once aroused, take care!

Finance

Taurus is very money-conscious. Wealth is more important to them than to many other signs. Wealth to a Taurus means comfort and security. Wealth means stability. Where some zodiac signs feel that they are spiritually rich if they have ideas, talents or skills, Taurus only feels wealth when they can see and touch it. Taurus' way of thinking is, 'What good is a talent if it has not been translated into a home, furniture, car and holidays?'

These are all reasons why Taurus excels in estate agency and agricultural industries. Usually a Taurus will end up owning land. They love to feel their connection to the Earth. Material wealth began with agriculture, the tilling of the soil. Owning a piece of land was humanity's earliest form of wealth: Taurus still feels that primeval connection.

It is in the pursuit of wealth that Taurus develops intellectual and communication ability. Also, in this pursuit Taurus is forced to develop some flexibility. It is in the quest for wealth that they learn the practical value of the intellect and come to admire it. If it were not for the search for wealth and material things, Taurus people might not try to reach a higher intellect.

Some Taurus people are 'born lucky' – the type who win any gamble or speculation. This luck is due to other factors in their horoscope; it is not part of their essential nature. By nature they are not gamblers. They are hard workers and like to earn what they get. Taurus' innate conservatism makes them abhor unnecessary risks in finance and in other areas of their lives.

Career and Public Image

Being essentially down-to-earth people, simple and uncompli-
cated, Taurus tends to look up to those who are original,
unconventional and inventive. Taurus likes their bosses to be
creative and original – since they themselves are content to
perfect their superiors' brain-waves. They admire people who
have a wider social or political consciousness and they feel that
someday (when they have all the comfort and security they
need) they too would like to be involved in these big issues.

In business affairs Taurus can be very shrewd – and that
makes them valuable to their employers. They are never
lazy; they enjoy working and getting good results. Taurus
does not like taking unnecessary risks and they do well in
positions of authority, which makes them good managers
and supervisors. Their managerial skills are reinforced by
their natural talents for organization and handling details,
their patience and thoroughness. As mentioned, through
their connection with the earth, Taurus people also do well
in farming and agriculture.

In general a Taurus will choose money and earning power
over public esteem and prestige. A position that pays more –
though it has less prestige – is preferred to a position with a
lot of prestige but lower earnings. Many other signs do not
feel this way, but a Taurus does, especially if there is nothing
in his or her personal birth chart that modifies this. Taurus
will pursue glory and prestige only if it can be shown that
these things have a direct and immediate impact on their
wallet.

Love and Relationships

In love, the Taurus-born likes to have and to hold. They are
the marrying kind. They like commitment and they like the
terms of a relationship to be clearly defined. More importantly, Taurus likes to be faithful to one lover, and they
expect that lover to reciprocate this fidelity. When this
doesn't happen, their whole world comes crashing down.

When they are in love Taurus people are loyal, but they are also very possessive. They are capable of great fits of jealousy if they are hurt in love.

Taurus is satisfied with the simple things in a relationship. If you are involved romantically with a Taurus there is no need for lavish entertainments and constant courtship. Give them enough love, food and comfortable shelter and they will be quite content to stay home and enjoy your company. They will be loyal to you for life. Make a Taurus feel comfortable and – above all – secure in the relationship, and you will rarely have a problem.

In love, Taurus can sometimes make the mistake of trying to control their partners, which can cause great pain on both sides. The reasoning behind their actions is basically simple: Taurus people feel a sense of ownership over their partners and will want to make changes that will increase their own general comfort and security. This attitude is OK when it comes to inanimate, material things – but is dangerous when applied to people. Taurus needs to be careful and attentive to this possible trait within themselves.

Home and Domestic Life

Home and family are vitally important to Taurus. They like children. They also like a comfortable and perhaps glamorous home – something they can show off. They tend to buy heavy, ponderous furniture – usually of the best quality. This is because Taurus likes a feeling of substance in their environment. Their house is not only their home but their place of creativity and entertainment. The Taurus home tends to be truly their castle. If they could choose, Taurus people would prefer living in the countryside to being city-dwellers. If they cannot do so during their working lives, many Taurus individuals like to holiday in or even retire to the country, away from the city and closer to the land.

At home a Taurus is like a country squire – lord (or lady) of the manor. They love to entertain lavishly, to make others feel secure in their home and to encourage others to derive the same sense of satisfaction as they do from it. If you are invited for dinner at the home of a Taurus you can expect the best food and best entertainment. Be prepared for a tour of the house and expect to see your Taurus friend exhibit a lot of pride and satisfaction in his or her possessions.

Taurus likes children but they are usually strict with them. The reason for this is they tend to treat their children – as they do most things in life – as their possessions. The positive side to this is that their children will be well cared for and well supervised. They will get every material thing they need to grow up properly. On the down side, Taurus can get too repressive with their children. If a child dares to upset the daily routine – which Taurus loves to follow – he or she will have a problem with a Taurus parent.

Horoscope for 2010

Major Trends

Last year was a banner career year – for many of you it was a life-time high. There will be a little bit of a lull early in 2010 – to give you some time to digest, and acclimate to your success – and then, boom! You go even higher. Another amazing career year coming up.

Last year you worked hard and played hard – you managed to have some fun. This year it is not so easy. With career success comes more work and you will have to 'carve' out leisure time – even when you can't seem to find any.

Spirituality has not been a major interest for some time, but this year we see big changes – not only short term, but on a long-term level. Two powerful planets – Jupiter and Uranus – make brief visits to your spiritual 12th house and this will activate your spirituality in a very powerful way. You will not feel the full brunt of this in 2010 (unless you were born early in the sign of Taurus – April 20–22) but will start feeling it from 2011 onwards.

With Jupiter moving into your 11th house this year, this is a year for friendships, for involvement with groups and organizations and group activities. A happy area of life. New and prominent friends are coming into your life. This was a happy and active area last year and the trend is continuing.

Health was good last year and will get even better this year as Jupiter moves away from a stressful aspect to you. More on this later.

In 2009 Pluto – a long-term planet – made a major move into your 9th house. This began a long-term interest in religion, philosophy and higher education. This trend continues in the year ahead. There is a detox – a purification – going on in your religious and philosophical beliefs. Two eclipses in your 9th house this year further reinforce what we say. Religious and philosophical beliefs – your view of the world and life – will get tested, and many deeply held beliefs will fall by the wayside.

Pluto's move into Capricorn in 2009 brought important changes in love attitudes – especially for singles. This is a long-term trend. Love is looked at from a more practical perspective – in a bottom-line kind of way – the way an experienced older person might look at it. This year Pluto will be camping out on an eclipse point (the lunar eclipse of June 26th) for many months – and this is going to test existing relationships. More on this later.

Your most important interests in the year ahead will be children, fun and creativity (from April 8th to July 22nd), home and family (until June 7th), health and work (from January 1st to April 8th and from July 22nd to December 31st), foreign travel, religion, higher education, legal issues, career, friends, friendships, group activities and organizations, and spirituality (from May 28th to September 10th).

Your paths of greatest fulfilment this year are religion, foreign travel, higher education and legal issues, friendships, groups activities and organizations (from January 18th to June 6th and from September 10th to December 31st).

Health

(Please note that this is an astrological perspective on health and not a medical one. In days gone by there was no difference; these perspectives were identical. But nowadays there can be quite a difference. For the medical perspective, please consult your doctor or health practitioner.)

Except for Neptune, the major long-term planets (the slow-moving ones) are either making nice aspects to you or leaving you alone. A wonderful health signal. Energy and vitality should be high. Health should be good. Of course there will be periods in the year where health and energy are not up to their normal levels, but these periods will be temporary – caused by short-term transits – and are not trends for the year. When these stressful transits pass, your natural good health returns. (We will cover these short-term trends in the monthly reports.)

Reflexology

Try to massage the whole foot on a regular basis, but pay extra attention to the points highlighted on the chart. When you massage, be aware of 'sore spots', as these need special attention. It's also a good idea to massage the ankles and top side (as well as the soles) of the feet.

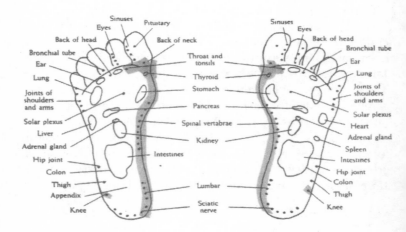

Saturn will be in and out of your 6th house of health this year (but mostly in). First off, this shows that health is important to you and that, for the most part, you are paying attention here – you are not ignoring health issues. Also it shows that you willingly take on daily disciplined health regimes. (Perhaps you are attributing your good health to these regimes, but your health would be good even without them.) Third, it shows that you are exploring the metaphysical aspects of health – the power of prayer, thinking right and a positive attitude. You get wonderful results from these kinds of therapies.

You are, for the next 2 years, evolving a good philosophy of health and disease – a more accurate philosophy – and this will be a big help to you. This is too big a subject to discuss here – but you should study the metaphysical literature on this subject (books by Ernest Holmes, Emmet Fox, Joseph Murphy, Florence Shinn and Mary Baker Eddy, just to name a few.)

Your health is good, but you can make it even better. This is done by paying special attention to the following parts of the body:

- neck and throat (neck massage is powerful for you, as much tension tends to collect there. Cranial sacral therapy would be good, too)
- kidneys and hips (hips should be regularly massaged)
- spine, knees, bones, gallbladder and overall skeletal alignment.

Since these are your most vulnerable areas, problems – should they happen – would most likely begin there – so you can nip them in the bud by being more vigilant.

Natrium sulphate is a wonderful homoeopathic remedy. The bull, swan and dove are healing power animals. Try to be around them if you feel under the weather.

With Venus as your health planet you should always examine your love life, marriage and friendships if you feel under the weather. Disharmony in love tends to have a dramatic impact on physical health – the spiritual root cause of health problems. Restore the harmony in your love life and chances are that your health problem will dissolve – the energy supporting the problem will no longer be there. Even if you need the services of a health professional, healing will go proceed more quickly and easily.

Venus, as our steady readers know, is a fast-moving planet. She moves through the entire horoscope in any given year. Thus there are many short-term health trends in your chart – these are discussed in the monthly reports.

Home and Family

Mars spends an unusual amount of time in your 4th house this year – over 5 months! (His normal transit is 1½ to 2 months in any given house.) This shows that there is much activity going on here.

On the most basic level, this indicates extensive repairs or construction going on in the home. Some of you are probably building a new home from scratch. Many of you are investing in exercise and sports equipment and making the home as much a gym as a home. Many are buying guns or other defensive kinds of equipment for the home. You want to make it like a fortress – impregnable.

These are all good things. But there are other issues involved here as well. It shows that tempers are flaring in the home. Perhaps there is much conflict between family members. Your challenge – and it will be daunting – is to keep the peace here.

It would also seem wise to accident-proof and childproof the home during this period (January 1st to June 7th). Keep matches and lighters away from children. Be more aware of sharp objects, such as knives or razor blades, and make sure children can't get near them. Are there nails sticking out of your rugs? Is that shelf too low or too sharp? Take an inventory. Be more mindful at home and more patient – for Mars can lead to accidents if one is not careful. Check your electrical wiring and see to it that it is in good order.

If you take simple precautions you can prevent many problems developing.

Mars is your spiritual planet. His position in the 4th house shows various things. Some of you might be expressing philanthropy by taking in strangers or showing hospitality to strangers – not so advisable during this period. It is only advisable if intuition commands it.

Some family members of appropriate age are joining the military or police force. There is a noble motive behind what they do. Others (and this seems more likely parents or parent figures) are having surgery this year.

Family members are becoming more spiritual during this period, and while this is a good thing it can also be a source of conflict with other family members – in fact, it is a classic source of conflict. There can also be conflicts over your friends or with your friends. Try to be soft-spoken and not provocative when dealing with family members. Take a few deep breaths and count to ten before answering.

Your spouse or current love (and children, too) wants to move or enlarge the home (or perhaps buy an additional home). You are cool about it. This could happen from June 6th to September 10th. Parents or parent figures are doing extensive repairs in the home. Siblings are better off not moving in spite of their spouses' desires. There is space where they are if they manage it properly.

Finance and Career

Your 2nd house of finance is not a House of Power this year. So you seem content with the way things are going. You have no need to make major changes. This tends to be a status-quo kind of year. Keep in mind, though, that the empty money house (for the most part) also gives you much freedom to shape your finances according to your desires – and since Taurus is always interested in money there is more financial freedom this year.

With fast-moving Mercury as your financial planet, earnings and earning opportunities tend to come to you in a variety of ways and means. It all depends on where Mercury is at a given time and the kinds of aspects he is receiving. We'll discuss these in the monthly reports.

Your financial planet will go retrograde four times this year – this is unusual. Generally he retrogrades three times in a given year. Thus, in the year ahead you will need to do more financial homework and exercise more caution than usual.

Steady readers know that when your financial planet goes retrograde it is time to review your finances – to see where improvements can be made. It is not time for important decision making. Mercury's retrogrades this year are from January 1st–15th, April 18th to May 11th, August 20th to September 12th and December 10th to 30th. We will discuss this further in the monthly reports.

The real headline, like last year, is your career. You did well last year and will do even better in the year ahead. Jupiter and Uranus are pretty much conjunct (travelling together) from May 15th through September. This shows sudden, meteoric success – promotions, pay rises, advancement. Many of you will attain sudden fame in the year ahead. How much fame depends on your status and stage in life. Whatever your stage, it is safe to say that you will become more well known than in the past year. Sudden, unexpected career opportunities will come your way. Many of you will have happy career changes. These things usually lead to more money, but money *per se* doesn't seem the objective.

Career success seems to come from friends in the right places who are helping you. It would be a good idea (from a career perspective) to be more involved in professional, trade or social organizations.

Jupiter rules your 8th house of inheritance. Thus an inheritance is likely in the coming year. Hopefully nobody has to actually die. It can come through being named in someone's will or being named as an executor, or through trust funds and the like.

This position also shows being 'suddenly' out of debt. Or having a sudden – a large – increase in your line of credit. Investors can come to you suddenly out of the blue as well.

From an investment perspective, high-tech companies, new inventions, airlines, bonds and the bond market are all favourable this year. In general property, telecommunications, transport and media are favourable for you.

Meteoric success can be just as stressful as meteoric failure. Your challenge will be to handle this in a calm and balanced way – not to let it go to your head. Be thankful and appreciative, but keep your feet planted firmly on the ground.

Love and Social Life

Your 7th house of love and marriage is not a House of Power this year. Normally this would show satisfaction with the status quo – and thus no major changes here. Singles would remain single, marrieds would remain married. By the way, this is the way Taurus likes things. Status quo is a happy state for Taurus.

But, as we mentioned earlier, your love planet will be eclipsed in the coming year – and not only that, it will be camping out on this eclipse point for many months. You might want the status quo, but change is definitely happening. Your marriage or current relationship (especially if it is your first marriage) is getting tested by the eclipse. (This applies to business partnerships as well.) Generally this brings out the dirty laundry in a relationship – the problems that have been repressed or suppressed. If the relationship is basically sound, it survives and even gets stronger. But if the relationship was flawed from the start, it can dissolve.

There are a few issues happening here. First, your love planet made a major move last year from happy-go-lucky Sagittarius to sober and conservative Capricorn. This changed your needs and attitudes in love. Love was basically happy-go-lucky and fun-loving for the past 15 years. Now, suddenly, it is more practical. You, or your beloved, are thinking differently about the relationship. And this creates stress. In some cases there is a feeling that the passion has gone out of the marriage – that you and your beloved have lost the 'spark', that you are just going through the motions coldly and mechanically – that, perhaps, the marriage is just a convenience and not a real romance. Third, the eclipse is happening. Sometimes the testing comes from dramas in the life of your partner or beloved – health issues or surgery – and is not the fault of the relationship *per se*.

Somehow or other the spark has to be reignited. With your kind of chart – with Pluto as your love planet – good sex will cover many sins. But this of itself won't be enough. Material gifts and material support are important. And with your love planet in the 9th house – foreign journeys, second honeymoons, taking courses together as a couple, worshipping together as a couple – will also be a big help.

For singles, this eclipse of the love planet can actually signal a marriage – a change in your marital condition. With your love planet now in Capricorn, let love develop slowly – don't try to test it. (The eclipse will test things on its own without your help.) While it is good to be practical in love and to want security, don't go overboard and just marry for convenience (you are sorely tempted now) – those things rarely bring happiness in the long term. Sexual chemistry is always important for you, but also look for someone who is 'philosophically' compatible – someone who looks at life in a similar way to you.

You find love and social opportunities at educational or religious settings – at university or a university lecture – at church, synagogue, ashram or mosque – in foreign countries and perhaps with foreigners. You gravitate to foreign people these days – they are more exotic. Good education and refinement are also important to you. Love is seldom a smooth ride, but this year it seems even more bumpy than usual.

Those in, or working on, their second marriage also have a bumpy ride, as two dynamic planets – Saturn and Uranus – make stressful aspects to your love planet. Relationships are being tested.

Those working towards their third marriage have fabulous opportunities this year – it is likely to happen.

Friendships are much smoother and easier than romance. This, like last year, is a banner year for friends. New and prominent – high-status – people enter your circle of friends.

Self-improvement

As mentioned earlier, spirituality is going to be very important in coming years. In 2010 you will only feel the first inklings – the first stirrings – of it, especially those of you born early in the sign. But in 2011 (and for years after) all of you will be deeply involved.

In fact we could go so far as to say that spirituality in coming years will be your single most dominant interest. For Uranus is your career planet – it is the planet of success on one level, but also the planet that shows your main purpose in life. His move into the 12th house, therefore, is very significant. There are many levels to this interpretation.

First off, you are going to be more idealistic about your career. You are going to want a career that helps the planet as a whole – something that blesses all of life. Career will not just be about personal success or ego gratification. (This has been happening in your life for some years and will only get stronger with time.) Second, even a mundane career will be enhanced by your involvement in charitable activities and altruistic causes. It's a very curious thing: While you apparently deny yourself and help others – donate time and money for altruism – your career and public image are magically enhanced. There are all sorts of scenarios as to how this happens – you make important contacts as you do these things, you develop a good public reputation, superiors make note of your activities – perhaps most importantly, you pay off negative karma which might have been hindering you. When a person acts altruistically with no thought of personal gain, then, as Emerson said, 'the universe conspires to make it happen'. All the powers of heaven will scramble to pay it, and if it can't be paid in one way it will be paid in another.

For those of you already advanced on a spiritual path, this transit is showing something even deeper. That spirituality itself – doing your spiritual practices and exercises – *is* your career and purpose – everything else in life must be subservient to that. At first blush this seems outlandish. What do my breathing exercises, chanting, prayer, meditation or asana practice have to do with my career? Plenty. These spiritual practices change your whole vibration and atmosphere. This changes the vibration of all whom you contact or associate with. And this actually changes the world. Someone in trouble comes into your aura and you are able to dispense help and healing – and this can have huge ramifications. You walk into a shop where perhaps a robbery or murder is about to happen and, because of your positive energy, it doesn't happen. You sit next to someone on a bus or train – someone who is perhaps ready to commit suicide – and your mere presence, just the vibrations that you emanate, heal and soothe this person. These events are not things you read about in the newspapers – the 12th house is all about secret, behind-the-scenes activities – but they are nevertheless real. It is the 'secret service' of life.

Uranus moving into your 12th house also has other messages. It shows dramatic changes in your spiritual attitudes, ideals and practices. Those not yet on the path will get on it. Those already on the path will change teachers and practice. Easterners might choose a Western path. Westerners might switch to the Eastern path. It also shows that the 'spiritual side' of astrology will become more interesting (Uranus rules astrology).

There are many, many valid paths to ultimate reality. But with Uranus in the 12th house you need a more scientific and rational approach. Mere faith (though important) and emotional exaltation (also important) will not be enough for you. You need to understand what is happening on a scientific level. There are many paths that deal with this – esoteric astrology, hermetic science, kabbalah (in the Western tradition) and jnana yoga (in the Eastern tradition). These will be things to explore in the years to come.

Month-by-month Forecasts

January

Best Days Overall: 4, 5, 13, 14, 23, 24
Most Stressful Days Overall: 2, 3, 8, 9, 16, 17, 30
Best Days for Love: 4, 5, 8, 9, 13, 14, 15, 23, 25, 26
Best Days for Money: 4, 5, 6, 7, 13, 14, 16, 17, 18, 23, 24, 25, 26, 27
Best Days for Career: 1, 9, 10, 16, 17, 19, 20, 28, 29

You begin your year with 70 to 80 per cent of the planets above the horizon – the 'day' side of your year. Not only that, but on the 20th you enter a yearly career peak, as your 10th house becomes ultra-powerful. Family is always important to you, but you can serve them best by succeeding in your outer ambitions – being the good provider. Focus on your career and de-emphasize home and family. Interesting, the family seems supportive in your career goals – this is what they want from you. It's also good to focus on the careers of individual family members in a supportive way. The status and prestige of the family as a whole get elevated this month.

This is a month where a shift in the planetary power is happening. By the 20th the Eastern (sunrise) sector of the horoscope becomes stronger than the Western, social sector. This creates psychological changes for you. You are becoming more independent and more in charge of your life. You have less need of other people. You can achieve your goals independently if they don't co-operate. You are in a period where you have the power to create circumstances as you like them.

There is a solar eclipse in your 9th house on the 15th. This eclipse seems benign for you – it actually makes nice aspects to you. Still, it won't hurt to take a reduced schedule anyway – people in general are not up to par during an eclipse – why expose yourself to this when you don't have to?

This eclipse will bring up the dirty laundry in the family circle, and family members are likely to be more temperamental. Be more patient and understanding. With knowledge of what is going on, we can't always stop events but our understanding makes us more philosophical about them – and we don't make matters worse. This eclipse (and there will be others in the year ahead) will test your religious and philosophical beliefs – a process that is going on all year. This is good. It tests your faith. Many people claim that they have faith until a big situation comes along – then, suddenly, they discover they had none. The good thing here is that once you understand your weakness you can correct it. For university or graduate students this eclipse brings changes in their educational plans or within their school (shakeups in the school's hierarchy, and rules). Sometimes heavy construction goes on that disrupts your normal study or routine. A legal matter (if you are involved in this kind of thing) will take a dramatic turn.

Though you are honoured and successful in your career, your financial planet, Mercury, is retrograde until the 15th. This won't stop earnings but will probably create weird delays and glitches. Avoid major financial decisions until after the 15th.

February

Best Days Overall: 1, 9, 10, 11, 19, 20, 21, 28
Most Stressful Days Overall: 5, 6, 12, 13, 26, 27
Best Days for Love: 1, 2, 3, 5, 6, 9, 14, 15, 19, 24, 25, 28
Best Days for Money: 1, 4, 5, 11, 12, 14, 15, 22, 23, 24
Best Days for Career: 6, 12, 13, 16, 25

Overall health is good, but try to rest and relax more until the 18th. The demands of career are taking all your energy. Delegate tasks where possible. Enhance health by paying more attention to your spine, knees, teeth, bones, gallbladder, skeletal alignment, hips and kidneys all month. Until the 11th pay more attention to your ankles and calves (massage them and give them more support when exercising) and to your feet from the 11th onwards (foot massage will be unusually powerful).

By the 18th, most career goals (at least of a short-term nature) are attained and your focus turns to friendships and group activities. This is an exciting and happy area of life all year, but especially during this period. You are meeting new and significant friends now, friends who are almost 'like family' to you.

There is a nice financial windfall on the 27th and 28th as the Sun and Jupiter travel together (this can happen a few days before or after as well). Your spouse, partner or current love also has a windfall. This period is also good if you are negotiating a loan or mortgage or want to attract outside investors to your projects. Seems like you are spending more on the home or family during this period as well. During this period Mercury and Neptune are travelling together, suggesting an excellent financial intuition. A flash of insight and inspiration comes to you.

On the 10th Mercury, your financial planet, crosses your Midheaven. This shows that money comes to you through a pay rise or through your good professional reputation. Parents or parent figures seem unusually supportive, too.

Love is happy this month. Jupiter is making fabulous aspects to your love planet all month, bringing love opportunities with friends or at group activities or organizations. When Mercury crosses the Midheaven there is a non-serious romantic opportunity with a boss or person of power. There is another happy love encounter from the 15th to the 17th as Venus and Jupiter travel together. This encounter seems sexual in nature but could lead to more than that. A friend either gives you a good financial idea or provides some opportunity on the 27th–28th. Your financial intuition is very sharp during this period.

The New Moon of the 25th occurs in your 10th house and is going to clarify your career, your relations with your bosses and with your parents or parent figures.

March

Best Days Overall: 1, 9, 10, 19, 20, 27, 28
Most Stressful Days Overall: 4, 5, 11, 12, 25, 26, 31
Best Days for Love: 5, 6, 7, 9, 16, 17, 18, 19, 25, 26, 27
Best Days for Money: 4, 5, 14, 15, 21, 22, 23, 24, 25, 26, 31
Best Days for Career: 5, 11, 12, 15, 24

Like last month, the main headline is your social life – especially friendships. Definitely a month to be involved in group activities and with social or professional organizations. It is not only important careerwise, but financially (and lovewise) as well. In fact, for many years now your friendships have been your main mission in life. You are here for your friends.

The 11th house is the house of fondest hopes and wishes. With so many benefic planets in this house you are manifesting your fondest hopes and wishes – and so this is a happy month. Of course, as soon as you manifest them, new ones will come into the picture – the wheel of life, the round of creation – never stops.

Love is happy, too. It is happy for all of you, but especially for those of you working on your third marriage. There are serious opportunities now (and last month, too). There are some bumps in the road to love. Be more patient with your beloved on the 11th, 12th, 20th, 25th and 26th.

Finances are happy this month, too. Again, friends are very involved here. The good use of technology is important from the 2nd to the 17th. Not only that, but your technological expertise boosts your bottom line. Don't be afraid to spend on technology to upgrade or improve – it is a good investment. On the 17th your financial planet moves into Aries, your 12th house. Be careful of rash spending or rash financial decisions. When intuition is on, these decisions will be good, but if you are not in the 'correct state' you could get hurt. Intuition will, for the most part, be good – and you need to follow it.

Taureans are down-to-earth, practical people. Generally (this has been my experience) they have some problems understanding the spiritual aspects of wealth. They like 'tangible' things that can be touched and felt. But this is a month – from the 17th onwards – for going more deeply into these things. There is no contradiction between spiritual wealth and tangible wealth – it is merely a question of cause and effect. Spiritual wealth – the precipitation of spiritual substance – is the cause of 'tangible' wealth – and thus must be given priority.

This is a month for more charitable giving as well.

On the 20th as the Sun moves into your 12th house you enter a more spiritual period. Those of you already on the path will have breakthroughs and insights. Those not on the path will experience more dream activity and many weird coincidences that can't be explained logically. The seeds of future spiritual development are being planted now.

April

Best Days Overall: 5, 6, 15, 16, 24, 25
Most Stressful Days Overall: 1, 8, 9, 22, 23, 28, 29
Best Days for Love: 1, 5, 15, 16, 24, 25, 28, 29
Best Days for Money: 1, 5, 10, 11, 15, 16, 17, 18, 19, 20, 24, 28, 29
Best Days for Career: 2, 7, 8, 9, 11, 12, 20, 21, 29

Relationships with your children (or those who are like children to you) have been difficult for the past 2 years. For the past few months you've seen some improvement, but now Saturn retrogrades back into your 5th house and relationships become challenging again. The good news is that these difficulties are short term. The children have needed to take on more responsibilities and this is generally not comfortable. Some have been suffering from low self-esteem and perhaps depression. Be more patient with them for the next few months.

The planets are now in their most extreme Eastern position – especially from the 20th onwards. Thus you now have maximum independence – maximum power to create circumstances as you desire them to be – maximum ability to have life on your terms. Create, and create wisely. Later on, circumstances will show whether your creations have been wise or unwise, for you will have to live with the consequences for a time.

On the 20th the Sun crosses your Ascendant and so you enter a yearly personal pleasure peak (one of several this year). This is a time for getting in shape and for enjoying all the pleasures of the senses. Also there seems more involvement with family and with a parent or parent figure. He or she is coming to stay or is very devoted to you these days. Family support seems good, but on the other hand there is a feeling that you are not your own person – that familial support comes with a price.

Health is excellent now – especially after the 20th. You can enhance it even further by paying more attention to your neck and throat (regular neck massage is powerful) until the 25th and to your lungs, arms and shoulders (regular arm and shoulder massage is good) from the 25th onwards.

On the 2nd your financial planet, Mercury, crosses your Ascendant. This brings money – more than usual – to you, and also brings very interesting financial ideas. Mercury will spend most of the month ahead in Taurus (from the 2nd onwards) and this is a signal of prosperity. Financial opportunities are seeking you out; you don't have to run after them. (Job opportunities are also seeking you out – though last month was stronger for this than now.) Try to make major purchases or important decisions before the 18th, as Mercury starts to retrograde then.

Love maintains the status quo this month, though your personal magnetism and charisma are certainly attractive. A fun-and-games love opportunity comes to you this month – but it doesn't seem serious. This person seems involved in your financial life. There is a more serious romantic opportunity from the 5th to the 7th.

66666

66666666666666

May

Best Days Overall: 2, 3, 4, 12, 13, 21, 22, 30, 31
Most Stressful Days Overall: 5, 6, 19, 20, 25, 26
Best Days for Love: 2, 3, 5, 6, 12, 15, 16, 21, 25, 26, 29, 30
Best Days for Money: 2, 8, 9, 12, 14, 15, 18, 21, 25, 26, 30
Best Days for Career: 5, 6, 9, 18, 26

Jupiter and Uranus are travelling together this month. This brings financial windfalls for your spouse, partner or current love. Also it can bring you sudden and unexpected insurance or royalty payments. There is a sudden opportunity to pay off debt or to borrow if you need to. Investors can mysteriously appear if you have good ideas. A parent or parent figure has a windfall as well.

Uranus moves into your 12th house of spirituality at the end of the month. This will bring lightning flash-like intuitions, inspirations and revelations to you – sudden spiritual breakthroughs. Also it shows that you are making important and dramatic changes in your spiritual life – in your practice and in your attitudes.

You are still in a yearly personal pleasure peak until the 21st. Enjoy the party. Taureans are famous for their ability to enjoy the carnal pleasures – so this is a happy period.

On the 21st as the Sun enters your money house you begin a yearly financial peak. Prosperity will be good all year, but this is one of the high points of the year. And with your financial planet moving forward after the 11th, your financial confidence and clarity are increased. I always like property for Taurus – in all of its various ramifications – but I especially like it this month. Good sales and marketing – good PR, good use of the media – is always important to you, but this month especially so. Investors might want to look at the beauty industry – art, jewellery, antiques, perfumes, fashion – for profit ideas. Also telecommunications, transport and media companies. Finance is the major focus from the 21st onwards.

Health is still excellent this month. You can enhance it further by paying more attention to your lungs, arms and shoulders (until the 20th) and to your stomach and breasts afterwards. Arm and shoulder massage – overall air purity – is important until the 20th. Afterwards, diet becomes more of an issue for you.

Your foreign travel planet, Saturn, has been retrograde for many months. This month it starts moving forward on the 30th. Best to schedule foreign travel after the 30th. Legal and educational issues – and decisions – are best delayed until after the 30th as well.

Pluto, your love planet, started to retrograde on the 7th of last month and will be retrograde this month and for some months to come. This is a good time to review your marriage and social life with a view to improving things. Not a good time to make major love decisions.

Pluto stays retrograde for many months. This doesn't mean that your love life comes to a halt. Singles will still date and there will be many social opportunities – only you don't rush into things. You let love develop as it will.

June

> Best Days Overall: 9, 10, 17, 18, 26, 27
> Most Stressful Days Overall: 1, 2, 15, 16, 21, 22, 29, 30
> Best Days for Love: 4, 5, 9, 13, 14, 18, 21, 22, 24, 25, 26
> Best Days for Money: 5, 6, 10, 11, 12, 15, 19, 20, 24
> Best Days for Career: 1, 2, 5, 6, 15, 24, 29, 30

You are still in a yearly financial peak (Taurus heaven) until the 21st. Mercury, your financial planet, moves speedily this month. You cover a lot of ground financially and have good success and confidence. Finance is still the major interest until the 21st. Most of the financial trends of last month are still in effect now.

There is a lunar eclipse on the 26th in your 9th house. This will test your religious and philosophical beliefs. Events will happen that will show whether they are correct or not.

Also, your faith will be tested. Even your faith in correct beliefs. Events will happen that will show whether you really have the faith that you have long professed. This eclipse is basically a repeat of the last solar eclipse of January 15th. Students will make changes in their educational plans. The main difference between this eclipse and the one in January is that it occurs right on Pluto, your love planet. This will test not only love relationships and marriages but business partnerships as well. This doesn't mean that they must fail – only that major changes and adjustments will happen. Good relationships will go through a rough patch, but they will survive. It is the so-so relationships that are in real danger. Pluto (as mentioned last month) is still retro-grade, so don't make any hasty love decisions one way or the other (you will be sorely tempted, though).

The other major headline of the month is Jupiter's move into Aries, your 12th house. As mentioned in the yearly report, this has a major impact on you. Taureans are down-to-earth people. They are not against spirituality – many of them are truly spiritual – but they go with the evidence of their senses. Reality is what is tangible. Now you are being exposed to all kinds of spiritual phenomena – contacts with other-worldly creatures, spiritual beings, a prophetic dream life that seems as real as reality can be, uncanny intuitions, enhanced ESP abilities and many other things not mentioned. You will be in contact with spiritual teachers – guru types – now, too. The 'other world' – the world of the invisible – will be more interesting than the physical world! What a shock for Taurus! Many of you will find the spiritual path now.

The other major headline this month is the power in your 3rd house of communication and intellectual interests. By now you have achieved your financial goals – it is a prosper-ous month – and now you want to explore the fruits of financial success. It buys you time to develop your mind and to study the things that interest you. On a more practical level it is excellent for sales, marketing and PR projects. Your mind and communication faculties are very sharp.

Health is good and will get even better after the 7th (as Mars moves out of Leo and into a more harmonious aspect to you). You can enhance your already good health even further by paying more attention to your stomach, breasts and diet (until the 14th) and to your heart afterwards.

July

> Best Days Overall: 6, 7, 15, 23, 24, 25
> Most Stressful Days Overall: 13, 19, 20, 26, 27
> Best Days for Love: 5, 6, 14, 19, 20, 23, 24,
> Best Days for Money: 1, 2, 3, 8, 9, 12, 21, 22, 31
> Best Days for Career: 3, 4, 12, 21, 26, 27, 31

A solar eclipse on the 11th is basically benign to you personally but seems to affect siblings, parents or parent figures and the family as a whole. This eclipse is basically a repeat (though not an exact one) of the last eclipse in this house on December 31st, 2009. The family and domestic pattern experience disruptions and changes. The home might be in need of repairs. Family members are more temperamental and passions will run high. Family members are having dramatic experiences in their lives. If possible, without being pushy, encourage family members to take a reduced schedule and avoid risky activities. This eclipse affects school children. They may change schools now or their educational plans. There are disruptions in the neighbourhood or in the lives of neighbours as well.

The focus is on the family this month – but especially from the 23rd onwards. Issues with children will start to improve after the 21st as Saturn leaves your 5th house.

Health is mostly good – especially until the 23rd. After that try to rest and relax – maintain high energy levels. Enhance your health by paying more attention to your heart (all month) and to your small intestine from the 10th onwards. After the 21st, start paying more attention to your spine, knees, teeth, bones, gallbladder and overall skeletal alignment (as mentioned in the yearly report). Though energy and vitality are not what you are used to, the problem is short term; you will feel a lot better next month.

Though you are past your yearly financial peak, finances still look good. Mercury, your financial planet, moves speedily this month. You are confident, covering a lot of ground and making fast progress towards your goals. You are spending more on the home and family this month, but can also earn from them as well. The family seems supportive. Home-based businesses look interesting and profitable. Family connections are profitable. Mind your spending from the 9th onwards – you seem more reckless than usual. Any financial deal or purchase from the 25th to the 27th needs more scrutiny. Get more disclosure.

You are, like last month, in a very strong spiritual period. This is a period for exploring spiritual healing. You will make good progress during this period.

Though most of the planets are below the horizon this month – not a period of great ambition – nevertheless very exciting career opportunities are happening for you of late: promotions, successes, honours, sudden advancements. These things may have happened in the past few months (from May onwards) but can still happen now. You can advance your career by getting more involved in charities and altruistic kinds of activities. Psychics, astrologers and gurus have important career guidance for you.

August

Best Days Overall: 2, 3, 11, 12, 20, 21, 30, 31
Most Stressful Days Overall: 9, 10, 15, 16, 22, 23
Best Days for Love: 2, 3, 4, 11, 13, 15, 16, 20, 22, 23, 29
Best Days for Money: 2, 5, 6, 9, 11, 12, 17, 20, 21, 27, 30, 31
Best Days for Career: 8, 9, 16, 22, 23, 26

There is an unusual amount of retrograde activity this month, Taurus – 40 per cent of the planets are retrograde all month, and 50 per cent from the 20th onwards. You are normally a very patient person, but even this virtue gets tested in the month ahead. This is a time to strive for perfection in everything you do – little mistakes or oversights can be magnified beyond what you can imagine. Shortcuts can be the long way round in the end. Go slow and steady and take nothing for granted.

Many eclipse points are getting re-stimulated this month as well, and it is good to be aware of these things. The re-stimulation of an eclipse point can often be as powerful as the actual eclipse itself. Venus, your ruling planet – and thus an important planet for you – re-stimulates eclipse points from the 4th to the 9th and from the 25th to the 28th. Avoid risky activities and be more mindful. Mars re-stimulates eclipse points from the 4th to the 9th and from the 25th to the 28th – the same advice applies. Mind your temper as well – avoid arguments and confrontations. Mars' re-stimulation can bring weird dreams or ESP experiences which shouldn't be taken too seriously. Saturn re-stimulates eclipse points from the 26th to 31st. This can bring changes in educational plans for students, and it might be better to reschedule foreign travel around this period.

With health needing watching until the 23rd, and all this eclipse phenomena going on, take it easy this month. Enjoy more quiet time at home. Have fun, but in a relaxed kind of way.

Career, as mentioned, is still very exciting – wonderful things are happening there – but keep your focus on family and their needs now. Work to maintain a state of emotional and domestic harmony. Your career planet retrogrades back into Pisces (where it has been for 7 or so years). It might seem to you that your career is moving backwards instead of forwards – but this is not the case. Many good things are happening behind the scenes. Charity and altruistic activities – as we have seen for many years – are still powerful ways to enhance your career and your public standing.

Your 5th house is powerful all month, but especially after the 23rd. You are in another yearly personal pleasure peak – a fun and creative period. Even money will come to you in

happy ways – and there is luck in speculations (I prefer
before the 20th than afterwards). Your financial planet
makes another one of his retrogrades on the 20th, so try to
wrap up important financial decisions or major purchases
before then.

September

Best Days Overall: 7, 8, 16, 17, 26, 27
Most Stressful Days Overall: 5, 6, 11, 12, 18, 19, 20
Best Days for Love: 2, 7, 11, 13, 14, 15, 16, 21, 26
Best Days for Money: 1, 2, 5, 7, 12, 16, 22, 27, 28, 29
Best Days for Career: 4, 12, 18, 19, 20, 22

Though your career planet is still retrograde and most of the
planets are still below the horizon – you are not that ambitious this period – very interesting and dramatic things are
happening in your career – perhaps unbeknownst to you,
behind the scenes. These seem very happy. There is sudden
advancement in store for you. Continue to enhance your
career by 'doing good' for the world, not just at your job.
Again we see sudden financial windfalls for parents or
parent figures, and they are likely to be generous with you.

You are still in one of your yearly personal pleasure peaks
until the 23rd, but your 6th house of work is also strong.
You need a good balance between work and play.

Mercury is retrograde until the 13th, so spend the time
reviewing your finances and financial management, and
execute on your plans after the 13th. Speculations are still
favourable this month, but after the 13th seems better than
before. Like last month, money comes to you in happy ways.
There is joy in the act of money-making. Often with these
aspects a night out on the town with important clients
produces more money than hours of tedious work.
Sometimes you are at the theatre or a party and make an
important financial connection. You are spending more on
health this month but can also earn from this field – especially those of you who are investors. Your financial planet

in your 5th house also shows that you are spending more on children (or those who are like children to you) or investing in them. But a child can come up with interesting financial ideas as well – or be the motivation or inspiration for greater earnings.

Though your health is good you still seem more focused on health issues this month. Your 6th house is very strong and will get even stronger after the 23rd. Most likely you are into healthy lifestyles or preventative kinds of medicine. You can enhance your already good health by paying more attention to your kidneys and hips (always important for you but especially until the 9th), to your spine, knees, teeth, bones, gallbladder and overall skeletal alignment (important all year),and to your head, face, skull and adrenal glands (until the 14th). After the 23rd focus on your heart as well. Emotional wellness is very important after the 23rd. Probably you will be more involved in the health of family members then, too.

Love is a mixed picture this month. On the one hand, Venus, your ruling planet (and the generic planet of love) moves into your 7th house on the 9th. You are more popular, more social, more proactive in love. You are going out of your way for your friends, spouse or current love. Yet Pluto is still camping out on an eclipse point, so existing relationships are being tested. Singles might be opting to change their marital status – Pluto on the eclipse point signals a dissatisfaction with the current status. Pluto will start to go forward on the 15th after many months of retrograde motion – and love issues will start to clear up.

October

Best Days Overall: 5, 6, 13, 14, 23, 24
Most Stressful Days Overall: 3, 4, 9, 10, 16, 17, 30, 31
Best Days for Love: 1, 5, 9, 10, 13, 18, 19, 23, 28
Best Days for Money: 2, 7, 10, 17, 19, 25, 26, 27, 28, 29
Best Days for Career: 2, 10, 16, 17, 19, 20, 29

Last month, on the 15th as Mars moved into Scorpio, the planetary power shifted from the bottom to the top half of your horoscope. Dawn is breaking in your year. You've had a good night's rest for the past 6 months and you are ready to face the day with new energy and enthusiasm. This energy will only increase in the coming months. It's time to let go of family and emotional issues for a while and start to pursue (implement) your career goals. As we have been mentioning for the past few months, there are dramatic things going on in your career – sudden advancements and successes – happy changes. You are like a rocket ship these days.

Also helping matters is the power in your 6th house of health and work. You are serious, sober, disciplined and hard-working. You are more than willing to earn your success. You are every employer's dream these days. (Those of you who employ others are attracting serious, hard-working people as well.) The problem now is that you can overdo things. You seem a little bit 'too' serious. Lighten up and have some fun as well.

Health is good and you can make it even better in the ways described last month. With your health planet in Scorpio, pay more attention to your colon, bladder and sexual organs. Detox regimes are more powerful than usual now. Good health is not about adding things to the body, but about getting rid of things that don't belong there.

Venus, your ruling planet, goes retrograde on the 9th – a rare retrograde for her. This could make you feel that you 'lack direction' – perhaps you feel confused. This is natural. It is only the cosmic signal that you need to review your personal goals and plans. Also a good time to review your health regime and the state of your physical body and personal appearance. Probably there are many things that can be done to improve these things; now is the time to look for them. With your attention all kinds of possibilities and solutions will come to you – and later, when Venus starts to move forward, you'll be able to implement them. Not a good idea to make drastic changes either to your image or health regime after the 9th. Wait till November 18th when things will be clearer.

Venus' retrograde is also a good time to review your self-esteem and self-concept. How do you think of yourself? Who do you think you are? What kind of image do you project to others? What can be done to improve things? (Confidence tends to be weaker when your ruling planet is retrograde.) When you upgrade your self-image and self-concept you will also be helping your relationships – we always attract who we are.

Finances look good. Your financial planet is moving speedily now, showing good financial judgement and confidence (personal confidence might not be that high, but this doesn't seem to affect finances). From the 1st to the 3rd there is luck in speculations. From the 3rd to the 20th money is earned through work – and since you seem more productive, this is a signal for prosperity. Social connections and networking seem powerful during this period. After the 20th it is a good time to pay off debt or refinance on better terms. Your spouse or partner seems more supportive.

November

Best Days Overall: 1, 2, 10, 11, 19, 20, 21, 28, 29
Most Stressful Days Overall: 5, 6, 12, 13, 26, 27
Best Days for Love: 1, 5, 6, 10, 13, 19, 23, 28
Best Days for Money: 6, 15, 16, 17, 22, 23, 25, 27, 28
Best Days for Career: 6, 12, 13, 16, 25

On October 23rd you entered a yearly social peak, and this is still in full swing now until the 22nd. Love is not perfect – there are bumps in the road – but it is active and there are many opportunities for singles. As we have seen for some months, you are more popular, you go out of your way for others, you put the interests of others ahead of your own. Singles have romantic opportunities with people from their past, from childhood and from family connections. There are intellectuals – writers, teachers, marketing people and glamorous types in your social circle. A business partnership could be forming this month as well. Singles find love opportunities at weddings, parties, hen nights and things of that nature. With Venus still retrograde until the 19th, avoid making major love decisions one way or another. By all means have fun, but go slow and steady.

There is more socializing with family these days, or entertaining from home. A wedding in the family would not be a surprise either.

Love is passionate and intense. There is great intensity. Both you and your beloved want to know each other on the deepest levels. This makes for high love experiences, but if not kept in check can lead to jealousy, possessiveness and many storms. There is a price to pay for passion when it goes negative.

Finances are good this month. Your social connections are once again important. You can have many financial opportunities as you attend parties and gatherings, and many of you are trying to integrate your financial life with your social life. Many of the parties you attend seem about business. On the 9th your financial planet moves into Sagittarius, your 8th house. Another good period for paying off debt or refinancing at better terms. You prosper as you help others to prosper. The financial interests of the other party should be paramount to you. There are financial opportunities with creative financing – with making money with other people's money. A good period to cut waste and expenses, too. Get rid of excess bank or brokerage accounts – consolidate. Get rid of excess possessions – things that you have no use for – detox and purify your financial life. Avoid speculating with other people's money.

Health is not what it should be these days. Overall health is good, but short term, until the 22nd, you need to rest and relax more. Listen to your body: It will tell you what is up. Enhance health in the ways described last month. Detox is still beneficial. Pay more attention to your heart until the 22nd.

There is a lot of water in the horoscope this month – often over 50 per cent of the planets will be in water signs. People will be kind and compassionate – the positive side – but also over-sensitive. Be more aware. Little things can set them off

– a facial expression, body language, rolling of the eyes, a seemingly innocent remark.

December

Best Days Overall: 7, 8, 17, 18, 26, 27
Most Stressful Days Overall: 3, 4, 9, 10, 11, 23, 24, 30, 31
Best Days for Love: 2, 3, 4, 7, 12, 17, 22, 25, 26, 30, 31
Best Days for Money: 4, 7, 13, 16, 19, 20, 23, 25, 31
Best Days for Career: 4, 9, 10, 11, 13, 22, 31

With Mars in your 8th house last month and this month, and with the 8th house powerful in general, you are in a more sexually active period. Love is one thing, sex is another. Love is being tested and many changes in existing relationships are happening – but your sex life seems unaffected.

In your chart, Mars is your spiritual planet. His position in your 8th house suggests that you are in a period for learning more about the spiritual dimensions of sex. Those already on the path might want to explore tantra or kundalini yoga which deals with these things. Others might want to work on elevating the sexual act from mere animal appetite to something higher. Those on the path will want to explore the mysteries of resurrection and ascension which come under the 8th house rulership. Others might learn of these things 'involuntarily' as the cosmos makes them aware of their mortality (this doesn't mean literal death, but confrontation with it in some form).

Like last month this is still a good period for detox, for getting rid of the excess in your life – things that you no longer need and which tend to clog up the works. This includes effete material in the body, old and useless possessions (sell them or give them to charity) and old, outmoded mental and emotional patterns. See how much better you feel as you do this.

This is a banner financial period for your spouse, partner or current love and they will tend to be more generous with you. With Mercury in conservative Capricorn, your financial judgement (always good) is even better. You are a savvy shopper who gets their money's worth. You make good long-term investment decisions. There are financial opportunities in foreign countries or with foreigners. But Mercury goes retrograde on the 11th, so best to wrap up your holiday shopping – and other large expenditures – before then. The job situation has also improved now that Venus is moving forward. Job-seekers should explore their social contacts for opportunities – these seem better than the traditional ways of looking for work.

There is a lunar eclipse on the 21st right on the border (the cusp) of your 2nd and 3rd houses. Probably the eclipse will have an impact on the affairs of *both* of these houses. Thus there are financial changes in store (but wait until next month before implementing them if possible). Students make changes in their educational plans and perhaps change schools. There are shakeups in the schools they attend. Communication equipment and cars will get tested – if there are problems you will find out about them now. Once again (and this has been happening all year) there are dramas with siblings and neighbours. This eclipse seems basically benign to you, but perhaps siblings should take a more reduced schedule – family members as well.

Health is good and will improve even more after the 21st. You can enhance it even further in the ways described last month. Venus (both your ruler and health planet) is now moving forward. Thus you can implement the changes you want to make to your health regime.

Love is more active this month – especially after the 21st. But there are still many bumps in the road and testings of existing relationships. Singles will have love opportunities in foreign lands or with foreigners. Family connections and family introductions also play an important role in love – especially after the 21st. You are meeting old flames from the past – reconnecting with them – in order to clear up unfinished business.

Continue to push forward with career goals. Much progress is being made. Next year will be even better than now.

Gemini

♊

THE TWINS
Birthdays from
21st May to
20th June

Personality Profile

GEMINI AT A GLANCE

Element – Air

Ruling Planet – Mercury
  Career Planet – Neptune
  Love Planet – Jupiter
  Money Planet – Moon
  Planet of Health and Work – Pluto
  Planet of Home and Family Life – Mercury

Colours – blue, yellow, yellow–orange

*Colour that promotes love, romance and social
  harmony* – sky blue

Colours that promote earning power – grey,
  silver

Gems – agate, aquamarine

Metal – quicksilver

Scents – lavender, lilac, lily of the valley, storax

Quality – mutable (= flexibility)

Quality most needed for balance – thought that is deep rather than superficial

Strongest virtues – great communication skills, quickness and agility of thought, ability to learn quickly

Deepest need – communication

Characteristics to avoid – gossiping, hurting others with harsh speech, superficiality, using words to mislead or misinform

Signs of greatest overall compatibility – Libra, Aquarius

Signs of greatest overall incompatibility – Virgo, Sagittarius, Pisces

Sign most helpful to career – Pisces

Sign most helpful for emotional support – Virgo

Sign most helpful financially – Cancer

Sign best for marriage and/or partnerships – Sagittarius

Sign most helpful for creative projects – Libra

Best Sign to have fun with – Libra

Signs most helpful in spiritual matters – Taurus, Aquarius

Best day of the week – Wednesday

Understanding a Gemini

Gemini is to society what the nervous system is to the body. It does not introduce any new information but is a vital transmitter of impulses from the senses to the brain and vice versa. The nervous system does not judge or weigh these impulses – it only conveys information. And does so perfectly.

This analogy should give you an indication of a Gemini's role in society. Geminis are the communicators and conveyors of information. To Geminis the truth or falsehood of information is irrelevant, they only transmit what they see, hear or read about. Thus they are capable of spreading the most outrageous rumours as well as conveying truth and light. Geminis sometimes tend to be unscrupulous in their communications and can do great good or great evil with their power. This is why the sign of Gemini is symbolized by twins: Geminis have a dual nature.

Their ability to convey a message – to communicate with such ease – makes Geminis ideal teachers, writers and media and marketing people. This is helped by the fact that Mercury, the ruling planet of Gemini, also rules these activities.

Geminis have the gift of the gab. And what a gift this is! They can make conversation about anything, anywhere, at any time. There is almost nothing that is more fun to Geminis than a good conversation – especially if they can learn something new as well. They love to learn and they love to teach. To deprive a Gemini of conversation, or of books and magazines, is cruel and unusual punishment.

Geminis are almost always excellent students and take well to education. Their minds are generally stocked with all kinds of information, trivia, anecdotes, stories, news items, rarities, facts and statistics. Thus they can support any intellectual position that they care to take. They are awesome debaters and, if involved in politics, make good orators.

Geminis are so verbally smooth that even if they do not know what they are talking about, they can make you think that they do. They will always dazzle you with their brilliance.

Finance

Geminis tend to be more concerned with the wealth of learning and ideas than with actual material wealth. As mentioned they excel in professions that involve writing, teaching, sales and journalism – and not all of these professions pay very well. But to sacrifice intellectual needs merely for money is unthinkable to a Gemini. Geminis strive to combine the two.

Cancer is on Gemini's solar 2nd house (of money) cusp, which indicates that Geminis can earn extra income (in a harmonious and natural way) from investments in residential property, restaurants and hotels. Given their verbal skills, Geminis love to bargain and negotiate in any situation, but especially when it has to do with money.

The Moon rules Gemini's 2nd solar house. The Moon is not only the fastest-moving planet in the zodiac but actually moves through every sign and house every 28 days. No other heavenly body matches the Moon for swiftness or the ability to change quickly. An analysis of the Moon – and lunar phenomena in general – describes Gemini's financial attitudes very well. Geminis are financially versatile and flexible. They can earn money in many different ways. Their financial attitudes and needs seem to change daily. Their feelings about money change also: sometimes they are very enthusiastic about it, at other times they could not care less.

For a Gemini, financial goals and money are often seen only as means of supporting a family; these things have little meaning otherwise.

The Moon, as Gemini's money planet, has another important message for Gemini financially: in order for Geminis to realize their financial potential they need to develop more of an understanding of the emotional side of life. They need to combine their awesome powers of logic with an understanding of human psychology. Feelings have their own logic; Geminis need to learn this and apply it to financial matters.

Career and Public Image

Geminis know that they have been given the gift of communication for a reason, that it is a power that can achieve great good or cause unthinkable distress. They long to put this power at the service of the highest and most transcendental truths. This is their primary goal, to communicate the eternal verities and prove them logically. They look up to people who can transcend the intellect – to poets, artists, musicians and mystics. They may be awed by stories of religious saints and martyrs. A Gemini's highest achievement is to teach the truth, whether it is scientific, inspirational or historical. Those who can transcend the intellect are Gemini's natural superiors – and a Gemini realizes this.

The sign of Pisces is in Gemini's solar 10th house of career. Neptune, the planet of spirituality and altruism, is Gemini's career planet. If Geminis are to realize their highest career potential they need to develop their transcendental – their spiritual and altruistic – side. They need to understand the larger cosmic picture, the vast flow of human evolution – where it came from and where it is heading. Only then can a Gemini's intellectual powers take their true position and he or she can become the 'messenger of the gods'. Geminis need to cultivate a facility for 'inspiration', which is something that does not originate in the intellect but which comes through the intellect. This will further enrich and empower a Gemini's mind.

Love and Relationships

Geminis bring their natural garrulousness and brilliance into their love life and social life as well. A good talk or a verbal joust is an interesting prelude to romance. Their only problem in love is that their intellect is too cool and passionless to incite ardour in others. Emotions sometimes disturb them, and their partners tend to complain about this. If you are in love with a Gemini you must understand why this is so. Geminis avoid deep passions because these would interfere with their ability to think and communicate. If they are cool towards you, understand that this is their nature.

Nevertheless, Geminis must understand that it is one thing to talk about love and another actually to love – to feel it and radiate it. Talking about love glibly will get them nowhere. They need to feel it and act on it. Love is not of the intellect but of the heart. If you want to know how a Gemini feels about love you should not listen to what he or she says but rather observe what he or she does. Geminis can be quite generous to those they love.

Geminis like their partners to be refined, well educated and well travelled. If their partners are more wealthy than they, that is all the better. If you are in love with a Gemini you had better be a good listener as well.

The ideal relationship for the Gemini is a relationship of the mind. They enjoy the physical and emotional aspects, of course, but if the intellectual communion is not there they will suffer.

Home and Domestic Life

At home the Gemini can be uncharacteristically neat and meticulous. They tend to want their children and partner to live up to their idealistic standards. When these standards are not met they moan and criticize. However, Geminis are good family people and like to serve their families in practical and useful ways.

The Gemini home is comfortable and pleasant. They like to invite people over and they make great hosts. Geminis are also good at repairs and improvements around the house – all fuelled by their need to stay active and occupied with something they like to do. Geminis have many hobbies and interests that keep them busy when they are home alone.

Geminis understand and get along well with their children, mainly because they are very youthful people themselves. As great communicators, Geminis know how to explain things to children; in this way they gain their children's love and respect. Geminis also encourage children to be creative and talkative, just like they are.

Horoscope for 2010

Major Trends

Last year – especially the latter part of the year – was a banner career year, and this trend continues in the year ahead. You are on a roll – going from glory to glory and from achievement to achievement. This is the main headline of the year ahead. You will need to learn to cope with success.

Pluto's move out of your 7th house last year has stabilized your love and social life considerably. For many years love has been stormy. The cosmos was detoxing your love life and marriage – and this was not always pleasant. Many of you lost husbands, wives and dear friends or have been divorced over the past 15 years. But now things are quieter. You are clear in love matters. You know what you want and what you need. You know the difference between real love and its imitation. The love that comes now will be good. You have paid your dues. More on this later.

Your social life in general is becoming more exciting. You will only feel the beginnings of this in the year ahead as Uranus makes a brief visit to your 11th house of friends. But in coming years you will feel this more strongly. Many existing friends will leave the picture and new ones will come in. Your whole circle of friends will be changing.

The past 2 years have been difficult on the home front. You took on more responsibility – more burdens. It was not safe for you to express your real feelings. Perhaps you felt physically or emotionally cramped at home and with the family. Most of this is over with, but you have a brief revisit from April 8th to July 22nd as Saturn moves back into the

4th house. The cosmos will give you a 'final exam' to see if you've learned your lessons – and then it will leave you alone.

Saturn moved in to your 5th house on October 30th of last year and will be there for most of the year ahead. Thus the cosmos is going to set your children (or those who are like children to you) in straight order. It will set your relationship with them in order and this means you might have to be more firm and disciplined with them. Being overly kind at the wrong times can be destructive to a child's character and development, and this is the kind of a year where you go more deeply into these things.

Pluto in your 8th house shows a deeper interest in sex, birth, death, past lives, reincarnation, life after death and occult studies. This is going to be a very long-term trend. Along with this you will be confronting death on a psychological level – perhaps through dreams or through events that happen in your life. The cosmos is calling you to a deeper understanding of this. When you learn the truth about death, you learn the truth about life.

Your most important areas of interest in the year ahead will be communication and intellectual interests (January 1st to June 7th), home and family (April 8th to July 22nd), children, creativity and fun (January 1st to April 8th and July 22nd to December 31st), sex, death and rebirth, transformation, personal reinvention and occult studies, religion, philosophy, higher education and foreign travel, career, and friends groups, organizations and group activities (May 23rd to September 10th).

Your paths of greatest fulfilment will be sex, death and rebirth, transformation, personal reinvention and occult studies, religion, philosophy, higher education and foreign travel (until February 18th), career, and friends groups, organizations and group activities (May 23rd to September 10th).

Health

(Please note that this is an astrological perspective on health and not a medical one. In days gone by there was no difference; these perspectives were identical. But nowadays there can be quite a difference. For the medical perspective, please consult your doctor or health practitioner.)

Overall health and vitality, though not perfect, is steadily improving – and this is the important thing. Last year was better than 2008 and 2010 is better than 2009. Next year will be better than this year.

Uranus, which has been making stressful aspects to you, will leave its stressful aspect for a few months – from May 28th to August 14th. Saturn, which has been stressing you for 2 years now, will mostly be making harmonious aspects to you (however, for a few months – from April 8th to July 22nd – it is in stressful aspect).

Overall, health is reasonable. You can, if you like, make it even better. Pay more attention to the following parts of the body:

- heart
- colon, bladder and sexual organs
- spine, knees, teeth, bones, gallbladder and overall skeletal alignment.

Pluto is your health planet. Last year he moved out of Sagittarius and into Capricorn and will be in Capricorn for the next 15 or so years. This brought long-term changes in your health attitudes and regimes. Many of these changes seem positive. You are more disciplined with regards to your health – you seem willing to take on daily disciplined health regimes and healthy lifestyles. You are interested in long-term cures rather than 'quick fix' solutions. However, you are more conservative in health matters – and seem afraid to experiment with new therapies or new modalities that could help you. You are interested in therapies that are 'well tested' and that have stood the 'tests of time'. Even those of you who are into alternative medicine are interested in the traditional forms of it.

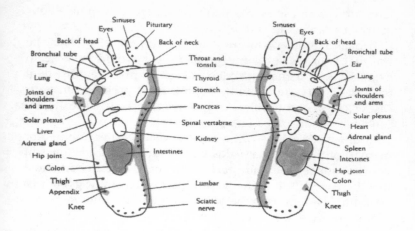

Reflexology

Try to massage the whole foot on a regular basis, but pay extra attention to the points highlighted on the chart. When you massage, be aware of 'sore spots', as these need special attention. It's also a good idea to massage the ankles and top side (as well as the soles) of the feet.

Pluto rules the colon, bladder and sexual organs. Hence their importance in your overall health. Safe sex and sexual moderation are important for everyone, but for you especially. Pluto rules surgery and many of you see this as a solution to health problems. But detox, also ruled by Pluto, would be in many cases equally effective.

While Pluto was in Sagittarius your liver and thighs needed more attention, as these organs are ruled by Sagittarius. But now with Pluto in Capricorn, your spine, knees, teeth, bones, gallbladder and overall skeletal alignment are important – and for the long term. Regular visits to a chiropractor or osteopath would be a good idea – the vertebrae of your spine need to be kept in alignment. Therapies such as Alexander Technique, Feldenkreis Method or Rolfing would be good. Yoga is excellent for your spine and it would be wise to focus more on the asanas that strengthen your spine. (Do your normal routine, but spend more time with the asanas that strengthen your spine – your instructor can guide you in this.)

If health problems occur – and if you want to clear the spiritual root cause of the problem – it would be wise to examine your sexual attitudes and sexual practice. Misuse of the sexual force tends to be behind most problems in your case. Correct the problem and chances are that the health problem will dissolve of its own weight.

Your health planet will camp out on an eclipse points for many months this year – this would show major changes in your health regime and practice. In some cases it can show health scares. But with overall energy basically good this year, they will probably be only scares and nothing more.

Kali muriaticum and Calcium phosphate are excellent homoeopathic remedies for you. Turtles, eagles, scorpions and alligators are healing power animals – their medicine is beneficial on a health level.

Home and Family

Home and family have been important for some years now and continue to be important for a few months this year. Saturn has been in your 4th house for some years. This has brought a reorganization and re-structuring not only of the physical home but of the family and family relationship. In many cases there has been a death in the family (Saturn rules your 8th house of death). In other cases it wasn't a physical death *per se*, but the death of a family relationship as it existed. Perhaps the family broke up. In many cases you 'died' inwardly to the family – only to be reborn on a better level.

This was the true purpose of this transit: to transform, detox and purify the family relationship and the domestic situation – to make it more ideal and perfect. But while the process was happening it wasn't pleasant.

Most of the rough spots are over with. Saturn left the 4th house on October 29th of 2009. But this year it returns for a few months – from April 8th to July 22nd – so that you can tie up loose ends and deal with things that you haven't yet dealt with.

Saturn, as mentioned earlier, also brought increased family responsibilities and burdens. While these were probably unpleasant, you emerged from it a better person – a stronger character. You have a few more months of this in 2010.

Moving was not advisable for the past few years, nor does it seem advisable this year. Though you feel cramped in the home as it feels that you don't have enough space, the fact is that you do if you organize the space better.

Many of you made major renovations in the home in the past 2 years, and if not it can happen this year as well. We're not talking about superficial things – like repainting or buying new curtains – but heavy construction – ripping out wires and plumbing, knocking down walls and the like.

With the ruler of the 8th house in the 4th house, the symbolism suggests getting rid of old household possessions, selling them or giving them away. A thorough house-cleaning should be done. Be ruthless. If it is something that you don't use or rarely use, get rid of it or give it to charity. (By the way, this will liberate much needed space in your home.)

Those of you who understand psychic energy will go further than this – you will not only do a physical house-cleaning, but a psychic/spiritual house-cleaning as well. You will clean the home of negative geo-pathological fields, negative energy vortexes or disembodied entities that might have been attracted there. When you do this, the whole atmosphere of the house will change. There are many ways to do this and those of you who are psychically aware know them. But if not you can call professionals – shamans or priests – who will do it for you. There are many dowsers who specialize in this sort of thing as well.

A parent or parent figure has been having a rough 2 years – perhaps it is depression or ill-health, or just feeling their age. But this is mostly over with. Another parent figure has been restless and nomadic – needing to explore his or her own personal freedom. This other figure is having a very prosperous year and will be travelling much. A sibling is making major renovations in the home and would also benefit from both a thorough physical and psychic/spiritual house-cleaning. Children too. (This seems to run in the family these days.)

Finance and Career

Your 2nd house of finance is not a House of Power this year, Gemini, thus you basically seem satisfied with the status quo. Normally this would show a status-quo kind of year, but with two eclipses happening in your money house – one, the lunar eclipse of December 31, 2009, very much in effect this year, the second a solar eclipse on July 11, 2010 – there will be many a financial change. Forced change.

These changes will ultimately be for the good, but while they're happening they tend to be unpleasant. Sometimes these things involve mere inconvenience – you have to change banks and thus change all your direct debits and BACS payments, or you change brokers or accountants. But sometimes the disruptions are more than that – a sudden expense comes that you weren't ready for. Or perhaps you decide on a big purchase that forces you to rearrange your investments or planning.

Overall, though, earnings will be status quo.

The main headline this year is your career. Jupiter crosses your Midheaven on January 18th and will be in your 10th house of career most of the year ahead. This brings outer success, promotion, elevation, honour and glory – each according to their stage in life. Most of you will not become 'household names' in the year ahead, but for sure you will be better known and regarded than in the past year.

When career is going well, pay rises also come. Elders, authority figures, parents and bosses are supportive of your career goals. Partners and friends likewise.

Career has been unstable for many years, with many shifts and sudden changes, but this year (and in coming years) you seem to have found your niche – your groove. You have less need for change. You are on a path and sticking to it.

Jupiter is your love planet. His move through your 10th house shows many interesting things. First off that you have friends in high places who are helping you. You can advance (and probably will advance) your career through social means – through attending or hosting the right kind of parties and through meeting people who can help you. Your social grace, your ability to get on with others, your personal likeability are probably playing more of a role in your success than your actual abilities. In the year ahead these qualities are prized by the powers that be. Keep in mind that social connections can open doors for you, but in the end you have to perform.

One parent or parent figure is prospering greatly this year (and seems supportive of you), the other parent or parent figure is more tight financially – reorganizing finances in the year ahead. If these two figures are together (which is not always the case) they are in conflict about finances – and how to manage them. One wants to spend, the other wants to conserve.

Your spouse or current love is supportive careerwise and seems very personally involved. He or she needs to be careful of debt and needs to follow the financial intuition. Children of appropriate age also need to cut down on debt and be more conservative financially. Siblings have passed through some major financial trials in the past 2 years and the year ahead looks much easier for them.

Love and Social Life

Your love and social life look happy and active in the year ahead. Very exciting. And there are periods in the year (as your love planet travels with Uranus) where it is like a soap opera or roller-coaster ride. It seems to me that you will have a successful social year.

Jupiter, your love planet, will be in your 10th house. This shows that love and marriage are very important to you. For many months in the coming year it will actually be the 'most elevated' planet in the horoscope – which shows your 'highest aspiration'. This importance that you place on it – this interest – will enable you to deal with the various challenges that arise.

Your needs and desires in love are a bit complicated this year. Jupiter in the sign of Pisces would make you very idealistic. You would be more interested in the 'pure feeling of love' than in practical considerations. But Jupiter in the 10th house of career shows a practical side that is equally strong. So when you meet someone where the chemistry is good, where the love feeling is there, your practical side might not be happy – e.g. he or she has no status, no money, is not from the 'right' family, etc. Conversely, when you meet someone of high status – the good provider, etc. – your idealistic side complains 'there is no passion here,' etc. It is like having two people in the same body looking at things from opposite perspectives and arguing with each other – difficult to please both sides. Your ideal love this year would be someone who could please *both* sides of your nature – someone who is a poet, creative, spiritual, idealistic, but yet has money and status. This is not so easy to find, but this year you are likely to meet up with these kinds of people.

With Jupiter as your love planet you always like someone who is educated and refined. You are allured to academics, religious people and foreigners. You have a need for philosophical compatibility. And this year is no different. But as Jupiter moves through spiritual Pisces, the spiritual dimension becomes more important this year. You not only need philosophical compatibility but also spiritual compatibility – someone who is on your spiritual path, who shares your spiritual ideals and values. You can have great physical chemistry, but if the spiritual compatibility is lacking there will be problems.

Generally you find love and social opportunities in foreign countries or in religious or educational settings – at college or while taking courses or attending lectures, or at university functions or religious functions. Often love opportunities come through the matchmaking efforts of professors, priests or pastors. This is still true in the year ahead. But this year love opportunities happen as you pursue your career goals and perhaps with people involved in your career. This year you have the aspects for the classic office romance – a romance with a superior or boss. Status and power turn you on – but as mentioned there needs to be more than that.

Since Jupiter will be travelling with Uranus for many months in the year ahead, love can happen suddenly and out of the blue. A lightning flash from above. This is a year for 'love at first sight'. The only problem with this is that love can end just as suddenly, too. It introduces instability in your love life. Existing relationships can suddenly break up due to meeting a special someone very suddenly.

Jupiter will be in your 11th house of friendships for a few months this year – from June 6th to September 10th. During this period love opportunities will happen at groups or organizations – and perhaps something that was just a friendship develops (suddenly and unexpectedly) into something more.

This is a good love year for those working on either their first, second or third marriages. Those in or working towards their fourth marriage have a status-quo year.

Self-improvement

Saturn will be in two houses of your horoscope this year. Most of the time he will be in your 5th house of fun, creativity and children. But he will spend a few months – from April 8th to July 22nd – in your 4th house.

His return to your 4th house – where he has spent the last 2 years – shows that the reorganization of your home and family life (but most especially your emotional life) is still not over. You are in a situation where it is not safe to express how you really feel. You are between a rock and a hard place. If you express your true feelings, you will alienate family members. If you repress them, you run the risk of depression – or worse – physical pathologies that arise from depression. Worse, you probably won't succeed in repressing your feelings for too long – and when they *do* get expressed

it will be an avalanche – in many cases totally out of proportion to the event that triggered it.

But there is a third way. Express you feelings, but in a
harmless way. Write them out or talk them out into a tape
recorder. Don't hold anything back. When you have
finished, erase the tape or throw the paper out (don't play
back what you've recorded or reread what you've written).
You will feel much better and no one close to you will have
been hurt or alienated.

This period is not only one for physically cleaning the
house, as mentioned, but also for emotional house-cleaning.
Old possessions (emotional patterns, memory patterns, traumas from past experiences) that are no longer serving you
should go. They are just clogging up the works. This is really
what the cosmos wants from you.

Saturn in your 5th house (where he will be for most of
the year) has various interpretations. Much depends on how
you view life. If you view the object of life to be pleasure –
sensual pleasure and its pursuit – this transit will certainly be
difficult. For it shows a need to limit these things – manage
them better and get them under control. When you consider
that you are in a very powerful career year, this need to limit
recreational activities is understandable – you need to focus
on serious issues like success.

But if you view life as a process of 'character building' – of
building a 'temple' that a higher power can use in the world
– then this transit will actually be very helpful to you. You
will limit certain kinds of sensual pleasures so that you can
experience more refined, higher types of pleasure. The
cosmos is not interested in having you walk around with a
hair shirt or in sackcloth and ashes – it is the very antithesis
of this. But it has more pleasures to offer you than the
commonly accepted ones. So it might limit you on the
sensual level in order to expand you on different levels.
There is always a compensation in life.

For those of you in the creative arts this transit will force
you to be more disciplined in your approach – it will force
you to be more detail-orientated in your creativity – to

create based on system and order and not solely on inspiration. You will learn to create regardless of the mood of the moment.

Learning to discipline children – in a right and proper way – will also be one of the lessons of this transit. To leave children without limits or to let them run the show (as is becoming the norm here in the US) could be considered a form of child abuse. To over-discipline them can verge on cruelty and create a generation of cruel people. There is a delicate balance here and you will learn it these next 2 years.

Month-by-month Forecasts

January

Best Days Overall: 6, 7, 16, 17, 25, 26
Most Stressful Days Overall: 4, 5, 11, 12, 18, 19
Best Days for Love: 4, 5, 6, 7, 11, 12, 13, 14, 15, 16, 17, 18, 25, 26, 27
Best Days for Money: 1, 4, 5, 6, 7, 13, 14, 15, 16, 17, 18, 25, 26, 27, 28
Best Days for Career: 7, 17, 18, 19, 26

You are in the 'day' time of your year as the year begins. A stunning 70 per cent, and sometimes 80 per cent, of the planets are above the horizon. Your 10th house of career becomes very powerful after the 18th, while your 4th house of home and family is basically empty (only the Moon moves through there on the 4th and 5th). This is the time to focus on your career and outer goals and to pursue them with boldness and confidence. Let family and emotional issues go for a while – de-emphasize them. You are in a period of great outer success. Jupiter crosses your Midheaven on the 18th (and many of you will feel this even earlier than that), the classic signal of career success and 'worldly favour'. You lead a charmed life careerwise. There are pay rises, promotions and even honours awaiting you.

Most of the planets are in the Western sector as the year begins, but this will change very soon. A strong social month as well. Jupiter is your love planet. His position at the top of the chart (the Midheaven) shows success in love as well as in your career. Your spouse, partner or current love is also prospering and successful – also elevated – and is supportive of your career goals. Singles have very interesting love opportunities with people 'at the top' – people of power and status, bosses, people who can (and do) help your career. You have the aspects for 'office romance'. After the 18th you can further your career through social means – through attending or hosting the right parties with the right people. You have a knack for meeting (socially) just the right people who can help you. Many a marriage will happen this month.

A solar eclipse on the 15th occurs in your 8th house. Your partner is prospering now, as we've mentioned, but will also make very important and dramatic financial changes. These changes will occur over a period of about 6 months – but they will be dramatic. Siblings and neighbours have dramas in their lives. The cosmos will make you aware of your mortality – this doesn't mean literal death, just a kindly reminder that death does exist and is something to be confronted and dealt with. Students (younger than university age) will have changes of school or changes in their educational plans. Oftentimes there are shakeups in the school they are attending. Cars and communication equipment get tested.

Health is good and you can enhance it further according to the ways mentioned earlier. This hasn't changed. Detox is unusually powerful during this period as well.

Finances are status quo – the real action is happening in your career.

February

> Best Days Overall: 2, 3, 12, 13, 22, 23
> Most Stressful Days Overall: 1, 7, 8, 15, 16, 28
> Best Days for Love: 2, 3, 4, 5, 7, 8, 14, 15, 24, 25
> Best Days for Money: 2, 3, 4, 5, 13, 14, 15, 24, 25
> Best Days for Career: 3, 13, 14, 15, 16, 23

Career is getting better and better. You go from glory to glory – from success to greater success. A heady feeling. Some 70–80 per cent of the planets are above the horizon. Jupiter, the planet of luck and expansion, is comfortably camped out in your 10th house of career. On the 11th Venus will cross your Midheaven, bringing social success and new and powerful friends – also spiritual guidance related to your career. And on the 18th, the Sun crosses the Midheaven and enters your 10th house of career – this initiates a yearly career peak. A career peak in a strong (overall) career year. Go boldly towards your goals and reach for the stars. You have a lot of help. You can safely de-emphasize home and family now – you can serve them best by succeeding in your outer life. You have a special success careerwise on the 27th and 28th – a meeting with a superior goes well. A happy career turn happens.

Overall the month ahead looks very happy. Until the 18th, your 9th house is very powerful. This brings optimism, the expansion of your horizons, happy travel and educational opportunities. For students it brings success in their studies. The Hindu astrologers consider the 9th house to be the luckiest of all the houses.

Health is good but after the 18th start to rest and relax more. Pace yourself. Keep energy levels high. Yes, career demands are strong, but try not to overdo things. Make sure you get a good night's sleep. Enhance your health after the 18th in the ways mentioned earlier, but also pay more attention to your heart.

Career is a much stronger interest than mere money – and you are right to think this way. Career success, a good professional reputation, good public standing, will eventually lead to money. Nevertheless there are some happy financial experiences this month. The New Moon of the 14th and 15th not only clarifies educational and legal issues but brings a nice windfall as well (sometimes it brings opportunity). It also brings very powerful financial intuition or interior revelation. Look for it. On the 27th and 28th the Sun travels with Jupiter (makes a conjunction), a classic signal of prosperity – but short term.

Love also seems very happy. With Jupiter at the top of your chart (near the Midheaven), love and social activities are important and high on your agenda. You put your partner or spouse on a pedestal these days and he or she appreciates it. You are still mixing with the high and mighty, people of power and prestige – and these people are helping you. Singles still have opportunities at the office or with people involved in their careers. On the 15th–17th there is a meeting with someone very spiritual and creative – someone you consider marriage material. However, it could just be fun and games. Neither you nor the other is sure.

March

    Best Days Overall: 2, 3, 11, 12, 21, 22, 29, 30
    Most Stressful Days Overall: 1, 6, 7, 14, 15, 27, 28
    Best Days for Love: 4, 5, 6, 7, 14, 15, 16, 17, 23, 24, 25, 26, 31
    Best Days for Money: 4, 5, 14, 15, 23, 24, 25, 31
    Best Days for Career: 3, 12, 13, 14, 15, 22, 30

Many of the trends that we wrote of last month are very much still in effect. You are still in the midst of a yearly career peak, much career progress is being made and there is much outer success in your life. Continue to give the focus there and de-emphasize home and family issues. Do what you need to do with the family, but keep your focus on your career.

We have a lot of water in the horoscope this month. Both the love planets in your horoscope are in water signs (Jupiter, all month; Venus, until the 7th). People – and especially romantic interests – are more sensitive now, much more than usual. You need to watch your facial expressions, body language and speech. Even stray dark thoughts – thoughts that come involuntarily – are picked up by your beloved, and there is a strong reaction to them. Keep your love feelings pure. Be more patient and understanding. Try not to make a bad situation worse by defending yourself or attacking the other party. Their sensitivities are their sensitivities. It is what it is.

The good part of this is that you will be experiencing highs and nuances in love that few people ever experience. It is precisely this sensitivity that allows for this.

Health needs more watching now – especially until the 20th. Enhance your health in the ways discussed last month. The same health trends are in effect.

The New Moon of the 15th once again brings happy (and substantial) financial windfalls and opportunities. It will boost your career even further and bring sudden – unexpected – material good. (Sometimes people spend more than usual under this aspect, too.) Your ruler, Mercury, starts to travel with Jupiter from the 7th to the 9th. This too brings happy windfalls – prosperity. In this case it also brings a very happy romantic experience. For marrieds it shows more romance within the marriage, happy social invitations and the meeting of new friends. For singles it indicates meeting a special someone – or a person that you would consider 'marriage material'.

By the 20th career goals have been basically achieved (in the short term, anyway) and your focus shifts to friendships, group activities, networking and involvement with organizations. This is a happy month both in terms of friendships and on a romantic level.

April

Best Days Overall: 8, 9, 17, 18, 26, 27
Most Stressful Days Overall: 3, 4, 10, 11, 24, 25, 30
Best Days for Love: 1, 3, 4, 5, 10, 11, 15, 16, 19, 20, 25, 28, 29, 30
Best Days for Money: 1, 3, 4, 10, 11, 13, 14, 19, 20, 24, 28, 29
Best Days for Career: 9, 10, 11, 18, 27

Saturn retrogrades back into your 4th house of home and family on the 3rd. There are important family responsibilities to deal with now – and perhaps a renovation or repair of the home. But keep your career in focus. Most of the planets are still above the horizon, and your 10th house of career is still a lot stronger than your 4th house. There is still much success happening – perhaps a foreign journey or a few journeys (career related) this month (and in the months ahead).

The planetary power is now mostly in the Eastern sector of your horoscope – the sector of Self. The planets will reach their maximum Eastern position next month. So you are independent now (more than usual) and have the power to create conditions as you like them – and you should. It is a time to create your own happiness and let the world adapt to you rather than vice versa.

You are still in a very social period. Your 11th house of friends and group activities is still strong until the 20th. Friendships are a lot happier. New friends are coming into the picture.

This is also a very spiritual month. Your 12th house of spirituality is very strong all month, but especially after the 20th. Career is demanding and exciting to be sure. Family responsibilities also weigh on you. But still it is good to make some time for your spiritual studies – your meditation and inner work. It is the best gift you can give to yourself. As you do this you will find that, rather than wasting time, this will *create* time – your work and duties will flow more smoothly and be done in a fraction of the normal time.

A good month for getting involved in charities and altruistic activities. You will probably 'just naturally' desire more
seclusion – and this is normal. Good to go on spiritual
retreats or religiously-orientated pilgrimages. We mentioned
that you are probably travelling related to your career, but if
you can fit in a religious pilgrimage or retreat it would be
wonderful.

When the 12th house is strong there are more supernatural kinds of experiences happening – whether you are on the
path or not. Those on the path understand what these things
are and smile. They are generally joyous things. Those not
on the path scratch their heads in bewilderment, but
remember the incidents. The cosmos is planting seeds for
future growth in these folk.

Now that Saturn has moved back into Virgo (on the 3rd),
pay more attention to your health. Rest and relax more.
Delegate tasks wherever possible. Maintain high energy
levels. Enhance your health in the ways mentioned earlier,
and also start paying more attention to your heart. Reduce
stress and worry as much as possible (another good reason
for getting involved in your spiritual studies – meditation is
the best natural way to reduce stress and lower blood pressure.)

May

   Best Days Overall: 5, 6, 15, 23, 24
   Most Stressful Days Overall: 1, 7, 8, 9, 21, 22, 27, 28
   Best Days for Love: 1, 5, 6, 8, 9, 15, 16, 18, 25, 26, 27, 28
   Best Days for Money: 2, 3, 8, 9, 12, 13, 17, 18, 23, 25, 26
   Best Days for Career: 6, 7, 8, 9, 16, 24

Jupiter (your love planet) and Uranus are more or less
conjunct all month. They are travelling together now. The
conjunction will be most exact towards the end of the
month – but you will feel this all month. This is a very
dynamic aspect that will be in effect for the next few
months. There are sudden travel opportunities to foreign

countries. Students hear unexpected good news about university or graduate school. Love is like a rocket ship – you soar in the heavens. Singles find love suddenly and unexpectedly. New – and very exciting – friends come into your life. Existing relationships can be severely tested. Perhaps there are rivals for your affections or the affections of your beloved. There is good news on the legal front (if you are involved in these kinds of things). There are major religious and philosophical breakthroughs.

Those involved in a marriage would be wise to give their partner as much space as possible so long as it isn't destructive. It might be wise to do unconventional things together as a couple – perhaps travel to some exotic, remote location. The relationship needs some change. Same old, same old will not cut it. Use your creativity.

Business partnerships are also being tested. But new and sudden ones can happen as well.

Health still needs watching but will improve after the 21st. Continue to enhance your health in the ways mentioned earlier, and pay more attention to your heart. Worry is said to be (by spiritual healers) the root cause of most heart problems. Worry is so common that we consider it 'normal'. Yet from the spiritual perspective it is considered a pathology. If there is something positive to be done about a situation – then by all means the positive action should be taken. But if not, what does the worry accomplish? It only saps your energy.

Uranus' entry into your 11th house on the 28th signals many changes in your friendships and social circle. Now – and for the next few months – you are getting a foretaste of the future. The full-blown transit will happen next year. Your whole social circle will be different as the years progress. Old friends are leaving the scene and new ones are coming in.

On the 21st the Sun crosses your Ascendant and enters your sign. This signals a yearly personal pleasure peak. A time for pampering the body, for enjoying good food and sensual pleasures, for getting your body and image into shape.

Finances are good, but will get better after the 20th as Venus enters your money house. Venus brings gifts of intuition and luck in speculations. Happy money comes to you.

You are still mingling with the high and mighty.

June

Best Days Overall: 1, 2, 11, 12, 19, 20, 29, 30
Most Stressful Days Overall: 4, 5, 17, 18, 24, 25
Best Days for Love: 4, 5, 6, 13, 14, 15, 24, 25
Best Days for Money: 1, 2, 5, 6, 11, 12, 13, 14, 15, 21, 24
Best Days for Career: 2, 4, 5, 12, 20, 30

Jupiter and Uranus are still travelling together and much of what we wrote of last month is still in effect now. Love is exciting. Love happens at first sight. You are bold in love – fearless. You jump into relationships quickly. However, keep in mind that love is also highly unstable. The one you love today, might not be around tomorrow. And the reverse is also true. You might feel passionate today, but tomorrow feel nothing. The mood swings in love are very severe. But, no matter. You are undaunted. New love seems ever available.

For marrieds the advice we gave last month is still valid. Do the unconventional.

Love attitudes seem different this month, though. For most of the year you've favoured people of power and prestige – good providers – those who could help your career. Now you want friendship with your beloved. You want a relationship of peers – of equals. You want to be experimental in love. You want to throw out all the old rule books and see what works for you. You are allured by people of different cultures and ethnicities – the more exotic, the better you like them.

On the 28th of last month Uranus left your 10th house of career. On the 6th of this month, Jupiter will follow. On the 10th, the planetary power shifts from the upper to the lower half of your horoscope. Thus career goals seem to have been achieved – you have been successful this year – now it's time

to pay attention to your family and emotional life. Of course
you will still have a career, but pursue it more 'internally' –
through setting goals, dreaming about them, visualizing
them. In due course, as the new day breaks in your year,
they will manifest quite naturally. Now find your point of
emotional harmony and function from there.

You are still in a yearly personal pleasure peak until the
21st. Enjoy. On the 21st, as the Sun moves into your money
house, you enter a yearly financial peak. The most prosperous period of your year. Your focus is on money, and what
you focus on tends to happen. Use your intellectual and
communication skills to create wealth, either through writing, teaching, blogging, sales, marketing or PR. Investments
in these kinds of companies – media, telecommunications or
transport – property too – all seem interesting. Many
creative kinds of ideas are coming to you after the 14th.

Health is much improved now, but still needs watching.
Continue to enhance health in the ways we've discussed in
previous months.

A lunar eclipse on the 26th brings job changes. If you
employ others, or have others who report to you, there is
instability with these people – there will be turnover
happening. This lunar eclipse forces change (as every one
does) – this time in your financial planning and strategy.

July

Best Days Overall: 8, 9, 17, 26, 27
Most Stressful Days Overall: 1, 2, 15, 21, 22, 28, 29, 30
Best Days for Love: 3, 5, 12, 14, 21, 22, 23, 24, 31
Best Days for Money: 1, 2, 3, 10, 11, 12, 20, 21, 31
Best Days for Career: 1, 2, 9, 18, 27, 28, 29, 30

More long-term financial changes coming up this month.
Last month's lunar eclipse affected finances because the
eclipsed planet was your financial planet – the Moon. Now
there is a solar eclipse in your money house, which is again
affecting finances. Two eclipses back to back have an impact

on money. Some deep changes are needed in your financial planning and thinking. Income (or people that you've relied upon) may not be as reliable as you thought. Investments or jobs that seemed reliable might also not be reliable.

Eclipses also force change from 'good' things. Major luck (which has been happening careerwise) can be just as disruptive – and time-consuming – as bad things. People often change their banks, brokers, financial planners and accountants under these aspects. Often, evidence of financial mismanagement – either personal or with those entrusted with your money – surfaces, and changes have to be made. Sometimes there is an unexpected expense that forces a rearrangement of the financial affairs. There are many scenarios as to how things can happen. But, in the end, the changes are for the good – though not always comfortable while they are happening.

The eclipsed planet, the Sun, is also your communication planet. Thus, as we saw in January, this eclipse tests your car and communication equipment. There are dramatic events in the lives of siblings and neighbours. Siblings should be encouraged to take a reduced schedule and to avoid risky activities. Though this eclipse is basically benign to you, it won't hurt to take a reduced schedule as well.

The good news this month is that in spite of the financial shakeups and turmoil, you are prospering. You are still well into your yearly financial peak until the 23rd. Your native gifts of communication – your mental agility – lead you on the path to profits. Just be yourself and prosperity will happen.

Your 3rd and 4th houses are also powerful this month. Again, the cosmos is urging you to be your natural self – to expand your mind and your knowledge – to learn and to teach others. Gemini heaven.

There is more focus on the family now – and this is as it should be. Career goals have been achieved, and with your career planet retrograde there's not much more to be done. Career issues will need some time for resolution. This is a month for renovating or beautifying the home – for entertaining from home as well.

Saturn leaves his stressful aspect with you on the 23rd. And overall, health and energy will be much improved. Continue to enhance your health even further by following the methods outlined in the general overview of the year.

Your love planet goes retrograde on the 23rd. Love is still exciting and unstable, but perhaps now is a good time for review. Look at where you stand, review your options and see where improvements can be made. Singles will continue to date and have fun – and there are many sudden opportunities, especially at group activities or organizations – but commitment is another matter. Let love develop slowly. (Not so easy with your love planet in Aries.)

August

Best Days Overall: 5, 6, 13, 14, 22, 23
Most Stressful Days Overall: 11, 12, 17, 18, 25, 26
Best Days for Love: 3, 4, 9, 13, 17, 18, 22, 23, 27
Best Days for Money: 1, 7, 8, 9, 17, 18, 27, 29, 30
Best Days for Career: 6, 14, 24, 25, 26

There's a lot of retrograde activity this month – including the retrograde of your ruler, Mercury. Some 40 per cent of the planets are retrograde and, after the 20th, it's 50 per cent. Try to be more perfect in everything you do. Don't take the little things or details for granted. Little imperfections can cause undue delays. Work slower but more perfectly.

You are still in Gemini heaven until the 23rd. Your normally sharp mind is even sharper now. You inhale information like the air. Still great for teaching, learning, sales or marketing. The challenge for you is not to overdo the communication and speech thing – very easy to do right now. Phone bills could be astronomical if you're not careful.

Your 4th house is still very powerful and most of the planets are still below the horizon. Your career planet is still retrograde. So, like last month, focus on the family and the emotional life. Get into your emotional comfort zone and function from there. Pursue career goals by the methods of the night – you are entering the midnight of your year. The methods of night are subjective rather than objective. One creates the internal, psychological conditions for success rather than pursuing them in an outer way. You dream, you visualize, you fantasize, you imagine yourself to be where you want to be in your career. Later on, through very magical, mysterious means, the forces of nature – and the planetary powers – will manifest these things.

Your love planet is in hot and fiery Aries – which wants everything yesterday. There is an impatience in love. Yet your love planet is retrograde, which suggests a slowing-down of the pace of love. Not so easy to handle. There is a sense of frustration here – but if you understand what is going on, it is easier to handle. Yes, you have a passion for someone or vice versa, indulge – but let love develop as it will. Don't rush into commitments. A love affair has a crisis from the 7th to the 10th. True love will weather it easily. You need to work harder during this period to show warmth and love to others.

Health once again needs more watching after the 23rd. Pay more attention to your heart. Rest and relax more. Get enough sleep. Apply the methods described in the general overview section.

The lunar eclipse of June 26th was announcing job changes; these could still happen. There could be big changes in the conditions of the workplace or the rules at work as well. Job-seekers have good opportunities all month but especially after the 23rd. Job changes or opportunities need more study these days. Your work planet has been retrograde for some months.

Finances are status quo this month. The Moon waxes from the 10th to the 24th and this will be your strongest financial period this month. There is a nice windfall on the 1st and the 27th.

September

Best Days Overall: 1, 2, 9, 10, 18, 19, 20, 28, 29
Most Stressful Days Overall: 7, 8, 13, 14, 15, 21, 22
Best Days for Love: 2, 5, 11, 12, 13, 14, 15, 21, 22
Best Days for Money: 3, 4, 5, 7, 8, 12, 17, 22, 28
Best Days for Career: 2, 10, 19, 20, 21, 22, 29, 30

Last month Uranus, after his brief foray into your 11th house, retrograded back into your 10th house of career. This month, on the 10th, Jupiter follows suit. So important career developments are happening and the demands of your career have increased. But along with this, most of the planets are still below the horizon and your 4th house of home and family is still powerful until the 23rd. So you need to balance home and career – the demands of your domestic life with the demands of your ambitions. Most of your focus should still be on the family and your personal emotional well-being. But you will be shifting more energy to your career. One time you will lean one way and another time another way – like a seesaw. Looks like there is more travel related to your career.

Health still needs watching until the 23rd. See our discussion of last month. But this month also pay attention to your kidneys and hips after the 8th and to your head, face, skull and adrenal glands after the 15th. Vigorous physical exercise is good after the 15th, as your muscles need to be kept in tone.

The two planets that rule communication in your horoscope are in the 4th house; this suggests various things. One, you are installing communication equipment in the home – or perhaps upgrading it. Family members are buying cars or communication equipment. A good period to communicate with family members in a deep way – to have family discussions and the like (but wait until Mercury goes forward on the 12th). Ever since Saturn left Virgo in July, things at home have been improving. A sense of heaviness and depression has left you. A parent or parent figure feels better. Both parents (or parent figures) are prospering this month.

With your love planet's move back into Pisces you are shifting love gears yet again. For the past few months you have been headstrong and aggressive in love – leaping into relationships rashly. You have been a love-at-first-sight kind of person. But now you are more cautious. For the past few months you wanted friendship with your beloved. But now you are once again (as in the beginning of the year) into status and power. You are turned on by power, by people who can help your career. Once again there are love opportunities at the office, with bosses or superiors or those involved in your career. You are turned on by people you can look up to and respect. With your love planet back in Pisces, be more aware of the sensitivities of your beloved. He or she is more easily hurt now.

Finances are basically status quo. The Moon waxes from the 8th to the 23rd and this should be, overall, your strongest financial period this month. You will have more energy and enthusiasm for finance.

On the 23rd you enter another yearly personal pleasure peak. Enjoy.

October

Best Days Overall: 7, 8, 16, 17, 25, 26, 27
Most Stressful Days Overall: 5, 6, 11, 12, 18, 19
Best Days for Love: 1, 2, 9, 10, 11, 12, 18, 19, 28, 29
Best Days for Money: 1, 2, 7, 10, 17, 19, 27, 28, 29
Best Days for Career: 8, 17, 18, 19, 27

Retrograde activity is still strong this month, but a little easier than last month. Mercury, your ruler, goes forward on the 3rd and you have more confidence and direction in your life. Still, the overall pace of events slows down. Like last month, don't take things for granted – dot your 'i's and cross your 't's – mind the details.

You are still in one of your yearly personal pleasure peaks until the 23rd. Thus you are exploring the fun side of life. Work is important – your 6th house is powerful, too – but you are having more fun. And this is how it should be.

Children seem a burden. A child, or someone who is like a child to you, seems gloomy and depressed, and needs more discipline. He or she is going through a personal transformation – a transformation of the body and image. Perhaps there is surgery or a near-death experience in this child's life. This personal transformation is a process that will go on for the next 2 years or so.

Love affairs, marriages and partnerships continue to be tested. But with your love planet still retrograde, avoid making major love decisions. You are still in a 'review' period in love. Nevertheless there are plenty of love opportunities for singles – and, like last month, these happen at work, as you pursue career goals and with people involved in your career. Foreigners also seem interesting. Love can also happen in educational or religious-type settings.

Health looks good this month. There is great improvement. Perhaps this is due to the focus that you are giving it. Vigorous physical exercise is still good until the 23rd. Your kidneys and hips (regular hip massage is good) need more attention all month. Your heart needs more attention after the 23rd (work to reduce stress and lower blood pressure). Your lungs, arms and shoulders should be given more attention after the 21st (regular arm and shoulder massage would be wonderful). Be careful of over-stimulating your mind as this can lead to insomnia and nerve disorders.

Venus makes one of her rare (once in two-year) retrogrades this month – beginning the 8th. This adds to the love uncertainties discussed earlier. Many people will be experiencing reversals in their love life this month – it's sort of in the air – so don't feel that you have been 'specially singled out'. In your chart, Venus rules your spiritual life. So dreams and intuitions need more verification – you might be seeing correctly but not interpreting correctly. Avoid making drastic changes to your spiritual regime.

There is a lot of water in the horoscope this month – at times as much as 70 per cent. This is huge. People, overall, are more sensitive – not just in love, but in general. Matter-of-fact statements of truth could be seen as 'cruel' and not taken the right way. You have to be more aware of other people's feelings these days.

November

Best Days Overall: 3, 4, 12, 13, 22, 23
Most Stressful Days Overall: 1, 2, 7, 8, 14, 15, 16, 28, 29
Best Days for Love: 5, 6, 7, 8, 13, 15, 16, 23, 25
Best Days for Money: 5, 6, 15, 16, 24, 25, 26
Best Days for Career: 6, 14, 15, 16, 17, 27, 28

Retrograde activity will almost disappear this month. The month begins with 40 per cent of the planets retrograde, but it will end with only one planet retrograde. Thus 90 per cent of the planets will be in forward motion. This shows that many deadlocked issues are now resolved. There is a new decisiveness both personally and on a world level. The pace of events quickens. For you, this forward motion is a big boon to your love and social life – both Venus (the generic love planet) and Jupiter (your actual love planet) start moving forward on the 18th. By then you will know whether you want to stay in or out of an existing relationship, or how far you want to take it. Love is basically happy early in the month but there are so many doubts and fears about it. The forward motion of the love planets will resolve these things.

For singles, love awaits them as they pursue their career goals and with people involved in their career. The aspects for the office romance are still strong. You are still mixing with the high and mighty.

On the 22nd, you enter a yearly social peak. Romance is in the air. There are at least three people you are involved with or where there is potential for involvement. One is intellectual, the other more athletic and the third a combination of the two.

Career is starting to dominate your attention again. On the 22nd the planets shift once again to the 'day' side of your horoscope – from the lower half to the upper half. This is the sunrise of your year. Dawn. If you have done your inner work, it is as if you have awakened from a good night's sleep and are ready to meet the challenges of the day with renewed energy and enthusiasm. Your actions will be more powerful.

There is still much success happening in your career. There is travel related to your career – foreign travel. In fact, your willingness to travel is a big factor in your success.

Health needs more watching after the 22nd. Pay more attention to your heart (all month), and to kidneys, hips, lungs, arms, shoulders and small intestine (until the 9th). The ways discussed in the yearly report are also good (these are in effect for the entire year). The main thing is to maintain high energy levels. Get enough sleep. Focus on essentials and let lesser things go. Rest when tired.

Finances are status quo this month. But financial energy will be stronger from the 6th to the 21st as the Moon waxes. You can schedule yourself accordingly.

December

Best Days Overall: 1, 9, 10, 11, 19, 20, 28, 29
Most Stressful Days Overall: 5, 6, 12, 13, 26, 27
Best Days for Love: 2, 4, 5, 6, 12, 13, 22, 23, 31
Best Days for Money: 4, 5, 13, 16, 21, 22, 23, 26, 31
Best Days for Career: 2, 11, 12, 13, 20, 29

This month, for a few days, we actually have 100 per cent of the planets moving forward. And even after the 10th (when Mercury retrogrades) there will still be 90 per cent of the planets in forward motion. A huge percentage. The pace of events quickens – both personally and for the world at large. True, you might be personally indecisive after the 10th, but this will not slow down your career, love life or finances. You might not feel as confident as normal. And perhaps there are unresolved dilemmas with the family. These are temporary. Review your home and family life and see where improvements can be made. After the 30th you can make them.

A lunar eclipse on the 21st occurs right on the border (the cusp) of your 1st and 2nd houses. Thus both houses will be affected. There are financial changes – perhaps sudden, unexpected expenses arise – things you didn't figure on – and you are forced to change course or shift money around. These financial shifts may come from unexpected windfalls, too – either way, you are forced to pay more attention to your financial situation.

This eclipse (which occurs as your ruler is retrograde) will also bring on a redefinition of your personality and image. Often this leads to a new wardrobe – a new look, a new way of presenting yourself.

You are still in the midst of a yearly social peak and seem very successful both socially and in your career (the two are intertwined these days). Your personal indecisiveness doesn't seem to affect your popularity, however. Perhaps it even enhances it. Humility is a quality admired by many people. You put others first.

This is also a more sexually active month – especially after the 21st.

You end the year as you began, with your 8th house very powerful. A period for getting rid of the excess in your life – excess in the physical body (through detox or fasting) or excess possessions or mental and emotional baggage. The theme of the 8th house is – when in doubt, remove. Keep only what is necessary for the foreseeable future. The excess is just clogging up the works and preventing the new and the fresh – the pristine and the pure – from coming in.

Health still needs watching until the 21st. Pay more attention to your heart (until the 21st) and to your kidneys and hips all month. Also refer to our health discussion in the yearly report.

Cancer

♋

THE CRAB
*Birthdays from
21st June to
20th July*

Personality Profile

CANCER AT A GLANCE

Element – Water

Ruling Planet – Moon
   Career Planet – Mars
   Love Planet – Saturn
   Money Planet – Sun
   Planet of Fun and Games – Pluto
   Planet of Good Fortune – Neptune
   Planet of Health and Work – Jupiter
   Planet of Home and Family Life – Venus
   Planet of Spirituality – Mercury

Colours – blue, puce, silver

*Colours that promote love, romance and social
  harmony* – black, indigo

Colours that promote earning power – gold,
  orange

Gems – moonstone, pearl

Metal – silver

Scents – jasmine, sandalwood

Quality – cardinal (= activity)

Quality most needed for balance – mood control

Strongest virtues – emotional sensitivity, tenacity, the urge to nurture

Deepest need – a harmonious home and family life

Characteristics to avoid – over-sensitivity, negative moods

Signs of greatest overall compatibility – Scorpio, Pisces

Signs of greatest overall incompatibility – Aries, Libra, Capricorn

Sign most helpful to career – Aries

Sign most helpful for emotional support – Libra

Sign most helpful financially – Leo

Sign best for marriage and/or partnerships – Capricorn

Sign most helpful for creative projects – Scorpio

Best Sign to have fun with – Scorpio

Signs most helpful in spiritual matters – Gemini, Pisces

Best day of the week – Monday

Understanding a Cancer

In the sign of Cancer the heavens are developing the feeling side of things. This is what a true Cancerian is all about – feelings. Where Aries will tend to err on the side of action, Taurus on the side of inaction and Gemini on the side of thought, Cancer will tend to err on the side of feeling.

Cancerians tend to mistrust logic. Perhaps rightfully so. For them it is not enough for an argument or a project to be logical – it must feel right as well. If it does not feel right a Cancerian will reject it or chafe against it. The phrase 'follow your heart' could have been coined by a Cancerian, because it describes exactly the Cancerian attitude to life.

The power to feel is a more direct – more immediate – method of knowing than thinking is. Thinking is indirect. Thinking about a thing never touches the thing itself. Feeling is a faculty that touches directly the thing or issue in question. We actually experience it. Emotional feeling is almost like another sense which humans possess – a psychic sense. Since the realities that we come in contact with during our lifetime are often painful and even destructive, it is not surprising that the Cancerian chooses to erect barriers – a shell – to protect his or her vulnerable, sensitive nature. To a Cancerian this is only common sense.

If Cancerians are in the presence of people they do not know, or find themselves in a hostile environment, up goes the shell and they feel protected. Other people often complain about this, but one must question these other people's motives. Why does this shell disturb them? Is it perhaps because they would like to sting, and feel frustrated that they cannot? If your intentions are honourable and you are patient, have no fear. The shell will open up and you will be accepted as part of the Cancerian's circle of family and friends.

Thought-processes are generally analytic and dissociating. In order to think clearly we must make distinctions, comparisons and the like. But feeling is unifying and integrative.

To think clearly about something you have to distance yourself from it. To feel something you must get close to it. Once a Cancerian has accepted you as a friend he or she will hang on. You have to be really bad to lose the friendship of a Cancerian. If you are related to Cancerians they will never let you go no matter what you do. They will always try to maintain some kind of connection even in the most extreme circumstances.

Finance

The Cancer-born has a deep sense of what other people feel about things and why they feel as they do. This faculty is a great asset in the workplace and in the business world. Of course it is also indispensable in raising a family and building a home, but it also has its uses in business. Cancerians often attain great wealth in a family type of business. Even if the business is not a family operation, they will treat it as one. If the Cancerian works for somebody else, then the boss is the parental figure and the co-workers are brothers and sisters. If a Cancerian is the boss, then all the workers are his or her children. Cancerians like the feeling of being providers for others. They enjoy knowing that others derive their sustenance because of what they do. It is another form of nurturing.

With Leo on their solar 2nd house (of money) cusp, Cancerians are often lucky speculators, especially with residential property or hotels and restaurants. Resort hotels and nightclubs are also profitable for the Cancerian. Waterside properties allure them. Though they are basically conventional people, they sometimes like to earn their livelihood in glamorous ways.

The Sun, Cancer's money planet, represents an important financial message: in financial matters Cancerians need to be less moody, more stable and fixed. They cannot allow their moods – which are here today and gone tomorrow – to get in the way of their business lives. They need to develop their self-esteem and feelings of self-worth if they are to realize their greatest financial potential.

Career and Public Image

Aries rules the 10th solar house (of career) cusp of Cancer, which indicates that Cancerians long to start their own business, to be more active publicly and politically and to be more independent. Family responsibilities and a fear of hurting other people's feelings – or getting hurt themselves – often inhibit them from attaining these goals. However, this is what they want and long to do.

Cancerians like their bosses and leaders to act freely and to be a bit self-willed. They can deal with that in a superior. Cancerians expect their leaders to be fierce on their behalf.

When the Cancerian is in the position of boss or superior he or she behaves very much like a 'warlord'. Of course the wars they wage are not egocentric but in defence of those under their care. If they lack some of this fighting instinct – independence and pioneering spirit – Cancerians will have extreme difficulty in attaining their highest career goals. They will be hampered in their attempts to lead others.

Since they are so parental, Cancerians like to work with children and make great educators and teachers.

Love and Relationships

Like Taurus, Cancer likes committed relationships. Cancerians function best when the relationship is clearly defined and everyone knows his or her role. When they marry it is usually for life. They are extremely loyal to their beloved. But there is a deep little secret that most Cancerians will never admit to: commitment or partnership is really a chore and a duty to them. They enter into it because they know of no other way to create the family that they desire. Union is just a way – a means to an end – rather than an end in itself. The family is the ultimate end for them.

If you are in love with a Cancerian you must tread lightly on his or her feelings. It will take you a good deal of time to realize how deep and sensitive Cancerians can be. The smallest negativity upsets them. Your tone of voice, your irritation, a look in your eye or an expression on your face can cause great distress for the Cancerian. Your slightest gesture is registered by them and reacted to. This can be hard to get used to, but stick by your love – Cancerians make great partners once you learn how to deal with them. Your Cancerian lover will react not so much to what you say but to the way you are actually feeling at the moment.

Home and Domestic Life

This is where Cancerians really excel. The home environment and the family are their personal works of art. They strive to make things of beauty that will outlast them. Very often they succeed.

Cancerians feel very close to their family, their relatives and especially their mothers. These bonds last throughout their lives and mature as they grow older. They are very fond of those members of their family who become successful, and they are also quite attached to family heirlooms and mementos. Cancerians also love children and like to provide them with all the things they need and want. With their nurturing, feeling nature, Cancerians make very good parents – especially the Cancerian woman, who is the mother *par excellence* of the zodiac.

As a parent the Cancerian's attitude is 'my children right or wrong.' Unconditional devotion is the order of the day. No matter what a family member does, the Cancerian will eventually forgive him or her, because 'you are, after all, family'. The preservation of the institution – the tradition – of the family is one of the Cancerian's main reasons for living. They have many lessons to teach others about this.

Being so family-orientated, the Cancerian's home is always clean, orderly and comfortable. They like old-fashioned furnishings but they also like to have all the modern comforts. Cancerians love to have family and friends over, to organize parties and to entertain at home – they make great hosts.

Horoscope for 2010

Major Trends

Last year Pluto moved into your 7th house of love after 15 or so years in your 6th house. A major change. Your love life, social life, friendships, marriage and business partnerships are getting a thorough cosmic detox. Those of your born early in the sign of Cancer (June 21st–26th) are (and have been) feeling this most strongly, but in coming years all of you will start to experience it. Last year's trend is continuing.

There are two (and we can stretch and say three) eclipses in your own sign this year. And this shows major redefinitions of the personality, the self-concept (how you think of yourself) and the image (and how you present yourself to others). If you haven't been careful in dietary matters, these eclipses often bring on physical detoxes. More on this later.

This year two powerful planets make major – but brief – visits to your house of career. Jupiter moves in from June 6th to September 10th – a very happy and pleasant transit – and Uranus moves in from May 28th to August 14th. Those of you born early in the sign of Cancer will feel this strongest, but in coming years all of you will feel it. This is bringing major career changes – perhaps even a new career path – to many of you – and this year, at least, it looks happy and successful. More on this later.

Religion, philosophy, foreign travel and higher education have been important to you for many years, and this trend continues in the year ahead – perhaps even stronger than in years past. This is a year for foreign travel and success in higher education. It is an especially happy aspect for students or university applicants.

Saturn moved into your 4th house of home and family in late October of last year and will spend most of the year here in this house. (It moves back briefly into your 3rd house from April 8th to July 22nd.) So there is a need for taking on more responsibility at home. More on this later.

Your most important areas of interest in the coming year are finance (from January 1st to June 7th), communication and intellectual interests (April 8th to July 22nd), home and family (January 1st to April 8th and July 22nd to December 31st), love, romance and social activities, sex, life and death, death and rebirth, past lives and occult studies, religion, philosophy, higher education and foreign travel, and career (May 28th to September 10th).

Your paths of greatest fulfilment this year are love, romance and the social life, sex, life and death, death and rebirth, past lives, occult studies (January 1st to February 18th), and religion, philosophy, higher education and foreign travel (January 18th to June 6th and September 10th to December 31st).

Health

(Please note that this is an astrological perspective on health and not a medical one. In days gone by there was no difference; these perspectives were identical. But nowadays there can be quite a difference. For the medical perspective, please consult your doctor or health practitioner.)

This is a unique kind of year. Not so easy to catalogue or pigeonhole. Three major long-term planets change signs for brief periods this year. Most of them are leaving you alone, but when they change signs this could create some temporary problems. Happily this period is brief – from July 22nd to August 14th – but it seems intense. Pluto, Saturn, Uranus, Mars and Jupiter are all in stressful aspect to you and these are not powers to be trifled with. Be sure you take a more relaxed schedule during this period. Rest and relax more and keep your focus on the essentials of your life. Let the unimportant go.

For most of the year there are two long-term planets in stressful aspect on you – Saturn and Pluto. So health, in general, needs more watching. The problem this year is that with your 6th house of health empty you are tempted to ignore your health – and you shouldn't. You will need to force yourself to pay more attention here.

The good news is that there is much you can do to enhance the health. Pay more attention to the following areas of your body:

- heart
- ankles and calves (early in the year until January 18th – regular ankle and calf massage is good – give them more support when exercising)
- liver and thighs (regular thigh massage is good)
- feet (foot massage, see our chart, is powerful this year – especially from January 18th to June 6th and from September 10th to the end of the year)
- head, face and skull (regular scalp and face massage is good – cranial sacral therapy as well).

Since these are your most vulnerable areas, problems – should they happen – would most likely begin there. So keeping them healthy and fit is sound preventative medicine.

Reflexology

Try to massage the whole foot on a regular basis, but pay extra attention to the points highlighted on the chart. When you massage, be aware of 'sore spots', as these need special attention. It's also a good idea to massage the ankles and top side (as well as the soles) of the feet.

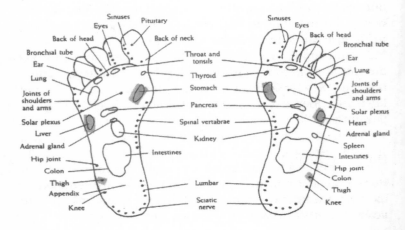

Your health planet is Jupiter. He is a long-term planet. Generally he stays in a sign for a whole year. But this year he moves through three (!) signs and houses of your horoscope – highly unusual. Thus at different times you need different kinds of therapies. While he is in Aquarius (January 1st–18th) the thighs and calves are important. When he moves into Pisces (January 18th to June 6th and September 10th to December 31st), your feet become important. Try to wear shoes that are sensible, that fit right and don't knock you off-balance. When he moves into Aries (June 6th to September 10th) the head and face become important.

In general, Jupiter rules religion, metaphysics and philosophy. So you are someone who benefits from metaphysical types of therapy – prayer and speaking of the word. Sessions of praise and worship, study of scripture tend to be healing for you. Also it is always important for you to have a clear and correct philosophy of health and disease – to understand how disease comes to be and how it manifests in the body (it goes much deeper than what they teach in medical school).

While Jupiter is in Aquarius you will continue your experimental tendencies of last year. Most of you will gravitate to alternative kinds of medicine. You will continue learning how you function – by trial and error and experiment.

With Jupiter in Pisces most of the year, the spiritual dimensions of healing will be important – exploring the power of the divine to heal the body directly with no intermediaries. More on this later.

While Jupiter is in Aries you will be more into physical fitness. Good health will be more than just 'no symptoms' – it means being able to jog or bike X amount of miles as well. Physical exercise is wonderful therapy during this period. Overall muscle tone is important.

Home and Family

Home and family are always important interests for you, but in the year ahead even more so. Saturn will spend most of the year in your 4th house. So this is a year for taking on even more family responsibility, for reorganizing the home, for better management of the family and the daily domestic routine.

The cosmos is working to set a 'correct order' in the home and family situation. Perhaps you have been lackadaisical in this area – too permissive, too lax. Now you will have to be more disciplined and organized.

Your spouse or partner seems very ambitious – focused on the career – and this can mean extra burdens for you.

Moves in the year ahead are not advisable. The horoscope is saying you have plenty of room where you are if you manage your space better. Furniture can be shifted, family members shuffled around, and space-saving devices are available.

While it is generally not advisable to apply corporate systems to the home, there are some good points to it. Things get done in the most efficient way. A little of this might be good in the year ahead – but don't go overboard. Setting up an efficient order will not be easy – you can expect resistance and more than a little rebellion from family members – but stick to it.

Saturn is the ruler of your 7th house of love, marriage, social activities and beauty. His presence in your 4th house suggests that you will be doing more entertaining from home and beautifying the home in the year ahead. There is a need to improve the aesthetics of the home. This seems very successful in the year ahead, for Saturn is in his most exalted position, in the sign of Libra.

For singles this can show a live-in relationship. The boyfriend or girlfriend comes to live with you. Also it shows that there are marriages happening in the family.

A parent or parent figure can be coming to stay for a while. This person seems to be making major renovations in his or her own home, and probably needs a place to stay. The marriage of this parent or parent figure is getting tested from May 28th to August 14th – and also in coming years. Siblings seem to have a status-quo year. Children of appropriate age are likely to move – in a sudden kind of way – from May 28th to August 14th. But this can also show renovations in the home.

The health of the parents or parent figures seems good. They might be feeling their age, or feeling depressed, but there is good news on the health front for them. Siblings need to explore the spiritual dimensions of health in a deeper way – also they benefit from vigorous physical exercise. Your spouse or partner needs to rest and relax more and pay more attention to health from May 28th to September 10th. Children would benefit from new and cutting-edge kinds of therapies – they are more experimental in health matters this year.

Finance and Career

Mars, which generally stays in a sign for 1½ months, will spend 5 months in your money house. If you consider that he has been in your money house the last 3 months of last year, this is a Mars transit of almost a year! Personally I have never seen anything like this. Highly unusual.

But this is suggesting many things. You are more proactive on the financial level. Working harder. You believe that you create wealth, create markets, through your personal efforts. You are aggressive in finances – risk-taking. You can be an impulsive spender and investor the first 5 months of the year. Some of this is very good. When your intuition is on, your 'impulses' and decisions are successful – your risk-taking works out – but if you are tired or off you can be hurt by this. Be especially careful of rashness from January 1st to March 10th during Mars' retrograde (very rare). Do more homework on both finance and in your career.

The purpose of this highly unusual transit is to develop a financial fearlessness. To overcome financial fear, to develop courage. This doesn't mean that you do foolhardy things. But only that you make the moves that need to be made without fear.

Mars also happens to be your career planet. So his unusual stay in your money house shows various things – elders, authorities and parent figures are supportive on a financial level. Money comes to you through pay rises. Your relations with the government play an important role in prosperity – government regulators and the like. But money can also be earned through government contracts or from companies that earn through government contracts.

For the first 5 months of the year (and it was true the latter part of last year, too) you define success in financial terms – not in terms of status or prestige. The more money you make, the more successful you feel. If you have two job opportunities – one pays well but is not very prestigious, while the other is prestigious but doesn't pay that well – you will choose the higher-paying position.

On the career front we see many major changes going on. Those of you born early in the sign of Cancer (June 21st–24th) will feel it very strongly in the year ahead. Those of you born later in the sign will have 'announcements' – promptings, feelings – of coming career changes, most likely in the year ahead. The status quo at your company, your job, your industry is being shaken up. Bosses are retiring, shuffled or being fired. The industry as a whole is shaken up. The rules are changing. Ultimately this is all very good. You are getting 'liberated' – probably in dramatic ways – to pursue the career that really fulfils you. The career that you were born to have. Those of you born early in the sign can expect sudden promotions and pay rises. The symbolism of the horoscope is 'sudden success'. Those of you born later in the sign will experience this in 2011.

There are job changes in the year ahead as well. Those of you who employ others will have to deal with employee instability and turnover. All these things seem like 'bolts from the blue' – they happen suddenly and unexpectedly.

Love and Social Life

As mentioned earlier, Pluto is now in your 7th house for many years to come. This trend is only in its beginning stages. There is a detox happening in your marriage, love and social life. This detox will not only purify your existing relationships (and also business partnerships) but will detox your attitudes to love and marriage. It is leading you – eventually, and through trials and dramas – to your own ideal of love and marriage, your personal ideal. You will get a first-hand glimpse of the attitudes and expectations that are blocking this from happening.

Many a marriage will fail in coming years, but many will survive and become stronger because of this purification. Much depends on the strength of your commitment and on the basic soundness of your relationship. Fundamentally good ones will easily survive.

Your love planet will spend most of the year in the romantic sign of Libra – a good signal for love and romance. Though Saturn tends to be practical about love – seeks stability, security, earning power and the like – in Libra he becomes more romantic. Once the 'practical issues' are settled, Saturn can be quite romantic – and this is what is happening.

For a few months this year Saturn will retrograde back into Virgo – from April 8th to July 22nd – and this will be a more difficult love period. The tendency will be to 'criticism and exaction' and this is not good for romance. Though you might not be engaging in this, you can attract partners who are. Lighten up a bit. Perfection is something we work towards, it is a goal to be achieved, a path to walk – don't expect it instantaneously.

Saturn will mostly be in your 4th house. This shows that family values, the ability to share feelings with another, emotional intimacy and emotional support are what you look for in a mate. Since the 4th house rules a parent figure (in a woman's chart it is the father, in a man's chart it is the mother) you will be attracted to parent figures.

Love opportunities will tend to happen close to home this year. No need to travel far and wide looking for love – it is there in the neighbourhood (especially from April 8th to July 22nd) or through family connections and at family gatherings. There are also love opportunities at lectures, educational settings and neighbourhood gatherings (from April 8th to July 22nd).

For the past 2 years mental and intellectual compatibility was important in love – and this will be the case while

Saturn returns to Virgo this year. But mostly now it is about emotional intimacy.

Some people feel that a romantic night out means going to the hot spots, the clubs or cabarets or theatre. But for you it could mean attending a lecture together, taking a course or just spending a quiet evening at home.

Those of you in or working towards their first marriage have a status-quo kind of year (though there is some crisis in the summer). Those working towards their second marriage have wonderful opportunities this year and it is likely to happen – either an actual marriage or a relationship that is like a marriage. Those working towards their third marriage have a status-quo kind of year. Marrieds will likely stay married and singles will likely stay single.

Friendships seem status quo for all of you.

Self-improvement

Saturn has been in your 3rd house for some years now – and will spend a few months here again in 2010. As mentioned in previous years, this is a time for setting your mind, your thinking and communication in right order. Disorderly or undisciplined speech gets punished – not tolerated by those around you. It is a time to think more deeply about things before you speak. Listen more, speak less. You will be amazed how much you learn by this practice. Also, many of you will find that you are mentally unsatisfied by superficial learning. When you study anything you want to go deeply into it. Thus, learning – real learning – will tend to be slower. For students – especially in our culture – this can be a problem. Depth of understanding is not usually rewarded. But your rewards will be interior ones – you will really know any subject that you study.

Saturn in your 4th house – for most of the year – brings other lessons. On the worldly level it brings a reorganization of the home and family situation. Tough love will be required and it must be handled 'just so' – in a very balanced way. Order in the home is a form of love and service –

though it seems uncomfortable. Chaos will do more damage than a justly applied discipline.

On a deeper level it is a time to reorganize – set into right order –your emotional life. You will find that many moods or feelings are not acceptable to those around you. Perhaps they were in the past, but not so now. You are called on to manage your feeling nature – but this needs to be done correctly. Repression of feeling is not the answer as it leads to depression and even physical illnesses. Unbridled expression is also not the answer as it sets negative vortexes into motion that will come back to you. This only amplifies the negativity in your emotional life.

But there is another way – and we have been writing about this for years, in the various reports. Express your feelings – but in a harmless way. Get them out of your system without 'downloading' them on others. There are many ways to do this. Write them out on paper and then throw the paper away. Talk them out into a tape recorder and then erase the tape. Say a little prayer, in your own words, asking that these negative patterns and feelings be removed from you for ever – you will be answered. Be careful that you don't reread what you've written or replay the tape. What you let out is considered a 'psychological bowel movement' and you would no more want to take this back into yourself than you would an actual bowel movement!

Also it will be very good to learn the positive ways to manage your moods and your feeling nature. This is done through prayer and meditation. A prolonged focus on something positive, elevating and ennobling will dispel anger and sadness. Praise and worship – of whoever your deity is – is a very quick way out of negative states. Singing, chanting and colour meditation also work very well. If you experiment with these various techniques you will find what works best for you.

There is a 'touch and let go' exercise in my book *A Technique for Meditation* that is very powerful for cleansing and releasing negative states.

Month-by-month Forecasts

January

Best Days Overall: 1, 3, 4, 18, 19, 28
Most Stressful Days Overall: 6, 7, 13, 14, 21, 22
Best Days for Love: 4, 5, 6, 13, 14, 15, 16, 25, 26
Best Days for Money: 2, 3, 4, 5, 6, 7, 13, 14, 15, 16, 17, 18, 25, 26, 27, 30
Best Days for Career: 2, 3, 11, 12, 21, 22

A very eventful and turbulent month, Cancer. You are still under the effect of the lunar eclipse of the 31st of last month and there is a solar eclipse on the 15th of this month. Both of these eclipses are powerful on you, so take a reduced schedule – a few days before and after. Avoid risky activities wherever possible. Of course, do the things that you need to do – no one should lose their job or get a divorce over this – but the unnecessary should be re-scheduled.

Every lunar eclipse affects your body, image and personality and this one is no different. If anything it is even stronger than usual, for it occurs in your 1st house. So, you are changing your image and redefining yourself. Probably you will be getting a new wardrobe and new accessories as you present a 'new look' to the world. If you haven't been careful in dietary matters, there could be a detox of the body as well.

Though this eclipse affects your personal self – your self-concept – it will inevitably affect your relationships as well. We attract according to who we are. And as you change yourself, you begin to attract different people into your life. Old people can be repelled and new types attracted (much depends on how radical the change is).

The solar eclipse on the 15th tests relationships – marriage and friendships. The eclipse occurs in your 7th house of love. Good relationships will survive and get even better – the dirty laundry that comes up will be cleansed, allowing the relationship to thrive. But flawed relationships probably won't.

Every solar eclipse affects your finances, and this one is no different. You are forced by circumstances to make long-needed changes either in your thinking, planning or strategy. Finances undergo a 'reality check'.

Your year begins in the midst of a yearly social peak. You are in the mood for romance. You are going out more, attending more parties and social gatherings, attending weddings, etc. But your love planet, Saturn, will start to retrograde on the 13th, counselling more caution in love. By all means, date, go out and have fun, but important love decisions should be avoided. You begin (on the 13th) a period of 'review' of your love and social life. This is an interior process. See what can be done to improve your happiness socially – perhaps there are improvements that can be made in your behaviour towards others, or in the kinds of friends that you want to attract. Take your time to attain social clarity now.

Finances are a little stressed, but this is short term. Parents or parent figures are mulling over financial aid – not yet clear what they want to do. There is a need to work harder, overcome more obstacles, to attain your financial goals. If you are willing to overcome the challenges – put in the extra work – the month ahead can be prosperous indeed.

February

Best Days Overall: 5, 6, 15, 16, 24, 25
Most Stressful Days Overall: 2, 3, 9, 10, 11, 17, 18
Best Days for Love: 2, 3, 9, 10, 11, 12, 14, 15, 22, 24, 25
Best Days for Money: 2, 3, 4, 5, 13, 14, 15, 24, 25, 26, 27
Best Days for Career: 7, 17, 18, 26

Your year begins with most – 70 to 80 per cent – of the planets above the horizon. So, you are in the 'daytime' of your year. Day is for overt, outer activity – activity in the world – for pursuing your career and outer objectives. Family is always important to you (it is really the reason why you pursue a career) but now is a time for focusing on your career. We see the importance of your career in other ways, too. Mars, your career planet, is forming the handle of a 'bucket chart' this month and last month. It is the way – the handle – by which you lift up your entire life and circumstances now. It is also the way you make money. The retrograde of Mars (last month as well) shows a need to review your career and to see how you can improve things. There are many career developments happening behind the scenes, but to you it seems that there are delays. You need to be more careful of how you communicate to superiors, bosses and authority figures – don't take things for granted. Give your career more focus, but don't be dismayed if results have a 'delayed reaction' – your work and your focus will not be lost or wasted.

Your year begins with most of the planets in the Western, social sector of the chart. Thus you are in a period where you are developing, honing and refining your social skills. Personal independence is not the vital factor for success – it is more about your 'people skills' and your likeability. Adapt to situations now – later on in the year there will be more freedom and power to change your conditions.

A very happy financial windfall comes on the 14th–15th (the New Moon). It not only brings money or financial opportunity, but intuition and revelation about your personal financial condition. Sometimes this revelation is worth more than actual money as it leads to wealth. A foreign journey could manifest during this period as well – or the opportunity to travel. Students are having success in their studies. Religious and philosophical breakthroughs happen. Another happy financial windfall happens on the 27th and 28th – there is luck in speculations then, too. A happy job opportunity comes for job-seekers. Inspired ideas come to you on the 27th and 28th as well – intuition is very sharp then.

In finance, work to help others prosper until the 18th. Keep the financial interests of others paramount in your mind. A good period to pay off debt and cut expenses.

Consolidate your bank or brokerage accounts – get slimmer and trimmer financially. This is a good period for borrowing money, for accessing outside capital or for dealing with tax or estate issues, too.

March

    Best Days Overall: 1, 3, 4, 18, 19, 28
    Most Stressful Days Overall: 2, 3, 9, 10, 16, 17, 29, 30
    Best Days for Love: 2, 5, 6, 9, 10, 11, 16, 17, 21, 25, 26, 29
    Best Days for Money: 4, 5, 14, 15, 23, 24, 25, 26, 31
    Best Days for Career: 6, 16, 17, 25

Most of the planets are still above the horizon, and this month – from the 7th onwards – your 10th house of career becomes powerful and active. Never lose your focus on your family, but pay more attention to your career. Many wonderful things are happening this month. First off, Mars, your career planet, starts moving forward after many months of retrograde motion. (It has been retrograde since the beginning of the year.) So, career plans and career goals are much more clear now. You have a clear direction. Your good professional reputation (and you need to guard this) is the source of profits and financial opportunity (this too has been the case since the beginning of the year). Moreover, as Venus, Mercury and the Sun move into Aries (on the 7th, 17th and 20th respectively) they not only energize your 10th house of career, but make fabulous and benefic aspects to Mars, your career planet. So this is a month of great career success. There is promotion, elevation, honour and recognition for your achievements. Pay rises are likely now too. (Sometimes we don't see these things immediately, but the events that happen now set the course for pay rises in the future.) Beginning the 20th you enter a yearly career peak as well. (You are in the noontime of your year.)

Your 9th house is very powerful this month – powerful and happy. Your mental horizons are expanding. You have many religious and philosophical breakthroughs – happy ones. There is great interest in theology – and with these kinds of aspects, many people actually prefer a good theological discussion to a night out on the town. Amazing but true. There is a joy in these things. Students are succeeding in their studies. There is foreign travel – or the opportunity for foreign travel now. There are happy educational opportunities. Job-seekers have many happy opportunities – either in foreign countries or with foreign companies. The 9th house is considered by many (especially the Hindu astrologers) to be the most fortunate of all the houses. So this is a happy month – a prosperous month, as earnings will increase – an optimistic month. A healthy optimism is vital to success.

Your love life is still under review. There are stresses this month, but these should not be considered 'punitive' but 'revelatory' – the cosmos is showing you the nature of your challenges – highlighting them as if on a huge bill board – this makes it easier for you to resolve them.

Health needs watching after the 20th. Pay more attention to your heart then. Do whatever you can to reduce stress and to maintain high energy levels. Enhance your health along the lines mentioned in the yearly report.

April

Best Days Overall: 1, 10, 11, 19, 20, 28, 29
Most Stressful Days Overall: 5, 6, 13, 14, 26, 27
Best Days for Love: 5, 6, 7, 15, 16, 25
Best Days for Money: 1, 3, 4, 10, 11, 13, 14, 19, 20, 22, 23, 24, 28, 29
Best Days for Career: 3, 13, 14, 22, 30

Spring is here. The Sun is in Aries – the sign of action – and 90 per cent of the planets are in forward motion until the 18th. The pace of events quickens. Progress is rapid. This is the time (and I like the 14th the best) for releasing new projects or products into the world. There is much cosmic momentum behind you. The wind is at your back propelling you forward.

You are still in your yearly career peak until the 20th and much happy progress is being made now. There is much career success these days as the planets in your 10th house are still making nice aspects to your career planet, Mars.

Problems at home are easing up temporarily as Saturn retrogrades out of your 4th house on the 3rd. All the more reason for focusing on your career.

Finances are basically good though there are some bumps in the road from the 14th to the 16th. Don't panic. Things will work out. These surprises will lead to positive changes. Challenges are the cosmos' way of opening new doors of opportunity for you.

As we saw last month, and for the entire year, your good professional reputation is vital for your prosperity. Don't do anything that would tarnish it. Keep it uppermost in your mind. Bosses, elders, parents and parent figures (and perhaps the government as well) are supporting your financial goals. If you have issues with the government, this is a good time to deal with them. These figures are more supportive before the 20th than afterwards, so try to resolve issues with them – or make your requests – early in the month.

Love is more challenging this month. The good news is that you are more analytical and rational in your love attitudes. With your love life still under review, it is good that you can see all the little flaws and imperfections – this will enable you to make things more perfect. However, in your relations with your spouse or current love (or prospective love), try to avoid destructive criticism and an attitude of 'exaction'. This will kill off any chance of romance – the wrong faculties are being used. Analysis is good when you are alone and reviewing things. Not when you are in actual romantic moments. No question you will have to work harder to show your natural warmth to others. You might be projecting – unconsciously – a feeling of 'coldness' and distance.

Romance might be challenging, but friendships seem happy and this is the theme of the month after the 20th.

May

Best Days Overall: 7, 8, 9, 17, 18, 25, 26
Most Stressful Days Overall: 2, 3, 4, 10, 11, 23, 24, 30, 31
Best Days for Love: 2, 3, 4, 5, 6, 14, 15, 16, 22, 25, 26, 30, 31
Best Days for Money: 2, 3, 8, 9, 12, 13, 18, 19, 20, 23, 25, 26
Best Days for Career: 1, 10, 11, 19, 20, 27, 28

A financial disagreement with a boss, parent, or parent figure will resolve itself by the 21st. Finances are good but will get even better after the 21st. Career success is important and it is happening, but try not to be too money conscious early in the month. Succeed, get promoted and the money will naturally follow. Try not to make too many assumptions about your career, your industry or company – big changes are on the way, upsets and surprises, beginning the 28th. This will open doors for you next month. There are job changes in the works – sudden and dramatic. Job-seekers have sudden opportunity.

By the 28th most of the planets will be in the Eastern sector of your horoscope, so this is a time for more independence and personal initiative. Stop relying on others for your happiness (and don't waste time blaming others – the time for this is past) – you are in charge of your happiness. You have the power now to create conditions as you like them to be – to design them according to your specifications. The world wants your happiness and will conform to you rather than the other way round.

Continue to focus on your career and outer objectives. Family issues seem easier these days and don't require too much attention. With Pluto now retrograde, avoid making major decisions involving children. There needs to be more study here – your judgement might not be realistic.

Your 11th house of friends is very powerful until the 21st. Thus this is a socially strong month. Good to be involved in group activities and being there for your friends (they will be there for you as well). This is a month – especially until the 21st – for manifesting your fondest hopes and wishes – especially in your financial life. Perhaps you won't manifest all of them now, but you will manifest some and make good progress towards your bigger goals.

Friendships seem happy but love and romance is more challenging. As mentioned last month, you need to work harder – make conscious effort – to project warmth and love towards others. You are by nature a loving person, warm and affectionate. But it is probably not coming through as it should these days. So make the extra effort. If you do, your love life will start becoming much easier. It is probably not ideal – there is conflict after the 21st – but at least you won't be making a difficult situation even worse. Again, be careful of judgemental and destructive criticism.

Venus moving into your sign on the 20th will certainly help your social life if you are single. It brings personal beauty, a sense of style, a physical grace and elegance to your body and image. You dress more attractively and project more glamour. Also helping your love life is the fact that the Moon will spend more time in your 7th house this month than usual – 5 days instead of the normal 2–3 days. This shows that you are making more social efforts and going out of your way for other people. Your love planet is still retrograde, so avoid making major love decisions one way or another. Your marriage, current love relationship and social life in general are still under review.

June

Best Days Overall: 4, 5, 13, 14, 21, 22
Most Stressful Days Overall: 6, 7, 19, 20, 26, 27
Best Days for Love: 4, 5, 10, 13, 14, 18, 24, 25, 26, 27
Best Days for Money: 1, 2, 5, 6, 11, 12, 15, 16, 21, 24
Best Days for Career: 6, 7, 8, 17, 26, 27

Jupiter is travelling with Uranus this month – a rare occurrence that only happens every 14–15 years or so. Not only that, but Jupiter moves into your 10th house of career – bringing success, sudden new job opportunities, sudden advancement and promotion. There are also happy financial windfalls coming to you from the 21st onwards as your financial planet crosses your Ascendant and enters your 1st house. These windfalls could also happen suddenly and unexpectedly. Perhaps you spend more during this period as well. You and your spouse or partner don't agree about finances, but the problem is short term. It passes by the 25th or thereabouts.

This is a month where you seem to be in the 'sweet spot' financially – especially after the 21st. Financial opportunities seek you out rather than vice versa. You project an image of wealth and are probably spending more on yourself – your image. You invest in yourself – the wisest investment there is.

Until the 21st you are in a strong spiritual period. Perhaps the strongest of your year. These are times when the doors to the invisible world stand open for you. No matter what your situation or condition – no matter what is going on in your outer life – spirit can handle it. Its energies are not of this world. They come from a heavenly dimension of perfection, and when invited into your life will just naturally create perfection. This is a month (until the 21st) where you will be experiencing much supernatural phenomena. Your dream life will be more active and prophetic, ESP will be strong and there will be many synchronistic-type experiences – strange coincidences that can't be explained logically. (They are very logical from the spiritual perspective, however – nothing at all illogical about them.)

This is also a wonderful period to review the past year in a sober and honest way. Where were you mistaken? Where did you fail? Where did you succeed? Where do you want to go from here? Correct your mistakes (religious people would say 'make atonement') and set new and happy goals for the year ahead. Your upcoming birthday is your personal new year and will set the tone for the coming year for you.

On the 21st, as the Sun enters your sign, you enter a yearly personal pleasure peak. A time for giving the body the pleasures that it needs. The body is not our enemy but our friend – our faithful companion in life. It's time to give yours a little indulgence. Of course, if you overdo it, you will pay a price for this later on.

A lunar eclipse on the 26th affects children and those who are like children to you. They are forced to change their image, self-concept and the way they present themselves to the world. Probably children will have dramas in their lives, too – many of these are merely love messages from above to force them to make necessary changes or correct behaviour. This eclipse, once again, tests the marriage or current relationship. But now with your love planet in forward motion, you are in a better position to make love decisions that need to be made.

Avoid speculations from the 19th to the 27th.

July

    Best Days Overall: 1, 2, 10, 11, 19, 20, 28, 29, 30
    Most Stressful Days Overall: 4, 5, 17, 23, 24, 25, 31
    Best Days for Love: 5, 7, 14, 16, 23, 24, 25, 26
    Best Days for Money: 1, 2, 3, 10, 11, 12, 13, 20, 21, 31
    Best Days for Career: 4, 5, 6, 7, 15, 16, 24, 25, 31

A solar eclipse on the 11th is an almost exact replay of the lunar eclipse of December 31, 2009 (which has been in effect until last month). It brings financial changes – changes in financial thinking, planning and strategy. Probably you were making decisions under the incorrect or incomplete assumptions; the eclipse will straighten this out. There can be sudden expenses (or sudden windfalls) or career developments behind these changes – nevertheless, you need to spend more time and energy on finance than you usually would. Since this eclipse occurs in your 1st house it brings a redefinition – a re-evaluation – of your self-concept, the way you think about yourself, the way that you want others to see you. As mentioned earlier, every time we change ourselves – our definition of self – we automatically have an impact on our love life and relationships. For we always attract who we are – yes, this is a bitter pill to swallow sometimes, but it is true. Change yourself and you change your social circle almost automatically.

Children are difficult to handle now – they too are going through changes – be more patient. Lend a helping hand where possible, but otherwise let the process continue.

This eclipse is strong on you, so take a reduced schedule. As our steady readers know, you don't stop your life completely and hide in a hole. No, you do the necessary but re-schedule the unnecessary. You avoid or re-schedule risky or stressful kinds of activities – such as surgery or foreign travel and the like.

Career is going great guns – sudden advancement, happy job changes, promotions and honours are still happening, but it is time to shift more attention to your family and emotional issues. On the 21st the planetary power once again shifts from the upper to the lower half of your horoscope. The sun is setting in your year and you enter the night. For some people this is uncomfortable, they are more in tune with the 'day' – with outer, objective activity. But for you this is happy. You are a classic night person (of course your personal horoscope calculated specifically for your date and time of birth could modify this). Going down memory lane, reviewing the past, is almost a form of entertainment for you. Some people like the clubs and theatres. But you enjoy a past-life regression or prenatal regression just as much. Delving into moods and emotions is more than just therapeutic – it is entertainment. So you will have no problem in pursuing your outer goals by the ways of night – by dreaming, visualizing, setting goals – by internal means rather than external ones. You, more than anyone, know the value and healing power of the night.

You are into another prosperous month. Until the 23rd financial opportunities are seeking you out. You only have to show up. After the 23rd you enter a yearly financial peak – one of the most prosperous periods in your year. Happy job opportunities come from the 22nd to the 26th – but study them more carefully. Those who employ others find good employees then, too.

August

Best Days Overall: 7, 8, 15, 16, 25, 26
Most Stressful Days Overall: 1, 13, 14, 20, 21, 27, 28
Best Days for Love: 3, 4, 13, 19, 20, 21, 22, 23
Best Days for Money: 1, 9, 10, 17, 18, 27, 29, 30
Best Days for Career: 1, 4, 5, 13, 22, 23, 27, 28

Be careful of a power struggle in love early in the month (it could have happened late last month as well). Another testing of the marriage and current relationship. Take a few deep breaths and count to 10 before answering provocations.

A parent seems in conflict with your spouse or partner as well.

Career is still exciting but the demands of the home and family are even stronger. You have a nice balancing act on your hands this month. (Next month it will be easier.)

Things at home are stormy. Passions are running high with family members. Parent or parent figures seem overly meddling. However, Venus entering your 4th house shows that there are opportunities to create harmony. This is a good month to renovate or beautify the home – try to do it before the 20th, as Mercury goes retrograde then.

Health needs more watching this month. Pay more attention to your head, face and skull (head and face massage will be wonderful). Cranial sacral therapy is good, too. Also focus on your heart. Work to reduce stress and tension. Avoid excess worry (easier said than done). If there is something constructive to be done, of course do it – but let go of the worry. It does nothing to help your situation. Of course rest and relax more and maintain high energy levels – this is probably the most important thing. Your health planet is retrograde now, so avoid making drastic changes to your diet or health regime – when energy is low it is very tempting to make big changes, we grasp at straws. Better to do your homework first, though.

You are still well into your yearly financial peak until the 23rd. This is your month for financial stardom. People measure how well they are doing by comparing themselves to you. You are (and have the potential to be) the 'gold standard' for others.

After the 23rd the focus shifts to communication and intellectual interests. Generally after a financial peak we feel 'sated'. We want to enjoy our money. We want to do things that we normally couldn't afford – like expand the mind, study things that interest us and learn. The whole point of money is to give a person freedom to develop the mind. This takes free time – leisure.

On a more mundane level, sales, marketing, media activities and good use of the media are important on a financial level. Money is earned through trading, buying and selling, retailing and things of that nature.

Love is improving as your love planet has moved into romantic Libra. But love is still being tested.

September

Best Days Overall: 3, 4, 11, 12, 21, 22
Most Stressful Days Overall: 9, 10, 16, 17, 23, 24, 25
Best Days for Love: 1, 2, 9, 11, 16, 17, 18, 21, 28
Best Days for Money: 5, 6, 7, 8, 12, 17, 22, 28
Best Days for Career: 2, 10, 11, 20, 21, 23, 24, 25

Career, though still very promising, is less important now. All the planets involved in your career are retrograde this month. So you can take a breather (safely, without missing opportunities) and focus on home and family. This is still a good period for entertaining from home, beautifying the home or doing construction or major renovations. Passions among family members are still running high and your job is to stay centred and calm – a point of peace in the centre of the chaos. Merely observe – not only the passions of family

members, but your own. Great psychological progress will
be made this way.

This is a period where your work is to find your point of
emotional harmony – but this will be a challenge these days.

Health needs watching, too – perhaps even more than last
month. Keep in mind our discussion of last month.

Finances seem status quo. The money house is empty
(only the Moon visits on the 5th and 6th). Like last month
you can enhance profits through good sales, marketing, PR
and advertising. Important to get the word out – to educate
people – about your product or service. After the 23rd,
family seems more supportive financially. Parents or parent
figures especially. Family connections or family businesses
boost the bottom line. You are spending more on the home
and family – but they are a source of support as well.
Investors should look at the health industry, telecommunications, transport and media until the 23rd, and to property
and the beauty industry afterwards. A business partnership
or joint venture seems likely after the 23rd. The opportunity will certainly be there. On the 27th to 29th there are
some financial upheavals and changes, but they are short
term.

Love is being severely tested this month. Saturn, your
love planet, is camping out on an eclipse point (the lunar
eclipse of June 26th) all month. Good relationships will
survive, of course, but it's a bumpy ride. Be more patient
with family members and your beloved.

A child (or child figure in your life) is beginning to find
direction in his or her life now. There is a job opportunity
coming to him or her after the 15th. Also there is love in his
or her life after the 8th. There is more confidence and self-
esteem. Personal appearance is much improved as well.

Singles will find love opportunities close to home –
through family connections or through introductions made
by family members. Old flames can come back into the
picture, too. The past is unusually alluring now that there
are so many planets in your 4th house. Nothing wrong with
exploring the past or enjoying it – the only danger, now, is

living in the past. Life always marches on. Every hour is new and unique.

October

Best Days Overall: 1, 2, 9, 10, 18, 19, 28, 29
Most Stressful Days Overall: 7, 8, 13, 14, 21, 22
Best Days for Love: 1, 7, 9, 13, 14, 16, 18, 19, 26, 28
Best Days for Money: 2, 3, 4, 7, 10, 17, 19, 27, 28, 29, 30, 31
Best Days for Career: 1, 9, 19, 20, 21, 22, 30

Most of the planets are now in the Western, social sector of your horoscope. Your focus is on other people and getting on with them. Personal independence, though a great virtue and something to be admired, is not the road to success these days – likeability, personal charm, the ability to get others to co-operate with you – these bring success. You need the good graces of others. So you are training your social skills now. You are sort of stuck (for the meantime) with the conditions you created during your independent phase – for better or worse. You have to adapt yourself as best you can to the way things are. Down the road – in the Spring of 2011 – you will have another period of personal independence and you will be able to create anew. (It's not that you can't create new conditions now – it's just harder to do.)

This is good for your love life. Love is much improved this month. Saturn is in romantic Libra, his most exalted position. And now Saturn has moved off the eclipse point. If your marriage or current relationship survived last month, it can pretty much survive anything. You gravitate to people who have strong family values – like yours. You like the niceties of romance, but also need emotional nurturing, emotional sharing and emotional compatibility. Emotional intimacy is as important as physical intimacy. Like last month (and for most of the past year) love opportunities come close to home, from family connections, family gatherings or family introductions. Romantically, you are still allured by the past – there are some good points to this – but the downside is getting stuck in old patterns – repeating the same old, same old love patterns over and over. In many cases this leads to reunions with old flames. Or, more likely, meetings with people who have the same patterns and characteristics as old flames.

Home and family is the main focus this month. On the 22nd, as the Sun enters your 5th house, you're in another yearly personal pleasure peak.

Health is much improved – and you seem to be paying more attention here – especially after the 27th. Physical exercise is excellent after the 27th. Pay more attention to your head, face, skull (after the 22nd) and your heart (all month). Your liver, thighs and feet are important all year. As in the past few months, avoid making major, dramatic changes to your diet or health regime without due study and research.

Job-seekers have opportunities, but they need more homework as your work planet is still retrograde.

Finances are happy this month. There is luck in speculations (after the 22nd). Money comes in happy ways and you seem to enjoy the act of money-making – it is a pleasure as much as any other. When your financial planet is in the 5th house, money-making becomes more fun than a night out on the town. But you are also spending more on leisure activities as well – and on your children (or children figures in your life). Until the 22nd money is earned through the family and family connections – you are spending more on the family and home as well.

November

Best Days Overall: 5, 6, 14, 15, 16, 24, 25
Most Stressful Days Overall: 3, 4, 10, 11, 17, 18
Best Days for Love: 3, 4, 5, 10, 11, 12, 13, 22, 23
Best Days for Money: 5, 6, 15, 16, 25, 26, 27
Best Days for Career: 7, 17, 18, 27, 28

Health is much improved this month, but with Saturn still stressing you out, you need to watch your energy and focus only on the essentials in your life. Still you are feeling much better and more energetic than last month. Also you seem more focused on health these days – especially after the 22nd. You are into exercise and healthy lifestyles. You are working for financial good health as well as physical good health. You spend more on health and health issues but can also earn from these fields. Enhance your health through physical exercise, through paying more attention to your head, face, and skull (regular scalp and face massage is powerful), your heart (after the 22nd) and your lungs, small intestine, arms and shoulders (after the 8th). Mental health – the health of the mental body – is important after the 8th. Keep your speech constructive. Give your mind the exercise it needs. Strive for intellectual purity. Errors in the mind not only cause all kinds of suffering in worldly affairs, but if held, can actually manifest as a physical pathology. Spiritual healing becomes important after the 8th – you go more deeply into it – and it is powerful for you.

This is a month for both working hard and playing hard. Both the 5th and the 6th houses are strong. There is the natural joy that comes from doing what you love and indulging in entertainments, and then there is a joy in productive service – in work. You will explore both this month.

When the 6th house is powerful it is good to do all those 'boring' detail-orientated tasks that you generally dislike – getting your accounting straight, reviewing your tax situation, fixing your computer or installing the new software that needs to be installed – things of that nature.

Love is good this month. Much improved over the past few months. But it more or less maintains the status quo. The testings in your marriage or current relationship seem to be resolved.

Job-seekers have good success this month. There seem to be many opportunities. I like after the 18th better than before the 18th – Jupiter, your work planet, starts moving forward then and your judgement will be better.

Until the 22nd there is luck in speculations, and money is earned in happy and fun kinds of ways. You are spending – like last month – on leisure activities and on children. Parents are investing more in their children – more than usual. But children are also more supportive of financial goals and can have interesting wealth ideas. After the 22nd you earn the old-fashioned way, through work and practical service.

December

Best Days Overall: 3, 4, 12, 13, 21, 22, 30, 31
Most Stressful Days Overall: 1, 7, 8, 14, 15, 16, 28, 29
Best Days for Love: 1, 2, 7, 8, 10, 12, 20, 22, 28, 31
Best Days for Money: 4, 5, 13, 16, 23, 24, 26, 31
Best Days for Career: 6, 14, 15, 16, 17, 26

Health needs more watching this month – especially after the 21st. Happily you are more focused on health now – more health conscious – and you seem on the case. You are not ignoring things. Enhance health by paying more attention to your heart (all month), your head, face, skull and musculature (until the 8th), and through physical exercise (until the 8th). Your lungs, small intestine, arms and shoulders become important after the 18th. Regular shoulder and arm massage will be good – this will help not only these parts but your entire body. As always, work to maintain high energy levels. Keep your petrol tank full.

There is a lunar eclipse on the 21st that is strong on you – especially those of you born early in the sign of Cancer. It occurs right on the border – the cusp – of Gemini and Cancer – your 12th and 1st houses. Thus it will have an impact on both these houses. It brings spiritual changes – revelations that cause you to change your practice, teachers and spiritual attitudes. Dreams will be active, but not very trustworthy, during this period and you shouldn't give them too much weight. Every lunar eclipse affects on your body, your image and your self-concept, but this one even more so (it is right near your 1st house) – so once again you get the opportunity to redefine yourself – to reinvent yourself on a better and happier level. As our steady readers know, changes in the self-concept produce changes in the image and wardrobe – and tend to affect relationships as well. If your spouse, partner or current love can adjust to these changes, or if the changes are pleasing to them, all well and good. But if the changes are displeasing, the relationship will get tested. If you were born between July 22nd and 25th, take a reduced schedule and avoid risky activities.

You end your year as you began it – in a yearly social peak. Of course, most people are socializing more at this time of year – but for you it's more than most. Again we see people of power and prestige – the high and mighty – in your social sphere. Wealthy people as well. Singles have many options and opportunities. The menu seems big. Business partnerships or joint ventures are probable after the 21st. Your social connections are like money in the bank. And, with most of the planets in the Western sector your wealth and success come from the good graces of others and not so much because of your skills or personal initiative. Likeability and social grace are more prized than actual ability. There is luck in speculations from the 20th to the 25th – but only speculate under intuition. Be careful of overspending during this period and do more homework on investments or major purchases. There can be some short-term financial disagreements with your beloved towards the end of the month – but these will pass.

Leo

♌

THE LION
Birthdays from
21st July to
21st August

Personality Profile

LEO AT A GLANCE

Element – Fire

Ruling Planet – Sun
    Career Planet – Venus
    Love Planet – Uranus
    Money Planet – Mercury
    Planet of Health and Work – Saturn
    Planet of Home and Family Life – Pluto

Colours – gold, orange, red

*Colours that promote love, romance and social
    harmony* – black, indigo, ultramarine blue

Colours that promote earning power – yellow,
    yellow-orange

Gems – amber, chrysolite, yellow diamond

Metal – gold

Scents – bergamot, frankincense, musk, neroli

Quality – fixed (= stability)

Quality most needed for balance – humility

Strongest virtues – leadership ability, self-esteem and confidence, generosity, creativity, love of joy

Deepest needs – fun, elation, the need to shine

Characteristics to avoid – arrogance, vanity, bossiness

Signs of greatest overall compatibility – Aries, Sagittarius

Signs of greatest overall incompatibility – Taurus, Scorpio, Aquarius

Sign most helpful to career – Taurus

Sign most helpful for emotional support – Scorpio

Sign most helpful financially – Virgo

Sign best for marriage and/or partnerships – Aquarius

Sign most helpful for creative projects – Sagittarius

Best Sign to have fun with – Sagittarius

Signs most helpful in spiritual matters – Aries, Cancer

Best day of the week – Sunday

Understanding a Leo

When you think of Leo, think of royalty – then you'll get the idea of what the Leo character is all about and why Leos are the way they are. It is true that, for various reasons, some Leo-born do not always express this quality – but even if not they should like to do so.

A monarch rules not by example (as does Aries) nor by consensus (as do Capricorn and Aquarius) but by personal will. Will is law. Personal taste becomes the style that is imitated by all subjects. A monarch is somehow larger than life. This is how a Leo desires to be.

When you dispute the personal will of a Leo it is serious business. He or she takes it as a personal affront, an insult. Leos will let you know that their will carries authority and that to disobey is demeaning and disrespectful.

A Leo is king (or queen) of his or her personal domain. Subordinates, friends and family are the loyal and trusted subjects. Leos rule with benevolent grace and in the best interests of others. They have a powerful presence; indeed, they are powerful people. They seem to attract attention in any social gathering. They stand out because they are stars in their domain. Leos feel that, like the Sun, they are made to shine and rule. Leos feel that they were born to special privilege and royal prerogatives – and most of them attain this status, at least to some degree.

The Sun is the ruler of this sign, and when you think of sunshine it is very difficult to feel unhealthy or depressed. Somehow the light of the Sun is the very antithesis of illness and apathy. Leos love life. They also love to have fun; they love drama, music, the theatre and amusements of all sorts. These are the things that give joy to life. If – even in their best interests – you try to deprive Leos of their pleasures, good food, drink and entertainment, you run the serious risk of depriving them of the will to live. To them life without joy is no life at all.

Leos epitomize humanity's will to power. But power in and of itself – regardless of what some people say – is neither good nor evil. Only when power is abused does it become evil. Without power even good things cannot come to pass. Leos realize this and are uniquely qualified to wield power. Of all the signs, they do it most naturally. Capricorn, the other power sign of the zodiac, is a better manager and administrator than Leo – much better. But Leo outshines Capricorn in personal grace and presence. Leo loves power, where Capricorn assumes power out of a sense of duty.

Finance

Leos are great leaders but not necessarily good managers. They are better at handling the overall picture than the nitty-gritty details of business. If they have good managers working for them they can become exceptional executives. They have vision and a lot of creativity.

Leos love wealth for the pleasures it can bring. They love an opulent lifestyle, pomp and glamour. Even when they are not wealthy they live as if they are. This is why many fall into debt, from which it is sometimes difficult to emerge.

Leos, like Pisceans, are generous to a fault. Very often they want to acquire wealth solely so that they can help others economically. Wealth to Leo buys services and managerial ability. It creates jobs for others and improves the general well-being of those around them. Therefore – to a Leo – wealth is good. Wealth is to be enjoyed to the fullest. Money is not to be left to gather dust in a mouldy bank vault but to be enjoyed, spread around, used. So Leos can be quite reckless in their spending.

With the sign of Virgo on Leo's 2nd house (of money) cusp, Leo needs to develop some of Virgo's traits of analysis, discrimination and purity when it comes to money matters. They must learn to be more careful with the details of finance (or to hire people to do this for them). They have to be more cost-conscious in their spending habits. Generally, they need to manage their money better. Leos tend to chafe under financial constraints, yet these constraints can help Leos to reach their highest financial potential.

Leos like it when their friends and family know that they can depend on them for financial support. They do not mind – even enjoy – lending money, but they are careful that they are not taken advantage of. From their 'regal throne' Leos like to bestow gifts upon their family and friends and then enjoy the good feelings these gifts bring to everybody. Leos love financial speculations and – when the celestial influences are right – are often lucky.

Career and Public Image

Leos like to be perceived as wealthy, for in today's world wealth often equals power. When they attain wealth they love having a large house with lots of land and animals.

At their jobs Leos excel in positions of authority and power. They are good at making decisions – on a grand level – but they prefer to leave the details to others. Leos are well respected by their colleagues and subordinates, mainly because they have a knack for understanding and relating to those around them. Leos usually strive for the top positions even if they have to start at the bottom and work hard to get there. As might be expected of such a charismatic sign, Leos are always trying to improve their work situation. They do so in order to have a better chance of advancing to the top.

On the other hand, Leos do not like to be bossed around or told what to do. Perhaps this is why they aspire so for the top – where they can be the decision-makers and need not take orders from others.

Leos never doubt their success and focus all their attention and efforts on achieving it. Another great Leo characteristic is that – just like good monarchs – they do not attempt to abuse the power or success they achieve. If they do so this is not wilful or intentional. Usually they like to share their wealth and try to make everyone around them join in their success.

Leos are – and like to be perceived as – hard-working, well-established individuals. It is definitely true that they are capable of hard work and often manage great things. But do not forget that, deep down inside, Leos really are fun-lovers.

Love and Relationships

Generally, Leos are not the marrying kind. To them relationships are good while they are pleasurable. When the relationship ceases to be pleasurable a true Leo will want out. They always want to have the freedom to leave. That is why Leos excel at love affairs rather than commitment. Once married, however, Leo is faithful – even if some Leos have a tendency to marry more than once in their lifetime. If you are in love with a Leo, just show him or her a good time. Travel, go to casinos and clubs, the theatre and discos. Wine and dine your Leo love – it is expensive but worth it and you will have fun.

Leos generally have an active love life and are demonstrative in their affections. They love to be with other optimistic and fun-loving types like themselves, but wind up settling with someone more serious, intellectual and unconventional. The partner of a Leo tends to be more political and socially conscious than he or she is, and more libertarian. When you marry a Leo, mastering the freedom-loving tendencies of your partner will definitely become a life-long challenge – and be careful that Leo does not master you.

Aquarius sits on Leo's 7th house (of love) cusp. Thus if Leos want to realize their highest love and social potential they need to develop a more egalitarian, Aquarian perspective on others. This is not easy for Leo, for 'the king' finds his equals only among other 'kings'. But perhaps this is the solution to Leo's social challenge – to be 'a king among kings'. It is all right to be royal, but recognize the nobility in others.

Home and Domestic Life

Although Leos are great entertainers and love having people over, sometimes this is all show. Only very few close friends will get to see the real side of a Leo's day-to-day life. To a Leo the home is a place of comfort, recreation and transformation; a secret, private retreat – a castle. Leos like to spend money, show off a bit, entertain and have fun. They enjoy the latest furnishings, clothes and gadgets – all things fit for kings.

Leos are fiercely loyal to their family and of course expect the same from them. They love their children almost to a fault; they have to be careful not to spoil them too much. They also must try to avoid attempting to make individual family members over in their own image. Leos should keep in mind that others also have the need to be their own people. That is why Leos have to be extra careful about being over-bossy or over-domineering in the home.

Horoscope for 2010

Major Trends

Last year was a banner love and social year – and the trend continues in the year ahead. Love is exciting, dramatic and unpredictable – a soap opera – just the way you like things. Many of you married in the past year, or got involved in serious kinds of relationships – those of you who haven't still have wonderful aspects in the year ahead. But hold on to your hat, love is a roller-coaster ride – never a dull moment!

Mars moved into your own sign October 17th of last year and was there until the end of the year. This year Mars will be in your sign until June 7th. This is a highly unusual Mars transit – he will have been in your sign for almost 8 months instead of his normal 1½- to 2-month transit. This is a good health indicator as it gives more energy and drive. It shows that you will be more athletic, more into physical exercise for the first 5 months of the year. And since Mars rules your 9th house many of you will be travelling and more involved with higher education, religion and philosophy. Many of these journeys and educational opportunities will happen suddenly and dramatically. For students going to university this is a happy aspect as it shows that universities are pursuing you rather than vice versa.

Jupiter moving into your 8th house in the year ahead shows that this is a year for paying off debt – or refinancing on better terms. For those of you of appropriate age it is a more sexually active year as well. When Saturn moved away from your money house last year, there should have been an increase in earnings – many financial burdens were lifted. Saturn will return to the money house for a few months, but will spend most of the year in the 3rd house. There are still some financial lessons to be learned, but most of it is over. The cosmos will 're-test' you briefly to see how far you've come. More on this later.

Your most important interests in the year ahead will be the body, image and personal pleasures (until June 7th), finance (April 8th to July 22nd), health and work, love, romance and social life, sex, birth and death, reincarnation, life after death, occult studies, the deeper things of life, and foreign travel, religion, philosophy and higher education (until September 10th).

Your paths of greatest fulfilment will be health and work, sex, birth and death, reincarnation, life after death, occult studies, the deeper things of life, and foreign travel, religion, philosophy and higher education (from May 28th to September 10th).

Health

(Please note that this is an astrological perspective on health and not a medical one. In days gone by there was no difference; these perspectives were identical. But nowadays there can be quite a difference. For the medical perspective, please consult your doctor or health practitioner.)

If your health was good last year (and it should have been) it will be even better in the year ahead. In 2011 it gets better still. Though your health is good, it seems that you are also paying more attention – especially since last year as Pluto moved into your 6th house. I would read this as being more involved in prevention – such as detox and emotional healing.

Your health planet, Saturn, spends time in two signs and houses this year. This shows some changes (temporary) in your health regime, doctors and diet.

You can do much to enhance your already good health – make it even more perfect. This is done by paying more attention to the following parts of the body:

- spine, knees, teeth, bones, gallbladder and overall skeletal alignment (regular back massage and regular visits to a chiropractor are always good for you and this year is no different. Always a good idea to give the knees more support when exercising.)
- small intestine (from April 8th to July 22nd)
- kidneys and hips (most of the year – from January 1st to April 8th and from July 22nd to December 31st – regular hip massage is good – there are many reflex points there that strengthen both the kidneys and the back)
- colon, bladder and sexual organs (safe sex and sexual moderation is important this year and for many years to come).

Since these are your most vulnerable areas, problems, if they happen, would most likely begin there. Thus, keeping them healthy and fit is good preventative medicine.

The beauty of the horoscope is that it not only shows us how to deal with health issues on a pragmatic, physical way, but also reveals likely root causes of problems. And since we can't talk about a real healing unless root causes are dealt with, the horoscope is a valuable tool in real healing.

In your horoscope there are a few possible root causes of problems. With your health planet in Libra most of the year, love problems – problems in the marriage or with friends – are a likely root cause – and should be looked at if problems arise. Family and emotional disharmony are another likely root cause (your family planet, Pluto, is in your 6th house of health). So, to get a deep (and rapid) healing – even if you need a health professional – it is good to bring these areas of life into harmony.

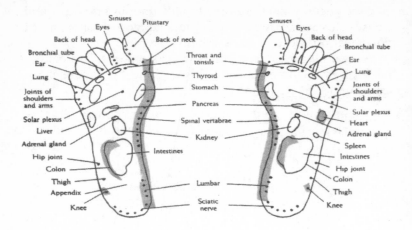

Reflexology

Try to massage the whole foot on a regular basis, but pay extra attention to the points highlighted on the chart. When you massage, be aware of 'sore spots', as these need special attention. It's also a good idea to massage the ankles and top side (as well as the soles) of the feet.

As mentioned, your health planet will be in two signs and houses this year. While he is in your money house (from April 8th to July 22nd), financial problems and worries can be a root cause of health problems – if you allow this. But the horoscope is even going more deeply than this – it is saying that there is a need to look at your financial attitudes, at how you handle money. Perhaps you are using it as a form of power or using it in some harmful manner – this can be a root cause of problems.

When your health planet is in the 3rd house (January 1st to April 8th and July 22nd to December 31st) overall mental health is important. There is a need to give the mental body its due – give it exercise, give it expression, give it good nutritious mental food (true information, ideas of truth, uplifting ideas, etc.). Your mental diet becomes almost as important as your physical diet – perhaps more so. Also you need to be careful to use your mind and communication faculties properly – think when necessary and then turn the mind off. Speak when necessary, but not overly much. Overuse of these faculties drains precious energy which would be used for healing and regeneration.

Home and Family

Your 4th house of home and family is not a House of Power this year, Leo. Usually this shows a status-quo kind of year. But this year, I'm not so sure.

Pluto, your family planet, will get eclipsed on June 26th and will stay camped out on this eclipse point for many months. This shows big and perhaps dramatic changes in the home and family relationship. A parent or parent figure undergoes some kind of crisis – this can be health-related or, more likely, an identity crisis. Dramatic events are happening with this person. Such a transit also tends to signal major repairs in the home and crisis within the family unit itself. Of course one should never look at these things as 'punishment' – only a cosmic detox of impurities. This will lead to better and happier conditions at home and with the family.

Venus, which usually stays in a sign and house for 1 month, will spend 3 months (on and off) in your 4th house in the year ahead. (It moves in on September 8th, stays there until November 8th, retrogrades back into your 3rd house until December 1st and then moves back into your 4th house from December 1st for the rest of the year.) This suggests various things. A parent or parent figure is coming for an extended stay. You will be working more from home. You will be very focused on the family – it will be your highest priority – during these periods. Also it suggests more entertaining from home and that a redecoration – a beautification – of the home is happening. For singles this suggests a live-in relationship. This will be an excellent period for creating more harmony with the family, mending fences and the like.

Parents or parent figures are either moving or doing major repairs and renovations in the home – perhaps even both. One of them will be, as we mentioned, redefining the

personality and changing the image and self-concept –
usually this results in a change of wardrobe, a change in the
image that they project. In health matters one of the parent
figures seems ultra-conservative – gravitating to orthodox
medicine – while the other is totally experimental, gravitating to alternative therapies. The conservative one needs to
pay more attention to their spine, knees, gallbladder and
overall skeletal alignment. Both need to pay more attention
to their kidneys and hips.

Children have been moving around for some years now –
an unstable domestic life. Another move – this time a happy
one – will happen this year. Their period of the nomadic life
is soon to end. They seem ready to settle down.
Grandchildren of appropriate age are having a status-quo
kind of year. Siblings are doing heavy renovations in the
home and are dealing with deep psychological issues – a
stormy home life in the year ahead.

If you are planning major repairs or heavy construction in
the home it will probably happen after June 26th, but the
period from September 14th to November 22nd seems best.
If you are planning redecorations of the home – cosmetic
kinds of things like repainting or buying new carpets or
curtains, or buying objects of beauty for the home –
September 8th to November 8th and December 1st to 31st
seem best.

Finance and Career

Neither your 2nd house of finance nor your 10th house of
career are Houses of Power this year. Thus you have no
impelling urges to make change in these areas. You seem
content with the status quo and this is usually how things
turn out.

The lack of power in these houses also gives you more freedom in these areas. The cosmos doesn't push you one way or
the other – and for those of you who have strong career or
money houses in your personal natal chart (cast specifically
for your date and time of birth) this would be a good sign.

This freedom gives you the ability to shape and mould your finances and career according to your specifications.

Jupiter, the planet of abundance, will move through your 8th house this year. This shows various things. In many cases this will show an inheritance. In other cases, it will show that you are remembered in someone's will or appointed executor of a will. Often it shows earnings through a trust fund or other similar arrangement.

Jupiter moving through the 8th house shows that your spouse, partner or current love is having a banner financial year – and that he or she is more generous with you. In general, your partners and friends are prospering in the year ahead.

Jupiter in the 8th house shows a 'fortunate' ability to access outside capital. If you have good ideas there are investors out there ready to help. Your line of credit will increase. You will have good fortune in creative kinds of financing – i.e. borrowing or refinancing at lower, more favourable rates. This is also a good year for getting out of debt. Those of you involved in tax or insurance issues should have a fortunate result.

Mercury, your financial planet, goes retrograde four times this year – a bit unusual. Generally he retrogrades only three times in a given year. So this is a year where you need to do more financial homework than usual – especially during those periods (January 1st to 15th, April 18th to May 11th, August 20th to September 12th, and December 12th to 30th). When the financial planet is retrograde there is a tendency to financial delays, errors or weird glitches – so there are more of these kinds of things than usual. Just be patient. It is not the end of the world when these things happen. If you have understanding, you smile and deal with the delays.

Mercury, as our steady readers know, is a fast-moving planet. Only the Moon moves faster than him. Thus money and earnings opportunities come to you in a variety of ways and through a variety of people and conditions. It all depends where Mercury is at a given time. These short-term trends will be dealt with in the monthly reports.

Siblings are making major financial changes and seem to have financial upheavals and crises this year. It will all turn out well – but the road is rocky. They especially need to be careful of debt. There are career changes in store for them as well. Parents or parent figures are having a status-quo kind of financial year. Children of appropriate age also need to be careful of debt. They are getting tested in financial matters in the year ahead. Grandchildren of appropriate age are having a status-quo year.

Love and Social Life

Both your 7th and 8th houses are strong this year. They have been strong for many years, but especially now. As we mentioned, with Jupiter moving through your 7th house of love and marriage in 2009, many of you married or entered into serious kinds of relationships. Business partnerships also happened. This happy social trend continues in the year ahead. Those of you who are still single or uncommitted are likely to find that special someone later on this year. Jupiter will be travelling with your love planet for a good part of the year.

Your powerful 8th house shows a year of greater sexual activity – more than usual. This too is a signal for romance. Whatever your age or stage in life, libido will be stronger than usual.

Jupiter will be travelling with Uranus (in varying degrees of exactitude) from May to early October. This brings sudden, dramatic, exciting love experiences – out of the ordinary – to you. You are always a 'love at first sight' kind of person, but now more so. This can bring sudden breakups with a current love, with simultaneous encounters with a new love. The highs of love are ultra-high. The sky is the limit. You are meeting people beyond your highest fantasy – people you thought didn't exist or who were 'beyond' you. There can be – especially for singles – serial love affairs this period. Every time you think you have met Mr or Ms Right, someone new comes along. It's as if the 'doors of heaven' open up in your love life and you see what is attainable and possible for you. Why should you settle for less? The only problem here is instability. If you can keep this new relationship going – perhaps by giving it more work – marriage could happen.

Existing romances will become more honeymoonish – more romantic, more fun – during this period. You will do 'out of the ordinary' things as a couple – perhaps travel to exotic locales or go on a religious pilgrimage or things of that nature. Your whole love life will partake of the nature of the miraculous and you are likely to remember this period for many years to come.

Love is about fun this year. You feel that a relationship has to be fun – a way of adding to the joy of life. You are not too keen on the burdens and responsibilities of love these days. This will perhaps come in the future, but not right now. The person who can show you a good time is the person that allures you. Physical and sexual chemistry are also important, if not the main, attractions. With these attitudes, when difficult times come you (or your partner) want out: 'I didn't sign up for this … this is no fun,' etc.

Love opportunities happen at the usual places – your usual haunts – places of entertainment, resorts, clubs, casinos, theatres, and at parties and social gatherings. From May 28th until August 14th opportunities come in foreign lands, in educational or religious/spiritual settings.

This is a good year for those working on either the first or second marriages. Those working towards their third or fourth marriage are having a status-quo year.

Self-improvement

Financial discipline is perhaps one of the hardest lessons for the Leo mentality. Leos are big earners and big spenders. Money is to be enjoyed and not hoarded. Though Leo is very creative and generally loves the arts, the art of financial management is not one of their arts. So, for the past 2 to 3 years, as the cosmos has called you to learn these things – your financial life has been difficult. Basically you are over

most of this, but from April 8th to July 22nd you will be able
to see how well you've done. Saturn retrogrades back into
your money house and you must start managing your
money better – start budgeting and make smarter spending
decisions. The object here is not to make you a 'skinflint' but
to show you how to be in control of your money rather than
letting money control you. Budgeting and a regular savings
and investment plan is not about 'lack and limitation' but
more about 'beauty'. Beauty is right proportion in all things.
Our physical bodies, surroundings and affairs should be
beautiful – just as the cosmos is beautiful – and so should
our financial lives. Proportional spending and investing
brings beauty to that area of life. If you think of yourself as a
creative artist creating beauty in your financial life, the
lesson will go better and more easily.

The next lesson – and this will be for most of this year and
all of next – is about mental and communication discipline.
Another difficult lesson for Leo. Leo believes in free expression. What you see is what you get. What they feel, is how
they express it. They are open and honest. This is an endear-
ing and wonderful quality. But in thinking and communication, you will need to do more homework. Just because you
feel deeply about something – some subject – doesn't make
it so. And just because you feel like talking and emoting
doesn't mean that it's always the right thing to do. Speech is
an awesome power with awesome consequences. We know
this just from observing everyday life. Someone tells you
something that's not true and you might act on it and experience loss or harm. Some innocent person can suffer the
loss of his reputation because of reckless speech. But the
power of speech, when understood on a spiritual level, is
even stronger than this. Every word creates 'psychic entities'
– actual creations on other levels. And if they are the product of false, hateful, malicious speech, these entities
contribute to the psychic pollution of the planet – they are
like quasi-living beings that go out and do good or do
damage, depending on the type of words spoken. It's as if
every human is creating his or her own heaven or hell, word

by word and thought by thought. So this is a time to get this in order.

Metaphysicians assert that you can trace every condition in your life – good or bad – to some word that was spoken. When you speak, you are literally creating your future. So you want to make sure that your speech is true (if you are conveying information) and helpful and constructive to others.

Saturn in your 3rd house of communication for most of the year is going to make you more conscious of these things. He will slow you down a bit, make you think and pause before you speak and consider the ramifications of the power you are setting loose.

Month-by-month Forecasts

January

Best Days Overall: 2, 3, 11, 12, 21, 22, 30
Most Stressful Days Overall: 8, 9, 16, 17, 23, 24
Best Days for Love: 1, 4, 5, 9, 10, 13, 14, 15, 16, 17, 19, 20, 25, 26, 28, 29
Best Days for Money: 4, 5, 6, 7, 13, 14, 16, 17, 18, 23, 24, 27
Best Days for Career: 4, 5, 13, 14, 15, 23, 24, 25, 26

Your year begins on a fitting note: dawn is breaking in your year. By the 20th the planetary power shifts from the 'night' side of the chart to the 'day' side. You've just, figuratively speaking, had a refreshing night's sleep, and now (by the 20th) you are ready to face the day – ready to pursue your outer worldly goals. Dreams, visions, emotions are not important *per se* – it's about putting them into action now. Pursue your career and the family and domestic situation will more or less take care of itself.

Your year begins on a serious note: your 6th house of health and work is the most powerful. But it is good now to achieve your work goals and also all those little odds and ends – such as accounting, fixing appliances and getting your health in order. This will make you ready to enter a yearly social peak on the 20th with a clear mind and greater confidence.

Last year was a banner love year and the trend continues in the month ahead. Jupiter leaves your 7th house on the 18th (which signals greater sexual activity), but Venus and the Sun move into the 7th house to replace it. A month for romance, parties, dating and social gatherings. Generally people attend more weddings when the 7th house is strong (and they also tend to get married themselves). Many of you married last year, and wedding bells can still ring in the month ahead (and year ahead). You are popular now. You are more self-effacing than usual, but this increases your popularity. You are not trying to 'lord' it over others, but are going out of your way to please them. You are the life of the party. Others like having you in their homes and at their parties.

You are no shrinking violet in love, either. You are aggressive and proactive. If you like someone they know it – you go after them directly. You're not sitting around waiting for the phone to ring.

Health needs more watching after the 20th. Overall health is good. But this is not one of your best periods – a short-term issue. Rest and relax more and listen to the body. Pay more attention to your heart (after the 20th) and in the ways outlined in the yearly report. Keep energy levels high and do your best to reduce stress and worry (meditation and spiritual work is great for that). Take a reduced schedule during the solar eclipse period of the 15th as well.

Mars is in your 1st house for many months to come. There are some good points about this. You are energetic, dynamic and magnetic. You project great sex appeal (regardless of your age or stage – there will be more than usual). But you need to mind your temper and be careful of haste and impatience.

A foreign journey is best delayed now – if possible.

Finances are status quo – but your financial planet is
retrograde until the 15th. So avoid major financial decisions
until after the 15th.

February

Best Days Overall: 7, 8, 17, 18, 26, 27
Most Stressful Days Overall: 5, 6, 12, 13, 19, 20, 21
Best Days for Love: 2, 3, 6, 12, 13, 14, 15, 16, 24, 25
Best Days for Money: 1, 4, 5, 11, 12, 14, 15, 22, 23, 24,
    28
Best Days for Career: 2, 3, 14, 15, 19, 20, 21, 24, 25

Last month's solar eclipse announced job changes and a
redefinition of your personality, self-concept and personal
image. Generally this leads to wardrobe changes – you
present yourself, you package yourself, in a new and better
way. Those of you who employ others are experiencing
instability with them – probably there is turnover happening. Though this eclipse happened last month, its effects are
felt this month (and for the next 6 months) as well.

You are still well into your yearly social peak until the
18th. One of the happiest and most active social periods of
your year. Your popularity and social grace are still very
strong. If you haven't met a special someone yet, it could
easily happen this month – just in the normal ways: at parties,
weddings or social gatherings. Singles have a sizable menu to
choose from now. There are happy love opportunities from
the 15th to the 17th and on the 27th and 28th. Career is
elevated – there is success – from the 15th to the 17th as well.

Your 8th house has been powerful since the 18th of last
month. This month it becomes even more powerful. So
libido is roaring (and for a Leo this is saying a lot). It would
be normal to be more sexually active with these aspects; the
question for you is: will you fritter away grand opportunities
by over-indulgence? Or will you use this 8th house energy
to detox and purify your body, pay off debt, settle tax issues
and get rid of old emotional and mental patterns that are

holding you back – re-invent yourself according to the 'you' that you dream of being?

These questions are especially pressing for those on the spiritual path. For it is the sex energy – the libido – that enables a person to hold to the path and make progress. If it is wasted (through excess) the progress won't happen.

With the 8th house strong, the cosmos will make you aware of your mortality – it will show you (in its own way and in a way that you understand) that life, here on earth, is short – not guaranteed – and that we should be attending to the things we were born to do.

Your spouse, partner or current love is prospering and more generous with you. He or she is having a banner financial year – but this month is one of the strongest in his or her year. This is a month where you can prosper through inheritance, trust funds or creative financing. Your financial planet is now moving forward and your financial judgement is good. But with these aspects you need to keep the financial interests of others paramount. You prosper only insofar as you help others to prosper. A business partnership or joint venture could happen after the 10th.

Health is much improved after the 18th, but until then refer to our discussion last month.

March

> Best Days Overall: 6, 7, 16, 17, 25, 26
> Most Stressful Days Overall: 4, 5, 11, 12, 19, 20, 31
> Best Days for Love: 5, 6, 11, 12, 15, 16, 17, 24, 25, 26
> Best Days for Money: 1, 4, 5, 14, 15, 23, 24, 25, 26, 27, 28, 31
> Best Days for Career: 5, 6, 16, 17, 19, 20, 25, 26

Since the beginning of the year most of the planets have been in the Western, social sector of your horoscope. This trend continues in the month ahead. You are in a period for developing social skills. Yes, you are royalty, but you must rule with kindness and consensus. Leadership is not for the leader, it is a form of service to other people. Even leaders can't always create conditions as they like them – all too often, like other people, they must adapt as best they can to the status quo. You are in one of those periods now. In a few months this will change, but for now adapt and cultivate your social skills.

Your 8th house is still powerful this month until the 20th. Keep in mind our discussion of this last month. Personal finance is more or less status quo. Your focus should be the prosperity of others, then your own prosperity will follow naturally. This is karmic law. There is a nice financial windfall from the 7th to the 9th – speculations seem very favourable during this period as well. You are spending on entertainment or entertainment equipment. Avoid speculations on the 20th – a short-term financial problem is just that – short term. Doesn't seem serious. Earnings increase after the 17th, but rash financial decisions or rash purchases can be costly. Income or earning opportunities come from abroad or from foreigners or foreign companies. Events in foreign lands help earnings. Job-seekers need more patience this month. Your work planet is retrograde and stressfully aspected. The next few months will be better for job-seeking than now. Your spouse, partner or current love is prospering greatly – a prosperous month in a prosperous year.

Your 9th house becomes powerful after the 2nd. This ignites many different interests on different levels. On the mundane level there is a yen for foreign travel and a kind of jet-set lifestyle (each in proportion to his or her status in the world). On another level it brings an interest in philosophy and higher education. A very good period for university or graduate students – they are succeeding in their studies. On a higher level this shows an interest in religion and theology – ministry. This is a month for studying scripture or other sacred writings – the mind opens to it easily. Religious students will have breakthroughs.

Health is good this month and will get even better after the 20th. You can enhance it even further by following the discussion of this in the yearly report. Your health planet is

still retrograde, so it is a time for review of your diet or overall health regime, not for making major changes.

Mars is still in your sign. You are energetic and magnetic –
and this will only increase after the 20th. You are more
athletic and performing at your personal best levels. Sex
appeal is strong and others take notice. Love is still happy.
The New Moon of the 15th brings a happy romantic experience – sudden and unexpected.

April

> Best Days Overall: 3, 4, 13, 14, 22, 23, 30
> Most Stressful Days Overall: 1, 8, 9, 15, 16, 28, 29
> Best Days for Love: 2, 5, 8, 9, 11, 12, 15, 16, 20, 21, 25, 29
> Best Days for Money: 1, 5, 10, 11, 15, 16, 19, 20, 24, 25,
>   28, 29
> Best Days for Career: 5, 15, 16, 25

Health is still wonderful until the 20th; after that rest and
relax more. Overall health is still very good, this is just not
one of your better periods. No need for panic. Rest and relax
more. Focus on the important things in your life and let
lesser things go. Reduce stress wherever possible (meditation
is great for this). Your health needs change this month as
well. Your health planet retrogrades back into Virgo from
Libra. So enhance health by paying more attention to your
small intestine (diet is probably more important now) and to
your heart (after the 20th). Continue to avoid making
dramatic changes to your health regime (though you will be
tempted) as your health planet will be retrograde all month.
The good part of this is that with your health planet in Virgo,
your understanding of health issues will be more astute.
Your own innate healing power will be stronger. Your gut
instincts about health will be good.

Avoid risky activities from the 14th to the 16th. Be patient
if people are misrepresenting you. You need to define yourself for yourself and not let others do it for you.

Your 9th house is powerful until the 20th so refer to our

discussion of this last month.

Career is the main headline this month. Your 10th house is strong. Mercury will cross your Midheaven on the 2nd (and you could feel it even before then) – this brings pay rises and financial support from bosses, elders and parents or parent figures. Finance is high on your agenda – you focus on it – and this in itself brings more prosperity. Your good professional reputation is important in finance as well. Referrals will come to you. There are financial opportunities with the government or government contractors. (Good relations with the government also seem very important – more than usual – during this period.) On the 20th the Sun crosses the Midheaven and enters your 10th house of career. This initiates a yearly career peak. You are elevated, honoured, appreciated and promoted. You are on top of the world – above everyone in your world (the place where you always feel you belong). You have power and authority – only use it properly. Better not to have power than to abuse it. This is a nice aspect in that you are honoured for who you are as a person, not just your career achievements.

If you're planning on foreign travel, better to do it before the 20th than afterwards. Earlier in the month – as early as possible – is best. If you are applying to college or university the advice is the same: do it early in the month.

Love is very happy all month. A current relationship is more romantic – almost honeymoonish. Singles are meeting new and marriageable types of people. New friends are coming into the picture. Marriage can still happen for singles. The only problem in love is possible infidelity – both you and your beloved have ample opportunities – the temptations are great.

May

Best Days Overall: 1, 10, 11, 19, 20, 27, 28
Most Stressful Days Overall: 5, 6, 12, 13, 25, 26
Best Days for Love: 5, 6, 9, 15, 16, 18, 25, 26
Best Days for Money: 2, 8, 9, 12, 18, 21, 22, 25, 26, 30
Best Days for Career: 5, 6, 12, 13, 15, 16, 25, 26

Though health and energy could be better (things will improve after the 21st) nevertheless many wonderful things are happening for you. A very exciting and happy month. Your social life shines on all its levels and dimensions.

Your financial planet is still retrograde until the 11th so, where possible, avoid making major purchases, investments or financial decisions until the 11th. Your financial life is under review now. Judgement is not up to its usual standards. There are all kinds of X factors that you might not be aware of. Mercury's retrograde will not stop earnings, but will tend to slow them down. Earnings come from your career – pay rises or the support of parents (or parent figures), elders or bosses. Your good professional reputation is still very important and you should guard it. Better to take a short-term loss than tarnish your reputation.

You are still in the midst of a yearly career peak. Your ruling planet is the most elevated in the horoscope and this describes you. You are on top, where you belong – in power, in authority, above everyone in your world. You are making great career progress now.

Usually people in power are not liked. Always they have to make choices and there are people who will be angry at their choices – even if they are good. Yet you seem very popular this month. Your love life is electric – incandescent. You soar to the heights. You experience the impossible. Sudden love opportunities come to you out of the blue. You meet your 'ideals' in love. Even existing relationships become more honeymoonish – and this is a great month for cementing your marriage by going on a second honeymoon. Singles find romance in foreign countries or with foreigners – educational or religious events are also romantic in nature.

The problem in love – as we saw last month – is that both you and your beloved have ample opportunity – you both have your admirers. In a way this is good – it tests your commitment to each other.

For singles this is a love-at-first-sight kind of period. You will understand the 'lightning bolt' that occurs between two people when they recognize each other and what they are to each other. This recognition comes from a place totally above the personality – it is supernatural in nature. Everyone experiences this kind of thing sometime in their life; it's your turn now.

June

    Best Days Overall: 6, 7, 15, 16, 24, 25
    Most Stressful Days Overall: 1, 2, 9, 10, 21, 22, 29, 30
    Best Days for Love: 1, 2, 4, 5, 6, 13, 14, 15, 24, 25, 29, 30
    Best Days for Money: 5, 6, 10, 11, 15, 17, 18, 19, 20, 24
    Best Days for Career: 4, 5, 9, 10, 13, 14, 24, 25

A very spiritual month. The two most spiritual houses of the horoscope – the 9th and the 12th – become powerful this month. Uranus moved into your 9th house on the 28th of last month; Jupiter joins him on the 6th. These are two very powerful and dynamic planets, so the 9th house is 'super–energized' now – all month. On the 21st the Sun (your ruling planet) enters the 12th house, and on the 25th Mercury joins him.

Love is still soaring. You are having peak love experiences these days – perhaps lifetime peaks. Love, foreign travel, religion and education are the most fun kinds of things these days. A good theological discussion is more interesting than a night out on the town. The visit of a guru or minister is more important – more exciting – than the visit of a rock star.

This is a month for many supernatural kinds of experiences. The fact that you are in love – in a state of harmony and bliss – is helping matters – it becomes easy to experience these things. They are always happening, but we tend to be unaware. Now you are aware. In fact, your current love relationship, the current state of your love life, could be described as supernatural – above the norm.

A great month for going on religious or spiritual-type pilgrimages or retreats (with your beloved).

In the next 2 months you will be having your birthday, which for you is your personal new year. What happens on your birthday – your state of mind and emotion – will set the course for the entire year ahead (until your next birthday). So, after the 21st it is good to review your past year. Be honest and sober about it. Look at your successes and your failures. Look at your mistakes and make atonement for them (correct them). Have you hurt others this past year? Bring these things into harmony. Have others hurt you? Practise forgiveness. Set goals for the year ahead. Clear the decks so that you start your new year with a clean slate.

Health is much improved over last month.

A lunar eclipse on the 26th announces job changes and changes in the conditions of work. It also announces changes in your health regime and diet. People often change their doctors or therapists under these aspects. There are dramatic experiences in the lives of parents, parent figures and family members. The spiritual revelations you have been having are bringing change to your spiritual practice and attitudes.

July

Best Days Overall: 4, 5, 12, 13, 21, 22, 31
Most Stressful Days Overall: 6, 7, 9, 20, 26, 27
Best Days for Love: 3, 4, 5, 12, 14, 21, 23, 24, 26, 27, 31
Best Days for Money: 1, 2, 3, 12, 14, 15, 21, 22, 31
Best Days for Career: 5, 6, 7, 14, 23, 24

Since April when Saturn moved back (by retrograde) into your money house, finances have been problematic. There was and is a need to reorganize and get financially healthier. There were extra financial burdens or expenses that forced this reorganization. Important spending decisions had to be made – there was a 're-allocation' of resources happening. This is still going until the 21st of this month. You seem to have adjusted and made the right decisions. Last month, on the 7th, Mars entered your money house and this should have improved things – it brought increases in earnings. This month Mercury and Venus enter the money house enhancing earnings even further. You are in financial recovery now. And you haven't yet hit your peak – this will happen next month. The financial picture looks bright indeed. Saturn, the great teacher, set things up (perhaps through drama and crisis) so that when your new wealth came in, you could receive it and handle it.

The two planets involved in your love life are now retrograde. On the 21st Saturn makes a stressful aspect to these love planets. It will be a challenge to maintain the intensity of love that you've had for the past few months. Your love gets challenged and tested by circumstances – the demands of the workplace distract from your beloved. Perhaps there are health issues with your beloved. Your confidence in your love is also weakened a bit – perhaps there are doubts in your mind – 'Oh, it was all too good to be true,' 'It can't last,' 'We were both living in "cloud cuckoo land".' In a way this is good. Real love withstands any test. Insecurities and blockages need to be revealed so that you can correct them. Also, your love life is receiving more help than stress – especially from the 21st onwards. Keep the faith; help is on the way.

A solar eclipse on the 11th is relatively benign to you, but it won't hurt to take a reduced schedule. Every solar eclipse affects you, as the Sun is your ruling planet. Always it brings a redefinition of yourself – your self-concept, your image, the state of your body, your personal appearance. It's as if you get a chance to upgrade these things. This eclipse occurs in your 12th house and thus brings changes to your spiritual regime and practice. It can bring changes to spiritual or charitable-type organizations that you are involved with – shakeups and the like. Your spiritual attitudes and understanding – through revelation – get shaken up and tested.

On April 20th the planetary power shifted from the Western, social sector to the Eastern sector. This month the power is at its maximum Eastern position. Thus you are more independent now and have the power to create conditions as you like them (you have always had this power, but now it is more easily expressed). Your happiness is not dependent on others, but on yourself. Create your happiness now. The world will conform to you rather than vice versa.

On the 23rd you enter another one of your yearly personal pleasure peaks – Leo heaven. Enjoy.

August

Best Days Overall: 1, 9, 10, 17, 18, 27, 28
Most Stressful Days Overall: 2, 3, 15, 16, 22, 23, 30, 31
Best Days for Love: 3, 4, 8, 9, 13, 16, 22, 23, 26
Best Days for Money: 2, 9, 11, 12, 17, 20, 21, 27, 30, 31
Best Days for Career: 2, 3, 4, 13, 22, 23, 29, 30, 31

The pace of events slows down for you personally and for the world at large this month. Some 40 per cent (and, after the 20th, 50 per cent) of the planets are retrograde. A month to learn patience. There is a need to 'sit loose to life' and not force things. With the Sun in your 1st house this might be difficult for you – you want things in a hurry. But haste, hurry and shortcuts will only create even more delays.

You are still in Leo heaven – a yearly personal pleasure peak – until the 23rd. A time for fulfilling sensual fantasies and getting your body and image in shape.

Finances are more complicated this month. On the 23rd you enter a yearly financial peak – but Mercury, your financial planet, will be retrograde. Of course you should pursue your normal financial goals, but better to plan future earnings and strategy rather than enact them. Financial planning is vital to your success and this might be an excellent time to do some. This is a month where you spend on yourself and on your image. You adopt the image of wealth. You like to flaunt your wealth more these days.

Health is good this month but there can be some scares from the 26th to the 31st – seems to me that they will be just scares. This period could bring some turbulence at work as well. Perhaps a job change is in the offing.

The planetary power shifted (last month) from the upper to the lower half of your horoscope. So you are now in the 'night-time' of your year. Night is for sleeping and for regenerating the energy. Not for overt action but for internal kinds of action. (Internal actions – though we don't see them and they are not apparent to others – are nevertheless actions. And they are considered this way from a spiritual perspective.) Thus you should be visualizing career goals – dreaming about them, entering into the subjective feeling of their attainment – so that when day breaks in your year (in 2011) they will burst forth into manifestation with great naturalness and power. This is a time to shift your focus to your family and emotional life. Find and then function from your point of emotional harmony.

In our secular worldly culture, ambition is given more weight than emotional harmony. But this is error. One of the main blockages to prayer being answered is disharmony in the emotional body. A person with emotional harmony will have their prayers answered quickly and speedily – often within hours.

Your career planet, Venus, re-stimulates eclipse points from the 11th to the 14th and from the 25th to the 28th. This can produce some short-term crises in your career or with parents or parent figures.

Love is still happy but the pace of your social life has slowed a bit. The planets involved in your love life are still retrograde. Though you are still very much a love-at-first-sight kind of person, best not to make major love decisions (one way or another) right now. Your love life is under review.

September

Best Days Overall: 5, 6, 13, 14, 15, 23, 24, 25
Most Stressful Days Overall: 11, 12, 18, 19, 20, 26, 27
Best Days for Love: 2, 4, 11, 12, 18, 19, 20, 21, 22
Best Days for Money: 5, 7, 8, 12, 16, 22, 27
Best Days for Career: 2, 11, 21, 26, 27

Saturn camps out on the lunar eclipse point of June 26th all month (in a Square aspect). This is unusual. Thus there are job changes, upheavals at the workplace, instability with employees and perhaps some health scares. Overall, health still looks good as most of the planets are in harmonious aspect to you – probably you are changing your health regime and the diet. You can enhance your health even further by the ways mentioned in the yearly report.

Like last month, most of the planets are firmly below the horizon. Focus on family now. Pluto, your family planet, has been camped out on the lunar eclipse point of June 26th for many months – and so there are family crises – crises or drama with parents or parent figures as well. The family needs you these days. Venus moves into your 4th house on the 8th and Mars moves in on the 15th. A good period for making renovations or for redecorating the home. Also good for family gatherings and entertaining from home. Venus in the 4th reinforces what we said earlier about focusing on the family – it is actually your mission in life right now, the most important thing. Venus' presence in your 4th house also shows that you will be working more from home – making your home like an office. You pursue your career goals from home.

Earnings go easier and seem increased over last month. You are still in the midst of a yearly financial peak until the 23rd and Mercury, your financial planet, starts moving forward on the 12th. Financial judgement improves and is more astute. If you have done your financial review, you are set to leap into dynamic and powerful action from the 12th onwards.

Avoid foreign journeys (if possible) on the 1st. Avoid risky activities from the 27th to the 29th.

Your 3rd house of communication and intellectual interests is powerful all month, but becomes even stronger after the 23rd. This will be a good time to release mass-mailings or advertising campaigns. Also good to catch up on your e-mails and letters that you owe. Good for short-term travel (domestic travel) and for taking courses in subjects that interest you.

Love is more about physical intimacy this month – but philosophical and religious compatibility is still important.

Children seem to lack direction these days, and this is OK. Natural. Don't make important or hasty decisions about them yet. Time, and not your overt actions, will resolve these issues. When in doubt, do nothing.

October

Best Days Overall: 3, 4, 11, 12, 21, 22, 30, 31
Most Stressful Days Overall: 9, 10, 16, 17, 23, 24
Best Days for Love: 1, 2, 9, 10, 16, 17, 18, 19, 20, 28, 29
Best Days for Money: 2, 5, 6, 7, 10, 17, 19, 28, 29
Best Days for Career: 1, 9, 18, 19, 23, 24, 28

Venus, your career planet (and the planet that shows your *Dharma*, or mission in life) is still very much in the 4th house this month. Most of the planets are below the horizon and your 4th house of home and family becomes super-strong after the 23rd. A very clear message: Continue to focus on the family and your domestic situation. This is your 'career' right now. With Venus going retrograde (a relatively rare event) on the 8th, the outer career seems on hold, anyway. You are not going to miss opportunities. Get the home and family situation the way you want it – as best you can.

You are entering the 'midnight' of your year. Though by nature you are an extroverted person, these days you are more introverted. You exhibit some of the traits of the '4th house Personality'. There is a love for the past. A nostalgia for the 'good old days'. You want your emotional harmony and are less ambitious. Old memories and old situations come back into your life for your analysis. A very good month for psychological progress and for gaining deep psychological insight. Your personal past is not just something educational, but is entertainment – perhaps as much entertainment as a night out on the town. This phase will not last long – another month perhaps – but it is good for you to have the experience.

Midnight is for dreaming and planning the future. The earth dreams in the winter, and in the Spring the dreams come true. So it is with you. What you dream of now will happen in 6 or so months.

Finances are good this month. There is an important job opportunity on the 1st or 2nd. Your work planet has moved off the eclipse point and so the work situation seems more stable. Your financial planet, Mercury, is moving forward – and at a fast clip as well. So there is financial confidence and you cover much ground financially – you achieve a lot quickly. Until the 23rd you can enhance your earnings in the normal ways for you – through good sales, marketing, PR and advertising. The need is to get word out about your product or service. After the 21st, as Mercury moves into your 4th house, wealth comes through the family, family support or family connections. Investors will want to look at property. You spend more on the family but can earn through them as well. You spend more on the home as well. Financial intuition will be very good after the 21st, provided you are calm and in a state of peace. Avoid making financial decisions when you are angry, fearful or depressed.

The retrograde of Venus (the generic love planet of the horoscope) adds to the slow pace of love these days. Your love planets are still retrograde as well. This is not going to stop your very exciting love life, just slow it down a bit. You can enjoy a rich social life without having to make any major decisions one way or the other. Go slow in love. (Most probably you will be hearing tales of woe from people in your world. I wouldn't take it too seriously – Venus is just retrograde.)

Health needs more watching after the 23rd. Pace yourself. Rest when tired. Maximize your energy. Pay more attention to your heart and review the health section of the general overview above. On an overall level health is still good; this is just not one of your better periods.

November

Best Days Overall: 7, 8, 17, 18, 26, 27
Most Stressful Days Overall: 5, 6, 12, 13, 19, 20, 21
Best Days for Love: 5, 6, 12, 13, 16, 23, 25
Best Days for Money: 1, 2, 6, 15, 16, 17, 25, 27, 28, 29
Best Days for Career: 5, 13, 19, 20, 21, 23

Retrograde activity has been intense the past few months. The world – and probably your personal life – has been in a kind of gridlock. Things did happen, but with many delays. Happily this is soon to be over with. The month begins with 40 per cent of the planets retrograde, but will end with 90 per cent of them moving forward. Gridlock lifts. The pace of events quickens.

This is still a time to focus on the family. This is your mission, your *Dharma*. You need to be there for them. After the 9th your siblings become important and you need to be there for them, too. After the 22nd it is your children – or those who are like children in your life.

Career, as mentioned, is not that important now. Sure, you will not give up your career, but it can be de-emphasized. Since your career planet went retrograde on the 8th of last month, this is a time for a career review. An honest, sober appraisal of things. What do you like, what do you dislike? What can be reasonably changed, what can't be changed? What improvements can be made? This is not a time for major career decisions, but for mulling things over. Ideas and insights will come to you now that will help you. After Venus goes forward on the 18th of this month, you will be clearer as to what to do. The improvements you seek can now be visualized and worked on in internal ways. Your main career work (aside from your normal duties) should be to 'enter into the feeling' of the way you want things to be. This will naturally produce the results you desire.

Like last month we see more work from home. Pursuing your career from home. After the 9th good marketing and sales will enhance your career – also social methods such as attending the right parties, getting to know the right people, etc.

On the 22nd you enter another yearly personal pleasure peak – more Leo heaven. The good times are rolling. No one is better at exploring the 'rapture' side of life than you. You don't need lectures from an astrologer on how to do this.

Health still needs watching temporarily. Energy and vitality are not what they should be until the 22nd. Like last month, pay more attention to your heart and to the ways mentioned in the yearly report.

Finances come from family, parent figures or family connections until the 8th. After that there are opportunities in foreign countries or with foreigners. Earnings should increase after the 8th. There is luck in speculations. Your intuition is good. You have huge wealth ideas and goals. Money comes to you in happy ways. There is joy in the act of money-making. Making money vies with your night life in terms of joy. You are investing in your children, spending on them, but can also earn through them as well. In many cases it is the children who are motivating you financially.

December

Best Days Overall: 5, 6, 14, 15, 16, 23, 24
Most Stressful Days Overall: 3, 4, 9, 10, 11, 17, 18, 30, 31
Best Days for Love: 2, 4, 9, 10, 11, 12, 13, 22, 31
Best Days for Money: 4, 7, 13, 16, 23, 25, 26, 27, 31
Best Days for Career: 2, 12, 17, 18, 22, 31

Your love planet finally starts moving forward on the 6th after many months of backwards motion. Clarity is coming in love. It is safe to make major love decisions now. Your love life is still wonderful, though not as exciting as in May or June. Love can happen any time in any place. This month you seem more in the mood for love affairs than for serious committed love – but serious love is out there for those who want it. Love is expressed sexually these days. Good sex will cover many sins in a marriage, too. By itself, of course, it is not enough, but it goes a long way.

Love opportunities can come in strange ways this month – at funerals or wakes, or as you make a sympathy call to someone who has lost a loved one. What the world sees as morbid, is for you a venue of romance.

Health is much improved this month. Energy is high. You are up and optimistic. Also you seem more focused on health this month – especially after the 21st. Physical exercise from the 8th onwards will enhance your already good health even further. These days, good health for you means physical fitness. Enhance health even further by paying more attention to your head, face, skull, heart, colon, bladder, sexual organs, lungs, small intestine, arms and shoulders.

Your financial planet goes retrograde from the 10th to the 30th, so try to do your holiday shopping before the 10th. If you must shop afterwards, make sure the shop has a good returns policy. You need more protection for purchases now.

This month money comes the old-fashioned way, through work and practical service to others. Job-seekers have good success all month – but especially after the 21st. Continue to focus on the home and family; this is your mission now. You're building the psychological infrastructure of your career now. As we have seen in recent months, you are working more from home.

You are still in a good period for entertaining from home and for beautifying the home – redecorating or buying art objects for the home.

The lunar eclipse of the 21st occurs right on the border of your 11th and 12th houses. Thus, it will have an impact on the affairs of both these houses. Spiritual revelation causes changes in your spiritual practice and attitudes. There are shakeups in a charity or spiritual or altruistic organization you are involved with. Friendships get tested. There are dramas in the lives of friends. This eclipse is basically benign to you, but it won't hurt to take a reduced schedule anyway. People in general are not up to par during an eclipse period and you shouldn't take any unnecessary chances.

Virgo

ℳ

THE VIRGIN
Birthdays from
22nd August to
22nd September

Personality Profile

VIRGO AT A GLANCE

Element – Earth

Ruling Planet – Mercury
   Career Planet – Mercury
   Love Planet – Neptune
   Money Planet – Venus
   Planet of Home and Family Life – Jupiter
   Planet of Health and Work – Uranus
   Planet of Pleasure – Saturn
   Planet of Sexuality – Mars

Colours – earth tones, ochre, orange, yellow

*Colour that promotes love, romance and social
   harmony* – aqua blue

Colour that promotes earning power – jade
   green

Gems – agate, hyacinth

Metal – quicksilver

Scents – lavender, lilac, lily of the valley, storax

Quality – mutable (= flexibility)

Quality most needed for balance – a broader perspective

Strongest virtues – mental agility, analytical skills, ability to pay attention to detail, healing powers

Deepest needs – to be useful and productive

Characteristic to avoid – destructive criticism

Signs of greatest overall compatibility – Taurus, Capricorn

Signs of greatest overall incompatibility – Gemini, Sagittarius, Pisces

Sign most helpful to career – Gemini

Sign most helpful for emotional support – Sagittarius

Sign most helpful financially – Libra

Sign best for marriage and/or partnerships – Pisces

Sign most helpful for creative projects – Capricorn

Best Sign to have fun with – Capricorn

Signs most helpful in spiritual matters – Taurus, Leo

Best day of the week – Wednesday

Understanding a Virgo

The virgin is a particularly fitting symbol for those born under the sign of Virgo. If you meditate on the image of the virgin you will get a good understanding of the essence of the Virgo type. The virgin is, of course, a symbol of purity and innocence – not naïve, but pure. A virginal object has not been touched. A virgin field is land that is true to itself, the way it has always been. The same is true of virgin forest: it is pristine, unaltered.

Apply the idea of purity to the thought processes, emotional life, physical body, and activities and projects of the everyday world, and you can see how Virgos approach life. Virgos desire the pure expression of the ideal in their mind, body and affairs. If they find impurities they will attempt to clear them away.

Impurities are the beginning of disorder, unhappiness and uneasiness. The job of the Virgo is to eject all impurities and keep only that which the body and mind can use and assimilate.

The secrets of good health are here revealed: 90 per cent of the art of staying well is maintaining a pure mind, a pure body and pure emotions. When you introduce more impurities than your mind and body can deal with, you will have what is known as 'dis-ease'. It is no wonder that Virgos make great doctors, nurses, healers and dieticians. They have an innate understanding of good health and they realize that good health is more than just physical. In all aspects of life, if you want a project to be successful it must be kept as pure as possible. It must be protected against the adverse elements that will try to undermine it. This is the secret behind Virgo's awesome technical proficiency.

One could talk about Virgo's analytical powers – which are formidable. One could talk about their perfectionism and their almost superhuman attention to detail. But this would be to miss the point. All of these virtues are manifestations of a Virgo's desire for purity and perfection – a world without Virgos would have ruined itself long ago.

A vice is nothing more than a virtue turned inside out, misapplied or used in the wrong context. Virgos' apparent vices come from their inherent virtue. Their analytical powers, which should be used for healing, helping or perfecting a project in the world, sometimes get misapplied and turned against people. Their critical faculties, which should be used constructively to perfect a strategy or proposal, can sometimes be used destructively to harm or wound. Their urge to perfection can turn into worry and lack of confidence; their natural humility can become self-denial and self-abasement. When Virgos turn negative they are apt to turn their devastating criticism on themselves, sowing the seeds of self-destruction.

Finance

Virgos have all the attitudes that create wealth. They are hard-working, industrious, efficient, organized, thrifty, productive and eager to serve. A developed Virgo is every employer's dream. But until Virgos master some of the social graces of Libra they will not even come close to fulfilling their financial potential. Purity and perfectionism, if not handled correctly or gracefully, can be very trying to others. Friction in human relationships can be devastating not only to your pet projects but – indirectly – to your wallet as well.

Virgos are quite interested in their financial security. Being hard-working, they know the true value of money. They do not like to take risks with their money, preferring to save for their retirement or for a rainy day. Virgos usually make prudent, calculated investments that involve a minimum of risk. These investments and savings usually work out well, helping Virgos to achieve the financial security they seek. The rich or even not-so-rich Virgo also likes to help his or her friends in need.

Career and Public Image

Virgos reach their full potential when they can communicate their knowledge in such a way that others can understand it. In order to get their ideas across better, Virgos need to develop greater verbal skills and fewer judgemental ways of expressing themselves. Virgos look up to teachers and communicators; they like their bosses to be good communicators. Virgos will probably not respect a superior who is not their intellectual equal – no matter how much money or power that superior has. Virgos themselves like to be perceived by others as being educated and intellectual.

The natural humility of Virgos often inhibits them from fulfilling their great ambitions, from acquiring name and fame. Virgos should indulge in a little more self-promotion if they are going to reach their career goals. They need to push themselves with the same ardour that they would use to foster others.

At work Virgos like to stay active. They are willing to learn any type of job as long as it serves their ultimate goal of financial security. Virgos may change occupations several times during their professional lives, until they find the one they really enjoy. Virgos work well with other people, are not afraid to work hard and always fulfil their responsibilities.

Love and Relationships

If you are an analyst or a critic you must, out of necessity, narrow your scope. You have to focus on a part and not the whole; this can create a temporary narrow-mindedness. Virgos do not like this kind of person. They like their partners to be broad-minded, with depth and vision. Virgos seek to get this broad-minded quality from their partners, since they sometimes lack it themselves.

Virgos are perfectionists in love just as they are in other areas of life. They need partners who are tolerant, open-minded and easy-going. If you are in love with a Virgo do not waste time on impractical romantic gestures. Do practical and useful things for him or her – this is what will be appreciated and what will be done for you.

Virgos express their love through pragmatic and useful gestures, so do not be put off because your Virgo partner does not say 'I love you' day-in and day-out. Virgos are not that type. If they love you, they will demonstrate it in practical ways. They will always be there for you; they will show an interest in your health and finances; they will fix your sink or repair your video recorder. Virgos deem these actions to be superior to sending flowers, chocolates or Valentine cards.

In love affairs Virgos are not particularly passionate or spontaneous. If you are in love with a Virgo, do not take this personally. It does not mean that you are not alluring enough or that your Virgo partner does not love or like you. It is just the way Virgos are. What they lack in passion they make up for in dedication and loyalty.

Home and Domestic Life

It goes without saying that the home of a Virgo will be spotless, sanitized and orderly. Everything will be in its proper place – and don't you dare move anything about! For Virgos to find domestic bliss they need to ease up a bit in the home, to allow their partner and kids more freedom and to be more generous and open-minded. Family members are not to be analysed under a microscope, they are individuals with their own virtues to express.

With these small difficulties resolved, Virgos like to stay in and entertain at home. They make good hosts and they like to keep their friends and families happy and entertained at family and social gatherings. Virgos love children, but they are strict with them – at times – since they want to make sure their children are brought up with the correct sense of family and values.

Horoscope for 2010

Major Trends

The past 2 years have been difficult for you, Virgo. Two powerful long-term planets – Uranus and Saturn – have had a big impact on you. Uranus has been affecting you since 2002 and has completely revolutionized your life. The conditions of your life on almost every level – love, career, finance – are vastly different than in 2002 when this transit began. Saturn has been in your sign for the past 2 years and has challenged your health and in terms of your self-esteem. Things improved for you late last year as Saturn left your sign and moved into Libra. But this year he makes a return visit for a few months – April 8th to July 22nd. So you will need to watch your energy more during this period and take on more responsibilities.

Love has been highly unstable for many years. Uranus in your house of love has seen to that. There has been many a divorce or breakup since 2002. Many friendships have broken up as well. The trials and tribulations in love seem mostly over with. The year ahead looks like a banner social year. Many of you will marry or enter into significant, serious kinds of relationships. More on this later.

Health and work are always important to you, and in the past year even more so. This trend continues in 2010. Overall health is good – though you need more rest when Saturn moves into your sign. More on this later.

Sexual activity seems to increase in 2010 as well. Whatever your age or stage in life, the libido will be stronger than usual.

Last year as Pluto moved into your 5th house, children, fun and creativity became important. This trend continues in the year ahead. This whole area of life is getting a thorough cosmic detox. Love affairs, outside of marriage, get tested. Relations with children will become purer – but only after some purging of old issues. Personal creativity will improve.

Your most important interests in the year ahead will be the body and image (April 8th to July 22nd and August 23rd to September 23rd), finance (January 1st to April 8th and July 22nd to December 31st), children, fun and creativity, and health and work, also love, romance and social activities, sex, birth and death, life after death, reincarnation and occult studies (May 28th to September 10th), friendships, group activities, involvement with organizations (January 1st to June 6th).

Your paths of greatest fulfilment in 2010 will be children, fun and creativity, health and work (until January 18th), love, romance and social activities (January 18th to June 6th and September 10th to December 31st), sex, birth and death, life after death, reincarnation and occult studies (June 6th to September 10th).

Health

(Please note that this is an astrological perspective on health and not a medical one. In days gone by there was no difference; these perspectives were identical. But nowadays there can be quite a difference. For the medical perspective, please consult your doctor or health practitioner.)

As we mentioned earlier, you've had a few rough health years, Virgo. Two very powerful planets were stressing you out – Saturn and Uranus. Health should have improved last year as Saturn moved out of your own sign and Jupiter was in your 6th house of health for most of the year. Those of you who were having health problems should have heard some good news. Health is good this year though you will have a brief period (from April 8th to July 22nd) when Saturn retrogrades back into your own sign where health will need more watching. Happily health is always important to you and you will be on the case. This focus should avoid most problems. For most of the year (January 1st to April 8th and July 22nd to December 31st) health and vitality should be good.

You can make your health even better by paying more attention to the following parts of the body:

- ankles
- feet
- head, face and adrenal glands (from May 28th to August 14th)
- liver and thighs (from January 1st to 18th).

Uranus, your health planet, changes signs briefly this year and this is going to bring changes in your health regime and health needs. For most of the year Uranus will be in the sign of Pisces. Pisces rules the feet. Hence the importance of keeping your feet in good health. The fact that Neptune, the planet that actually rules the feet, is in your 6th house of health is another message of the importance of the feet. Foot reflexology, foot massage, foot bathing, hydro-massage for the feet are all wonderful therapies in the year ahead. Try as much as possible to wear sensible shoes, shoes that fit, shoes that don't knock you off-balance. Better to sacrifice fashion for comfort. If you can have both, all the better. When

Reflexology

Try to massage the whole foot on a regular basis, but pay extra attention to the points highlighted on the chart. When you massage, be aware of 'sore spots', as these need special attention. It's also a good idea to massage the ankles and top side (as well as the soles) of the feet.

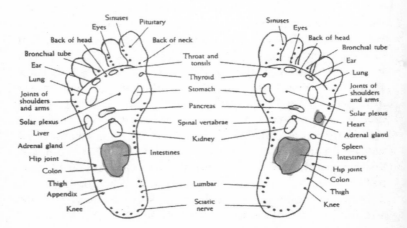

Uranus moves into Aries, a very major and rare transit (the last time it was there was 85 to 88 years ago) you will need to start paying more attention to your head, adrenal glands and face. Head and facial massage will become very beneficial then. This will be true in 2011 and for many years to come. I also like therapies such as cranial sacral therapy, which keeps the bones in the skull in correct alignment. This kind of therapy should be very powerful for years to come. When Uranus moves into Aries, health attitudes will also change. For many years the spiritual dimensions of healing have been very important and this will continue to a degree in the future. Neptune, the most spiritual of all the planets, is still in your 6th house, and Uranus will still be in Pisces for most of the year. But Uranus' shift into Aries shows that good health for you will mean physical fitness as well as no symptoms. You measure your health by how many miles you can run or jog, how many push-ups you can do, and things of that nature. So physical exercise becomes very important therapy this year and in future years. A day at the gym will often do you as much good as a visit to a health professional. Muscle tone becomes very important to your health.

As mentioned, the spiritual dimensions of health are still important for most of the year and you will be making very good progress in your understanding of these issues. You respond very well, as you have in past years, to spiritually-orientated therapies such as prayer, meditation, the laying-on of hands, reiki and the manipulation of subtle energies. Being 'prayed up' – in a state of connection with the higher power within you – is important not just for your spiritual life but for your health. Health problems, should they happen, will probably be coming from a place of disconnection. Now, this is true for everybody to some degree, but is very dramatically true for you. Therefore stay connected as much as possible. Also it is still very important to recognize that there is one and only one healer – the divine within you. Everything else that happens in healing is merely a side-effect of the action of this one healer. As you know, this one healer will often work through human instruments –

doctors, therapists or health professionals. But it is not limited to these and will often act directly on its own. It is fully capable of that. So, if health problems arise you need to explore your spiritual life. Bring that into order and chances are that your health problem will dissolve of its own weight. Intuition, as in past years, is still very important to your health. It is the moment-by-moment intuition that will lead you out of problems. Therapies that never worked for you before may now, in a given instance, work. Therapies that always worked for you before could now, in a given instance, fail. It is the intuition of the moment that is important. Uranus' move into Aries (your 8th house) from May 28th to August 14th is also giving us other messages. It shows the importance of safe sex and sexual moderation. The body has its normal sexual urges; it is a sexual creature born of the sexual act. These are easily fulfilled. But excess can cause problems. Also Uranus in the 8th tends to sexual experimentation. And though this is a good thing, if it becomes destructive it can have an impact on your health. You will need to be alert to that. If health problems arise while Uranus is in your 8th house you might want to look at your sexual attitudes and the use of your sexual force. Uranus in your 8th house also indicates that detox regimes will be very powerful, and should be looked at as a substitute for surgery in many cases.

Home and Family

Your 4th house of home and family is not a House of Power this year, Virgo, therefore the cosmos gives you a lot of freedom and latitude in how you want to shape this area of life. The cosmos is not pushing you one way or the other. Generally this leads to a status-quo kind of year. This year, however, I'm not so sure about that.

Two very unusual things are happening. Your family planet, Jupiter, moves extremely quickly this year – it will actually move through three signs and houses of your horoscope. Generally it stays in a sign and house for a whole year

– occasionally it will affect two signs and houses – but three? Very rare. This shows many different attitudes about the home – different ideas of how the home should be – different moods of family members and different needs of these family members.

While Jupiter is in your 6th house in Aquarius (until January 18th), the family as a whole seems health-conscious. There will be a great focus on healthy meals and healthy lifestyles. Probably there will be more consciousness of the environmental quality of the home, radiation in the home, the kind of insulation used in construction, etc. Also you will be trying to make your home like a mini-health spa (Virgo heaven). You will be buying health equipment and the like. (These trends were happening all of last year as well.)

When Jupiter moves into Pisces, your 7th house (January 18th to June 6th and September 10th to December 31st) there will be more of an emphasis on beautifying the home. Most likely you will redecorate, repaint, buy art objects for the home – perhaps a few times. You want to make it a place of aesthetic beauty as well as a place to live. Probably there will be more entertaining from home – more parties, more family gatherings. The home will become a social centre as well as a home. I wouldn't be surprised if there were marriages happening in the family as well.

When Jupiter moves into Aries in your 8th house (from June 6th to September 10th) it will be a great time to do a major house-cleaning – get rid of old possessions that you no longer need. You need to make room for the new things that want to come to you. You will also be buying athletic equipment for the home – making the home more like a gym. Extensive renovations could happen at this time, too.

The second unusual thing that is happening is that your family planet will travel with Uranus for many months in the coming year. The last time we saw something like this was in the early 1990s. This shows many things. Moves, for one thing. Renovations perhaps. A need for change in the home. High-tech gadgetry in the home. Sometimes people don't physically move but they live in different places for a long time (it is 'as if' they have moved). Family members can be very rebellious during this period and more difficult to handle. It will be a time to give family members maximum freedom and space – so long as it isn't destructive. (In some cases homes can break up or there can be 'rifts' in the family relationship.)

Learning emotional stability and calm will be the major challenge, then – for emotions will be either very high or very low. Both for you personally and for family members.

Basically, the cosmos is liberating you from unhealthy (not the good ones) family attachments. And sometimes it does this in dramatic kinds of ways.

After many years of Uranus opposing your Sun, you are quite used to sudden changes – so you are well able to handle the things that are coming.

Finance and Career

The main financial headline this year is Saturn's transit in your money house for most of the year. Saturn will retrograde out of there for a few months – April 8th to July 22nd – but he is the major influence here in 2010 and next year as well.

There are many messages here. On the most general level, Saturn – the great tester – is going to test your financial attitudes, abilities, strategies and judgement. Perhaps your plans were too optimistic – perhaps you didn't allow for unexpected contingencies – Saturn will show you your mistakes. Perhaps you haven't been managing your money effectively. Saturn will reveal that as well. Your financial life will get some 'rough treatment' to see how solid it is – how much stress it can take. In this treatment you will see some of your weaknesses and be able to make adjustments. Keep in mind, none of what is happening is punitive, only educational.

On a Wall Street there is a saying that 'everybody is a genius in a bull market.' When things are rosy and business is good, everyone seems smart in their own eyes. But it is in the down times, the bear markets when business is slow, that the real geniuses emerge. Now you will learn how much financial savvy you really have.

Saturn's intent is to set order – cosmic order – in your financial life. If you have been responsible in your financial affairs and conduct, this transit will only make you richer – and on a more enduring kind of level – a wealth that will last. But if you have been irresponsible in your finances – overcharged your credit cards, overspent, indulged in shady kinds of dealings – this transit can be very traumatic. For now the debts come due – the behaviour is disallowed – the piper must be paid. Yes, it might be unpleasant, but in the end your finances – both on a material level and in your attitudes and strategy – will be in the right order.

Saturn is the ruler of your 5th house of children, fun and creativity. So his move into your money house is giving us other messages as well. First off, you are probably spending more and investing more in your children. Spending more on fun- and leisure-type activities. Second, you can earn from these things as well. Children of appropriate age will be more supportive financially. And even younger children can come up with interesting financial ideas – or inspire you in a financial way. Many an entrepreneur has said that he got his multi-million pound idea just from watching his children.

Your personal creativity is a factor in wealth this year. And this could be where Saturn is pushing you. Explore your own creativity. Those of you already in the creative arts should have an excellent year. Your products are more marketable.

From an investment perspective – for those of you who have investment portfolios – commercial property, blue-chip type stocks, the art and beauty industry, industries that cater to children, casinos, resorts and entertainment are interesting investments in the year ahead.

Last year was an excellent year for job-seekers. Jupiter was in your 6th house bringing dream job opportunities. The year ahead also looks good. There are happy job changes coming – sudden and unexpected – from May to October as

Jupiter travels with your work planet. Those of you who employ others will have sudden employee turnover, but the end result is good – for there are replacements for whoever leaves. And good replacements, too.

Your 10th house of career is not a House of Power this year, and this tends to the status quo. Your position and public status will more or less be like last year. (Happy job changes don't necessarily move you up the career ladder.)

Love and Social Life

Last year – especially towards the end – was a fabulous love and social year. This trend continues in 2010. Perhaps even stronger.

The main headline is Jupiter's move into your 7th house of love and marriage. This always brings marriage (or business partnerships, joint ventures and things of that nature) or serious relationships that are like a marriage. Even for those of you who are too young to marry, you will meet people who are 'marriage material' – people you would consider marrying.

As mentioned earlier, ever since Uranus moved into your 7th house of love, your love life and social sphere in general have been quite unstable and chaotic. Oh yes, there has been love in your life, but it has been unstable and not likely to last. Many of you have been divorced and have been exploring the joys of social freedom. But now (actually since last year) you seem ready to settle down – to get serious. This time, this year, love looks much more stable than in previous years. For Uranus is getting ready to leave your 7th house of love – he has done his job; he has liberated you to pursue the social life of your dreams. He cleared the decks so that you can meet and have true love.

Many of you married last year or got involved in serious relationships. If you are still single, this is likely to happen in the year ahead as well.

You are allured by various kinds of people this year. One part of you is allured by health professionals or people involved in your health (and this has been a long-term trend). Office romances – romances with people you work with – have also been happening. But this year you are looking for someone highly educated, refined – more of a mentor type – than usual. Foreigners allure you. Romantic meetings can happen in foreign lands or in educational settings. You want someone you can look up to and respect. Women will gravitate to father figures. Men, to mother figures. Also, aside from all the other compatibilities in love, there is a need for emotional and philosophical compatibility. You want someone educated but with whom you can also share your feelings. Emotional intimacy is probably just as important as physical intimacy.

Religious-type settings also seem conducive for love this year.

The year ahead – especially from May 28th to September 10th – seems a more sexually active kind of year – another signal of a happy love life.

Those of you working towards or already in their second marriage are having a status-quo kind of year – though you will be more socially and sexually active. Marrieds will tend to stay married and singles will tend to stay single. Those in or working towards their third marriage, likewise.

There are weddings in the family as well.

Old flames from the past are coming back into your life – to resolve old issues.

There are two eclipses (and we can perhaps count three) happening in your 11th house of friends – so friendships are getting tested in the year ahead. The good ones will remain.

Self-improvement

For the past 2 years your body and image was the main focus for self-improvement. Saturn was in your own sign helping you to lose weight, take on disciplined health regimes and in general be more disciplined with your body. It was also a time for a reality check with your self-esteem. If self-esteem was too low or unrealistically low, Saturn raised you up. If self-esteem was too high, Saturn taught you some humility. The idea here was never punishment but more a sense of realism. A realistic sense of self will help you set realistic goals. You won't bite off more than you can chew. But neither will you do less than your potential. Saturn makes a return visit to your 1st house but only for a few months this year – from April 8th to July 22nd. So these lessons and opportunities will return for a while. But the major lesson, as mentioned, will be in your financial life. Saturn is going to set the whole thing into beautiful order. If you are overspending Saturn will keep you in check. On the other hand, if you have been under-spending or been overly miserly, Saturn will correct that, too. This is a time for managing your money – being in control of your money and not letting your money control you. This is the whole point. This is a time for intelligent budgeting and money management. Intelligent budgeting is not about lack but more about control and beauty. If you know that certain expenses will be coming up again and again, and because of your wise budgeting the money is there – there is a sense of peace. A sense of harmony. A sense of security. A sensible budget should include set-asides for a fun, happiness and joy. It is not a spartan kind of thing. Saturn will bring you a sense of proportion in your financial affairs. Proportion is the essence of beauty. If you are earning X amount, spending should be proportional. This will make your financial life not only satisfying, but beautiful as well. In the end Saturn wants to bring you long-term wealth. Wealth that will endure. Wealth that is secure. But this implies a sense of control. If the cosmos rains down riches upon you but your bucket is leaky, the riches will just leak out. Saturn is going to help you to seal any leaks in your bucket so when the wealth comes it stays there and goes where it should go.

For many years now Uranus has been bringing radical and dramatic changes not only in your career but in your love and social life is well. The main lesson for many years has been learning to cope with dramatic change while not losing your equilibrium or centre. This lesson is just about over – you have another year of it but it's winding down. By now you have learned to make change your friend. The next lesson will be in your sexual life – you will feel it for a few months this year from the May 28th to August 14th but you will really start to feel it in coming years. Uranus moves into your 8th house of sex. This will begin a period of sexual experimentation. It will be as if all the rule books get thrown out and you are going to find out about this subject for yourself by trial and error. Now, experimentation is basically a good thing because it leads to all kinds of new knowledge. Especially, it leads to self-knowledge. It leads to what works and doesn't work for you personally. As in almost every other area of life, each of us is a law unto ourselves. We all function differently. Our job in life is to learn how we as individuals function, and in coming years you will apply this to your sexual life. Experimentation is responsible for every breakthrough in knowledge. On the other hand, for every new product produced in a lab there are a few blown-up laboratories. So it is very important that you keep your experiments positive and constructive.

Many of our readers are very deeply into personal transformation. And as Uranus moves into your 8th house there is going to be great experimentation in this area as well. There are many fine books on these subjects – many spiritual systems that deal with these things, with general rules and principles given – but in the end you will have to find out what works for you. And this is the time to do it.

Saturn is the ruler of your 5th house of speculation, so its move into your money house this year, and for 2011 as well, shows a tendency to speculate. Speculations in general should be favourable in the year ahead, however Saturn cautions not to get involved in casino like risk-taking but in more cautious, well-hedged, calculated kinds of risk-taking. Speculations done under intuition – by this we mean true intuition – will always work out. Speculations done blindly generally don't work out. So you will have to discern between true and false intuition in the coming year.

Month-by-month Forecasts

January

Best Days Overall: 4, 5, 13, 14, 23, 24
Most Stressful Days Overall: 11, 12, 18, 19, 25, 26
Best Days for Love: 4, 5, 7, 13, 14, 15, 17, 18, 19, 25, 26
Best Days for Money: 4, 5, 6, 7, 13, 14, 15, 16, 17, 18, 25, 26, 27
Best Days for Career: 4, 5, 13, 14, 23, 24, 25, 26

Even though we have a solar eclipse on the 15th which tends to shake things up – bring dramatic change, upheavals and the like – the month ahead seems basically happy for you. You begin your year in the midst of a yearly personal pleasure peak – so you are having fun, are involved in leisure activities and enjoying your life. Even as the Sun moves into your 6th house of work, which for most people would be a more serious period – I would read this as merely an extension of the party. Work, to you, is pleasure – good for its own sake. Too much idleness and fun are uncomfortable for you.

Also adding to the joy is Jupiter's move into your 7th house on the 18th. This brings romance, new friends, perhaps even marriage, business partnerships or joint ventures, and in general a more active social life – more parties, dating and social gatherings. This trend is in effect for most of the year ahead.

This seems a more sexually active month as well. Mars is the 'handle' of a 'bucket' chart. Your sexual abilities and sex appeal (or understanding of the sexual force) lift up your entire life. Of course there are other meanings here, too. Your ability to help others to prosper, your insights into the deeper things of life – such as reincarnation and depth psychology, life and death – also lift up your life.

A very happy romantic opportunity came your way last month, but it could still happen this month. This meeting has the potential for marriage. This also could indicate a possible business partnership as well.

Health looks good and with your 6th house of health powerful you are very much into health regimes and healthy lifestyles. Your normal interest in health – always strong – is more emphasized now. If there have been health problems in the past, there is good news on that front this month.

The solar eclipse of the 15th is basically benign to you, but it won't hurt to take it easy during this period anyway. People in general are not at their best during an eclipse period. This eclipse seems to affect your children and spiritual life. Spiritual revelation or new insight cause changes in your spiritual practice and regime. There are shakeups in spiritual or charitable organizations you are involved with. Spiritual attitudes and approaches change. There are dramas in the lives of children (or those who are like children to you). Avoid speculations during this period (though for the month as a whole these seem favourable).

February

Best Days Overall: 1, 9, 10, 11, 19, 20, 21, 28
Most Stressful Days Overall: 7, 8, 15, 16, 22, 23
Best Days for Love: 2, 3, 13, 14, 15, 16, 23, 24, 25
Best Days for Money: 2, 3, 4, 5, 14, 15, 24, 25
Best Days for Career: 1, 11, 12, 22, 23

You began your year with most of the planets below the horizon – the 'night' side of your horoscope. And this holds true for most of the month ahead. Thus, your focus should be more on the family, your domestic situation and your emotional well-being. Career can take a back seat. On the 18th as the Sun moves into Pisces, the upper half of the horoscope gets stronger – you are at the dawn of the year, but not quite. Next month the planetary power will shift to the upper half for many months ahead. That will be a time to start pursuing your outer ambitions.

You began the year with the Western sector of the horoscope strong. This trend is even stronger this month.
Personal initiative and independence are most wonderful
traits, but now they are less important. This is a time for
honing your social skills, for getting your way through co-
operation and consensus and for developing your likeability.
You seem successful at this. This is not a time for changing
your circumstances by direct action. Adapt as best you can to
situations. Your good comes to you through the good graces
of others.

Health and work are still paramount until the 18th –
Virgo paradise. Job-seekers had good success last month; this
trend continues in the month ahead. There is no shortage of
jobs or work opportunities – there are at least four and
maybe five. Those of you who employ others also have
success in hiring these days.

Health is good this month, but rest and relax more after
the 18th. Enhance health by paying more attention to your
heart, ankles and feet. Until the 11th pay attention to your
kidneys and hips. From the 10th onwards pay more attention to your lungs, small intestine, arms and shoulders. The
main thing is to maintain high energy levels. Let go of unimportant, draining things and focus on the things that are
really important to you.

On the 18th you enter a yearly social peak, in an already
strong social year. There is a special someone out there for
singles. There are happy love meetings or romantic experiences from the 6th to the 9th (as Venus, the planet of love,
travels with Neptune, your love planet) and on the 27th and
28th as your ruling planet, Mercury, travels with Neptune.
The 27th and 28th also bring wealth opportunities and
supernatural kinds of experiences. Those on the path receive
spiritual revelation – a downpouring of spiritual power and
insight. Your dream life will be active and prophetic at these
times.

Finance is not a major interest this month, nevertheless
there are some nice things happening. Until the 11th you
earn the old-fashioned way, through work and service. After

the 11th it is through spousal support or the good graces of a current love or friends. The 14th to the 17th bring windfalls, financial opportunities and happiness in love. Happy romantic meetings are likely this period as well.

March

Best Days Overall: 1, 9, 10, 19, 20, 27, 28
Most Stressful Days Overall: 6, 7, 14, 15, 21, 22
Best Days for Love: 3, 5, 6, 12, 14, 15, 16, 17, 22, 25, 26, 30
Best Days for Money: 2, 3, 4, 5, 6, 14, 15, 16, 17, 23, 24, 25, 26, 29, 30, 31
Best Days for Career: 4, 14, 15, 21, 22, 25, 26

Be more careful driving on the 11th, 12th, 20th, 25th and 26th. Cars or communication equipment could experience some mechanical difficulties as well.

Health still needs watching until the 20th. Enhance the health by paying more attention to your heart (until the 20th) and to your ankles, calves and feet (all month). Regular massage of your ankles, calves and feet will do wonders for you – it will strengthen your whole body.

Job-seekers have a wonderful opportunity (and it seems to come through a friend) on the 15th. Friends can also get jobs for themselves and will hear good news on the health front.

You are still in the midst of your yearly social and romantic peak. Marriages (or quasi-marriages) could happen. Singles have a large menu to choose from as the 7th house is chock-full of planets. You still gravitate to unconventional types of people – this has been a trend for many years – but now you want them to have family values as well. Emotional nurturing and emotional intimacy also seem very important these days. Existing relationships can be enhanced through more emotional sharing and support as well.

Last month and this month there were many planets in Pisces – Venus is still there until the 7th. People in general –

and especially lovers and friends – are more sensitive these days – 100-fold more than usual (we also have a lot of water in the horoscope this month). So tone down the criticism and judgement – even in your thoughts. Cut your lover and friends more slack. Little things will get huge reactions.

There has been a financial reorganization going on for many months now, but though you might feel the pinch there are still happy developments going on. Saturn in your money house can make you feel unduly pessimistic about finances. Beware of the tendency to imagine worst-case scenarios – yes, you need to be more sober and serious about money, but not depressed about it. Your spouse, partner or current love is financially supportive. Social connections are boosting the bottom line. After the 7th, focus on helping others to prosper. Think of the best financial interests of the other person in your financial dealings. Good to pay off debt and cut down on waste. There is good access to outside capital – either investors or through borrowing. If finances feel tight, creative financing techniques can buy you more time. There is a nice financial windfall or opportunity from the 7th to the 9th – this could come from a parent, parent figure, family member or family connection.

April

  Best Days Overall: 5, 6, 15, 16, 24, 25
  Most Stressful Days Overall: 3, 4, 10, 11, 17, 18, 30
  Best Days for Love: 5, 9, 10, 11, 15, 16, 18, 25, 27
  Best Days for Money: 1, 5, 10, 11, 15, 16, 19, 20, 25, 26, 27, 28, 29
  Best Days for Career: 5, 15, 16, 17, 18, 24

Mercury goes retrograde on the 18th. He is both your personal and career planet. Thus, though career is becoming increasingly important, you need to review things here and aspire to some clarity. If you take some time for a sober appraisal of things you will be in a wonderful position next month as you enter a yearly career peak.

Your 8th house has been powerful since the 20th of last month. It is still powerful until the 20th of this month. This has many meanings. It is a more sexually active month. Whatever your age or stage in life, libido will be stronger than usual. It is a period of prosperity for your spouse, partner or current love. There is greater spousal support. This is a good period to clean house (in both a literal and metaphorical sense). Get rid of excess possessions that you don't use and that just gather dust and clutter up your life. Get rid of mental and emotional patterns – ideas and feelings – that no longer serve your interests. Detox the body, the mind and the emotions.

There is also a stronger interest in all the deeper things of life – death, rebirth, reincarnation, life after death, occult studies and the like. In many cases, the cosmos chooses to remind a person of his or her mortality when the 8th house is strong. There is a need to come to grips with death on a psychological level – and the cosmos has many ways, creative ways, of enabling this. Sometimes through a personal near-death experience – but often with a near-death experience of someone close to you. The object is not to 'take you (or the other) out' – only to deliver a message.

For those of you on a spiritual path, the 8th house has deeper and more wonderful meanings to convey. All of us have areas of life that are in need of 'resurrection' – perhaps there are dead projects, dead investments or dead relationships that cause us grief. The 8th house energy can teach us how to 'resurrect' these things. Resurrection, which is seen by many as some 'miraculous' or other-worldly power – is actually one of the most natural things in the world, going on around us all the time. So, many of you will be bringing things or projects 'back from the dead'.

Saturn moves out of your money house and into your own sign on the 3rd; he will spend the next few months there. Health needs more watching now – but more next month than now. The good point here is that finances are improved. Venus, crossing your Midheaven on the 25th, brings windfalls and financial opportunities that come from your career (a pay rise) or through your good professional reputation, or through parents, parent figures, elders or bosses. Venus, your financial planet, will spend most of the month in your 9th house. This is considered a prosperous house. There are travel (and perhaps educational) opportunities related to your career.

May

Best Days Overall: 2, 3, 4, 12, 13, 21, 22, 30, 31
Most Stressful Days Overall: 1, 7, 8, 9, 15, 27, 28
Best Days for Love: 5, 6, 7, 8, 9, 15, 16, 24, 25, 26
Best Days for Money: 5, 6, 8, 9, 15, 16, 18, 23, 24, 25, 26
Best Days for Career: 2, 12, 14, 15, 21, 30

Your personal and career planet, Mercury, goes forward on the 11th. On the 21st, as the Sun crosses your Midheaven, you enter a yearly career peak. The timing couldn't be more perfect. Hopefully you have attained some clarity as to your career and career goals, and the situation that is going on in your company. Now you can leap into action and be powerful. You can further your career goals through getting involved in charities, community projects and altruistic kinds of activities. Your idealism and spirituality are valued and honoured. This is a month for wonderful career progress. There are happy job changes as well. Dream job opportunities – either with your present company or with another one – are happening. All sudden and unexpected.

With your career active, we are tempted to counsel letting go of home and family issues, but this doesn't seem possible this month. Moves – sudden and unexpected – and happy – seem on the horizon. This could be related to the job changes, but not necessarily so. Your current love could be moving in or you could be moving in with him or her. We see more working from home or involvement in a family kind of business. You are installing health equipment or gadgetry in the home.

Health needs watching after the 21st. Nothing serious on the horizon – just a period where your energy levels are not what they should be. You can enhance your health by paying more attention to your heart (do this by reducing stress and worry) and in the ways mentioned in the yearly report. On the 28th, your health planet moves into Aries, your 8th house. So there are changes in your health regime as well. Physical exercise and muscle tone become more important. Good health for you means physical fitness as well as 'no symptoms'. If there have been health problems in the past, there is good news on that front this month. There is good news on the health front for family members as well. After the 28th pay more attention to your head, face and skull – regular scalp and face massage is powerful. Detox regimes become more powerful after the 28th as well.

Your good professional reputation is still very important financially until the 20th. Pay rises and good support from parents or parent figures, bosses or elders are also helping. After the 20th family support is still good, but financial opportunities also come through friends and through involvement in professional or trade organizations. Networking brings profits.

Children – or those who are like children to you – are having a bit of a rough time now – their love relationships and friendships are getting tested.

June

Best Days Overall: 9, 10, 17, 18, 26, 27
Most Stressful Days Overall: 4, 5, 11, 12, 24, 25
Best Days for Love: 2, 4, 5, 12, 13, 14, 20, 24, 25, 30
Best Days for Money: 4, 5, 6, 13, 14, 15, 19, 20, 24, 25
Best Days for Career: 10, 11, 12, 19, 20

Many of the trends we wrote of last month are still very much in effect. You are still in the midst of a yearly career peak, yet home and family issues are also very important. There is a need to handle both and balance both – not so easy to do. You can't ignore either of these areas. Now you will swing one way, now the other – it's a dynamic kind of balance that is needed.

Moves could still happen this month – again, sudden and unexpected. In some cases you are living in different places for long periods of time and thus it is 'as if' you have moved. There are renovations going on in the home as well – perhaps multiple renovatioris. A parent or parent figure is exploring personal freedom these days and doesn't seem to want any 'burden' or responsibility. He or she is travelling much and leading a more nomadic kind of existence. He or she is testing the physical limits these days – hopefully in constructive ways. Yoga – a safe and constructive way to test the body's limits – would be wonderful for this person.

We saw you installing more health equipment in the home last month, but now you might be adding athletic equipment as well. Your home is becoming part gym and part health spa.

This is a month for both career and psychological break-throughs.

A lunar eclipse on the 26th will test a love affair and bring changes with children (or those like children to you). Things happen that change your relationship with them – many of these things can be quite normal: a move, graduation, marriage – but still it is disruptive. Happy things can be just as disruptive as negative things. Children are redefining their personality and self-concept – which normally leads to changes in their wardrobe and image.

Every lunar eclipse tests your friendships and this one is no different. Dramatic events are happening in the lives of children and friends.

Finances are good this month. Happy job changes can still happen. There is more working from the home. Your financial planet will be in your 11th house (the sign of Cancer) until the 14th, indicating good family support and support from friends. Like last month it is good to be more involved in trade or professional organizations. After the 14th, with your financial planet in the spiritual 12th house, your intuition is important. You go more deeply into the spiritual sources and dimensions of wealth.

Health still needs watching until the 21st. Keep in mind our discussion of last month. Mars moves into your sign on the 7th, which has many good points. You are more athletic, more magnetic and charismatic. You get things done quickly. But you need to mind your temper and avoid haste and rush.

July

Best Days Overall: 6, 7, 15, 23, 24, 25
Most Stressful Days Overall: 1, 2, 8, 9, 21, 22, 28, 29, 30
Best Days for Love: 1, 2, 5, 9, 14, 18, 23, 24, 27, 28, 29, 30
Best Days for Money: 3, 5, 12, 14, 16, 17, 18, 21, 23, 24, 31
Best Days for Career: 1, 2, 8, 9, 12, 21, 22

Last month the planetary power shifted to the East from the Western, social sector of your horoscope. This was an important shift. You are now in a period of greater independence. You have more control over your life and affairs. The challenge is to use this control in a positive way. Since the beginning of the year you've been cultivating your 'people skills' – social grace, getting things done through consensus and co-operation with others, adapting to situations rather than changing them. Now, your personal initiative matters. Who you are and what you can do is important. Time to take the bull by the horns and create the life you desire. Time to have life on your terms. Of course, others should always be respected and treated properly – beware the temptation to run roughshod over them – especially now with Mars in your own sign. You can be nice to others and still go your own way and carve out your own life.

Last month's lunar eclipse tested friendships; this month's solar eclipse on the 11th will do the same. It occurs in your 11th house of friends. This eclipse, like the last one, is basically benign to you, but a reduced schedule is still a good idea. People are not at their best during an eclipse period, and you don't need to be caught up in other people's issues. This eclipse can bring shakeups in organizations you belong to – either of a social, professional or charitable nature. It also brings changes to your spiritual regime and practice. If there are 'skeletons in your closet', they are likely to come out now – but never mind, it's good to deal with them and put them to rest now.

Health is improving now. Saturn leaves your sign on the 21st, enhancing your overall energy. Saturn will not return to your sign for another 28 years. He is effectively gone for good. Personal self-confidence and self-esteem are improving as well. By now, after 2 years of a Saturn transit in your own sign, your sense of self-esteem and self-worth is solid and realistic – neither overly inflated nor too low. Just right. You have a realistic sense of your own abilities and are ready to make better decisions.

With Saturn now in your money house for the next year 2 years, finances are getting reorganized – just as in the first few months of this year. You have to take on more financial responsibility – perhaps more burdens are placed on you and this forces you to manage your money better. In spite of this, this is a good financial month. Venus, your financial planet, will move into your own sign on the 10th, bringing windfalls and financial opportunities. Personal items will come to you – things like clothing or jewellery. You will spend more on yourself – your image and appearance. Your personal appearance will play a large role in earnings. You will project an image of wealth – or strive in that direction. Financial opportunities will seek you out rather than vice versa.

Your love planet has been retrograde since June. This hasn't stopped your love life – but there is a bit of a lull now. Your love life is under review. With Venus and Mars in your 1st house you certainly look good and are attractive – this isn't the issue. It has to do with your specific relationships and where they are going. Date and have fun, but avoid making important love decisions one way or the other.

August

Best Days Overall: 2, 3, 11, 12, 20, 21, 30, 31
Most Stressful Days Overall: 5, 6, 17, 18, 25, 26
Best Days for Love: 3, 4, 6, 13, 14, 22, 23, 24, 25, 26
Best Days for Money: 3, 4, 9, 13, 14, 17, 22, 23, 27
Best Days for Career: 2, 5, 6, 11, 12, 20, 21, 30, 31

You have been in a more intense spiritual period since the 23rd of last month; this trend continues in the month ahead – until the 23rd. This is a period for spiritual-type break-throughs – for insights and for the expansion of your inner understanding and knowledge. Great for spiritually-orientated retreats or pilgrimages, for prayer meetings and meditation seminars. Good now to review the past year, correct mistakes and set honest goals for what you want in the coming year. Your birthday represents your personal new year – a very important celestial event in your year. You want to begin your celestial new year with a clean slate.

On the 23rd, as the Sun crosses your Ascendant, you enter a yearly personal pleasure peak. But the focus on spirituality will still be there – the Sun is your spiritual planet. So you will have supernatural kinds of experiences all month: an active dream life, good ESP and a greater contact with the invisible world. Personal pleasure will come to you in supernatural kinds of ways as well. This is a good period to renew and 'burnish' your image in spiritual ways. You've done the gym and the physical exercise regimes last month, now you will be able to enhance your image through meditation, visualization and diet. Yoga also seems good this month.

Those on a spiritual path will be more involved in karma yoga – serving the divine through the body – through actions – not just meditatively.

Though finances are still being reorganized and re-structured – and probably you feel the pinch – this is still a good month financially. Until the 7th financial opportunities are still pursuing you. You are still cultivating the image of wealth, which is a good thing – it puts you into the vibrations of wealth and attracts all kinds of opportunities to you. After the 7th Venus will enter your money house, where she is more powerful on your behalf. There is more luck in speculations and there is an opportunity to earn money in happy ways (especially from the 7th to the 10th). You are spending more on children but can earn in this way as well. Children can have very interesting financial insights and ideas. You are earning more this month, but with Mars in your money house it seems best to channel extra earnings towards reducing debt. (If you need to borrow, these opportunities are there as well – but better to avoid borrowing for frivolous things.)

There are some financial bumps in the road from the 11th to the 14th and from the 25th to the 28th. These will force some needed changes in your thinking and strategy.

A love affair gets tested from the 26th to the 31st, and children may experience dramas in their lives.

Drive more defensively from the 4th to the 9th and from the 25th to the 28th. Mind your temper more, too – avoid arguments or confrontations.

September

Best Days Overall: 7, 8, 16, 17, 26, 27
Most Stressful Days Overall: 1, 2, 13, 14, 15, 21, 22, 28, 29
Best Days for Love: 2, 10, 11, 19, 20, 21, 22, 29, 30
Best Days for Money: 2, 5, 9, 10, 11, 12, 21, 22
Best Days for Career: 1, 2, 7, 16, 27, 28, 29

Love is active and happy, but still under review. There are many doubts to be resolved. Only time will resolve these things. Enjoy your love life, but avoid making major decisions one way or the other. Though you are still in a 'love at first sight' kind of period, let love develop slowly and as it will.

Moves and renovations of the home can still happen now, but probably require more thought and homework. There can be delays involved in these things.

A love affair (not a marriage) is being tested all month. If it is flawed, it will probably dissolve – or be on the road to dissolution. A good relationship will survive. Still, singles have many love opportunities.

Children (or those like children to you) are going through a turbulent period. Be more patient with them. They seem more temperamental. Older children are going through image and personality changes – ultimately for the better. A parent or parent figure is still nomadic and still exploring his or her personal freedom. Give this person as much space as possible.

Avoid speculations during this period – your planet of speculations camps out on an eclipse point all month.

Drive more carefully and defensively on the 1st and avoid temper-tantrums and confrontations.

You are still very much into your yearly personal pleasure peak until the 23rd. A time for enjoying the pleasures of the flesh and the good life. After the 23rd you enter a yearly financial peak. You are in one of the most prosperous periods of your year. Saturn in your money house demands hard-headedness and a certain realistic approach to finances. It wants you down to earth. But your spiritual planet moving through your money house counsels following your intuition and inner guidance. Often this latter attitude seems to contradict the 'realistic' approach, but in hindsight intuition always proves to have been the most 'practical' way to go. Getting the spiritual to jive – to harmonize – with the material aspects of wealth is quite a challenge, but it can be resolved. Manage what you have in a rational way, but with the understanding that, at any moment, spirit can supply you with more. When the 'more' comes you will adjust your budget accordingly. Still a good time to reduce debt and expenses until the 15th. Try to simplify your finances now – consolidate savings, current and brokerage accounts. Do you have three savings accounts when one will do? Consolidate.

Sales, marketing, PR and advertising become important in your financial life after the 8th. Good use of the media is important.

Health is good this month.

October

Best Days Overall: 5, 6, 13, 14, 23, 24
Most Stressful Days Overall: 11, 12, 18, 19, 25, 26, 27
Best Days for Love: 1, 8, 9, 17, 18, 19, 27, 28
Best Days for Money: 1, 2, 7, 8, 9, 10, 18, 19, 28, 29
Best Days for Career: 7, 17, 25, 26, 27, 28

Your chart makes two important patterns this month, Virgo, and this is so rare that it is worth discussing. From the 3rd to the 5th and from the 23rd to the 31st, your chart is a 'bucket' chart with the Moon as the 'handle'. This shows that family and friends are the way to lifting up your life. You look to these areas to lift you up. (By the way, since last month as the planets shifted to the bottom half of your horoscope, family has become more important and career less.) From the 7th to the 21st, your chart is a 'bowl' chart – this shows someone who has a need to give and to share with others. Your bowl is, symbolically speaking, full – and only as you empty it, by sharing and giving, can you refill it.

You are still in the midst of yearly financial peak. So there is prosperity now. You are working for it, no question – going the extra mile for clients, customers or bosses – but earnings are on the increase. Like last month, intuition is a major factor. You are going more deeply into the spiritual sources of supply while trying to keep both feet on the ground and not lose your realism. The spiritual perspective is that wealth is spiritual in nature and infinite. But Saturn in your money house declares that wealth is limited and must be apportioned and managed properly. Both perspectives are true. Wealth is infinite, but at any given time we have X amount to work with – X amount on hand – and that X amount needs to be handled wisely. On the 3rd Mercury moves into your money house and stays there until the 21st – another positive for finance. First it shows greater personal interest – always a prerequisite for success. But it also indicates that your mission in life – your main concern – is getting your finances in order and in achieving a modicum of security. Elders, bosses, parents or parent figures are supportive. Your good professional reputation brings referrals and other financial opportunities. The only problem now is that your financial planet, Venus, goes retrograde on the 8th. This won't stop your earnings, only slow things down a bit. But it is a time for a serious, sober review of your finances with a view to improving them. If you pay some attention here, sitting down with a pad and paper and jotting down your thoughts, many interesting solutions will come to you. When Venus goes forward next month, you can put these ideas into practice.

A child (or child figure in your life) meets a mentor or guru this month – looks like early in the month. This child has been through a lot in the past month, so this meeting is good. 'When the student is ready, the master appears.' Things go more easily for this child in the month ahead.

Your 3rd house of communication and intellectual interests is strong all month, but especially after the 23rd. Great to catch up on your phone calls, e-mails and letters. Touch base with people you haven't contacted in a while. Take courses in subjects that interest you. Time to feed and restock your mind.

Health is good and you can enhance it further in the ways discussed in the yearly report. Your health planet is retrograde (it has been retrograde for some months) so avoid making major changes to your diet or health regime without doing some serious homework first.

November

Best Days Overall: 1, 2, 10, 11, 19, 20, 21, 28, 29
Most Stressful Days Overall: 7, 8, 14, 15, 16, 22, 23
Best Days for Love: 4, 5, 13, 14, 15, 16, 23
Best Days for Money: 3, 4, 5, 6, 13, 15, 16, 23, 25
Best Days for Career: 6, 17, 22, 23, 27, 28

Like last month, your chart fluctuates from the 'bowl' to the 'bucket' type. It is a bucket on the 1st and 2nd and again from the 19th to the 28th. It is a bowl from the 3rd to the 17th. Review our discussion of this last month.

Your financial planet is still retrograde until the 18th, so your financial life is still under review. Earnings won't stop, but delays and sometimes irritating glitches happen. You need to make sure all financial dealings and purchases are 'perfect' – all the details, the small print in the contracts, the doubts, need to be handled. If you are doing the review we discussed last month you will be in a nice position to move forward on the 18th. Until then it might feel as if you are going backwards instead of forwards financially – but this is only appearances. Important financial developments are happening behind the scenes. Continue to enhance wealth through social contacts, partners or your spouse or current love. The beauty industry – art, fashion, jewellery, perfumes, antiques – are interesting paths to profits. You are probably spending more on these things as well.

Some 90–100 per cent of the planets are below the horizon of your horoscope. Your 10th house of career is basically empty (only the Moon visits there on the 22nd and 23rd) while your 4th house of home and family is very strong. Focus on the family and let your career go for a while (do what you need to do, but give your main attention to your family and domestic situation). In fact, from the 8th onwards, your mission – your spiritual career – is your family. Be there for them. Where possible take work home with you or work from home – this will give you more time with the family. (Many of you are doing this already.)

On the 28th of last month Mars moved into your 4th house. He is there all of this month. This has many meanings. First, there are important renovations or repairs going on in the home. Perhaps family members are having near-death kinds of experiences or encounters with death (this need not mean literally death). The family pattern seems threatened or disrupted. Family members or parent figures can be having surgery. All the more reason for you to be there for them.

Health needs more watching after the 23rd. Pay more attention to your heart, ankles, calves and feet. The health trends of the yearly report are still valid now. As always, when energy is not up to its usual standards you need to rest and relax more.

Your love life has been under review for many months now. On the 8th your love planet starts moving forward. And on the 18th, another planet involved in your love life (Jupiter) joins him. Clarity is returning. (Venus also starts moving forward on the 18th as well.) You more or less know where a given relationship stands and where you want to take it. Your love life is still very active this month, as it has been all year.

December

Best Days Overall: 7, 8, 17, 18, 26, 27
Most Stressful Days Overall: 5, 6, 12, 13, 19, 20
Best Days for Love: 2, 11, 12, 13, 20, 22, 29, 31
Best Days for Money: 1, 2, 4, 12, 13, 22, 23, 28, 29, 31
Best Days for Career: 2, 11, 19, 20, 29

Many of the trends we wrote of last month are still very much in effect. Family is the major interest and focus – and still your spiritual mission this month. Your job now is to be there for them in whatever capacity you can.

Also – consistent with having so many planets below the horizon and a strong 4th house – this is a time to find, and function from, your point of emotional harmony. Your inner state – your everyday mood – seems more important than mere outer success. When you are in emotional harmony, outer success will naturally happen in due course and at the right time. You will be more able to handle it – more stable with it – when it does happen.

A lunar eclipse on the 21st occurs right on the border of your 10th and 11th houses and will have an impact on the affairs of both these houses. Thus there are career changes, changes in your corporate hierarchy or industry. Friendships, once again, get tested (this has been happening all year – ever since the last lunar eclipse of December 31st,

2009) and there are dramatic – out of the ordinary – experiences in the lives of friends. Professional or trade organizations you belong to experience internal shakeups. Often your high-tech gadgetry gets tested as well. This eclipse is stronger on those of you born later in the sign of Virgo (September 15th to 23rd). If this is you, take a reduced schedule. With career matters wait until your career planet starts moving forward on the 30th before making important decisions – the eclipse has changed the landscape, but you need not be in a hurry – study the landscape further.

The lunar eclipse coincides with the beginning of another yearly personal pleasure peak. A time for parties, leisure activities, fun and games. A time for exploring the 'rapture' side of life. You have a better ability to get on with children these days, as you are more in touch with your own inner child. You can relate to them as an equal.

Your financial planet will be in the 3rd house all month – the obvious message here is to enhance your financial life with good ideas (and they will come to you) through good marketing, sales and use of the media. Get the message out about your product or service. Buying and selling, trading and retailing also seem like paths to profits. Your financial judgement is sound and keen these days. Purchases and investment decisions are likely to be good.

Health needs watching until the 21st. Pay attention to your heart. Make sure you get enough rest. Avoid burning the candle at both ends.

Libra

☲

Personality Profile

LIBRA AT A GLANCE

Element – Air

Ruling Planet – Venus
   Career Planet – Moon
   Love Planet – Mars
   Money Planet – Pluto
   Planet of Communications – Jupiter
   Planet of Health and Work – Neptune
   Planet of Home and Family Life – Saturn
   Planet of Spirituality and Good Fortune –
     Mercury

Colours – blue, jade green

*Colours that promote love, romance and social
   harmony* – carmine, red, scarlet

Colours that promote earning power –
   burgundy, red-violet, violet

Gems – carnelian, chrysolite, coral, emerald, jade, opal, quartz, white marble

Metal – copper

Scents – almond, rose, vanilla, violet

Quality – cardinal (= activity)

Qualities most needed for balance – a sense of self, self-reliance, independence

Strongest virtues – social grace, charm, tact, diplomacy

Deepest needs – love, romance, social harmony

Characteristic to avoid – violating what is right in order to be socially accepted

Signs of greatest overall compatibility – Gemini, Aquarius

Signs of greatest overall incompatibility – Aries, Cancer, Capricorn

Sign most helpful to career – Cancer

Sign most helpful for emotional support – Capricorn

Sign most helpful financially – Scorpio

Sign best for marriage and/or partnerships – Aries

Sign most helpful for creative projects – Aquarius

Best Sign to have fun with – Aquarius

Signs most helpful in spiritual matters – Gemini, Virgo

Best day of the week – Friday

Understanding a Libra

In the sign of Libra the universal mind – the soul – expresses its genius for relationships, that is, its power to harmonize diverse elements in a unified, organic way. Libra is the soul's power to express beauty in all of its forms. And where is beauty if not within relationships? Beauty does not exist in isolation. Beauty arises out of comparison – out of the just relationship between different parts. Without a fair and harmonious relationship there is no beauty, whether it be in art, manners, ideas or the social or political forum.

There are two faculties humans have that exalt them above the animal kingdom: their rational faculty (expressed in the signs of Gemini and Aquarius) and their aesthetic faculty, exemplified by Libra. Without an aesthetic sense we would be little more than intelligent barbarians. Libra is the civilizing instinct or urge of the soul.

Beauty is the essence of what Librans are all about. They are here to beautify the world. One could discuss Librans' social grace, their sense of balance and fair play, their ability to see and love another person's point of view – but this would be to miss their central asset: their desire for beauty.

No one – no matter how alone he or she seems to be – exists in isolation. The universe is one vast collaboration of beings. Librans, more than most, understand this and understand the spiritual laws that make relationships bearable and enjoyable.

A Libra is always the unconscious (and in some cases conscious) civilizer, harmonizer and artist. This is a Libra's deepest urge and greatest genius. Librans love instinctively to bring people together, and they are uniquely qualified to do so. They have a knack for seeing what unites people – the things that attract and bind rather than separate individuals.

Finance

In financial matters Librans can seem frivolous and illogical to others. This is because Librans appear to be more concerned with earning money for others than for themselves. But there is a logic to this financial attitude. Librans know that everything and everyone is connected and that it is impossible to help another to prosper without also prospering yourself. Since enhancing their partner's income and position tends to strengthen their relationship, Librans choose to do so. What could be more fun than building a relationship? You will rarely find a Libra enriching him- or herself at someone else's expense.

Scorpio is the ruler of Libra's solar 2nd house of money, giving Libra unusual insight into financial matters – and the power to focus on these matters in a way that disguises a seeming indifference. In fact, many other signs come to Librans for financial advice and guidance.

Given their social grace, Librans often spend great sums of money on entertaining and organizing social events. They also like to help others when they are in need. Librans would go out of their way to help a friend in dire straits, even if they have to borrow from others to do so. However, Librans are also very careful to pay back any debts they owe, and like to make sure they never have to be reminded to do so.

Career and Public Image

Publicly, Librans like to appear as nurturers. Their friends and acquaintances are their family and they wield political power in parental ways. They also like bosses who are paternal or maternal.

The sign of Cancer is on Libra's 10th house (of career) cusp; the Moon is Libra's career planet. The Moon is by far the speediest, most changeable planet in the horoscope. It alone among all the planets travels through the entire zodiac – all 12 signs and houses – every month. This is an important key to the way in which Librans approach their careers, and also to what they need to do to maximize their career potential. The Moon is the planet of moods and feelings – Librans need a career in which their emotions can have free expression. This is why so many Librans are involved in the creative arts. Libra's ambitions wax and wane with the Moon. They tend to wield power according to their mood.

The Moon 'rules' the masses – and that is why Libra's highest goal is to achieve a mass kind of acclaim and popularity. Librans who achieve fame cultivate the public as other people cultivate a lover or friend. Librans can be very flexible – and often fickle – in their career and ambitions. On the other hand, they can achieve their ends in a great variety of ways. They are not stuck in one attitude or with one way of doing things.

Love and Relationships

Librans express their true genius in love. In love you could not find a partner more romantic, more seductive or more fair. If there is one thing that is sure to destroy a relationship – sure to block your love from flowing – it is injustice or imbalance between lover and beloved. If one party is giving too much or taking too much, resentment is sure to surface at some time or other. Librans are careful about this. If anything, Librans might err on the side of giving more, but never giving less.

If you are in love with a Libra, make sure you keep the aura of romance alive. Do all the little things – candle-lit dinners, travel to exotic locales, flowers and small gifts. Give things that are beautiful, not necessarily expensive. Send cards. Ring regularly even if you have nothing in particular to say. The niceties are very important to a Libra. Your relationship is a work of art: make it beautiful and your Libra lover will appreciate it. If you are creative about it, he or she will appreciate it even more; for this is how your Libra will behave towards you.

Librans like their partners to be aggressive and even a bit self-willed. They know that these are qualities they sometimes lack and so they like their partners to have them. In relationships, however, Librans can be very aggressive – but always in a subtle and charming way! Librans are determined in their efforts to charm the object of their desire – and this determination can be very pleasant if you are on the receiving end.

Home and Domestic Life

Since Librans are such social creatures, they do not particularly like mundane domestic duties. They like a well-organized home – clean and neat with everything needful present – but housework is a chore and a burden, one of the unpleasant tasks in life that must be done, the quicker the better. If a Libra has enough money – and sometimes even if not – he or she will prefer to pay someone else to take care of the daily household chores. However, Librans like gardening; they love to have flowers and plants in the home.

A Libra's home is modern, and furnished in excellent taste. You will find many paintings and sculptures there. Since Librans like to be with friends and family, they enjoy entertaining at home and they make great hosts.

Capricorn is on the cusp of Libra's 4th solar house of home and family. Saturn, the planet of law, order, limits and discipline, rules Libra's domestic affairs. If Librans want their home life to be supportive and happy they need to develop some of the virtues of Saturn – order, organization and discipline. Librans, being so creative and so intensely in need of harmony, can tend to be too lax in the home and too permissive with their children. Too much of this is not always good; children need freedom but they also need limits.

Horoscope for 2010

Major Trends

Last year was a year of many major changes; this year there are even more changes in store. Last year Pluto, after spending 15 years or so in Sagittarius, moved into Capricorn, your 4th house, for good. This was a major transit as it affected both your family and financial life. Financial attitudes and behaviour are undergoing drastic change. It is as if your whole philosophy of wealth is being changed. More on this later.

Last year Saturn moved into your own sign towards the end of the year. This year he will spend most of the year in your sign, and this too has major health and energy implications and in terms of your body, physical appearance and image. More on this later.

This year we see other dramatic changes as well. Uranus, which has spent 7 to 8 years in your 6th house, will move out of there into your 7th house from May 28th to August 14th. This is going to change your love life dramatically and test many a marriage, business partnership or serious relationship. Those of you born early in the sign of Libra (September 23rd–25th) will feel this most strongly. But in coming years all of you will feel it. This brief transit this year is merely an announcement of things to come and should be looked at seriously.

Last year was a mixed kind of year. Yes it was a fun year – Jupiter was in your 5th house and you indulged in parties and entertainments and all kinds of leisure activities. But Saturn also moved into your own sign towards the end of the year and this toned you down a bit – forced you to take on more responsibilities and to get a little bit more serious about life. Jupiter was showing you a good time but Saturn was saying, 'Hold on, don't get too carried away, life is serious business.'

This year seems to be more of a work-orientated year, more of a serious year than last year was. Jupiter will move into the 6th house of work, and so you are less in a party mode and more in a work mode – more into achieving goals at work. There is still fun in your life – it is not *all* work and Neptune is still in your 5th house – but you shift more towards work and responsibility.

For job-seekers the year ahead is basically nirvana. Jupiter will bring all kinds of wonderful and happy job opportunities to you. Those of you who employ others will expand the workforce, and Jupiter's move into the 6th house should be considered a symbol of success.

Your major interests in the year ahead will be home and family, children, fun and creativity, health and work, love, romance and social activities (especially from May 28th to September 10th), the body, the image and physical appearance (from January 1st to April 8th and from July 22nd to December 31st), friendships, group activities and organizations (January 1st to June 6th), and spirituality (from April 8th to July 22nd).

Your paths of greatest fulfilment in the year ahead will be home and family, children, fun and creativity (until January 18th), health and work (January 18th to June 6th and September 10th to December 31st), and love, romance and social activities (June 6th to September 10th).

Health

(Please note that this is an astrological perspective on health and not a medical one. In days gone by there was no difference; these perspectives were identical. But nowadays there can be quite a difference. For the medical perspective, please consult your doctor or health practitioner.)

Health has been basically good these past few years and should be basically good in the year ahead. However, no question energy and vitality are not as they were last year. Saturn in your own sign shows that you need to watch your energy more. Further, Uranus starts to make a stressful aspect to you from May 23rd to August 14th. But this transit is very brief. Still it will be a good idea to rest and relax more, to use your energy wisely, avoid burning the candle at both ends, manage your time, delegate tasks wherever possible and try to do more with less through better planning.

Happily your 6th house of health has been strong for many years, but this year even more and so you will be paying attention to your health. It is a priority to you, as it should be, especially now. The main danger when the aspects are difficult is a tendency to ignore health, but this will not be the case with you.

There are many things you can do to enhance your health. Pay more attention and focus on the following parts of the body:

- feet
- ankles and calves
- liver and thighs.

Since these are your most vulnerable areas, any problems – if they were to arise – would most likely begin there, so keeping them healthy and fit is good preventative medicine.

Neptune is your health planet. In the physical body, Neptune rules the feet. Hence the importance of your feet in overall health. Foot reflexology, foot massage, foot baths, foot hydrotherapy are all wonderful therapies for you, Libra. You respond very well to these. Your health planet rules from the sign of Aquarius, which rules your ankles and calves. The planet that actually rules the ankles and calves, Uranus, occupies your 6th house for most of the year. Hence the importance of these parts of the body in your overall health.

Neptune rules your health from the 5th house. This gives us many messages, and these messages have been true for years now and we have written about them. There is a need to express your creative urges. If these are blocked for any reason it can actually have an impact on your physical health. So a creative hobby is not only fun but therapeutic for you. I especially like music, dance and creative writing. But anything which expresses your creativity will be good. The 5th house rules the fun of life. So you must avoid

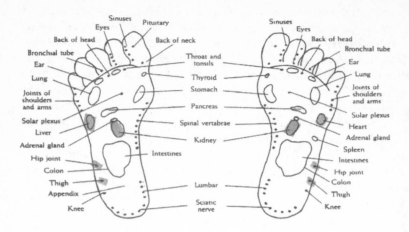

Reflexology

Try to massage the whole foot on a regular basis, but pay extra attention to the points highlighted on the chart. When you massage, be aware of 'sore spots', as these need special attention. It's also a good idea to massage the ankles and top side (as well as the soles) of the feet.

depression like the plague. Feelings of depression should be looked at as the first symptoms of disease and treated accordingly. Though this is a serious year, as mentioned, try not to get too serious. Make sure you have some fun. One can handle responsibilities in a cheerful way. If you feel under the weather, a night out on the town will often do you as much good as a visit to a health professional.

Neptune is the most spiritual of all the planets, so the message here is that you respond very well to spiritually-orientated therapies: prayer and meditation, reiki, the laying-on of hands, energy medicine, the manipulation of subtle energies are all powerful therapies for you. With the spiritual planet as your health planet the message is to stay 'prayed up' and in a state of grace. Spiritual disconnection is a probable root cause of any health problem. This is so for everyone to some degree, but especially so for you. Jupiter in your 6th house also shows the power of spiritual therapies, but more the power of prayer and speaking of the word. In the physical body Jupiter rules the liver and thighs, hence their importance in your overall health in the coming year. Thighs should be regularly massaged.

Saturn in your own sign in your 1st house shows this will be an excellent year for losing weight and getting in shape. Great for disciplined exercise regimes.

Home and Family

Your 4th house of home and family has become a House of Power ever since last year. It is a major focus in the year ahead. Not only is the 4th house strong but there will be two eclipses in that house in the coming year: a solar eclipse on January 15th, and a lunar eclipse on June 26th. There is going to be a lot of change and disruption. Keep in mind that none of this is punitive, only educational and corrective. In addition to the power in the 4th house, your home and family planet (Saturn) moves a bit erratically in the year ahead. It begins the year in your own sign of Libra but then retrogrades back into your 12th house from April 8th to July 22nd, and then back into Libra after July 22nd.

No question there is a lot going on here. Pluto in your 4th house is indicating many things. First off, it shows that on the physical level there are major renovations and repairs going on in the home, usually of a deep nature. On another level it is showing death or near-death experiences in the family or with family members. On another level it is showing a cosmic detox going on in the home, family and emotional life. Detoxes are not usually pleasant while they're happening, but in the end they are good. Your present situation is apparently not good enough for you, and the cosmos wants to improve it in a deep and profound way. We see you spending more on the home and on family members in the year ahead, for Pluto is your financial planet. The two eclipses in your 4th house will probably bring up the flaws in the home so that you can correct them, and these are probably expensive.

Saturn in your own sign shows that you are taking on more family responsibility, and that these responsibilities are perhaps burdensome to you. There are many scenarios of what could happen. A parent or parent figure comes to live with you or you must take responsibility for this person. Perhaps you feel that your family owns you and that you are not an independent person. The family obligations seem to be controlling you, not vice versa. However, Saturn is urging you to take on these responsibilities, not to shirk them but to handle them perfectly. In this process many wonderful things will happen for you, most notably for your character. You will grow as a human being. It seems to me that these extra family responsibilities are contributing to the detox and the change in the whole family structure that we see. It is as if you will have to relate to your family in a new and different way. Not that you will break with them, but that you will break the more instinctive ties and relate to them from a higher level in yourself. Family is a womb and a tomb, as some sages have said. It is a womb in the sense that it protects us when we are young. Very important. But when the time comes for the child to come out of the womb – it must leave. If it stays in the womb, the womb becomes a tomb, and it is the same with family. When the time comes for a person to become more of an individual, someone who thinks for him- or herself and takes charge of his or her own destiny, it might be necessary to leave the family fold. If one doesn't do that when the time comes, the family womb can become a family tomb.

There are other possible scenarios here, too. The family can be disrupted or broken up due to divorce – not so much on a personal level but between other family members – and this creates a breakup in the family unit. Sometimes this happens because of the death of a family member or near-death kind of experience, and sometimes because of squabbles within the family. It will be quite a challenge to keep things together, but your newfound family responsibility could be coming from some of these kinds of breakups and disruptions.

This is a year, and for many years to come, where you will be making deep and profound psychological progress. You will discover things that are quite amazing. These discoveries lead to greater emotional freedom and maturity.

A parent or parent figure seems to be having surgery. It could be cosmetic or something more serious. They should, of course, explore other alternatives. A parent or parent figure is very likely to move quite suddenly from May 28th to September 10th. Sometimes they don't actually move under this aspect; they just live in different places for long periods of time and it is as if they have moved.

As mentioned earlier, a parent or parent figure could be coming to stay with you or be under your personal care. If you are a parent, the scenario could be reversed – you may be called upon to pay special attention to one of your children. Both of the parents or parent figures in your life, mother and father, are having a dramatic crisis-filled kind of year. They will be redefining their personality, redefining their image, redefining the way that they think about themselves – their self-concept.

Children (of appropriate age) are having a status-quo family year – they will probably stay wherever they are right now. Siblings are likely to move in the year ahead, and this looks like a happy event. They are also likely to be investing in their home and buying expensive items for the home. Major renovations in the home of siblings would not be a surprise, either. Grandchildren of appropriate age would probably like to move but this doesn't seem advisable in the year ahead. Your spouse or partner is feeling restless, probably travelling around more than usual, and perhaps living in different places for long periods at a time.

Finance and Career

Neither your 2nd house of finance nor your 10th house of career is a House of Power this year, Libra. Normally this would indicate a status-quo kind of year – but other factors in your horoscope make us question this. Perhaps you are satisfied with the way things are, but forces out of your control are going to impose change. Pluto, your financial planet, will be eclipsed on June 26th and will be camping out on the eclipse point for many months. Thus you will be making long-term and very dramatic changes in your investments, in your financial planning, with your financial advisors and banks, and with your whole financial strategy. This can come about because of a crisis or a sudden expense or change in financial circumstance. The change that causes this need not be something bad; in fact, it can be something very good – you inherit a large sum of money or have some major windfall. And now you have to invest that money or change your financial planning as a result. Whichever way it happens, finances will be a major concern from June 26th and for the next few months thereafter.

(Venus, your planet of inheritance, spends an unusual amount of time in your money house this year. Normally she stays in a sign for about a month – she will be there on and off for 3 months. This may mean you will be named in someone's will or come into a trust fund, or gain a large insurance payment. It does not necessarily indicate that the inheritance comes through a death.)

The major financial change in your life happened last year as Pluto changed signs from Sagittarius to Capricorn. For many years you have been a kind of speculator, loose spender, a total optimist when it came to finances. Now you're going to be much more conservative. You're going to be careful about your spending. You're going to try to make your spending more proportional to your income. You're going to look for value for your pound. You're going to become much more risk-averse than you have been. You are more open to long-term investment and savings plans. You will be less allured by a quick profit and begin embracing a philosophy of gaining wealth through evolutionary rather than revolutionary means. All of this is basically good. Only sometimes people over do this. You need to discern sharply between financial caution, which is basically good, and financial fear, which is a pathology. This takes honest introspection.

Pluto in your 4th house also shows, as mentioned, spending more on the home and on the family and family members. It also indicates that you can earn from these things as well. The property field, either commercial or residential, looks interesting from a financial perspective. The family business (or businesses that are run like a family) also seem profitable and good. Family connections play a huge role in earnings. Family members will tend to be supportive of your financial goals. Parents and parent figures seem supportive as well. Since Pluto rules debt, mortgages, bonds and the bond market are also interesting paths to profits. There are many scenarios here. You can invest in mortgages or bonds. Or you can use creative financing techniques to make money in other ways. From an investment perspective the blue-chip type stocks seem the best – also the bonds of the blue-chip type companies.

As mentioned earlier, this is a great year for job-seekers and for those who employ others – there is good fortune in finding work or in employing others. Work is not only profitable but is going to be interesting, creative and exciting. You will earn and have fun at the same time.

Two (and perhaps three) eclipses occur in your 10th house of career – so although you might be satisfied with the status quo, outer events can bring career changes in the year ahead. (I say 'perhaps three' because the lunar eclipse on December 21st occurs right near the Midheaven, though technically it occurs in the 9th house.)

Love and Social Life

A lot of change – a lot of excitement – happening in your love life in the year ahead. Next year will be even more eventful, but you will feel the beginnings of it this year.

Jupiter and Uranus will move into your 7th house of love and marriage for a few months this year. Uranus will move in first – clearing the decks, creating change and upheaval in a current social situation. Current relationships, current marriages, current friendships will get tested. But Jupiter coming into this house on June 6th (until September 10th) expands your social life, brings new and important friends into the picture, and for singles shows a new and important relationship – something that happens suddenly. It's as if a 'bomb' explodes in your current social picture, obliterating all the patterns. And once that is done, new people come into your life. The obliteration is the prelude to the reconstruction.

For marrieds this can indicate various scenarios. The current relationship temporarily breaks up and then re-coalesces on better terms, or it breaks up and someone new comes in to take the place of the old.

Many a wedding bell will ring for Librans in the next 2 years.

There is another interesting thing happening in your love life this year, Libra. Mars, your love planet, will spend an unusual amount of time in your 11th house. Mars generally stays in a house from 1½ to 2 months (approximately). This year Mars will spend over 5 months in your 11th house, from January 1st to June 7th. This highly unusual transit suggests that you may become romantically involved with friends, or that a friend wants to become more than that. It will also show that romantic opportunities will come to you as you get involved with groups or organizations and group kinds of activities. This transit also indicates that the first 5 months of the year you want to be as much of a friend to your beloved as his or her lover. You want a relationship of peers, equals. It's not just the romantic relationship but your friendship that's important, too. Aside from this, romantic opportunities will come in the neighbourhood, with neighbours or in educational settings. Friendship is important but also intellectual compatibility, good communication and a need to respect and fall in love with your lover's mind as well as body. Those working towards their first marriage have very good opportunities this year and even better ones next year. Those working towards their second marriage seem to have a status-quo kind of a year: singles will tend to remain single and marrieds will tend to remain married.

Those working towards their third marriage have very interesting opportunities from January 1st to June 7th.

Singles will have many – and exciting – opportunities for love affairs in the year ahead – especially from May to September. These seem to happen at the workplace or with those involved in your health.

Self-improvement

For 2 years now Saturn has been in your 12th house of spirituality, and will remain there for a few more months in 2010. This has big implications in your spiritual life as it shows a need for daily discipline in your spiritual regime. It's necessary to take a more practical approach to spiritual issues. Spirituality in its deepest sense is not abstract, airyfairy or impractical. It is an exact science. It has vast practical implications. And this is a time for you to be going more deeply into these things. Correct knowledge of the spiritual nature of the universe and its relation to earthly affairs will revolutionize your notions of health, finance and love. For everything begins in the spiritual world. Little by little it manifests – much as empty space becomes a cloud of vapour, then rain, then ice. So too do spiritual ideas become increasingly solid, step by step. This is a time not only for more discipline in your various practices but also for taking a more scientific and rational approach to spirit. There are many paths that emphasize this – in the East it would be jnana yoga; in the West, hermetic science or kabbalah. I always like these paths for you, but especially these days.

Uranus has been in your 6th house of health for many years now and will be there for most of the year ahead. This shows, as mentioned, a more experimental approach to health and healing. On a deeper level it is showing that for the past 6 or 7 years you have been doing what everybody eventually needs to do – learning how you function healthwise in a personal way. No one is wired up exactly as you are. Things that work for other people might not work for you. Things that work for you might not work for other people. Our job – and your job – is to find out how we personally function. This is the way that will lead to true knowledge. And this is the lesson that is continuing in the year ahead.

Month-by-month Forecasts

January

Best Days Overall: 6, 7, 16, 17, 25, 26
Most Stressful Days Overall: 1, 13, 14, 21, 22, 28
Best Days for Love: 2, 3, 4, 5, 11, 12, 13, 14, 15, 21, 22, 25, 26
Best Days for Money: 4, 6, 7, 8, 9, 13, 16, 17, 18, 23, 27
Best Days for Career: 1, 4, 5, 13, 14, 15, 25, 26, 27, 28

You begin your year as the planetary power has just (in the past month) shifted from the East to the West. For the past 6 months or so you have been called upon to be more independent, less reliant on others, more self-motivated. Now you are called upon to exercise your natural Libra gifts – your social genius. For you this shift is very comfortable. You get your way through others and their good graces. Your likeability (always strong) is much more important than your actual abilities. You will handle the next 6 months well.

We see the importance of your social life in other ways, too. Your love planet, Mars, is the handle of a 'bucket' chart for most of the month (actually all month, but at times the Moon will join the picture). Thus, it is through your friends, partners and social connections that you 'lift up' your life. At other times (from the 1st to the 5th and from the 21st to the 30th) your career will be the way you lift up your life.

Your love planet is retrograde this month, so your love life is on review. Sure, you will date and socialize, but important love decisions should not be taken. Normally you are a 'love at first sight' kind of person (and even more so now with your love planet in Leo) but try to rein this in a bit – let love develop slowly over time.

There was a powerful lunar eclipse on you on the last day of last year – very much in effect now and for the next 6 months – and there is another strong eclipse on you on the 15th of this month. This is a solar eclipse. The last eclipse shows career changes and changes in the hierarchy of your company and perhaps in your industry. A parent or parent figure was very affected as well. This solar eclipse occurs in your 4th house and seems to affect the other parent figure in your life. It brings dramatic events in the life of this parent figure, too. The family and domestic pattern gets shaken up a bit – changes need to be made. There are family dramas. Emotions run high. Flaws in the home are revealed so that you can take corrective action. Your dream life will probably be more active, but don't give it much weight – this is psychic flotsam and jetsam stirred up by the eclipse. Friendships get tested.

Career is important, but family and your emotional life seem the main focus these days.

Prosperity looks good this month as your financial planet get much positive stimulation by other planets. The problem is that you are not too focused here, probably not giving finances enough attention. Very understandable, with all that is going on. Rest and relax more until the 20th.

February

Best Days Overall: 2, 3, 12, 13, 22, 23
Most Stressful Days Overall: 9, 10, 11, 17, 18, 24, 25
Best Days for Love: 2, 3, 7, 14, 15, 17, 18, 24, 25, 26
Best Days for Money: 1, 4, 5, 6, 9, 14, 15, 19, 24, 28
Best Days for Career: 2, 3, 13, 14, 24, 25

On the 20th of last month you entered a yearly personal pleasure peak which is still going on until the 18th. You've gone through much emotional turmoil of late; the antidote is to have some fun. Joy regenerates the emotional body.

Health is much improved this month as well. You seem focused on it this month – especially after the 19th. If you have had health problems in the past year, you should be hearing good news now.

Job-seekers have a banner month. The beginning of last month should have brought a very beautiful job opportunity, but there are more on the way now. The New Moon of the 14th not only clarifies relations with children and a current love affair, but brings a job opportunity as well. After the 18th there are at least four potential job offers. Not bad.

Those of you who employ others are expanding the work force this month (this will go on all year, but this month especially).

Your social life is still important as Mars is still the handle of a 'bucket' chart, but Mars is still retrograde so keep in mind our discussion of last month. Also, until the 18th love is more stressed out – there are more obstacles – you have to work harder to show your love and warmth to others. Children of appropriate age are having their marriages or relationships tested (this has been going on for the past few months). Your spouse or love is working hard to please the children these days, so there is hope.

Your dream life is very active on the 27th and 28th. There are supernatural kinds of experiences during this period as well. Intuition is excellent.

There are happy love opportunities from the 15th to the 17th – and these days also bring financial windfalls. There is a nice financial windfall on the 27th to the 28th as well. You have a happy travel opportunity from the 15th to the 17th.

There is a lot of air in your horoscope this month – and you are an air sign. The good news is that your mind and communication skills – always good, always sharp – get even better. But the problem here is the overstimulation of the mind. The mind starts to turn and turn without let-up. Also there will be a tendency to talk too much – to overdo a good thing. This can cause insomnia and other nervous problems. Meditation, yoga and spiritual practice will help you control these things.

March

> Best Days Overall: 2, 3, 11, 12, 21, 22, 29, 30
> Most Stressful Days Overall: 9, 10, 16, 17, 23, 24
> Best Days for Love: 5, 6, 16, 17, 25, 26
> Best Days for Money: 4, 5, 9, 14, 15, 18, 19, 23, 24, 27, 31
> Best Days for Career: 4, 5, 14, 15, 23, 24, 25

Looks like a happy time for love. The timing here is just exquisite. On the 10th your love planet starts moving forward after a few months of retrograde motion. On the 20th, as the Sun moves into your 7th house, you enter a yearly romantic and social peak. Thus, your social judgement is back to its usually high standard and you are ready for romance. If you have done your love and social review these past few months, your love life should be even better. For you are more clear about what you want and can make better choices. Love opportunities come through friends, groups or organizations. Group activities. People who might seem like just 'acquaintances' may want to be more than that. Love can come at spiritual or religious-type venues as well – at church, synagogue, ashram or mosque – at meditation seminars or spiritual retreats. Foreign countries and foreign people are alluring as well. With Saturn in your 1st house you may come off as being overly cold or serious – you will have to work harder to 'lighten up' and project warmth to others.

Until the 20th, you are working hard. You are in a serious period. But this hard work, this practical service, prepares the way for love – perhaps you feel more 'deserving' of love as well. You've fulfilled all your work obligations.

The New Moon of the 15th brings a love opportunity (but it doesn't seem serious – just a fling) with a superior or boss. A child has an interesting career opportunity.

Health needs more watching after the 20th. Pay more attention to your heart (all month), to your lungs, small intestine, arms and shoulders (from the 2nd to the 17th), to your kidneys and hips (until the 7th) and to your feet, ankles, thighs, calves and liver (all month).

Job-seekers still have an amazing month – many opportunities. People who employ others are still expanding the work force – and in a good way, too. There are interesting career opportunities seeking you out on the 2nd, 3rd, 29th and 30th – but especially on the 30th.

Those on the spiritual path will have a deep illumination from the 7th to the 9th. Writers will be very inspired. Sales and marketing people will be poetic.

Finances are more stressful than usual this month but these are just 'bumps in the road' – not long-term trends. You just need to work a little harder for financial goals than usual. The cosmos is demanding more from you.

April

Best Days Overall: 8, 9, 17, 18, 26, 27
Most Stressful Days Overall: 5, 6, 13, 14, 19, 20
Best Days for Love: 3, 5, 13, 14, 15, 16, 22, 25, 30
Best Days for Money: 1, 5, 10, 11, 15, 19, 20, 24, 28, 29
Best Days for Career: 3, 4, 13, 14, 19, 20, 24

Spring is here, and most of the planets (90 per cent until the 7th, 80 per cent from the 7th to the 18th, and 70 per cent thereafter) are moving forward this month. The pace of events quickens. Things get done in a hurry. A knotty problem that has plagued you for a few years can resolve itself in minutes these days.

You are still in the midst of a yearly social peak. Singles have opportunities for either serious, long-term romance or for flings. Flings seem to happen at the workplace, with co-workers, or with people involved in your health. Serious romantic opportunities come at parties, weddings, social gatherings or through friends and involvement with organizations. Friends or acquaintances want to become more than that.

Speculations are very favourable now and will become even more favourable next month. Of course, only speculate under intuition. Some of you are going to hit it very BIG – but the cosmos has many ways of helping you to prosper and is not limited to the casino.

Job-seekers still have outstanding opportunities and these can happen suddenly, out of the blue. Work is more fun these days. The joy aspect of work and the workplace is a big factor in your job decisions.

Family is very important all year, but last month the planetary power shifted from the lower to the upper half of your horoscope. Thus you are 'waking up' from your 'good night's sleep' now (symbolically speaking) and are ready to face the day – the outer world – with renewed energy.

Health still needs watching until the 20th. Pay more attention to your heart (until the 20th), to your liver and thighs (all month), and to your ankles, calves and feet (all month). The best medicine, as our steady readers know, is high energy. So do your best to keep energy levels as high as possible.

Saturn leaving your sign on the 8th is a plus for your energy, but you will feel the boost more after the 20th. Love is a bit more challenging after the 20th, but you are undeterred by this. Libras, more than most, can handle difficult relationships.

Your 8th house is powerful after the 20th, thus this is a strong (one of the strongest) financial period for your spouse, partner or current love. He or she will be more generous. Spousal support will be increased.

After the 20th you are into a more sexually active period. Libido will increase, regardless of your age or stage in life.

May

Best Days Overall: 5, 6, 15, 23, 24
Most Stressful Days Overall: 2, 3, 4, 10, 11, 17, 18, 30, 31
Best Days for Love: 1, 5, 6, 10, 11, 15, 16, 19, 20, 25, 26, 27, 28
Best Days for Money: 2, 3, 8, 9, 12, 18, 21, 25, 26, 29, 30
Best Days for Career: 2, 3, 12, 13, 17, 18, 23

Last month, on the 20th, you entered the 8th house segment of your year. One of the most mysterious, difficult to understand, yet wonderful periods in the year. When the 8th house is strong, events are always hidden, under cover, wrapped in mystery. Seeds die as they germinate, and from that death the new plant will emerge. May's flowers may come from April showers, but they also come from the secret process of death – the province of the 8th house. The petrol in your car 'dies' as you drive, but it is that very death, that transformation from petrol to fire, that makes the car go and takes you to your destination. This is a period for understanding death. Sounds morbid? Perhaps, but for those on the path it leads to a better understanding of life. A deeper understanding.

The cosmos has many ways to lead you to this understanding. Perhaps you will be attending more funerals. Perhaps you will have encounters with death in other ways – near-death experiences, brushes with the dark angel, dreams of death – things of this nature. The dark angel is saying, 'Look at me in a deeper way.'

There are many things in your life that you would like to see 'resurrected' – reborn, renewed. It could be your body or some bodily feature, some relationship, some business or financial project, investments that are under water. All of these things can be resurrected when you understand the meaning of death and its true function – when you allow the 8th house energy, so prevalent now in your horoscope, to teach you its mysteries.

Those on the path face a stark choice: they can squander this energy in sexual excess (we're not talking about normal sexual expression) or they can use this energy constructively to 'resurrect' themselves and their lives.

On a more mundane level this is a time for a good house-cleaning on all the levels – a cleansing of the body (through detox), a cleansing of the physical home through getting rid of excess or useless possessions, a cleansing of the mind and emotions, through ridding yourself of old mental and emotional patterns – this will liberate so much energy that resurrection will happen quite naturally.

When the Sun enters your 9th house on the 21st, you will be ready for the religious and philosophical breakthroughs awaiting you – these will be made possible by your detox work.

Uranus moves into your 7th house on the 28th and this, as mentioned in the yearly report, is going to test existing marriages or relationships. There are still many opportunities for flings this month – especially at the workplace.

June

   Best Days Overall: 1, 2, 11, 12, 19, 20, 29, 30
   Most Stressful Days Overall: 6, 7, 13, 14, 26, 27
   Best Days for Love: 4, 5, 6, 7, 8, 13, 14, 17, 24, 25, 26, 27
   Best Days for Money: 5, 6, 9, 15, 18, 21, 22, 24, 26
   Best Days for Career: 1, 2, 11, 12, 13, 14, 21

There is a need to watch your health this month – all month, but especially after the 21st. Jupiter has now joined Uranus in a stressful aspect with you. There is a strong lunar eclipse on the 26th that has an impact on you. Venus, your ruler, will re-stimulate an eclipse point from the 9th to the 11th. The best way to go through aspects like this is from your highest vibratory state. Keep energy levels high. Don't let little, petty things disturb you. Keep your focus on the important things in your life. Avoid risk-taking activities. Do what you need to do (career and love dominate the month) but re-schedule the unnecessary – or even avoid it. Enhance your health by paying more attention to your feet, ankles and calves – massage them regularly. Think less and talk less. Avoid needless arguments and confrontations that only drain energy. (One needless argument of 5 minutes can make you feel like you've been on a chain gang for 8 hours.)

Love is very exciting and dramatic this month. Jupiter joins Uranus in your 7th house of love and marriage. There are two scenarios here. One, your existing marriage or relationship gets severely tested. This doesn't seem to come from any basic incompatibility but rather from temptations to both parties – there are so many love opportunities now that the

strength of commitment gets tested. Two, the existing relationship becomes more romantic and honeymoonish.
Troubled relationships can be repaired or enhanced by doing
unconventional kinds of things as a couple – taking journeys
to spots usually not visited by people, or taking courses
together as a couple, re-opening the lines of communication
between you, cementing the mental bonds between you.
Give your partner as much space as possible so long as it isn't
destructive. With your love planet now in your 12th house of
spirituality (from the 7th onwards), intuition will guide you.

For singles love is less complicated and happier than for
marrieds. There are opportunities for serial love affairs. New
and exciting – unconventional types of people – come into
your life. Love happens suddenly, out of the blue, when you
least expect it. New social doors are opening up for you. It is
not a time for committed kinds of relationships – but for
dating and playing the field – taking advantage of being
single and unattached.

Business partnerships are getting tested as well.

Career is going great guns this month, too. On the 21st
you enter a yearly career peak and there is much progress
being made. Friends are succeeding and helping you out.
You know just the right people who can help you climb the
corporate or industry ladder. You are elevated this month.

The lunar eclipse of the 26th has an impact on your financial planet and brings important financial changes – not only
now, but for many months in the future. There is a re-engi-
neering of your investments, financial attitudes and strategy
going on. Also there are career changes – probably sudden
ones – happening.

July

Best Days Overall: 8, 9, 17, 26, 27
Most Stressful Days Overall: 4, 5, 10, 11, 23, 24, 25, 31
Best Days for Love: 4, 5, 6, 7, 14, 15, 16, 23, 24, 25, 31
Best Days for Money: 3, 6, 12, 14, 19, 20, 21, 23, 31
Best Days for Career: 1, 2, 10, 11, 20, 31

We have a bit of a replay of last month happening. Of course, no cosmic replay is ever exactly the same, but the patterns are similar. There are many planets in stressful alignment with you. There is another strong eclipse on the 11th – this time a solar eclipse – and there are more testings going on in your love life. Keep in mind our health discussion of last month. Continue to pay more attention to your feet, calves and ankles, and massage them regularly. Health and energy will improve after the 23rd, but still needs watching.

When the aspects are stressful, as they are now, it means that you need to work harder to achieve your goals than necessary. It is like a car driving up a steep hill. The car will make it up the hill, but will use more petrol and it will take longer. It helps to understand that the stresses are not your fault – just the cosmic weather. Try not to compare your performance with the times when the sun was shining and the wind was at your back.

Months like these are character-building periods. You learn the stuff that you are made of. Many of you will reach down deep and find resources – inner strengths – that you never knew you had. It took the stress to reveal these things to you. Similarly in love: We never know if love is real when everything is honeymoonish – love and harmony are just natural during those times. It is in the tough times, in the periods of testing, that we find out the depth of our love and commitment.

Like last month, love seems happier (though just as unstable) for singles than for marrieds. Freedom is a wonderful thing, but the other party also has freedom. It cuts both ways. So there are many flings this period – some might have potential for the long term – but you will find out about this later on, not now.

You are still in the midst of a yearly career peak. So push forward towards your career goals. You have friends in high places who are helping and supporting you.

When Uranus moved into your 7th house in May, a testing of friendships began. The solar eclipse of the 11th will further test friendships. Over the long haul – not straight away – you will be in completely different social circumstances than you are now. The cosmos, little by little, and perhaps in dramatic ways, is liberating you to find the love and social life of your dreams – but first the old attachments and bonds have to go. Those friendships that do survive will be so different as to be something 'new'.

This solar eclipse occurs in your 4th house so there are dramas with family members – emotional upheavals – temper-tantrums and the like. The family and domestic pattern gets tested or threatened.

Finances are still undergoing change – re-tooling – but they improve after the 10th.

August

Best Days Overall: 5, 6, 13, 14, 22, 23
Most Stressful Days Overall: 1, 7, 8, 20, 21, 27, 28
Best Days for Love: 1, 3, 4, 5, 13, 22, 23, 27, 28
Best Days for Money: 2, 9, 11, 15, 16, 17, 20, 27
Best Days for Career: 1, 7, 8, 17, 18, 29, 30

Health is improved over the past 2 months, but with Saturn back in your own sign, it still needs watching. Family responsibilities weigh on you. You are thinking of old age and perhaps feel older than your years. Your sense of self – your self-esteem and self-confidence – are getting a 'reality check' now and this is good. You are neither the 'worm of the dust' nor the 'high and mighty one' – events will show you your true place in the scheme of things. You are learning a true humility which brings power and success. If your self-esteem is too low, events will raise it up – show you that you are more than you think you are. If self-esteem is too high, unrealistically high, events – or perhaps meetings with genuinely high people – will adjust things. The good part is that you will undertake projects that are suited to your gifts and abilities. You won't bite off more than you can chew. This is a big factor in success.

In love, you are getting your way. The testings of love, the instability in your love life is subsiding a bit now. On the 15th Uranus retrogrades out of your 7th house of marriage. Your spouse, partner or current love is trying very hard. He or she is putting you first – putting the relationship first – putting your interest ahead of his or her own – is squarely in your corner. This is a big help and can save the relationship. With both Venus (your ruler) and Mars (your love planet) in your own sign of Libra, your natural social genius is even stronger than usual – and this is helping your love life as well. You are more up to the challenges that have arisen. You will need this genius from the 4th to the 9th and from the 25th to the 28th.

Singles need not do anything special for love these days – just show up. Love, and love opportunities, are seeking you out. They come to you.

Finances are good this month, though not a great priority. (This has been your financial weakness all year.) Your financial planet, Pluto, has been retrograde since April 7th, so your financial life is under review. Pluto was eclipsed in June and is camping out on this eclipse point all month. So, you know that changes have to be made and you are studying the best ways to do this. Of course, Pluto's retrograde doesn't halt your financial life – only slows things down a bit. Friends seem especially helpful from the 23rd to the 27th.

Avoid risky activities from the 11th to the 14th and from the 25th to the 28th. Avoid negative confrontations or power struggles as well. If you are provoked, take a few deep breaths before answering back.

September

Best Days Overall: 1, 2, 9, 10, 18, 19, 20, 28, 29
Most Stressful Days Overall: 3, 4, 16, 17, 23, 24, 25
Best Days for Love: 2, 10, 11, 20, 21, 23, 24, 25
Best Days for Money: 5, 7, 11, 12, 16, 22, 26
Best Days for Career: 3, 4, 7, 8, 17, 28

Mars re-stimulates the eclipse point of July 11 on the 1st, and may make your beloved more temperamental. Be more patient.

Saturn will camp out on an eclipse point (in Square aspect) all month; this indicates upheavals in the home, family issues and dramas with parents or parent figures. Sometimes this shows renovations or repairs in the home. Emotions run high in the family, it's up to you to stay centred and calm.

Friendships again get tested from the 27th to the 29th. Perhaps there are dramas in the lives of friends.

Jupiter and Uranus once again go exactly conjunct this month (they have been conjunct since May, but now it is more exact). There is luck in speculations and many of you will hit it big. Singles have opportunities for flings – non-serious love affairs – that happen suddenly and out of the blue. Children (or children figures in your life) prosper in sudden ways.

Last month, on the 23rd, you entered one of the strongest spiritual periods of your life. Your 12th house became powerful. This trend continues until the 23rd of this month. Now, power in the 12th house is not considered that fortunate when it comes to worldly affairs. The mood is more altruistic. Spiritual values become more important to you than worldly values. It's as if you look at events with different eyes and from a different place in yourself. The reason why this is considered unfortunate in a worldly sense is that spirit wants you to succeed in the world, but on its terms and in its way – not necessarily from the 3D perspective. So this is a month for spiritual revelation and breakthroughs: A month for experiencing the supernatural, rather than the natural. This is a time for a review of the past year and for correcting the mistakes of the past. A time for wiping the slate so that you can start your personal new year – your birthday – in a proper way. Curiously this will not harm your financial life, but enhance it – and in fact you are in a good financial period these days – one of the best in your year. In a moment – a trice, a twinkling – spirit can transform the knottiest financial problem into wealth and prosperity.

Health is much improved this month. Jupiter moves away from his stressful aspect to you. Last month Uranus did likewise. Your 1st house is filled with planets (50 per cent of them are either there or moving through there this month). Energy is high and you have enough to achieve any goal. Also you are in the period of maximum personal independence. You have the power, the will and the energy to change conditions to the way you like them. Your personal happiness is up to you – not others – now. If others don't go along with you (but it seems to me that they will), you can go off on your own.

October

   Best Days Overall: 7, 8, 16, 17, 25, 26, 27
   Most Stressful Days Overall: 1, 2, 13, 14, 21, 22, 28, 29
   Best Days for Love: 1, 9, 18, 19, 20, 21, 22, 28, 30
   Best Days for Money: 2, 5, 9, 10, 13, 19, 23, 29
   Best Days for Career: 1, 2, 7, 17, 27, 28, 29

You are in the midst of a yearly personal pleasure peak until the 23rd. Last month you experienced the pleasures of the inner life – the non-physical (though very real) pleasures of the spirit. Now you are experiencing the pleasures of the body. And there is no real contradiction, one leads to the other. Mental and emotional happiness will lead to physical happiness. Generally there is a danger of overdoing the good life – and the price for this is paid later on. But now with spartan, disciplined Saturn in your 1st house, this is not likely to happen. Your tendency will be to slimness. If you overindulge, you will diet or do things to make up for it.

Personal appearance was great last month and is good this month as well. The Sun in your sign gives you a sunny disposition, sex appeal and more energy and charisma – star power. With many of you there is some conflict about how to dress. Saturn counsels conservatism and dark colours. The

Sun likes to dress dramatically and flamboyantly. Saturn favours a low-key image and would hide your natural charms. The Sun likes to flaunt them. Some of you will alternate from one mode to the other. Others will be more flamboyant and dramatic but in a more low-key, toned down way.

Mercury enters your sign on the 3rd and stays there until the 21st. This brings glamour to the image. It brings an ability to change your image and body through spiritual means. Happy travel and educational opportunities come your way. You cultivate a 'smarter' image. People see you as more than just a 'party person' but as someone with intelligence.

You are in a period of maximum independence now. Create conditions to please yourself. Take the personal initiative to create your own happiness.

Friends are going out of their way to please you this month. They are catering to you. Friends are seeking you out, rather than vice versa. Your social life, like last month, is close to home – wherever you are. No need to do anything special or go anywhere special; it finds you.

Love is less active these days. On the 8th, Venus goes retrograde, so you need to become clearer as to what you want and what your goals are. Your body, your image, your wardrobe – your whole self-concept – is under review now. Your 7th house of love and marriage is now empty (for the most part) and social goals seem achieved for now. Like last month you find wealth alluring. The good provider, the one who can help you financially, is the one who interests you. The good news is that your spouse or partner (or current love) is helpful in this area. Singles find love opportunities as they pursue their normal financial goals or with people involved in their finances.

Finances are good this month. You enter a yearly financial peak on the 22nd. Your money house is powerful. Social connections, partners and your spouse are important financially. Business partnerships or joint ventures are likely this month. Friends are supportive and providing financial opportunity.

November

Best Days Overall: 3, 4, 12, 13, 22, 23
Most Stressful Days Overall: 10, 11, 17, 18, 24, 25
Best Days for Love: 5, 7, 13, 17, 18, 23, 27
Best Days for Money: 1, 5, 6, 10, 15, 16, 19, 25, 28
Best Days for Career: 5, 6, 15, 16, 24, 25, 26

Venus is still retrograde until the 18th, so your personal life, your personal goals, your image and wardrobe are still under review. Self-confidence is not what it should be – but this is not pathology – only the natural consequence of an inner review. By the 18th personal clarity and confidence returns. You know what you want, the image you want to project, and you go about manifesting it.

You are still in a yearly financial peak. So this is a prosperous period. Friends – people you meet at group activities or organizations – are helpful financially. Being up to date technologically is important. Don't be afraid to invest in upgrades and the like. You are still making important financial changes – Pluto is still camping out on an eclipse point – but you seem more confident and clear about what you are doing.

The love needs and attitudes changed late last month. Mars, your love planet, is now in your 3rd house and this gives many messages. Love opportunities happen in the neighbourhood, with neighbours, close to home. They happen at schools, lectures, seminars and educational settings. Siblings or their connections play a role in your love life. (The love life of siblings seems happy this month, too.) Material things are not that important in love these days. Now it is communication and shared intellectual interests. You gravitate to people you can talk to. Love is good communication – communication is a form of love. You need to fall in love with the person's mind as much as with his or her body. Troubled marriages can be helped through better communication and perhaps by taking courses together as a couple. There is a need to forge better relations in your mental bodies.

In general this is a month – after the 22nd – for the pursuit of intellectual interests and for communication. Since you are an air type, this is comfortable and happy for you. The danger for you is too much of a good thing – too much thinking and too much talking.

Job-seekers have good success this month. Neptune, your work planet, goes forward on the 7th and your 6th house is once again strong. There have been many happy job opportunities this past year, but now you are more clear about things – you have better discernment about which job to take.

Health is good this month. You can enhance it further by paying more attention to your ankles, calves, feet, thighs and liver. Regular massage of the thighs, calves, ankles and feet will be powerful.

December

Best Days Overall: 1, 9, 10, 11, 19, 20, 28, 29
Most Stressful Days Overall: 7, 8, 14, 15, 16, 21, 22
Best Days for Love: 2, 6, 12, 14, 15, 16, 17, 22, 26, 31
Best Days for Money: 3, 4, 7, 13, 17, 23, 25, 26, 30, 31
Best Days for Career: 5, 16, 21, 22, 26

The planetary power has been below the horizon for some months now. So family and emotional issues have been important – more important than your career. This month, with your 4th house becoming powerful after the 21st, home and family are even more important. Pursue career objectives by strengthening your domestic base, by attaining emotional harmony and through visualization, goal-setting and interior kinds of methods. These are the doors that are open now – and this is the most powerful way to proceed. When day breaks in your year – in the Spring of 2011 – you will be ready to pursue your career goals objectively – and they will go better.

In fact, with a lunar eclipse happening right near your Midheaven on the 21st, overt action might be counter-productive. The situation with your career is changing. You might be aiming at the wrong objective. This eclipse is strongest on those of you born early in the sign of Libra – from September 22nd to 25th. If you are one of these, take a reduced schedule during this period. Career changes are happening – and the rules of the game, the shape of the game, are changing. Perhaps you thought that the road to the top was through this executive or through a certain road. Now you discover that such-and-such an executive is no longer there and that road you wanted to pursue now leads to dead end.

As always, the lunar eclipse brings dramas with parents or parent figures. They are redefining themselves – their self-image and self-concept.

Family seems the centre of almost everything this month – even love. After the 8th, your love planet moves into the 4th house. It makes you nostalgic for old flames. You want emotional comfort, nurturing and intimacy with your beloved. Good talk is not enough anymore. You want real feelings – not abstractions. You give love by giving good emotional support, and this is how you feel loved. A quiet romantic evening at home is more satisfying than the hoopla of a night out on the town. The tendency is to 'mother–father' your beloved, and you'd like that treatment in return. This is a month for entertaining from home rather than attending parties elsewhere.

Finances will be good this month as your financial planet gets much positive stimulation. Again, friends, social contacts (this is your natural pattern), partners and family members seem supportive. Most of the financial changes and shifts are over with. Your financial house seems in order (relatively speaking).

Health needs more watching after the 21st. The main thing now is to maintain high energy levels – don't let yourself get overtired. Rest when tired. Pace yourself. Take frequent breaks and work to a rhythm. You'll get more done with taking breaks every 10 minutes than with trying to push through for an hour at a time. Enhance health in the ways discussed in the yearly report.

Scorpio

♏

THE SCORPION
*Birthdays from
23rd October to
22nd November*

Personality Profile

SCORPIO AT A GLANCE

Element – Water

Ruling Planet – Pluto
  Co-ruling Planet – Mars
  Career Planet – Sun
  Love Planet – Venus
  Money Planet – Jupiter
  Planet of Health and Work – Mars
  Planet of Home and Family Life – Uranus

Colour – red-violet

*Colour that promotes love, romance and social
  harmony* – green

Colour that promotes earning power – blue

Gems – bloodstone, malachite, topaz

Metals – iron, radium, steel

Scents – cherry blossom, coconut, sandalwood, watermelon

Quality – fixed (= stability)

Quality most needed for balance – a wider view of things

Strongest virtues – loyalty, concentration, determination, courage, depth

Deepest needs – to penetrate and transform

Characteristics to avoid – jealousy, vindictiveness, fanaticism

Signs of greatest overall compatibility – Cancer, Pisces

Signs of greatest overall incompatibility – Taurus, Leo, Aquarius

Sign most helpful to career – Leo

Sign most helpful for emotional support – Aquarius

Sign most helpful financially – Sagittarius

Sign best for marriage and/or partnerships – Taurus

Sign most helpful for creative projects – Pisces

Best Sign to have fun with – Pisces

Signs most helpful in spiritual matters – Cancer, Libra

Best day of the week – Tuesday

Understanding a Scorpio

One symbol of the sign of Scorpio is the phoenix. If you meditate upon the legend of the phoenix you will begin to understand the Scorpio character – his or her powers and abilities, interests and deepest urges.

The phoenix of mythology was a bird that could recreate and reproduce itself. It did so in a most intriguing way: it would seek a fire – usually in a religious temple – fly into it, consume itself in the flames and then emerge a new bird. If this is not the ultimate, most profound transformation, then what is?

Transformation is what Scorpios are all about – in their minds, bodies, affairs and relationships (Scorpios are also society's transformers). To change something in a natural, not an artificial way, involves a transformation from within. This type of change is a radical change as opposed to a mere cosmetic make-over. Some people think that change means altering just their appearance, but this is not the kind of thing that interests a Scorpio. Scorpios seek deep, fundamental change. Since real change always proceeds from within, a Scorpio is very interested in – and usually accustomed to – the inner, intimate and philosophical side of life.

Scorpios are people of depth and intellect. If you want to interest them you must present them with more than just a superficial image. You and your interests, projects or business deals must have real substance to them in order to stimulate a Scorpio. If they haven't, he or she will find you out – and that will be the end of the story.

If we observe life – the processes of growth and decay – we see the transformational powers of Scorpio at work all the time. The caterpillar changes itself into a butterfly, the infant grows into a child and then an adult. To Scorpios this definite and perpetual transformation is not something to be feared. They see it as a normal part of life. This acceptance of transformation gives Scorpios the key to understanding the true meaning of life.

Scorpios' understanding of life (including life's weaknesses) makes them powerful warriors – in all senses of the word. Add to this their depth, patience and endurance and you have a powerful personality. Scorpios have good, long memories and can at times be quite vindictive – they can wait years to get their revenge. As a friend, though, there is no one more loyal and true than a Scorpio. Few are willing to make the sacrifices that a Scorpio will make for a true friend.

The results of a transformation are quite obvious, although the process of transformation is invisible and secret. This is why Scorpios are considered secretive in nature. A seed will not grow properly if you keep digging it up and exposing it to the light of day. It must stay buried – invisible – until it starts to grow. In the same manner, Scorpios fear revealing too much about themselves or their hopes to other people. However, they will be more than happy to let you see the finished product – but only when it is completely wrapped up. On the other hand, Scorpios like knowing everyone else's secrets as much as they dislike anyone knowing theirs.

Finance

Love, birth, life as well as death are Nature's most potent transformations; Scorpios are interested in all of these. In our society, money is a transforming power, too, and a Scorpio is interested in money for that reason. To a Scorpio money is power, money causes change, money controls. It is the power of money that fascinates them. But Scorpios can be too materialistic if they are not careful. They can be overly awed by the power of money, to a point where they think that money rules the world.

Even the term plutocrat comes from Pluto, the ruler of the sign of Scorpio. Scorpios will – in one way or another – achieve the financial status they strive for. When they do so they are careful in the way they handle their wealth. Part of this financial carefulness is really a kind of honesty, for

Scorpios are usually involved with other people's money – as accountants, lawyers, stockbrokers or corporate managers – and when you handle other people's money you have to be more cautious than when you handle your own.

In order to fulfil their financial goals, Scorpios have important lessons to learn. They need to develop qualities that do not come naturally to them, such as breadth of vision, optimism, faith, trust and, above all, generosity. They need to see the wealth in Nature and in life, as well as in its more obvious forms of money and power. When they develop generosity their financial potential reaches great heights, for Jupiter, the Lord of Opulence and Good Fortune, is Scorpio's money planet.

Career and Public Image

Scorpio's greatest aspiration in life is to be considered by society as a source of light and life. They want to be leaders, to be stars. But they follow a very different road than do Leos, the other stars of the zodiac. A Scorpio arrives at the goal secretly, without ostentation; a Leo pursues it openly. Scorpios seek the glamour and fun of the rich and famous in a restrained, discreet way.

Scorpios are by nature introverted and tend to avoid the limelight. But if they want to attain their highest career goals they need to open up a bit and to express themselves more. They need to stop hiding their light under a bushel and let it shine. Above all, they need to let go of any vindictiveness and small-mindedness. All their gifts and insights were given to them for one important reason – to serve life and to increase the joy of living for others.

Love and Relationships

Scorpio is another zodiac sign that likes committed, clearly defined, structured relationships. They are cautious about marriage, but when they do commit to a relationship they tend to be faithful – and heaven help the mate caught or even suspected of infidelity! The jealousy of the Scorpio is legendary. They can be so intense in their jealousy that even the thought or intention of infidelity will be detected and is likely to cause as much of a storm as if the deed had actually been done.

Scorpios tend to settle down with those who are wealthier than they are. They usually have enough intensity for two, so in their partners they seek someone pleasant, hardworking, amiable, stable and easy-going. They want someone they can lean on, someone loyal behind them as they fight the battles of life. To a Scorpio a partner, be it a lover or a friend, is a real partner – not an adversary. Most of all a Scorpio is looking for an ally, not a competitor.

If you are in love with a Scorpio you will need a lot of patience. It takes a long time to get to know Scorpios, because they do not reveal themselves readily. But if you persist and your motives are honourable, you will gradually be allowed into a Scorpio's inner chambers of the mind and heart.

Home and Domestic Life

Uranus is ruler of Scorpio's 4th solar house of home and family. Uranus is the planet of science, technology, changes and democracy. This tells us a lot about a Scorpio's conduct in the home and what he or she needs in order to have a happy, harmonious home life.

Scorpios can sometimes bring their passion, intensity and wilfulness into the home and family, which is not always the place for these qualities. These traits are good for the warrior and the transformer, but not so good for the nurturer and family member. Because of this (and also because of their need for change and transformation) the Scorpio may be prone to sudden changes of residence. If not carefully constrained, the sometimes inflexible Scorpio can produce turmoil and sudden upheavals within the family.

Scorpios need to develop some of the virtues of Aquarius in order to cope better with domestic matters. There is a need to build a team spirit at home, to treat family activities as truly group activities – family members should all have a say in what does and does not get done. For at times a Scorpio can be most dictatorial. When a Scorpio gets dictatorial it is much worse than if a Leo or Capricorn (the two other power signs in the zodiac) does. For the dictatorship of a Scorpio is applied with more zeal, passion, intensity and concentration than is true of either a Leo or Capricorn. Obviously this can be unbearable to family members – especially if they are sensitive types.

In order for a Scorpio to get the full benefit of the emotional support that a family can give, he or she needs to let go of conservatism and be a bit more experimental, to explore new techniques in child-rearing, be more democratic with family members and to try to manage things by consensus rather than by autocratic edict.

Horoscope for 2010

Major Trends

Last year was a very important year in that your ruling planet Pluto moved out of Sagittarius and into Capricorn and will be in Capricorn for at least another 15 years. This shows a major shift from finance to intellectual interests and communication. You are in a period where you want to gain knowledge and express that knowledge to others – a period where you want to expand your mind. Presumably by now you are where you want to be financially; now it's time to enjoy the fruits of financial freedom – and for you that means cultivating your intellectual interests.

Many of you moved last year and the move looks happy. More moves could be in store in the year ahead. More on this later.

Job changes seem very likely to happen in the coming year and for years to come as Uranus makes a very important move from your 5th house to your 6th house from May 28th to August 14th. More on this later.

Mars will spend an unusual amount of time in your 10th house of career in the year ahead – it will be there from January 1st to June 7th, about 2½ times the length of his usual transit. This shows a lot of hard work, a lot of competition, a need to fend off threats to your status and position. More on this later.

Your personal planet, Pluto, gets eclipsed on June 26th and camps out on this point for many months. This indicates a long-term redefinition of your personality, your image and how you think about yourself. It tends to bring changes in your image, your presentation to others and how you dress. This is basically a healthy thing and we all need to do this every now and then. This is your year for it.

Saturn has been testing your friendships for a few years now and many have gone by the boards. Your good friends have remained but many of your flawed relationships are now over with. Your social life, your social circle, might be smaller than it used to be but it is certainly of higher quality. This testing continues for yet a few months in the year ahead from April 8th to July 22nd, and then will be over with.

Saturn's move into your 12th house, which began in late October of 2009, continues in the year ahead, making spirituality a major focus. This is a year for being more serious about your spiritual studies, your practices and about your spiritual ideals. More on this later.

Your major interests in the year ahead will be communication and intellectual interests, home and family, children, fun and creativity, health and work (from May 28th to September 10th), your career (January 1st to June 7th), friends, groups and organizations (from April 8th to July 22nd), and spirituality (January 1st to April 8th and July 22nd to December 31st).

Your paths of greatest fulfilment will be communication and intellectual interests, home and family (January 1st to 18th), children, fun and creativity (January 18th to June 6th and September 10th to December 31st), and health and work (June 6th to September 10th).

Health

(Please note that this is an astrological perspective on health and not a medical one. In days gone by there was no difference; these perspectives were identical. But nowadays there can be quite a difference. For the medical perspective, please consult your doctor or health practitioner.)

Health has been basically good the past few years and this trend continues in the year ahead. In fact, when Jupiter leaves its stressful aspect to you on January 18th, health and vitality should improve even further. Your 6th house of health is not a House of Power this year – except for a few brief months. For most of the year it will be empty. This too is a very positive health signal. You don't pay too much

Reflexology

Try to massage the whole foot on a regular basis, but pay extra attention to the points highlighted on the chart. When you massage, be aware of 'sore spots', as these need special attention. It's also a good idea to massage the ankles and top side (as well as the soles) of the feet.

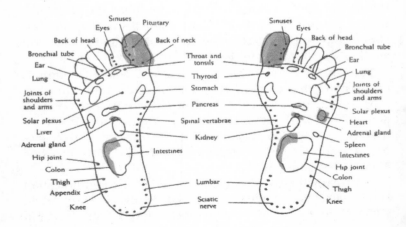

attention to health as there is no need to. You sort of take good health for granted.

Your 6th house will become strong from May 28th to September 10th as two long-term and powerful planets enter the 6th house. Since your overall vitality is good I just read this as a greater interest in health regimes and healthy lifestyles in general. Possibly you will be buying new kinds of health gadgets – high-tech kinds of things – during this period.

Good though your health is, you can make it even better by paying attention to the following parts of the body:

- colon, bladder and sexual organs
- head, face and scalp (regular head and face massage will be wonderful, not only helping your head and face but energizing your entire body, as your head and face contain reflexes to the entire body)
- ankles and calves (from May 28th to August 14th – give your ankles more support when you exercise and massage them regularly)
- liver and thighs (from June 6th to September 10th – thighs should be regularly massaged).

We mentioned earlier that your ruling planet, Pluto, will be eclipsed on June 26th and will be camping out on this eclipse point for a few months. From a health perspective this often indicates a detox of the physical body. This will be so if you haven't been careful in dietary matters. But this should not be confused with disease. It is strictly a kind of bodily cleansing. If you have been careful in dietary matters it will merely bring a redefinition of your personality and image, as mentioned earlier.

Mars is your health planet and he will spend an unusual amount of time in the sign of Leo this year. A normal Mars transit lasts between 1½ to 2 months on average. This transit will last over 5 months. Highly unusual. This would show a need to pay more attention to your heart, as Leo rules the heart. It would also indicate that a creative hobby would be very therapeutic – blocked creative urges could have an impact on your health. Physical exercise is always good for you. Good health for you means physical fitness. A good workout at the gym will often do you more good than a visit to a health professional. You are the kind of person who gets high on exercise. With Mars as your health planet, this is not a surprise.

Uranus moving into your 6th house of health from May 28th to August 14th is also giving us other messages. First, it shows that you are going to be making dramatic changes in your health regime and in your diet. You are going to start becoming much more experimental in health matters. Orthodox medicine is probably not for you. You will probably gravitate to alternative therapies or new, cutting-edge technologies.

Since Mars is a relatively fast-moving planet, your health and health needs will tend to vary quickly depending on where Mars is at any given time and the kind of aspects it is receiving. These short-term trends are covered in the month-by-month reports.

Home and Family

Your 4th house of home and family is a House of Power this year and has been a major House of Power for the past 7 years. Last year it was especially important, as Jupiter moved into that house and spent most of the year there. Jupiter is still in your 4th house as the year begins, but will move out of there on January 18th. However, Jupiter will be travelling with Uranus for many months in the coming year, and since Uranus is your home planet there are other happy things happening in the home this year, too.

Many of you moved last year. Many of you bought or sold homes in profitable ways. Many of you renovated or expanded your home so that it was 'as if' you had moved. Spending was heavier than usual on the home last year. I presume you were buying expensive items for the home. But also spending more on family members.

Because Jupiter will be moving with Uranus from May through September in 2010, more moves could happen in the year ahead. These could happen very suddenly and unexpectedly. Again, you might not actually physically move, but you could make renovations or alterations in the home so that it would be as if you have moved.

Last year the family circle expanded either through births or marriage. These trends are continuing in the year ahead. Often with this transit people meet people who are 'like family' to them, and this is the way the family circle expands.

For many years now – and we have written about this – you have been working to make the home as much a place of entertainment as a home. You have installed home theatres, sporting equipment, electronic gadgetry, music systems, games and toys and the like. This trend is continuing in the year ahead. In many cases this need to make the home more entertaining is coming from the children. But not necessarily. You are buying adult toys as well.

Last year – and the trend will continue in the year ahead – you were looking to 'make money' at home. Probably you installed the necessary equipment, the home office and the like, to make this possible. We see this happening in the year ahead as well. If anything, this tendency to work from home will be even more intensified in the year ahead as your home and family planet, Uranus, moves into your 6th house of work. This happens from May 28th to August 14th. At this time you will also be installing more health equipment and health gadgets in the home, and in general trying to make the home a healthier place to live in. For years home has been an entertainment centre; now home will become like a health spa.

You have the kind of home where you never really need to leave. Entertainment is there, health equipment is there, and all of your office needs. The home seems all-encompassing these days. All in all, your home and family situation seems happy and exciting.

You are very supportive of the family in financial and emotional ways, and the family is very supportive of you in the same ways.

A parent or parent figure is likely to come into a very large financial windfall from May through September. You could perhaps be involved in this.

Finance and Career

Though your 2nd house of finance is not a House of Power this year, and though normally this would indicate the status quo, your financial planet is making many important moves in the year ahead. Thus we do see many financial shifts, changes and progress.

Jupiter, your financial planet, actually moves through three signs and houses of your horoscope in the year ahead. This is, as we have mentioned, highly unusual. At most it will move through two signs and houses, and normally through only one sign and house in any given year. This year he moves through *three*. This indicates various things. You are making fast and rapid financial progress. You are covering a lot of ground. Financial opportunity will come to you in various ways and through various people in the year ahead.

You begin the year with Jupiter in your 4th house. As we have mentioned this indicates money from property, from the fortunate purchase or sale of a home, good family support especially from parents or parent figures, investments in the home, spending on the home and the family, and earning money from the home. When Jupiter moves into Pisces from January 18th to June 6th, and then again from September 10th to the end of the year, there will be a big change in your financial attitudes and strategy. First off you will become more speculative and risk-taking. And, speaking generally, speculations should be favourable in the year ahead. This would be a good year to invest modest sums in the lottery or other such kinds of speculation. (Of course you should always do this under intuition and never blindly.) Jupiter in your 5th house indicates 'happy' money, money that is earned in fun and joyous ways. Perhaps you are out on the golf course or at the theatre or some party and you meet at an important financial connection. Perhaps one of your children comes up with a bright idea that is worth a lot of money. Perhaps your love for your children inspires you to wealth. The act of money-making has to be enjoyable; it's not just about getting richer. And it seems that you will be successful at this. Your financial planet in spiritual Pisces is also giving us another very important message: the role of intuition in your financial life. Scorpios tend to be very intuitive and psychic but now you even more so, especially when it comes to finances. As our steady readers know, one flash of true intuition is worth many years of hard labour. So be alert to it and don't be afraid to act on it. Jupiter in the spiritual sign of Pisces also suggests that you will be delving more deeply into the spiritual dimensions of wealth. This is a huge subject and you should read as much as you can about it. But we can mention some of the main points. The spiritual dimensions of wealth acknowledge one and only one source of wealth: the divine within. Everything else that happens is just a side-effect of the activity of spirit. In spiritual wealth one cultivates an attitude of worshipping the power that produces wealth. The tangible things are side-effects – to worship them is seen as a form of idolatry. The worship is focused on the power that produces all these wonderful and happy material things.

Your challenge for most of the year will be to open the spiritual doors of supply rather than the natural ones. You will find that when spirit says yes, the world says yes and all the doors open up. When spirit says no, the world says no. This will be a time of more charitable giving – which, by the way, is one of the best ways to open up the spiritual doors. In the financial world, giving is the doorway to bankruptcy. In the spiritual dimensions of wealth, giving is the doorway to greater riches. But you must experiment here and learn this for yourself. My feeling here is that most of you will learn these lessons and emerge from the year much wealthier than when you began. For Jupiter will be travelling with the planet Uranus, and this conjunction tends to produce large and sudden wealth. Many millionaires are born under this aspect. And many have made their money under this aspect. So there are large financial windfalls in store for you in the year ahead.

On June 6th Jupiter moves into Aries your 6th house. It stays there until September 10th. This produces a whole different philosophy of wealth. First off you will be a much freer spender, perhaps even an impulse spender. Your financial optimism seems boundless. If you are learning to overcome financial fear, Jupiter in your 6th house also shows earning money the hard way: through work. You will be a more productive worker and thus earn more. The main danger during this period is financial rashness and impulsiveness. So try to think things through more before acting. When your intuition is on, your sudden and impulsive decisions will probably turn out beautifully – but if you are tired and not in the right emotional state this impulsiveness could be harmful to you. While Jupiter is in Aries you will be allured by the 'quick buck'. You will want wealth in a hurry. It will happen for many of you. But there are dangers here as well. There are many unscrupulous people who will exploit this urge for their own advantage. But Scorpios are great judges of other people and you should have no problem discerning this.

Jupiter in your 6th also indicates more spending on health, and also opportunities to earn from the health field.

This is a prosperous year ahead.

Love and Social Life

Your 7th house of love and marriage is not a House of Power this year, Scorpio, so the tendency will be to the status quo. Whatever your status, single or married, you seem content and have no need to make major changes. Generally this indicates that love and marriage are not major priorities for you this year as compared to other things in your life. This is the way the cosmos works – some years are love years, some years are money years, some are psychological years, some are spiritual years, etc., etc. This rotating priority of the cosmos ensures a well-rounded development as life goes on. Still, for singles we do see a very serious relationship brewing which begins September 8th to November 9th or from December 1st to the end of the year. Venus, your love planet, spends 3 months in your own sign. This is highly unusual. A normal Venus transit lasts 1 month. This year she will spend 3 months in your sign.

This suggests that love is looking for you during this period – and it will find you. This love seems of the marrying kind. It doesn't necessarily mean that you will marry, but the person that you meet will be marriage material – someone that you would consider marrying. Nothing special that you need to do; this person is coming to you. You just have to show up.

Venus will go retrograde this year. This retrograde, especially when you compare it to the other planets, is rare. With the exception of Mars, the other planets tend to retrograde every year, sometimes for many months. Venus only retrogrades once every 2 years, and since Venus is your love planet it has a stronger impact on you than on other people. During this period (October 8th to November 18th) love tends to feel like it's going backwards instead of forwards. Sometimes relationships break up under this aspect. It is a time for rethinking and reviewing your current marriage or relationship and your overall love life. This is a time for seeing where things could be improved, so that when Venus goes forward on November 18th you can start to implement these improvements. This period is no time for marrying or divorcing, nor for making important social or love decisions.

Saturn has spent a few years in your 11th house of friends, and this has tested friendships as we have mentioned earlier. You still have a few months of this in the year ahead, from April 8th to July 22nd. Then these lessons are over with. As we have mentioned you will probably be left with fewer friends, but the ones that you have will be good ones. This is the message of Saturn. Better one or two really good friends than hosts of lukewarm, phony ones.

Those of you who are in or working towards their second marriage are having your relationship tested as there are two eclipses in your house of marriage in the year ahead – and if we stretch we could say there are three eclipses, for the one on December 21st is right on the cusp of your house of second marriages. On the other hand, singles looking to marry for the second time could marry under these aspects as they indicate a change in marital status.

Those working towards their third marriage will have an easier time this year (as compared to the last 2 years) but the tendency is to the status quo.

Self-improvement

Spiritually you tend to gravitate towards teachings that emphasize love, love, love. This is all well and good, and certainly no one will argue that love is one of the great gateways to the divine and to deeper spiritual development. By nature you are a fierce warrior, not someone to be tampered with. Thus, learning to love unconditionally is very important spiritually. Spiritually speaking there are two dimensions to love. One is the love between two human beings. You are the type that feels close to the divine when you are in love. Nothing wrong with this. However there is a deeper kind of love that has little to do with romantic love. This is the unconditional love of the spirit. This love is not dependent on any outside object; it just is. This love is what opens the gates to the divine for you.

Since October of 2009 a new dimension of spiritual growth has opened up before you. Generally the spiritual paths that emphasize love, love, love are based on the emotions. With Saturn now in your 12th house of spirituality for most of the year ahead, there is a need to balance this with a rational, scientific approach. Emotion, even though it is love-based, is highly unstable. When one is in a good mood, one sees God and all the choirs of angels. But when one is in a bad mood, one feels, and can often behave, like an atheist. So taking your mind along for the spiritual journey is called for these days. There is a need for consciously understanding what you are doing and what you know.

Most of the love-based systems tend to be anti-intellectual. The mind, the intellect, is considered 'the great enemy'. But this year you will learn that the intellect is not your enemy but actually your friend and assistant on the path. It is not the mind that is your enemy but the impurities there, the false beliefs and false ideas. Cleanse the mind of these false ideas and the mind becomes your ally and friend on the path.

Those of you on the path already will find that you are called to teach others. Those who are still beginners will find a craving for intellectual knowledge of the path and of the spiritual world. This intellectual knowledge, while not being the actual experience of spirituality (because spirit is beyond any word or concept), nevertheless will give you more stability on the path. When you are in a bad mood, because of various reasons (many of them even astrological ones), your intellectual understanding will support your spiritual quest.

Also, a clear intellectual understanding of the spiritual world serves as a road map. The roadmap is not the actual trek, not the journey. However, a good roadmap is essential for taking the journey. This is especially true for those who are beginners on the path. Get yourself a good roadmap, a map that matches the territory to be traversed. Then when it comes time to actually make the journey, at least you'll know where you're going.

Month-by-month Forecasts

January

Best Days Overall: 1, 3, 4, 18, 19, 28
Most Stressful Days Overall: 2, 3, 16, 17, 23, 24, 30
Best Days for Love: 4, 5, 13, 14, 15, 23, 24, 25, 26
Best Days for Money: 6, 7, 11, 12, 16, 17, 18, 27
Best Days for Career: 2, 3, 4, 5, 13, 14, 15, 25, 26, 29, 30

Your year begins with 80 per cent (sometimes 90 per cent) of the planets below the horizon. You are in the 'night-time' of your year and should be focused on the home and family and your overall emotional well-being. But dynamic Mars in your 10th house of career is making very heavy career demands. You can't be with the family as much as you would like. A period of balancing between the two. Where possible, however – and this is a very personal and individual judgement – shift as much attention to the home and family as possible. This month – especially after the 20th – your family is your actual spiritual mission.

You have just come off (last month) a yearly financial peak. Now the focus is on communication and intellectual interests, until the 20th, and the home and family afterwards. You have achieved your basic financial goals and now it is time to enjoy the fruits of wealth: free time to develop your mind. When the 3rd house is powerful it is usually a good time for sales, marketing and PR projects – for launching these kinds of things. But this month, Mercury and Saturn are retrograde. Mercury, the generic ruler of communication, is retrograde until the 15th. Saturn, your actual planet of communication, starts to retrograde on the 13th. So this month might be better for *planning* sales and marketing projects rather than actually doing them. You can still take courses in subjects that interest you – the retrogrades won't affect that. But avoid buying major communications equipment now – this should be studied further.

A solar eclipse on the 15th will test communication equipment and bring changes to sales, marketing or PR plans – another reason to avoid launching these things now. This eclipse brings career changes and upheavals as well. It changes the 'gestalt' not only of your career, but also of your company and even your industry. There are dramas with parents or parent figures and siblings now – dramatic experiences in their lives. They are, for the next 6 months, redefining their personalities and self-concepts. (Often this happens because of slanders and innuendo from others.) Their self-esteem and self-confidence get some severe testing. This eclipse is basically benign to you – the shakeups help you, they clear your pathway – still, it won't hurt to take a reduced schedule during this eclipse period. Why ask for problems? People are not up to par during an eclipse period, so why get caught up in this?

Finances are good this month. A financial windfall or lucky speculation comes early in the month (it could have happened last month as well). Your financial intuition is super early in the month. On the 18th your financial planet moves into Pisces, your 5th house. Thus speculations will be favourable all year. Now your challenge is to make the act of money-making so pleasurable that you would rather do that than go out on the town. You will do it. The cosmos will show you how.

February

Best Days Overall: 5, 6, 15, 16, 24, 25
Most Stressful Days Overall: 12, 13, 19, 20, 21, 26, 27
Best Days for Love: 2, 3, 14, 15, 19, 20, 21, 24, 25
Best Days for Money: 4, 5, 7, 8, 14, 15, 24
Best Days for Career: 2, 3, 13, 14, 24, 25, 26, 27

Health is good overall but needs more watching this month, until the 18th. It needed more watching last month, from the 20th onwards. Nothing serious here, just not one of your better periods energetically. Rest and relax more. Don't panic over sudden aches or pains or sniffles. Lowered energy just makes you more vulnerable than usual. Keep your energy levels as high as possible. (Both home and career are very demanding these days – and this is part of the problem, too.) Pay more attention to your heart (reduce stress and worry) until the 18th, and to your head, face, skull and adrenals all month. Just because energy is not what it should be doesn't mean that you have to make major changes to your diet or health regime. Probably your current health regime is just fine – it is an energy issue, not a dietary one. Mars, your health planet, is retrograde all month (and it was retrograde last month as well). Study proposed new health regimes more carefully now. By the 18th, as energy returns, you will have little need to make dramatic changes.

Like last month, career and home are vying with each other for your attention. Both are demanding. And so, like a seesaw, you will shift attention from one to the other – now leaning one way, now another. You succeed in your career the old-fashioned way – through sheer hard work. Keep in mind that your spiritual mission now is the family and children (or those who are like your family or like your children to you). Whenever possible, be there for them. Also, this attention on the home and family will be favourable to your career – it will not harm it the way that you might imagine, and in certain respects will enhance it.

This month the planetary power shifts from the East to the Western sector of your chart. By now you have created conditions as you like them. You have had your season of independence. Now it is time to enjoy the fruits of this. You will live with your own creation. If you have created well, this Western shift will be pleasant; if not, you will see the errors and be ready to correct them on the next go round of independence – later on in the year. In the meantime, adjust and adapt to situations as best you can. This too is a skill in life – and a good one to learn.

This is a happy month for love. For marrieds the relationship becomes more honeymoonish. A foreign journey from the 15th to the 17th will do wonders to ease a troubled marriage or a marriage in the doldrums. Problems in the marriage can be resolved by just having more fun – doing fun things together as a couple.

For singles this month is about non-serious love – flings. There are many opportunities all month, but especially from the 15th to the 17th. The person who can show you a good time – the fun-loving, non-serious person – is the one you gravitate to now. Love doesn't always have to be so serious. There should be fun, laughter and lightness to it.

Finances are good, too. The 15th to the 17th not only brings happy love experiences, but also financial bonanzas – there is luck in speculations during this period. The 27th and 28th bring career success, elevation and financial increase as well.

On the 18th you enter one of your yearly personal pleasure peaks. A good thing, too. You seem to be working hard.

March

    Best Days Overall: 1, 3, 4, 18, 19, 28
    Most Stressful Days Overall: 11, 12, 19, 20, 25, 26
    Best Days for Love: 5, 6, 16, 17, 19, 20, 25, 26
    Best Days for Money: 4, 5, 6, 7, 14, 15, 23, 24, 31
    Best Days for Career: 5, 6, 16, 17, 18, 19, 20, 25, 26

Health is good right now. On the 10th your health planet, Mars, starts moving forward after months of retrograde motion. You are more clear about your health regime, diet and the overall state of your health. If there are changes to be made, your decisions will be better after the 10th. Also, on the 20th your 6th house of health becomes very strong. You seem to be paying more attention here. Exercise seems the major interest. You can enhance your already good health by paying more attention to your heart (all month), to your head, face and skull (all month), to your kidneys and hips (from the 7th onwards) and to your lungs, small intestine, arms and shoulders (from the 17th onwards). Scalp, face, hip, arm and shoulder massage is powerful these days.

Mars, moving forward, is very good for job-seekers and for those who employ others. There is more clarity as to what you want. Job-seekers have been 'directionless' for a few months, but now there is direction. After the 20th (perhaps even before) there are happy job opportunities coming. Parents, elders, your spouse, partner, social circle and connections are helpful now.

The year ahead is a strong party year, and you are still in a yearly personal pleasure peak until the 20th. You need to explore the joy of life now – it's not just about sensual pleasure, but almost a spiritual mission. You need periods of fun to get you ready for the more serious, work-orientated period beginning on the 20th. Andrew Carnegie's famous saying, 'in leisure there is luck' certainly applies to you these days. It is when you lighten up, relax, live the life that you love to live, that ideas and inspirations can come into you. When you are tense and serious, you block these things. Even serious work can be made more 'fun' – more like a game – without damaging productivity. In fact, it will enhance productivity.

Love is good this month, but there are ups and downs. Without the downs we would never appreciate the ups. Your love planet spent the last month in Pisces and will be in Pisces until the 7th. This makes you and your partner 1,000 times more sensitive in love than usual. When love is good between you, the highs are incredible – you experience all the little nuances that most people never get to experience. The problem is that if you're not careful – in unguarded moments – little things like facial gestures, voice tones, body language can be devastating to your lover. Even a brief negative thought that passes through your mind – seemingly innocent – can have devastating effects. You need to understand this and be more careful. The 2nd to the 5th brings sudden love opportunities or social invitations. Love happens out of the blue. On the 11th and 12th there is some conflict between you and your beloved. Try not to make things worse – work to minimize the negativity – the problem will soon pass. On the 7th your love planet moves into Aries and you become a 'love at first sight' kind of person. You become more aggressive in love – fearless. When your intuition is on, this is good. You go directly to your objective without the muss and fuss of all the courtship rituals. But if your intuition is off, there can be mistakes in love – bad choices. However, this is a month where you learn that there is nothing to fear in love, but fear itself. Pick yourself up and jump back into the fray.

April

Best Days Overall: 1, 10, 11, 19, 20, 28, 29
Most Stressful Days Overall: 8, 9, 15, 16, 22, 23
Best Days for Love: 5, 15, 16, 25
Best Days for Money: 1, 3, 4, 10, 11, 19, 20, 28, 29, 30
Best Days for Career: 3, 4, 13, 14, 22, 23, 24

Working hard and playing hard continue to be the main themes of the month. Your 5th house is still very strong, and your financial planet (Jupiter) is still camped out there. Speculations are favourable, but your hard work is just as important in earnings. You seem to be spending more on the family and children, but you could also earn from these things as well. Family seems very supportive financially. Children have interesting financial ideas – also they can inspire and motivate you to earn more.

Job-seekers and those who employ others are having good fortune now – like last month. Elders, bosses, parent or parent figures seem instrumental here.

On the 20th two important things happen. First, you enter a yearly social peak. There is more dating, more parties, more social gatherings. Whether you are married or single, your social life will expand. Second, the planetary power shifts from the lower, 'night' side of your horoscope to the upper, 'day' side. Thus there is a psychological shift happening. Sunrise is breaking in your year. You are awakening (symbolically speaking) from a good night's sleep. Dream time is over. Now you attain your goals through the methods of day – by direct, outer action. Career and outer success become ever more important for the next 6 or so months. Right now, as we have seen, since the beginning of the year you have attained success the old-fashioned way: through hard work. You've simply worked harder than your competitors and thus you've succeeded. After the 20th, hard work of itself is not enough. You need to know the right people, attract the right people who can help you – so it is good to promote your career through social means. Host or attend the right parties. Network more with friends. Your spouse, partner or current love has ideas or connections.

Career is going well but there are some bumps in the road – upheavals and changes – on the 14th to the 16th. There are probably dramas with parents or parent figures during this period, too. But these things will turn out well.

There are happy love experiences or romantic meetings from the 4th to the 6th. This can bring some happy social invitation as well.

A very happy career opportunity – or elevation – comes on the 25th–26th.

Health needs more watching after the 20th. Pay more attention to your heart, head, face and skull. Physical exercise is good, too, and you seem to be engaging in it. But the main thing, as our steady readers know, is to maintain high energy levels. Never allow yourself to get overtired – this makes you vulnerable to more serious ailments. A strong aura (the spiritual immune system) will repel any disease. But when energy drops, the aura weakens.

May

    Best Days Overall: 7, 8, 9, 17, 18, 25, 26
    Most Stressful Days Overall: 5, 6, 12, 13, 19, 20
    Best Days for Love: 5, 6, 12, 13, 15, 16, 25, 26
    Best Days for Money: 1, 8, 9, 18, 25, 26, 27, 28
    Best Days for Career: 5, 6, 12, 13, 15, 16, 25, 26

Jupiter and Uranus make a very rare (once in 14–15 years) conjunction in your 5th house. Jupiter is your financial planet. Thus this brings sudden wealth to you – large wealth – perhaps speculative wealth. How large depends on your age and stage in life. But it is unusual. Your whole financial picture changes in an instant. Also, you seem willing to try out different financial techniques and stratagems. You are throwing out all the rule books and seeing what works for you – and you seem very successful with this. Those of you in the creative fields – the arts – cash in on your creativity: a

book is published, paintings are sold or exhibited in a prominent way, music is sold and successful. Children (or those
who are like children to you), parents or family members
also prosper greatly. Many of you will achieve 'overnight'
success in an industry that is only in its infancy now – an
industry that is in its 'childhood' stage.

This trend is continuing for the next few months. It is a
very exciting time financially. Only keep in mind (and it
might be difficult during all this excitement) that this wealth
can be very unstable. It can come quickly and leave quickly.
So, protect as much of your earnings as you can – put the
money into some safe and conservative investments.

Uranus moves into your 6th house on the 28th, and this
signals job changes (perhaps a few of them). For those who
employ others there is turnover and general instability in
the staff. You never know who is available when.

You are still in the midst of a yearly social peak, so keep in
mind our discussion of this last month. This is a more
romantic kind of month, but the year as a whole seems more
about love affairs and flings rather than serious romance.
Marriage is doubtful for singles – though they will meet
'marriage material' this month.

Last month, on the 7th, Pluto (your ruling planet) went
retrograde. He will be retrograde for many more months.
This doesn't mean that your life stops. It only means that
your personal goals, your direction in life, your image, the
way your body looks, are under review for a while. Perhaps
you feel 'lacking in direction' on a personal level – this
would be normal. But this is a time where you are meant to
gain inner clarity about your direction – and time will bring
this clarity. Your self-confidence and self-esteem are not up
to their usual standards.

Health still needs watching until the 21st. Review our
discussion of last month. After the 28th pay more attention
to your ankles.

June

Best Days Overall: 4, 5, 13, 14, 21, 22
Most Stressful Days Overall: 1, 2, 9, 10, 15, 16, 29, 30
Best Days for Love: 4, 5, 9, 10, 13, 14, 24, 25
Best Days for Money: 5, 6, 15, 24, 25
Best Days for Career: 1, 2, 11, 12, 15, 16, 21

Jupiter is still travelling with Uranus and you are still in one of the most exciting financial periods of your life. Review our discussion of this last month. You will be hearing about a lot of 'instant' millionaires these days – and you could be one of them.

Last month on the 21st the Sun entered your 8th house – your favourite house – your most natural house. Thus you are in Scorpio heaven these days. You are prospering personally but your spouse, partner or current love is also prospering – and you are probably playing a big role in this. Your mission now is to help others prosper – to make others rich and to keep the financial interests of others uppermost in your mind.

The phenomena of the 8th house happen on various levels. On the mundane, worldly level, this brings opportunities to earn through creative financing and through attracting outside money to your projects – either through investors or borrowing. Debt, as you know, is a double-edged sword. Used constructively it enhances returns and expands the wealth. Used destructively – well, it destroys wealth.

Scorpios are fascinated by death. To a Scorpio, death is not a morbid thing. They love going to funerals and wakes – not that they wish anyone ill or dead – but it is enjoyable. A Scorpio can have as much fun at a funeral as on a night out on the town. Their job, on a spiritual level, is to educate the rest of us about the true meaning of death and what it is all about. I personally know many a Scorpio actively doing these things. When death is understood correctly, we will understand life more correctly and we will live differently –

without fear. This is a month where you go more deeply into this subject.

The process of resurrection is also ruled by Scorpio and the 8th house, and this is a month where you can practise this more and go more deeply into it. You will have more power to resurrect troubled relationships, projects, investments and the like – just follow your intuition and inner feeling.

Health is much improved over last month. You can enhance it further by paying more attention to your heart (until the 7th), small intestine (after the 7th), ankles and calves (all month), and your liver and thighs (from the 6th onwards). Ankle, calf and thigh massage is powerful now. With your 8th house strong until the 21st, detox regimes are also good.

A lunar eclipse on the 26th is strong on you, Scorpio, so take a reduced schedule during this period and avoid risk-taking or stressful activities. It occurs in Capricorn, your 3rd house, but it is a direct hit on Pluto, your ruler. Thus this eclipse will force you to redefine your image, personality and self-concept. You need to rethink (and then improve) these things. Perhaps there are areas of your personality or the way you think of yourself that are not up to your true standard – probably they have been operating uncon-sciously. Now they surface (usually other people bring them up in an unpleasant way) and you are forced to confront them. This eclipse will also change educational plans for students – in various ways. It can bring changes in school, changes in the main areas of study, or changes in the rules of a school. Cars and communication equipment will get tested by this eclipse as well.

July

Best Days Overall: 1, 2, 10, 11, 19, 20, 28, 29, 30
Most Stressful Days Overall: 6, 7, 13, 26, 27
Best Days for Love: 5, 6, 7, 14, 23, 24
Best Days for Money: 3, 12, 21, 22, 31
Best Days for Career: 1, 2, 10, 11, 12, 13, 20, 31

Basically a happy month. Your 9th house is powerful until the 23rd; this house is considered the happiest and most fortunate by the Hindu astrologers. Power in the 9th house brings an optimism which, of itself, leads to success. It's as if the planets are giving you 'happy vitamins' now. This is a month for happy travel and educational opportunities. Students at university or graduate school level are enjoying success in their studies or with their applications for university. Legal issues will tend to go well. The stars don't guarantee a 'win' – the individual merits of your case are still paramount – but it indicates 'best-case' scenarios.

Your career planet in the 9th house shows that your career is expanding and that there is much optimism about your career. Probably you will travel related to your career as well.

For those on the spiritual path, this is a month for religious and philosophical breakthroughs – and when these happen, oh, what joy! Teaching others what you know, sharing your wisdom, is your mission early in the month. This doesn't mean that you will go door to door or stand on a soap box in the middle of the road. No, people will come into your proximity – they will be drawn to you – and you will know by intuition what to share with them.

On the 23rd you enter a yearly career peak. Most of the planets are still above the horizon. Your 10th house of career will be powerful. Your family planet, Uranus, will start to retrograde on the 5th. Family issues will take time to resolve, so important decisions probably shouldn't be taken now anyway – focus on your career. After the 23rd, your mission is outer success. You can be of more service to others from a position of power than from a lowly position. Many of you might think that your ambitions now are strictly personal, but this is an illusion. The cosmos itself, working through you, desires your success.

There is a solar eclipse on the 11th that occurs in your 9th house. This eclipse, like the last one, is basically benign to you – it will clear obstructions on your path. Perhaps there was some 'bogey man' (symbolically speaking) on your path: the eclipse comes and lo, the 'bogey man' is gone. This eclipse will break career barriers and bring career changes – either within your present company or with a new one. It changes the hierarchy of your company, and in many cases of the entire industry. It brings dramatic events in the lives of parents, parent figures or bosses – often it forces a redefinition of their personality and self-concept. It brings educational changes for students at university or graduate school.

Health needs more watching after the 23rd. The demands of your career and the workplace are very strong. Work hard, but work smart, too. Delegate where possible. Organize your day so that you achieve the maximum with the minimum expenditure of energy. Keep your focus on essentials and let the frivolous go. Enhance health in the ways mentioned in the yearly report, but also pay more attention to your heart (after the 23rd), small intestine (until the 30th), and your kidneys and hips (on the 31st).

August

Best Days Overall: 7, 8, 15, 16, 25, 26
Most Stressful Days Overall: 2, 3, 9, 10, 22, 23, 30, 31
Best Days for Love: 2, 3, 4, 13, 22, 23, 29, 30, 31
Best Days for Money: 9, 17, 18, 27
Best Days for Career: 1, 9, 10, 17, 18, 29, 30

Finances are still very good. You are in the midst of a lifetime peak in many cases. But last month, on the 23rd, your financial planet (Jupiter) went retrograde. It will be retrograde all of this month and until November. This brings a bit of a lull in your financial life. Of course earnings will still come, but with more delays. Financial confidence and judgement are not up to their usual high standards. This is a time to put your financial life under review. This is the kind of time when you analyse the merits of different investments or plans, where you analyse your product or service and see where improvements can be made. Perhaps another bank is offering a higher rate of interest. Perhaps another brokerage house is offering better terms. But what about the small print? This is a time to study all these things – to crunch the numbers and weigh all the angles and intangibles. Take your time. Be thorough.

In general this is a time to avoid financial shortcuts. Strive to make every financial transaction perfectly. Don't take things for granted.

Moves and property investments (including major purchases for the home) can still happen these days as well. Again, with your home and family planet retrograde until December, these things need more study and planning. If you must do them, make sure you protect yourself adequately.

You are still in the midst of a yearly career peak and much progress is being made. The New Moon of the 10th is a particularly good career day. It boosts your career and also clarifies many issues.

Continue to watch your health more closely until the 23rd. Keep energy levels high. Review our discussion of this last month. Health needs particular attention from the 4th to the 9th and from the 25th to the 28th. Avoid stressful, risky activities. Drive more defensively and avoid arguments and temper-tantrums. These periods also bring disruptions at work or in the workplace. This month, enhance health through more attention to your kidneys and hips (massage the hips regularly). Also spiritual healing – prayer, meditation, the laying-on of hands, the manipulation of subtle energies – are particularly powerful this month. You will make great progress in your understanding of these things this month. (Many of you will be involved in healing ministry as well – using spiritual techniques to heal others.)

Love should get easier after the 7th. Until the 7th your love planet (Venus) is in Virgo, which is not her favourite position. (It's as if you take a Goddess of Beauty and force her to work emptying bed pans or cleaning floors – she can't express herself at her highest level.) On the 7th Venus enters Libra, a much more romantic position. You are able to express your natural warmth and love to others more easily

– and you will see the impact of this on your love life almost
instantly.

September

>   Best Days Overall: 3, 4, 11, 12, 21, 22
>   Most Stressful Days Overall: 5, 6, 18, 19, 20, 26, 27
>   Best Days for Love: 2, 11, 21, 26, 27
>   Best Days for Money: 5, 12, 13, 14, 15, 22
>   Best Days for Career: 5, 6, 7, 8, 17, 28

In July the planetary power shifted from the social, Western
sector to the independent East, and this trend is even more
pronounced this month. (Next month it will be stronger
still.) You are entering a period of maximum independence.
You are, figuratively speaking, in a position to 'make karma',
whereas for many months you were 'paying karma'. You
had to adjust to situations. Now you can create situations –
and you should.

Last month, on the 23rd, your 11th house of friends
became powerful. A strong social period. Not necessarily
romantic, but more about being a friend and enjoying the
fruits of friendship. Friends are helpful in your career. But
career is also boosted by being more involved with social,
professional or trade organizations. Networking – good use
of the internet and electronic media – your technological
savvy – is important to career success. Career success will be
boosted by your ability to work with groups in a harmonious
way. If you are weak in this area, now is the time to work on
this and improve your skills.

On the 23rd you enter one of the strongest spiritual periods in your year. A time for inner, spiritual progress and for
getting more in tune with the Higher Power within you. For
those on the path, this brings revelation and spiritual breakthroughs. It brings prophetic dreams and higher experiences
– with angels, masters and other cosmic beings. For those
not yet on the path, it brings 'head scratching' events –
things that can't be explained by logic – you don't feel well

one morning and don't go to work, and on that day there is some terrible accident either in the work environs or on your route. You know there was some power protecting you. A car cuts you off on the highway and forces you to slow down – and perhaps you are fretting and fuming about this – but in a few minutes you note that there is a police car right behind you. A power, a something, was looking out for you. These are love messages from above calling you to closer communion.

Love is happy this month. On the 8th Venus (your love planet) crosses your Ascendant and enters your 1st house. This not only brings love to you – but many other things. It brings beauty and glamour to your image. You dress more stylishly and your normal sense of style is enhanced – almost automatically. It brings things of beauty – art objects, fashion accessories and clothing – to you. You look great and other people take notice. They run after you. You have love on your own terms these days. Others are going out of their way to please you. Mars is also in your sign from the 15th onwards, and this too enhances your personal charisma and sex appeal. For job-seekers this indicates job opportunities seeking them out, rather than vice versa. No need to search the ads or send out hundreds of CVs – jobs are seeking you.

October

> Best Days Overall: 1, 2, 9, 10, 18, 19, 28, 29
> Most Stressful Days Overall: 3, 4, 16, 17, 23, 24, 30, 31
> Best Days for Love: 1, 9, 18, 19, 23, 24, 28
> Best Days for Money: 2, 10, 11, 12, 19, 29
> Best Days for Career: 3, 4, 7, 17, 27, 28, 30, 31

Love is still happy, but under review this month. Venus, your love planet, starts to retrograde on the 8th. Often this introduces all kinds of doubts and insecurities in a current relationship (even though it is basically good). Both you and your beloved seem to 'pull back' for a while. There is a need to review and see where improvements can be made. In

spite of Venus' retrograde, love opportunities are still seeking you out and you are still having love on your own terms.
Your spouse, partner or beloved is putting you first – is
squarely in your corner – in spite of all the doubts and insecurities. This is not a time to panic about love. It is a time to
proceed slowly – not force issues – let love develop as it will.

Spirituality could be said to be your main mission until
the 23rd. Your *Dharma*. Your true career. Your connection to
the Higher Power is the most important thing these days.
Your spiritual exercises, though seemingly undertaken
alone, have great power over not just your own aura but the
auras of those around you. In effect, therefore, this changes
the world. The real change that happens in the world takes
place far from the halls of Parliament or Congress – far from
the thrones of the high and the mighty. No, real change
happens in the secret chambers of an individual heart –
perhaps in some remote place, far from the halls of worldly
power. Some yogi in the Himalayas makes a spiritual breakthrough and the world is forever changed. Presidents and
prime ministers will (over time) merely 'rubber stamp' these
changes.

Emerson has said, 'the soul's communion with its source
is the highest event in nature' – and this is what many of
you are experiencing this month.

On a more mundane level, your career planet in your
12th house of spirituality this month shows that you can
(and should) enhance your career through involvement
with charities, causes and altruistic kinds of activities. You
will meet many 'powers that be' through these activities,
and other 'powers that be' will certainly take notice.

On the 23rd the Sun, also your career planet, crosses your
Ascendant and enters your 1st house. You begin a yearly
personal pleasure peak. A time to give your body the pleasures due to it. Your mission becomes to get your body and
image in shape – the way that you want them to be. The
truth is you look good this month. Venus is still in your sign
all month, enhancing your glamour and personal style. Mars
is in your sign until the 28th (almost all month) gives you

sex appeal, energy and personal dynamism. However, good though your appearance is, there are always improvements to be made and now is the time to make them.

You have a 'can do' attitude these days. Health is good. Seems like you are exercising more than usual and your muscle tone is good. You are fit.

Job and career opportunities are coming to you all month – no need to search all the want ads.

November

Best Days Overall: 5, 6, 14, 15, 16, 24, 25
Most Stressful Days Overall: 12, 13, 19, 20, 21, 26, 27
Best Days for Love: 5, 13, 19, 20, 21, 23
Best Days for Money: 6, 7, 8, 15, 16, 25
Best Days for Career: 5, 6, 15, 16, 26, 27

On the 23rd of last month the planetary power shifted from the upper to the lower half of your horoscope. From the 'day' side of the chart to the 'night' side. Time now to de-emphasize career and outer goals and focus on the family and emotional issues. Time to build the psychological infrastructure of future career success – your future goals and direction. A solid house needs a good foundation. You are working on this foundation these days.

Career opportunities are still running after you. And you can be more choosy about the various proposals.

You are still very much in the midst of a yearly personal pleasure peak until the 22nd. Sensual fantasies get fulfilled. This, by the way, is the nature of the universe. Every desire will get fulfilled, in its own time. In fact, this is the reason for many problems in the world, for even negative desires will get fulfilled as well – unless there is a counterforce nullifying them. This is the time for personal bodily desires to be fulfilled.

On the 22nd you enter a yearly financial peak. The timing here is perfect. On the 18th Jupiter, your financial planet, starts to move forward after many months of retrograde motion. Just in time. You are clear. Your financial judgement is sound. You are ready to leap into action and capitalize. Speculations have been favourable all year, but they become more favourable after the 22nd.

After the 22nd, as your career planet moves into the money house, it is as if it is your mission, your main purpose, is to acquire wealth. The cosmos wants you to be rich, but not in the selfish, egotistical way – in order to be more able to help others and to fulfil the plan of life. We need money to fulfil our plans. People in authority over you – parents or parent figures, bosses, elders and even government figures – are supportive financially. Your good professional reputation – your public standing – is also very important now. It brings referrals, offers and financial opportunities. If you have issues with the government, this is a good month to deal with them.

Health is good all month. You are spending more on health issues (probably athletic or exercise equipment) but can also earn from this field, too. Good health this month means more than just 'no symptoms' or physical fitness – it means good financial health as well.

Love is still under review until the 18th. On the 9th Venus retrogrades back into Libra, your 12th house. This indicates various things. Love is more idealistic. There is a need to seek guidance on love from the spirit world – the Higher Intelligence. Psychics, astrologers, ministers, gurus and spiritual channels can all be of help these days – and probably will be involved in your love life and love decisions. Singles should avoid the bars and clubs in their search for love – they will do better in spiritual settings – meditation seminars, spiritual retreats, the yoga or tai chi studio and the like.

December

Best Days Overall: 3, 4, 12, 13, 21, 22, 30, 31
Most Stressful Days Overall: 9, 10, 11, 17, 18, 23, 24
Best Days for Love: 2, 12, 17, 18, 22, 31
Best Days for Money: 4, 5, 6, 13, 23, 31
Best Days for Career: 5, 16, 23, 24, 26

A happy month ahead. Love is much improved over last month. Venus, your love planet, is back in your own sign and moving forward. A current relationship is back on track and happy. Doubts have been resolved. Your lover or spouse is in your corner, going out of his or her way to please you. Singles need not worry about love, either; it is still pursuing them. Nothing special needs to be done – just go about your normal business.

It is understandable that others would be pursuing you these days. Venus in your sign makes your personal appearance shine. You are glamorous and stylish. You exude grace and charm. Aphrodite has thrown her girdle about you, and even the gods in heaven are not immune. For many months now you have been working to change your image; this month you see the positive results.

You are still in the midst of a yearly financial peak. Prosperity is strong. There is luck in speculations. You have an innate optimism and confidence about earnings and financial judgement. Like last month, bosses, elders, parents or parent figures are supportive financially – both in concrete ways and in terms of providing opportunities. Pay rises are likely, too. This is the kind of month (last month as well) where career success is measured in pounds and pence – 'monetized'. Status, prestige and glory are not the issue for you – earnings are.

Health is wonderful now. You can enhance it further by paying more attention to your liver and thighs (until the 8th) and to your spine, knees, bones, gallbladder and skeletal alignment from the 8th onwards. Like last month, financial health is important to you until the 8th. Afterwards, mental health is important. There is a need to feed your 'mental body' and give it its needs. If you feel under the weather (unlikely), purge your mind of error. Think less and speak less. Energy and health will improve.

A lunar eclipse on the 21st occurs right on the border of your 8th and 9th houses. It will have an impact on both these houses. This eclipse is basically benign to you and is more or less a replay of the solar eclipse of July 11th. It can bring intimations of mortality – dreams of death and/or a need to face death on the psychological level. Sometimes it brings near-death experiences or other encounters with death. But Scorpio is not terrified by these kinds of things. Death holds little terror for the Scorpio – especially for those on the path. It is merely a doorway to another dimension – better and finer than this one. But still, it is a kindly reminder to get down to business – to take care of the important things in life and to re-order one's priorities in life. Students are again affected by this eclipse. It can bring changes in the school, in educational plans or in their area of study, or shakeups in the school they are attending. Legal matters will take a dramatic turn one way or another – especially if they have been stalled for a while.

Sagittarius

♐

THE ARCHER
Birthdays from
23rd November to
20th December

Personality Profile

SAGITTARIUS AT A GLANCE

Element – Fire

Ruling Planet – Jupiter
   Career Planet – Mercury
   Love Planet – Mercury
   Money Planet – Saturn
   Planet of Health and Work – Venus
   Planet of Home and Family Life – Neptune
   Planet of Spirituality – Pluto

Colours – blue, dark blue

Colours that promote love, romance and social
   harmony – yellow, yellow-orange

Colours that promote earning power – black,
   indigo

Gems – carbuncle, turquoise

Metal – tin

Scents – carnation, jasmine, myrrh

Quality – mutable (= flexibility)

Qualities most needed for balance – attention to detail, administrative and organizational skills

Strongest virtues – generosity, honesty, broad-mindedness, tremendous vision

Deepest need – to expand mentally

Characteristics to avoid – over-optimism, exaggeration, being too generous with other people's money

Signs of greatest overall compatibility – Aries, Leo

Signs of greatest overall incompatibility – Gemini, Virgo, Pisces

Sign most helpful to career – Virgo

Sign most helpful for emotional support – Pisces

Sign most helpful financially – Capricorn

Sign best for marriage and/or partnerships – Gemini

Sign most helpful for creative projects – Aries

Best Sign to have fun with – Aries

Signs most helpful in spiritual matters – Leo, Scorpio

Best day of the week – Thursday

Understanding a Sagittarius

If you look at the symbol of the archer you will gain a good, intuitive understanding of a person born under this astrological Sign. The development of archery was humanity's first refinement of the power to hunt and wage war. The ability to shoot an arrow far beyond the ordinary range of a spear extended humanity's horizons, wealth, personal will and power.

Today, instead of using bows and arrows we project our power with fuels and mighty engines, but the essential reason for using these new powers remains the same. These powers represent our ability to extend our personal sphere of influence – and this is what Sagittarius is all about. Sagittarians are always seeking to expand their horizons, to cover more territory and increase their range and scope. This applies to all aspects of their lives: economic, social and intellectual.

Sagittarians are noted for the development of the mind – the higher intellect – which understands philosophical, metaphysical and spiritual concepts. This mind represents the higher part of the psychic nature and is motivated not by self-centred considerations but by the light and grace of a Higher Power. Thus, Sagittarians love higher education of all kinds. They might be bored with formal schooling but they love to study on their own and in their own way. A love of foreign travel and interest in places far away from home are also noteworthy characteristics of the Sagittarian type.

If you give some thought to all these Sagittarian attributes you will see that they spring from the inner Sagittarian desire to develop. To travel more is to know more, to know more is to be more, to cultivate the higher mind is to grow and to reach more. All these traits tend to broaden the intellectual – and indirectly, the economic and material – horizons of the Sagittarian.

The generosity of the Sagittarian is legendary. There are many reasons for this. One is that Sagittarians seem to have an inborn consciousness of wealth. They feel that they are rich, that they are lucky, that they can attain any financial goal – and so they feel that they can afford to be generous. Sagittarians do not carry the burdens of want and limitation – which stop most other people from giving generously. Another reason for their generosity is their religious and philosophical idealism, derived from the higher mind. This higher mind is by nature generous because it is unaffected by material circumstances. Still another reason is that the act of giving tends to enhance their emotional nature. Every act of giving seems to be enriching, and this is reward enough for the Sagittarian.

Finance

Sagittarians generally entice wealth. They either attract it or create it. They have the ideas, energy and talent to make their vision of paradise on Earth a reality. However, mere wealth is not enough. Sagittarians want luxury – earning a comfortable living seems small and insignificant to them.

In order for Sagittarians to attain their true earning potential they must develop better managerial and organizational skills. They must learn to set limits, to arrive at their goals through a series of attainable sub-goals or objectives. It is very rare that a person goes from rags to riches overnight. But a long, drawn-out process is difficult for Sagittarians. Like Leos, they want to achieve wealth and success quickly and impressively. They must be aware, however, that this over-optimism can lead to unrealistic financial ventures and disappointing losses. Of course, no zodiac sign can bounce back as quickly as Sagittarius, but only needless heartache will be caused by this attitude. Sagittarians need to maintain their vision – never letting it go – but they must also work towards it in practical and efficient ways.

Career and Public Image

Sagittarians are big thinkers. They want it all: money, fame, glamour, prestige, public acclaim and a place in history. They often go after all these goals. Some attain them, some do not – much depends on each individual's personal horoscope. But if Sagittarians want to attain public and professional status they must understand that these things are not conferred to enhance one's ego but as rewards for the amount of service that one does for the whole of humanity. If and when they figure out ways to serve more, Sagittarians can rise to the top.

The ego of the Sagittarian is gigantic – and perhaps rightly so. They have much to be proud of. If they want public acclaim, however, they will have to learn to tone down the ego a bit, to become more humble and self-effacing, without falling into the trap of self-denial and self-abasement. They must also learn to master the details of life, which can some-times elude them.

At their jobs Sagittarians are hard workers who like to please their bosses and co-workers. They are dependable, trustworthy and enjoy a challenge. Sagittarians are friendly to work with and helpful to their colleagues. They usually contribute intelligent ideas or new methods that improve the work environment for everyone. Sagittarians always look for challenging positions and careers that develop their intellect, even if they have to work very hard in order to succeed. They also work well under the supervision of others, although by nature they would rather be the supervisors and increase their sphere of influence. Sagittarians excel at professions that allow them to be in contact with many different people and to travel to new and exciting locations.

Love and Relationships

Sagittarians love freedom for themselves and will readily grant it to their partners. They like their relationships to be fluid and ever-changing. Sagittarians tend to be fickle in love and to change their minds about their partners quite frequently.

Sagittarians feel threatened by a clearly defined, well-structured relationship, as they feel this limits their freedom. The Sagittarian tends to marry more than once in life.

Sagittarians in love are passionate, generous, open, benevolent and very active. They demonstrate their affections very openly. However, just like an Aries they tend to be egocentric in the way they relate to their partners. Sagittarians should develop the ability to see others' points of view, not just their own. They need to develop some objectivity and cool intellectual clarity in their relationships so that they can develop better two-way communication with their partners. Sagittarians tend to be overly idealistic about their partners and about love in general. A cool and rational attitude will help them to perceive reality more clearly and enable them to avoid disappointment.

Home and Domestic Life

Sagittarians tend to grant a lot of freedom to their family. They like big homes and many children and are one of the most fertile signs of the zodiac. However, when it comes to their children Sagittarians generally err on the side of allowing them too much freedom. Sometimes their children get the idea that there are no limits. However, allowing freedom in the home is basically a positive thing – so long as some measure of balance is maintained – for it enables all family members to develop as they should.

Horoscope for 2010

Major Trends

Last year was very much an educational year – a year for pursuing intellectual interests, for expanding the mind, taking courses and perhaps teaching others. Students, especially in the pre-university years, should have been very successful last year. Writers and teachers should also have had a very good year.

In the year ahead the focus will be more on home and family – discovering, and sometimes rediscovering, the pleasures of a happy family life and family harmony. This will be a bit of a shift for you because Sagittarians are travellers and not necessarily homebodies. But this year the cosmos is going to give you greater appreciation of these things. More on this later.

This year is also going to be more of a fun year, and 2011 will be even more fun than 2010. Your ruling planet, Jupiter, will move into your 5th house from June 6th to September 10th. Uranus will also be in that house from May 28th to August 14th. So not only are you going to have fun but you're going to have it in new, experimental and unconventional kinds of ways.

For singles these transits are showing love affairs – but non-serious ones. And perhaps quite a few of them.

Don't think that you will be stuck at home all year – your 9th house of foreign travel is very strong until June 7 and you will be doing much travelling in the year ahead. This power in the 9th house is also very good for university students or those applying to university or graduate schools. The aspects look very favourable for you.

Those of you involved in legal issues should also have a fortunate result, though there looks to be much conflict involved.

Your major interests in the year ahead will be finance, communication and intellectual interests, home and family, and children, fun and creativity (May 28th to September 10th), and religion, philosophy, higher education and foreign travel (from January 1 to June 7).

Your paths of greatest fulfilment in the year ahead will be finance, communication and intellectual interests (from January 1st to 18th), home and family (from January 18th to June 6th and from September 10th to December 31st), and children, fun and creativity (June 6th to September 10th).

Health

(Please note that this is an astrological perspective on health and not a medical one. In days gone by there was no difference; these perspectives were identical. But nowadays there can be quite a difference. For the medical perspective, please consult your doctor or health practitioner.)

Last year, as Saturn left Virgo, your overall health and vitality should have improved dramatically. This trend will continue in the year ahead, however for 3 months Saturn will move back into Virgo and into a stressful aspect with you. This will be a period (April 8th to July 22nd) for watching your energy more, resting and relaxing when tired, pacing yourself and organizing your time and your energy better. But if you've got past the last 2 years you certainly know how to do these things – you have had good training.

Your 6th house of health is not a House of Power this year, Sagittarius, and I read this as a positive health signal. You can sort of take good health for granted as there is nothing really wrong. You have no real need to focus overmuch on health.

You can make your good health even better by paying more attention to the following parts of the body:

- liver and thighs
- kidneys and hips
- heart
- Thighs and hips should be regularly massaged.

Since your health planet (Venus) is a fast-moving planet, and in the course of a given year she will move through all the signs and houses of your horoscope, your health needs will change month to month depending on where Venus is at any given time and the kind of aspects she is receiving. These short-term trends are dealt with in the monthly reports.

However, we should mention that Venus is going to spend an unusual amount of time in your 12th house of spirituality – from September 8th to November 8th and from December 1st to 31st. (A normal Venus transit is 1 month, here she will stay in your spiritual 12th house for 3 months.) This indicates

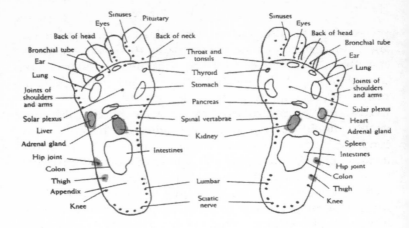

Reflexology

Try to massage the whole foot on a regular basis, but pay extra attention to the points highlighted on the chart. When you massage, be aware of 'sore spots', as these need special attention. It's also a good idea to massage the ankles and top side (as well as the soles) of the feet.

that you will be going more deeply into the spiritual dimensions of health. This is another huge, huge subject and we can only discuss the main points here. Basically you will benefit from spiritually-orientated therapies – therapies such as prayer and meditation, the laying-on of hands, reiki, energy medicine and the manipulation of subtle energies.

Intuition will be very important in the maintenance of health. You have to be open to the intuition of the moment and not the rule books or how-to books. Your intuition will guide you unerringly to the exact therapy or thing that you need.

Home and Family

Uranus has been in your 4th house for many years now, and on January 18th Jupiter, your ruling planet, will join it and stay there for most of the year.

Thus your 4th house of home and family is a major House of Power in the year ahead. Many of you have moved in recent years, perhaps a few times. Your home has been a work in progress – never finished. Always it is being upgraded and improved, much in the way that people update their software and computer systems. You have been restless on an emotional level and often this has expressed itself in moves and renovations. You are looking for your dream home – and every time you think you have found it, something new and better reveals itself. But in the year ahead you seem successful. You find your dream home, or dream domestic situation.

Moves, happy ones, are very likely in the year ahead. But these seem more stable. Once you have made it, this will be it. You are likely to stay where you are for many years.

Jupiter in your 4th house is not only showing moves, but big investments in the home. The purchase of expensive items for the home, renovations of the home. Quite often this indicates the purchase of additional homes or additional properties. The whole domestic sphere expands in the year ahead.

Your family circle expands through marriage or new births, and through meeting people who are 'like family' to you.

Family life, which has been erratic and unstable for many years, starts to become much happier in the year ahead. There have been many breakups in the family and family situation in past years. Things are settling down. The new pattern that has emerged seems much more pleasant than it has been. Family support looks excellent and you are also supportive of the family. There is good teamwork this year. Parents or parent figures are not only emotionally support-ive but also financially supportive.

A parent or parent figure is prospering greatly in the year ahead and thus seems more generous with you and with other family members. Another parent figure, who has been having a rough time for the past 2 years, seems to have an easier time this year. All of this is helping the family harmony.

As we have mentioned, you are a world traveller. So the simple pleasures of domestic harmony and family support have never been that important to you. This year you learn what wonderful things they are.

Jupiter, your ruling planet, will move into your 5th house from June 6th to September 10th. For women of appropriate age this shows greater fertility. For Sagittarians of any age it indicates more involvement with children or those who are like children to you.

Children seem more difficult to handle in the year ahead, especially from May 28th to August 14th. They are more rebellious and need more freedom. And you need to give them space, so long as it is not destructive.

A parent or parent figure is prospering, as we have mentioned, and also doing a lot of travelling in the year ahead and in general leading the good life. If there have been marital problems between your parents, this year there are opportunities for reconciliation.

Children of appropriate age are all over the place. Very nomadic. Living in different places for long periods of time. Very unsettled but they seem happy in this unsettledness. Your spouse or partner probably doesn't want to move in the year ahead; you're the one who wants to, and probably you will prevail. Siblings are having a status-quo domestic year. Grandchildren of appropriate age likewise.

Finance and Career

Finance has become very important in your horoscope since last year as Pluto moved into your money house. It will remain there for many years to come. This shows – and this is a long-term trend – that a cosmic detox is going on in your financial life. You are in a period where you learn how to prosper by cutting back. By cutting expenses, by reducing waste, by paying off debt and reducing interest expense. Now this is somewhat difficult for a Sagittarius. For you are very free spenders and tend not to be cost conscious. But you are in a period where these lessons will need to be learned. For you, now, it's not so much about earnings *per se*, but about reducing needless expense. Many things you are spending on are probably not necessary. But this will require hard analysis on your part.

Pluto, of course, rules debt generically. So this indicates that you can earn through creative financing, through attracting outside investors to your projects, and through the correct use of debt. The correct use of debt, a very interesting subject, will be another important lesson for you. Strive to avoid destructive debt, which will only make you poorer, and cultivate constructive debt, which will enhance your earnings many times over. Constructive debt is when you borrow to invest in assets that will go up in value and will bring you returns much larger than the cost of your debt. Destructive debt is when you borrow for things that will go down in value or actually disappear in value such as clothing or a holiday or a night at the theatre. Those things will soon vanish and you will be stuck paying the bill. Constructive debt will actually make you rich. A writer borrows to buy an expensive computer with all the peripherals. Yes, he or she borrows for this, but this computer will produce, over time, much more money than the computer has cost. This is constructive debt. Businessmen will borrow, sometimes on the public markets, to build a factory that will produce earnings far in excess of the amount they are borrowing. This is constructive debt.

Pluto also rules inheritance, estates, royalties, trust funds and insurance payments. Thus, money can come to you in these ways as well.

Many of you will be planning your estates now – and in future years. Taxes are also a big issue for you and are influencing many financial decisions and strategies.

Saturn, your money planet, does some strange gyrations in the coming year. It begins the year in the sign of Libra, your 11th house, and spends most of the year there. But for a few months, from April 8th to July 22nd, it retrogrades back into your 10th house. Then it goes forward again into the 11th house. So you might be backtracking in financial issues in the year ahead, perhaps reviewing some of the moves you've made in previous years.

Your money planet in the 11th house shows various things. It indicates that your social contacts, your friendships, are very important in your earnings. It often shows someone who has rich friends, people who are willing to provide financial opportunities and contacts. It indicates that you can earn money through being involved in professional or trade organizations. Good friends are like money in the bank and you will learn this lesson very well this year and in future years. Social wealth is also a form of wealth.

I see the year ahead as very prosperous, Sagittarius. Saturn in Libra for most of the year is in his most exalted position. Saturn expresses himself at his full potential in the sign of Libra. And this is a picture of your earning power – you are expressing your earning power at your highest level – not only that but you seem to be very comfortable in the way you are earning money, and this is very important, too. You will probably be spending more on art and beauty products and the like. You'll spend on them and you can also earn from them. Works of art are not only pleasant to have around, but if you are savvy, they make very good investments.

Saturn back into Virgo, where it has been for the past 2 years, will make you a much more careful shopper. You will be more conservative; you will get value for your pound. Also it shows that bosses, superiors and elders are financially supportive. It indicates that your good professional reputation is a huge factor in your earnings and you should guard it zealously. For those of you who invest, the health field should be explored during this period. With Jupiter in your 4th house for most of the year, the property field also seems very interesting and money can come from the fortunate purchase or sale of a home or from family support.

Now Sagittarians perhaps more than any of the signs have the best and most spiritual consciousness of wealth. It seems to be innate and inborn in the sign. But now that Pluto, your spiritual planet, is in your money house for many years, you will go even deeper into the spiritual dimensions of wealth. Yes, you know and understand a lot, but there is always more. Make sure you follow your intuition in the coming years.

In the year ahead there are two eclipses in your money house, which indicates major financial change – but change that is good in the end. These alterations are disruptive (perhaps uncomfortable) while they're happening but they're ones you've long needed to make and now the cosmos is forcing you to make them.

Love and Social Life

Your 7th house of love, marriage, and social activities is not a House of Power this year, Sagittarius. As our steady readers know, this tends towards the status quo: Marrieds will tend to stay married and singles will tend to stay single. The cosmos isn't pushing you one way or the other. You pretty much have the freedom to shape your love and social life as you will. The problem is not with freedom but with your lack of interest.

However there are many opportunities for love affairs in the year ahead, as we have mentioned earlier. These opportunities occur spontaneously, out of the blue, in shocking and surprising ways. These opportunities will come to you whether you are married or single. For singles this is an exciting time (May 28th to September 10th). For marrieds this will test their relationship, test their love and commitment to their partner. One never knows the depth of one's love or commitment to another until one is sorely tempted. And these temptations will come your way in the year ahead. This doesn't mean that you must succumb to them, but they will illumine your heart and who you are.

Those of you who are in their second marriage will also have the kind of testing that we mentioned previously. Also the relationship will be tested in other ways, as there seems to be a power struggle going on in the marriage. Best to avoid this if possible, or at least minimize it.

Those of you who are working towards their second marriage will have very nice opportunities from January 1st to June 7th. And I wouldn't be surprised if it happens in a foreign land, or in a religious or educational setting. Those working towards their third marriage need patience; a marriage now is not advisable. Those in their third marriage will see it tested in other ways. If you are in your third marriage it will take some work on your part to make things less cold and mechanical – to inject some warmth and passion back into the relationship.

Mercury, your love planet, is a fast-moving planet. During the course of the year he will move through all the signs and houses of your horoscope. Thus, events in your love life – the circumstances of love, the way that it comes to you – tend to change month to month depending on where Mercury is at any given time and the aspects that he is receiving. We will discuss these short-term trends – and there will be many of them – in the monthly reports.

We should mention that your love planet will be retrograde for much longer and more frequently in 2010 than usual. Generally Mercury retrogrades three times in a given year. This year it will be four times. This indicates that there are more 'glitches' and delays in love than usual. More tendencies to miscommunication and misunderstanding. Keep in mind that Venus, the generic ruler of love, also goes retrograde in the year ahead (one of her rare retrogrades). This reinforces what we are saying. Make efforts – special efforts – to communicate properly with your spouse, partner or current love. Don't automatically assume that your beloved got your message, or that you got your beloved's message. Confirm, confirm, confirm.

These many retrogrades show that this is a year for reviewing your love life, your marriage and your general social situation. Look for places where improvements can be made. Then when the love planets are moving forward – or perhaps next year – you can set about implementing your decisions.

Self-improvement

For the past 2 to 2½ years Saturn has been in your 10th house of career. Probably this was a difficult career period. You will have been forced to take on many new responsibilities, probably had demanding kinds of bosses, and needed to earn your success through hard work and sheer merit. Careerwise the cosmos was not giving you any breaks. To the degree that you earned your success, that was the degree to which you succeeded. Most of these lessons are over this year, but you will have a little more of this from April 8th to July 22nd as Saturn retrogrades back into your 10th house. As you probably have learned by now, do not shirk responsibility, do not avoid it, rather embrace it. Pick up the load, lift up the burden, build your muscles. It is precisely these kinds of unpleasant pressures that will shape you as a person and build your career.

Saturn will spend most of the year ahead in your 11th house of friends. This indicates that your friendships will be getting tested. Many of them will probably not survive the next 2 years. Only the really good ones, the sound ones, will survive. Your circle of friends will probably shrink in the next 2 years, but what remains will be good. The main lesson of this transit is learning the art of forgiveness. Friends will probably disappoint you. People that you thought were friends were not as you thought them to be. Probably there will be hurts, resentments and grudges. These need to be worked on spiritually and removed. We are not responsible for what people do to us, we are only responsible for how we deal with these issues. We are responsible for our own energy. And this is an important lesson. That people behave in ways that we would rather they didn't, is not the issue. Their actions will generate their own karma. But if you allow their actions to embitter you, you allow them to generate negative momentum in your emotional body and then it is your problem. Forgiveness does not whitewash the actions. We forgive the people, but not the actions. The actions are what they are. Yes, they were wrong and we don't whitewash. But we forgive the people because we understand the pressures and motivations that made them act as they did. This is a great distinction. If you can learn forgiveness – true forgiveness, from your heart and not just your mouth – you will have a much wider and better circle of friends than ever before.

Saturn is not only testing friendships but is also testing your own attitudes about friendship. Often we are disappointed by friends because we have not been a true friend ourselves. So this is a time for examining your ideas and ideals of friendship – what it really means to be a friend. In astrology we have a wonderful definition that I have never seen topped. In astrology the 11th house of friends is also the house of fondest hopes and wishes. It is not an accident that the 11th house rules both of these areas of life. It is a message that a true friend is someone who wishes for you your own fondest hopes and wishes and is ready and willing to make them come true. Anything less than that falls short of the ideal of friendship and needs work. Here you have a good measurement of how to judge your friendships – and how you are as a friend.

Month-by-month Forecasts

January

> Best Days Overall: 2, 3, 11, 12, 21, 22, 30
> Most Stressful Days Overall: 4, 5, 18, 19, 25, 26
> Best Days for Love: 4, 5, 13, 14, 15, 23, 24, 25, 26
> Best Days for Money: 6, 7, 13, 14, 15, 16, 17, 18, 25, 27
> Best Days for Career: 4, 5, 13, 14, 23, 24

Your year begins in the midst of a yearly financial peak. Money is the main headline of the month ahead. Some 50 per cent of the planets are either in your money house or moving through there this month – a huge percentage. This shows great personal focus, great drive, a great 'fire in the belly' to achieve earnings goals. There is no difficulty you can't surmount, no mountain you can't climb, in pursuit of your goals. This is 90 per cent of success.

Still, finances are complicated this month. Saturn, your financial planet, will start to retrograde on the 13th. This will not stop your gangbuster earnings, only slow things down a bit. You will need to be more perfect – especially in the little details – in all your financial transactions. So-called shortcuts might not be shortcuts at all – in fact, they can delay you even further. Avoid them. Better to be the tortoise going step by step, slowly and methodically, than the hare. The hare will only have to retrace his steps later on. (Being the tortoise is not your style, but this is one of the spiritual lessons of the month.)

There is a solar eclipse on the 15th that occurs in your money house as well. (There will be another one in this house later in the year – June 6th.) This indicates a need to change your financial thinking and strategy. Perhaps an unexpected expense happens, or a client you thought you could rely on, can't be relied on. Events happen to force changes in your strategy and approach.

But these new changes require more thought. The eclipse coincides (pretty much) with Saturn's retrograde. So finances need to be reviewed. Different financial scenarios need to be worked out. Numbers have to be crunched. Doubts need to be resolved. All of this takes time.

This eclipse, overall, is benign to you. It affects students – at university or graduate level – and their educational plans. Many will change area of study or educational establishment they attend. Their study regime can also get disrupted. The lecturer whose module you wanted to take is not there and there is someone else doing the seminars.

Whatever your religion – even if your religion is secular and materialistic – there are crises of faith now. Your beliefs get tested. And this is a good thing.

On the 18th Jupiter, your ruler, moves into your 4th house. So home and family – emotional and psychological issues – become important to you for the year ahead. There have been many family upheavals in recent years – perhaps even actual breakups of the family. Your personal attention is now needed.

February

    Best Days Overall: 7, 8, 17, 18, 26, 27
    Most Stressful Days Overall: 1, 15, 16, 22, 23, 28
    Best Days for Love: 1, 2, 3, 11, 12, 14, 15, 22, 23, 24, 25
    Best Days for Money: 2, 4, 5, 9, 10, 11, 12, 14, 15, 22, 24
    Best Days for Career: 1, 11, 12, 22, 23, 28

You began your year with 70 per cent (and sometimes 80 per cent) of the planets below the horizon – in the lower half of your horoscope. On the 18th of last month Jupiter, your ruler, entered your 4th house. On the 18th of this month the Sun will enter this house. Your 10th house of career, by contrast, is empty – only the Moon will visit there on the 1st and 28th. A very clear message from your horoscope: You are in the 'night-time' of your year. Focus on the family – be there for them – mend family fences. Find, and function from, your point of emotional harmony. Feeling right is more important than 'doing right' – if you feel right, you will do right.

Career is a dynamic, lifelong project. It has its phases – active and passive – its own rhythmic breath – just as anything in the universe has. You are now in a more passive phase. This doesn't mean that you have given your career up – no, you are just getting a good night's sleep. The pause that refreshes and renews. Yes, there are many things that you would like to do in life – but pursue them by the ways of the night – by dreaming about them, visualizing them, setting goals and, most importantly, entering into the 'feeling' of their achievement. This is very powerful. When day breaks in your year, these things will manifest naturally and easily.

Love is better than last month. Last month your love planet was retrograde until the 15th. This month the love planet is moving forward all month. Until the 10th love opportunities happen as you pursue your normal financial goals – and with people involved in your finances. Love is practical, down to earth. The basics are important. You are turned on by material gifts and material support. You gravitate to traditional types of people. Love is slow and cautious. But after the 10th, this changes. You like the unconventional in love – unconventional people and unconventional relationships. You like people who think 'outside the box'. Marrieds can enhance their relationships by doing unconventional kinds of things together as a couple. Same old, same old is just boring. The romantic spark has to be rekindled. Singles want friendship with their beloved, not just romance. After the 10th romantic opportunities happen in educational settings – in schools, at lectures or seminars – also in the neighbourhood. Love is close to home.

A happy travel opportunity comes on the 27th and 28th. Students hear good news. Job-seekers have great opportunities from the 15th to the 17th. There is a romantic meeting with an old flame or through a family connection on the 27th and 28th.

Health needs watching these days, but especially after the 18th. Rest and relax more, pace yourself, rest when tired. Respect the messages that your body is giving you. Enhance health in the ways mentioned in the yearly report, but also pay more attention to your heart (all month), your calves and ankles (until the 11th) and to your feet (from the 11th onwards). Foot, ankle and calf massage is powerful this period.

March

Best Days Overall: 6, 7, 16, 17, 25, 26
Most Stressful Days Overall: 1, 14, 15, 21, 22, 27, 28
Best Days for Love: 4, 5, 6, 14, 15, 16, 17, 21, 22, 25, 26
Best Days for Money: 2, 4, 5, 8, 9, 10, 11, 14, 15, 21, 23, 24, 29, 31
Best Days for Career: 1, 4, 14, 15, 25, 26, 27, 28

Your 4th house of home and family is even stronger than last month. Most of the planets are below the horizon (70 to 80 per cent). Your 10th house of career, by contrast, is empty – only the Moon visits there on the 1st, 27th and 28th. Thus the focus is on the home, family and your emotional life. Review our discussion of this last month. This month your career planet, Mercury, also enters your 4th house (from the 2nd to the 17th) – this shows that it is your actual spiritual mission – your *Dharma* – to be there for the family and to deal with emotional issues. It is the most important thing these days.

Great psychological progress will be made now. You will get insights into your moods and feelings. You will see why you feel as you do. For many (especially those on the path) there will be greater dominion over their emotional nature – one of the great dominions one can aspire to.

The main challenge these days is dealing with the heightened sensitivity of other people – family, your beloved and people in general. We have a lot of water in your horoscope this month (40–50 per cent) and a lot of power in the sign of Pisces. Little things – tone of voice, facial expression, a rolling of eyes, body language and even stray dark thoughts (not expressed) can have a huge impact on others. Any little thing that changes the energy has an impact on others and they respond to it. You need a lot of control over your mind and feelings during this period.

This condition is in effect all month, but especially until the 20th. After that, as the Sun moves into Aries, the sensitivities are reduced. On the 20th, you enter a yearly personal pleasure peak – a party period, a time to explore all the various pleasures of life. And not just physical, sensual pleasures, but the pleasures of creativity, of being like a child, carefree and fancy free – the pleasures of the arts and sport and things of that nature.

Sagittarius loves travel, and these pleasures will open up as well. (I have noticed that regardless of their financial situation, Sagittarians manage to travel everywhere – one way or another. Income has little to do with it.)

Health improves after the 20th, but still needs watching. Pay attention to your heart (all month) – work to reduce stress and needless worry. Until the 7th, pay attention to your feet. After the 7th pay more attention to your head, face and skull. Regular scalp and face massage will do wonders after the 7th – also vigorous physical exercise is good.

Finances are still under review. Saturn, your financial planet, is still retrograde. Earnings are happening, but more slowly. Not to worry, though, many things – positive things – are going on behind the scenes.

Love is status quo this month. On the 7th–9th there is a happy romantic meeting or experience. For marrieds there is more romance in the marriage and perhaps some happy social invitations. After the 17th singles are more interested in flings than in serious kinds of romance.

April

Best Days Overall: 3, 4, 13, 14, 22, 23, 30
Most Stressful Days Overall: 10, 11, 17, 18, 24, 25
Best Days for Love: 5, 15, 16, 17, 18, 24, 25
Best Days for Money: 1, 5, 6, 7, 10, 11, 16, 19, 20, 25, 28, 29
Best Days for Career: 5, 15, 16, 24, 25

Saturn, still retrograde, moves back into Virgo on the 3rd. Health needs more watching now – three long-term planets are now stressing you out. Happily the short-term planets are either leaving you alone or making harmonious aspects. Pay more attention to your heart (all month), your kidneys and hips (all month), your neck, throat and jaw (until the 25th – neck massage will be powerful) and your lungs, arms and shoulders (after the 18th).

This move by Saturn also increases the demands of your career. Home and family are still dominant now, but you will have to juggle more between the two – the family and your career. Bosses can be more demanding these days. Nit-picky. Never satisfied. But this can be used to your advantage.

Don't complain (though the temptations are great). Give the boss more than he or she asks for – go the extra mile. If the deadline is the 10th, submit your work on the 5th. If they ask for two hours' overtime, offer three. If you are being paid X amount an hour – give $2X$ an hour worth of service. This invokes a spiritual law that is unstoppable and will lead to greater career success in the future. Doing this will not be easy – but with creativity you can.

With health more delicate now you need to drop the frivolous from your life and focus on the important things. This will liberate more time and energy for the family and your career.

You are in a party period until the 20th – but, given your situation, keep your entertainments wholesome – non-draining. There are pleasures that sap your energy and pleasures that enhance it – focus on the latter.

The good news this month is that health is important to you – high on your list of priorities. You are focused here – and this focus will probably avert many potential problems.

Last month the planetary power shifted to the West – the social sector of your horoscope. This is a time for cultivating your social skills – your likeability and your ability to gain the co-operation of others. Personal initiative, though a wonderful trait, will not lead to success these days. Your good comes through the good graces of others.

Love is playful and non-serious until the 2nd. After that, love is about service – doing for your beloved. Love is practical and down to earth. The roses and good times are not that important. Service endures. Moonlit walks on the beach, though pleasant, are ephemeral. Love opportunities happen at work or as you pursue your health goals. Co-workers and people involved with your health, health professionals in general, are alluring you. Your love planet goes retrograde on the 18th – a pretty regular occurrence which you have been through many times. A time to review your relationship (or lack of one) and social life in general. A time to analyse and look for ways to improve things.

Finances are good this month – especially after the 19th. But they are still under review. Keep in mind our discussion of this in the January report.

May

Best Days Overall: 1, 10, 11, 19, 20, 27, 28
Most Stressful Days Overall: 7, 8, 9, 15, 21, 22
Best Days for Love: 2, 5, 6, 12, 14, 15, 16, 21, 25, 26, 30
Best Days for Money: 2, 3, 4, 8, 9, 14, 18, 22, 25, 26, 30, 31
Best Days for Career: 2, 12, 21, 22, 30

A very exciting month – a month of many dynamic personal changes. Your ruler makes a very rare conjunction with Uranus – this only happens once every 13–15 years. This indicates sudden moves – perhaps many of them – a nomadic, vagabond type of existence. You are visiting many different places – not homeless but at home everywhere. On a certain level this is Sagittarius heaven.

This conjunction also shows sudden financial good – on a large scale. Seems to me that you are getting a new car or new communication equipment – or both. Expensive items.

This is a period (and it will continue for the next few months) where you are testing the limits of your body. Basically a good thing – this is how we learn about ourselves. Yoga or tai chi would be excellent now as these are safe and constructive ways to test your limits. But some of you will insist on being 'daredevils' anyway.

No one loves personal freedom more than Sagittarius, but right now this passion for personal freedom is strong even by your standards – some would say 'it's ridiculous' – and I'm sure you'll hear this from other people.

On the 21st the planetary power makes a major shift from the lower half of your horoscope to the upper half – day is breaking in your year and it is time to focus on your career and outer goals. Another major change.

Uranus makes a major move into your 5th house on the 28th – this only happens once every 88 or so years. For parents it indicates some problems handling children – they are more rebellious these days (but then again, so are you). Give them as much space as possible so long as it isn't destructive. Children (or those who are like children to you) are also being experimental with their bodies – testing their limits. Yoga might be good for them as well.

On the 21st you begin a yearly social peak. Love is active and happy. Singles are probably best advised not to marry these days – your need for personal freedom doesn't make for stable relationships – but you will meet 'marriageable' types of people now. Probably you will be attending more weddings as well. Those who are involved romantically with Sagittarians need to give them a lot of space. The relationship will go better if you do different and unique kinds of things as a couple.

Health needs more watching after the 21st. Pay more attention to your heart, kidneys, hips, lungs, arms and shoulders (all month) and to your stomach and breasts after the 20th.

Bosses and superiors are still stern and demanding; this is another reason why you want to 'break out' and explore personal freedom.

Your financial life is good, but still under review. Earnings are better before the 21st than afterwards. Afterwards you just need to work harder for them.

June

Best Days Overall: 6, 7, 15, 16, 24, 25
Most Stressful Days Overall: 4, 5, 11, 12, 17, 18
Best Days for Love: 4, 5, 10, 11, 12, 13, 14, 19, 20, 24, 25
Best Days for Money: 5, 6, 10, 15, 18, 24, 26, 27
Best Days for Career: 10, 11, 17, 18, 19, 20

You are still in the midst of a yearly social peak until the 21st. There are many love – and even marriage – opportunities for singles. But you don't seem serious. You want freedom and good times. Jupiter, your ruler (still travelling with

Uranus, by the way) moves into your 5th house of fun on the 6th. Commitment doesn't seem likely. Like last month these feelings are being caused by demanding bosses and career responsibilities. You need to cut loose in other ways. This is a month for serial kinds of love affairs – flings.

Continue to mind your health more until the 21st. Rest and relax where possible. Maintain high energy levels. Enhance your health in the ways described last month. Diet is more of an issue until the 14th. Your stomach seems more sensitive.

Finances are stressful until the 21st. But these are short-term stresses. The overall trends are good. Your financial planet started moving forward on the 30th of last month – so your financial judgement is good and you have a new sense of clarity. Your professional reputation – your good name – is ultra-important financially, so guard it well. Elders, bosses and parents might be tough on you – demanding – but they are supporting your financial goals. There is luck in speculations, too. Your personal creativity seems marketable.

A lunar eclipse occurs in your money house – a repeat (though not exact) of the solar eclipse of January 15th. This eclipse, like the last one, shows financial changes, but this one is easier in the sense that you are clearer and more confident about what to do. Your financial planet was retrograde during the last eclipse; now it is moving forward. This eclipse affects the finances of your spouse, partner or current love as well. They, too, are making dramatic financial changes. This eclipse makes you more aware of your own mortality. There are encounters with death, perhaps some near-death experiences (not actual death) – all designed to help you deal with this on a psychological level. Perhaps surgery will be recommended to you. Always get a second opinion. This eclipse has an impact on Pluto, your spiritual planet. This indicates changes in your spiritual regime and practice. Generally this comes from interior revelation, which always produces change. You've reached one level and now need to work in another way to go to the next level. This eclipse seems stronger on you personally than the last one – take a reduced schedule.

There are some health scares from the 9th to the 11th, but these will just be 'only scares'. Probably there will be dramas in the lives of friends, the testing of friendships as well. There are some disturbances at work or upheavals in the workplace. Employers will experience instability with their staff.

Avoid foreign travel from the 21st to the 23rd.

July

> Best Days Overall: 4, 5, 13, 21, 22, 31
> Most Stressful Days Overall: 1, 2, 8, 9, 15, 28, 29, 30
> Best Days for Love: 1, 2, 5, 8, 9, 12, 14, 21, 22, 23, 24
> Best Days for Money: 3, 7, 12, 16, 21, 23, 24, 25, 26, 31
> Best Days for Career: 1, 2, 12, 14, 15, 21, 22

Health is much improved this month. And when Saturn moves into Libra on the 21st – away from his stressful aspect to you – health and energy will improve even further. Also helping matters is your health planet's elevation in your horoscope after the 10th. This shows that health is an important priority – something you aspire to – and thus you give it more attention. You can enhance your health even further by paying more attention to your kidneys and hips (regular hip massage is good), your heart (reduce stress and worry) until the 21st, and the small intestine from the 10th onwards. Diet becomes more of an issue after the 10th as well.

Jupiter and Uranus are still travelling together, still bringing much excitement and change into your life. Love affairs happen suddenly and out of the blue – though these things are not serious or long term – very unstable. You are having fun in unconventional kinds of ways. There is much travel – both domestic and foreign this month – Sagittarius heaven.

A solar eclipse on the 11th adds more spice to the picture. Basically this eclipse is benign to you – last month's eclipse was stronger – but still take it easy during this period. Since your travel planet is eclipsed, perhaps you should schedule your foreign travels for either side of this period.

This eclipse affects students (again). It brings more changes in their educational plans and schools.

There are shakeups in your church, synagogue or ashram. Religious beliefs and attitudes get tested. Faith itself (perhaps you didn't have as much as you thought) gets tested. This eclipse will reveal to you what you really believe in your heart – not what you are professing with your mouth. This is useful, since we can then take steps to correct things.

This eclipse occurs in your 8th house, and thus you confront death in various ways – generally in a psychological kind of way – but borderline people (those hovering between life and death) can make the transition around this time. Your spouse or partner (who is prospering this month) is forced to make dramatic and long-term financial changes. Those who are in the process of planning their estates make changes to their will or to these plans. (This was true in last month's eclipse as well.)

Children of appropriate age are having their marriage or love relationship tested these days. There are dramatic experiences in their lives from the 28th to the 31st.

A love affair seems in trouble from the 28th to the 31st.

Finances are improving this month. Mars travels with Saturn (your financial planet) towards the end of the month. This brings luck in speculations and opportunities to earn money in happy ways. Creative projects are marketable now.

August

Best Days Overall: 1, 9, 10, 17, 18, 27, 28
Most Stressful Days Overall: 5, 6, 11, 12, 25, 26
Best Days for Love: 2, 3, 4, 5, 6, 11, 12, 13, 20, 21, 22, 23, 30, 31
Best Days for Money: 4, 9, 13, 17, 19, 20, 21, 22, 27
Best Days for Career: 2, 11, 12, 20, 21, 30, 31

Some 60–70 per cent of the planets are above the horizon this month. Your 10th house is powerful all month (it was strong last month as well) while your 4th house of home and family only gets strong after the 15th. A clear message from the cosmos: focus on your career – the activities of the day – and let family and emotional issues go for a while. When you 'do right' – succeed, achieve your goals – you will 'feel' right.

Great career progress was made last month, and the trend continues. On the 23rd you enter a yearly career peak – you are in the midday of your year – operating at maximum power and authority.

You can enhance your career in various ways. Be ready to take any courses that relate to your career – be ready to further your education. Also be ready to travel at a moment's notice. Be a good mentor to those beneath you, and a good student to those above you. Social skills are unusually important to your career as well. Your likeability is as much, if not more, an asset as your competence. Be ready to attend or host the right kind of parties and meet the right kind of people.

There is some uncertainty in your career after the 20th as Mercury, your career planet, starts to retrograde. This won't stop your career progress, but only slow things down a little. Be extra careful – take extra precautions – when communicating to superiors or those beneath you. Take pains not to be misunderstood. You might want to review your career after the 20th to see where improvements or adjustments can be made. Important career decisions should be studied more – delay them until next month when Mercury starts to move forward again.

Health again needs more watching after the 23rd. You had a brief holiday last month, but now you must keep watch again. Keep energy levels high. Focus on the really important things in your life and let lesser things go. Take positive and constructive action and refuse to worry or fret. This will save much energy (and improve your blood pressure and heart health as well). Pay more attention to your heart, kidneys, hips (all month) and small intestine (until the 7th). Social disharmony tends to be a root cause for health problems in general. After the 7th it is even more pronounced. If health problems should arise, work to bring your social life – relations with friends – into harmony and chances are that the health problem will just dissolve of its own weight.

Eclipse points are getting re-stimulated this month – often, these re-stimulations can be as powerful as the actual eclipse. Venus, your health planet, re-stimulates eclipse points from the 11th to the 14th and from the 25th to the 28th – this can bring some health scares, job changes, disturbances at the workplace and the testing of friendships. Saturn re-stimulates an eclipse point from the 26th to the 31st – bringing financial changes and surprises. Mars re-stimulates eclipse points from the 4th to the 9th and from the 25th to the 28th. Avoid risk-taking activities then – drive more carefully. A love affair will get tested. Children will have dramatic kinds of experiences. A child or child figure redefines his or her personality and image.

September

Best Days Overall: 5, 6, 13, 14, 15, 23, 24, 25
Most Stressful Days Overall: 1, 2, 7, 8, 21, 22, 28, 29
Best Days for Love: 1, 2, 7, 11, 16, 21, 27, 28, 29
Best Days for Money: 1, 5, 9, 12, 16, 17, 18, 22, 28
Best Days for Career: 7, 8, 16, 27

Your financial planet, Saturn, camps out on an eclipse point all month (with varying degrees of exactitude). A big reorganization of your financial life is happening. This will ultimately be good – you long needed to do this, and now you are forced into it by events. Investments get re-shuffled. Banks, brokers and financial planners get changed. Perhaps your bank or broker creates new and unpleasant rules, and this forces change. People you thought were reliable in your finances might not be as reliable as you thought, so that you have to change plans or strategies. Strategies that may have worked for you in the past, suddenly are not working. Happily Saturn is moving forward and your financial judgement is sound and your decision-making should be good.

You are still in the midst of a yearly career peak until the 23rd. On the 12th Mercury, your career planet, starts to move forward. If you have done your review, you will be ready to make the important career decisions that need to be made. It might seem to you that you've been moving backwards in your career, but this was just an illusion. Sometimes you have to go backwards in order to go forwards – even in backward motion there are important developments behind the scenes.

The good news about your career is that bosses are less demanding of you. They have eased up on you.

Health still needs watching this month. Rest and relax more. Pace yourself. Don't allow yourself to get overtired. Pay more attention to your heart, kidneys and hips (all month) and to your colon, bladder and sexual organs (after the 8th). Detox regimes are powerful after the 8th. Perhaps surgery is recommended as a solution after the 8th, but detox will often do as much good. Always get second opinions on these things. Spiritual healing and spiritual healers are powerful after the 8th as well.

Avoid speculations on the 1st and from the 27th to the 29th. Drive more carefully and defensively on the 1st.

Jupiter, your ruler, retrogrades back into your 4th house of home and family on the 10th. (Uranus retrograded back into this house last month on the 15th.) So career is important, but so is home and family. You are doing a balancing act between the two – this tends to be stressful. Another reason to be more careful healthwise.

Jupiter and Uranus continue to travel together. You are still nomadic, restless and vagabondish. A wanderer – and happy to be a wanderer. Your religion is personal freedom these days, and this creates problems in love – in current relationships. As mentioned earlier, those involved with Sagittarians romantically need to give them a lot of space.

Friendships – non-committed kinds of relationships – go much better and more easily than the committed ones. You don't seem in the mood for commitment – and you haven't been for a long time.

October

Best Days Overall: 3, 4, 11, 12, 21, 22, 30, 31
Most Stressful Days Overall: 5, 6, 18, 19, 25, 26, 27
Best Days for Love: 1, 7, 9, 17, 18, 19, 25, 26, 27, 28
Best Days for Money: 2, 7, 10, 13, 14, 16, 19, 26, 29
Best Days for Career: 5, 6, 7, 17, 28

Pluto, your spiritual planet, was eclipsed on June 26th. Since that time it has been more or less camping out on this eclipse point. So there is much change, reorganization and refining going on in your spiritual life (also with charitable or altruistic organizations you are involved with). Pluto was retrograde until the 14th of last month. So for many months there has been a need to subject dreams, hunches and intuitive messages to scrutiny. Not that your intuition couldn't be trusted, but your interpretation could have been amiss. The fault is never with the spirit, which is perfect, but with us. Happily this is over with. And now that you are entering one of the most spiritual periods of your year (after the 22nd), it is comforting to know that your intuition is on form and that you are understanding what is given you.

Pluto on the eclipse point also brought many changes in the health regime of your spouse, partner or current love – perhaps job changes as well. At least now, with Pluto moving forward, there is more clarity in these areas.

You are in a month for spiritual breakthroughs of all sorts – for encounters with supernatural beings – angels and masters – for great inner progress. Some 50 per cent of the planets – a huge percentage – will either be in or moving through your 12th house this month. It would only be normal to crave more seclusion. Sleep is often more interesting than being awake – there is more going on. Dreams happen in Technicolor – very vivid. Some are so vivid that they can affect the physical body – for good or ill. (Bad dreams can change the sugar levels and other chemical balances of the body. Good dreams can actually cure diseases.)

This is a month (from the 23rd onwards) for more prayer, meditation, spiritual retreats, religious-type pilgrimages, spiritual seminars and the like. A time to take a bit of a holiday – to the degree that you are able – from everyday, worldly concerns.

There is love in your life, but – as we have seen for many months now – you are in the mood for personal freedom. You don't mind free, uncommitted flings – but the ones that restrict freedom are irksome. This doesn't bode well for marriage or serious relationships. By definition, these things are a restriction – a limitation – on personal freedom. However, if you find someone who thinks like you, serious love can happen.

From the 3rd to the 21st love opportunities come through friends and through your involvement with groups and organizations. You sort of want friendship with your beloved as well as romance. After the 21st love opportunities happen in spiritual settings – the prayer meeting, the yoga retreat, the charity ball – things of that nature. Love is very idealistic from the 21st onwards. A non-serious love opportunity (a fling, really) comes to you after the 23rd. He or she pursues you.

Finances are good. There is a nice windfall on the 1st–2nd. There is luck in speculations during this period. A foreigner or foreign investment is profitable.

November

Best Days Overall: 7, 8, 17, 18, 26, 27
Most Stressful Days Overall: 1, 2, 14, 15, 16, 22, 23, 28, 29
Best Days for Love: 5, 6, 13, 17, 22, 23, 27, 28
Best Days for Money: 3, 4, 6, 10, 11, 12, 13, 15, 16, 22, 25
Best Days for Career: 1, 2, 6, 17, 27, 28, 29

Your spiritual period and inner growth continue this month
– until the 22nd. Many of you are leading a supernatural
(rather than a natural) life. The supernatural becomes the
natural for you. This is a good period now (last month, too)
to review your past year in a sober and honest way, evaluate
your performance – what has been achieved, what is left to
be done – correct mistakes, forgive those who need to be
forgiven, and set new goals for the coming year. For, in
astrology, we consider your birthday to be your personal
new year; you should have the same approach to your birthday as you have to the actual New Year.

Finances are good. Saturn, your financial planet, is
moving forward – progress is being made – and receiving
good aspects. Earnings come in the ways mentioned in the
yearly report – through friends, involvement in organizations and groups, and your technological savvy and expertise. Investments in technology – upgrades of your
technology – in the latest software and the like are good
investments. Online kinds of businesses are good as well.

On the 22nd, as the Sun crosses your Ascendant, you
enter another yearly personal pleasure peak. This peak is
different from the previous one in that the focus is mostly on
the body – the physical pleasures of the body. A time for
leading the good life – and no one needs to teach Sagittarius
how to do this. A month where you need to watch your
weight more. This period also brings foreign travel – one of
your great loves. You are not only a 'jet-set' person right
now, but also a mentor to others – a mentor to those
beneath you in knowledge and a disciple to those above you.

You are now entering one of the most independent periods of your year – a time to have life on your terms – to
create the conditions of your own happiness. Others are
always important, and we never run roughshod over them –
but your happiness is in your own hands. If others don't go
along with you (highly unlikely now), you can go your own
way.

Love, both serious and not, pursues you this month. You
have your pick as to what you want – perhaps you will have

a little of both. Your spouse, partner or current love goes out of his or her way to please you.

Health is good this month, but overall still needs watching. With Mars in your own sign, you might want to bite off more than you can chew. Still, you are athletic (more so than usual) and charismatic. There is much sex appeal to your image – more than usual (and this applies to all, whatever your age or stage in life). Haste, impetuousness and temper need to be watched – these can lead to accidents or fights.

Last month your health planet went retrograde on the 8th. Venus is still retrograde until the 18th of this month – so avoid making major changes to your health regime until after the 18th.

Job-seekers need to do more homework before accepting opportunities. Things are not what they seem.

December

Best Days Overall: 5, 6, 14, 15, 16, 23, 24
Most Stressful Days Overall: 12, 13, 19, 20, 26, 27
Best Days for Love: 2, 7, 12, 16, 19, 20, 22, 25, 31
Best Days for Money: 1, 4, 7, 8, 10, 13, 20, 23, 28, 31
Best Days for Career: 7, 16, 25, 26, 27

You are still in the midst of a yearly personal pleasure peak. Health and energy are basically good, but if you overdo the good life there is a price to be paid later on. Health can be enhanced even further by paying more attention to your heart, kidneys, hips, colon, bladder and sexual organs. Safe sex is particularly important to your health this month. Avoid sexual excess. Listen to your body. Spiritual healing is powerful this month as well. You will go more deeply into your knowledge of this subject and will respond well to these kinds of therapies – meditation, prayer, invocations of healing spirits and beings, the laying-on of hands and things of this nature. Probably you will be involved in spiritual healing for others as well.

Love affairs, both serious and non-serious, meet with some temporary bumps in the road. Your love planet camps out – makes a station – on Pluto from the 5th to the 16th. This can cause a temporary separation or breakup in a current relationship. Love seems to go backwards. Things are disclosed that were hidden – and they need to be digested. If the relationship is basically sound, it will survive – but give it time. Mercury will be retrograde until the 30th. Avoid major love decisions until then. Your lover or partner is still devoted to you and seems to want you.

Last month the planetary power shifted from the upper half to the lower half of your horoscope. Night has fallen in your year. Day is over – a new phase begins. Time to let go of your outer goals and work on the family and your emotional well-being. Now it's important to feel right and to be in inner harmony. Lack of harmony, according to the sages, is the number one reason why believers suffer delays in the answer to prayer. If there was enough inner harmony, they say, prayers are answered instantly. Review our discussion of this in the January report.

On the 21st you enter a yearly financial peak. Finances have been basically good this year, and now they will get even better. The main challenge now is over-spending – either on travel or fun. The good news is that you have the money to spend.

A lunar eclipse on the 21st further tests a current relationship or marriage – avoid making major decisions one way or the other until the 30th. Your spouse, partner or current love is forced to make important financial changes. Those of you involved in estate planning are making important changes here. Those who are inheriting money see forward movement in the courts or with administrators. Many of you will be reminded of your mortality – a love message from above – to get more serious about life and to do what you came here to do.

Capricorn

♑

THE GOAT
Birthdays from
21st December to
19th January

Personality Profile

CAPRICORN AT A GLANCE

Element – Earth

Ruling Planet – Saturn
   Career Planet – Venus
   Love Planet – Moon
   Money Planet – Uranus
   Planet of Communications – Neptune
   Planet of Health and Work – Mercury
   Planet of Home and Family Life – Mars
   Planet of Spirituality – Jupiter

Colours – black, indigo

Colours that promote love, romance and social
   harmony – puce, silver

Colour that promotes earning power –
   ultramarine blue

Gem – black onyx

Metal – lead

Scents – magnolia, pine, sweet pea, wintergreen

Quality – cardinal (= activity)

Qualities most needed for balance – warmth, spontaneity, a sense of fun

Strongest virtues – sense of duty, organization, perseverance, patience, ability to take the long-term view

Deepest needs – to manage, take charge and administrate

Characteristics to avoid – pessimism, depression, undue materialism and undue conservatism

Signs of greatest overall compatibility – Taurus, Virgo

Signs of greatest overall incompatibility – Aries, Cancer, Libra

Sign most helpful to career – Libra

Sign most helpful for emotional support – Aries

Sign most helpful financially – Aquarius

Sign best for marriage and/or partnerships – Cancer

Sign most helpful for creative projects – Taurus

Best Sign to have fun with – Taurus

Signs most helpful in spiritual matters – Virgo, Sagittarius

Best day of the week – Saturday

Understanding a Capricorn

The virtues of Capricorns are such that there will always be people for and against them. Many admire them, many dislike them. Why? It seems to be because of Capricorn's power urges. A well-developed Capricorn has his or her eyes set on the heights of power, prestige and authority. In the sign of Capricorn, ambition is not a fatal flaw, but rather the highest virtue.

Capricorns are not frightened by the resentment their authority may sometimes breed. In Capricorn's cool, calculated, organized mind all the dangers are already factored into the equation – the unpopularity, the animosity, the misunderstandings, even the outright slander – and a plan is always in place for dealing with these things in the most efficient way. To the Capricorn, situations that would terrify an ordinary mind are merely problems to be managed, bumps on the road to ever-growing power, effectiveness and prestige.

Some people attribute pessimism to the Capricorn sign, but this is a bit deceptive. It is true that Capricorns like to take into account the negative side of things. It is also true that they love to imagine the worst possible scenario in every undertaking. Other people might find such analyses depressing, but Capricorns only do these things so that they can formulate a way out – an escape route.

Capricorns will argue with success. They will show you that you are not doing as well as you think you are. Capricorns do this to themselves as well as to others. They do not mean to discourage you but rather to root out any impediments to your greater success. A Capricorn boss or supervisor feels that no matter how good the performance there is always room for improvement. This explains why Capricorn supervisors are difficult to handle and even infuriating at times. Their actions are, however, quite often effective – they can get their subordinates to improve and become better at their jobs.

Capricorn is a born manager and administrator. Leo is better at being king or queen, but Capricorn is better at being prime minister – the person actually wielding power.

Capricorn is interested in the virtues that last, in the things that will stand the test of time and trials of circumstance. Temporary fads and fashions mean little to a Capricorn – except as things to be used for profit or power. Capricorns apply this attitude to business, love, to their thinking and even to their philosophy and religion.

Finance

Capricorns generally attain wealth and they usually earn it. They are willing to work long and hard for what they want. They are quite amenable to foregoing a short-term gain in favour of long-term benefits. Financially, they come into their own later in life.

However, if Capricorns are to attain their financial goals they must shed some of their strong conservatism. Perhaps this is the least desirable trait of the Capricorn. They can resist anything new merely because it is new and untried. They are afraid of experimentation. Capricorns need to be willing to take a few risks. They should be more eager to market new products or explore different managerial techniques. Otherwise, progress will leave them behind. If necessary, Capricorns must be ready to change with the times, to discard old methods that no longer work.

Very often this experimentation will mean that Capricorns have to break with existing authority. They might even consider changing their present position or starting their own ventures. If so, they should be willing to accept all the risks and just get on with it. Only then will a Capricorn be on the road to highest financial gain.

Career and Public Image

A Capricorn's ambition and quest for power are evident. It is perhaps the most ambitious sign of the zodiac – and usually the most successful in a worldly sense. However, there are lessons Capricorns need to learn in order to fulfil their highest aspirations.

Intelligence, hard work, cool efficiency and organization will take them a certain distance, but will not carry them to the very top. Capricorns need to cultivate their social graces, to develop a social style, along with charm and an ability to get along with people. They need to bring beauty into their lives and to cultivate the right social contacts. They must learn to wield power gracefully, so that people love them for it – a very delicate art. They also need to learn how to bring people together in order to fulfil certain objectives. In short, Capricorns require some of the gifts – the social graces – of Libra to get to the top.

Once they have learned this, Capricorns will be successful in their careers. They are ambitious hard workers who are not afraid of putting in the required time and effort. Capricorns take their time in getting the job done – in order to do it well – and they like moving up the corporate ladder slowly but surely. Being so driven by success, Capricorns are generally liked by their bosses, who respect and trust them.

Love and Relationships

Like Scorpio and Pisces, Capricorn is a difficult sign to get to know. They are deep, introverted and like to keep their own counsel. Capricorns do not like to reveal their innermost thoughts. If you are in love with a Capricorn, be patient and take your time. Little by little you will get to understand him or her.

Capricorns have a deep romantic nature, but they do not show it straightaway. They are cool, matter of fact and not especially emotional. They will often show their love in practical ways.

It takes time for a Capricorn – male or female – to fall in love. They are not the love-at-first-sight kind. If a Capricorn is involved with a Leo or Aries, these Fire types will be totally mystified – to them the Capricorn will seem cold, unfeeling, unaffectionate and not very spontaneous. Of course none of this is true; it is just that Capricorn likes to take things slowly. They like to be sure of their ground before making any demonstrations of love or commitment.

Even in love affairs Capricorns are deliberate. They need more time to make decisions than is true of the other signs of the zodiac, but given this time they become just as passionate. Capricorns like a relationship to be structured, committed, well regulated, well defined, predictable and even routine. They prefer partners who are nurturers, and they in turn like to nurture their partners. This is their basic psychology. Whether such a relationship is good for them is another issue altogether. Capricorns have enough routine in their lives as it is. They might be better off in relationships that are a bit more stimulating, changeable and fluctuating.

Home and Domestic Life

The home of a Capricorn – as with a Virgo – is going to be tidy and well organized. Capricorns tend to manage their families in the same way they manage their businesses. Capricorns are often so career-driven that they find little time for the home and family. They should try to get more actively involved in their family and domestic life. Capricorns do, however, take their children very seriously and are very proud parents, particularly should their children grow up to become respected members of society.

Horoscope for 2010

Major Trends

Last year could be considered a major watershed year for you, Capricorn. Pluto made a major move from Sagittarius into your own sign. Pluto will be in your sign for the next 15 or so years. This has major ramifications for you. Over the

long term, you are going to be redefining your personality
and self-concept. You will be into areas such as personal
reinvention and personal transformation. Not in a fly-by-
night kind of way, but as a long-term project. You are in it
for the long haul. This trend continues even more strongly
in the year ahead.

Last year was a banner financial year, Capricorn, and the
year ahead also looks amazingly prosperous. More on this
later.

Love was not a major interest last year and neither is it
the major interest in the year ahead. Sure, singles will go out
and date, etc., but it is not a burning desire. However, there
are two (and perhaps we can say three) eclipses in your 7th
house of love in the year ahead. This will test marriages,
business partnerships and friendships of the heart. More on
this later.

This year two major planets, Uranus and Jupiter, will
move into your 4th house of home and family, making this
area of life a dominant interest from May 28th to September
10th. There are major changes in the home and family, but it
seems to me that these will be very happy changes – changes
for the better. More on this later.

Saturn, your ruling planet, will spend most of the year
ahead in your 10th house of career, making this a very
powerful career year. You are on top, calling the shots, very
comfortable in this position, expressing yourself at your
highest potential. More on this later.

Your major interests in the year ahead will be the body
and image, finance, communication and intellectual interests, and home and family (from May 28th to September
10th), sex, birth and death, the deeper things of life, reincarnation, occult studies, debt and the repayment of debt, taxes
and estate issues, and religion, philosophy and higher education (from April 8th to July 22nd), and career (January 1st
to April 8th and July 22nd to December 31st).

Your paths of greatest fulfilment in the year ahead are the
body, the image, personal pleasure and finance (until
January 18th), communication and intellectual interests

(from January 18th to June 6th and from September 10th to December 31st), and home and family (from June 6th to September 10th).

Health

(Please note that this is an astrological perspective on health and not a medical one. In days gone by there was no difference; these perspectives were identical. But nowadays there can be quite a difference. For the medical perspective, please consult your doctor or health practitioner.)

Health is a little bit more delicate this year than it was last year. Two major planets are moving into stressful aspect with you in the year ahead, though not for the entire year. For example, Saturn is making a stressful aspect from January 1st to April 8th and then again from July 22nd to December 31st. He will spend most of the year in stressful aspect with you. Uranus will also start to make a stressful aspect to you from May 28th to August 14th. The good news is that Uranus will not be in stressful aspect for the whole year. Next year (2011) is another story and you will certainly have to pay more attention to your health and energy then. This year you are sort of getting an announcement of things to come.

The fact that your 6th house of health is not a House of Power indicates that health is basically good this year. Sure, energy might not be as strong as it was in the past 2 years, but we don't see major problems. You can sort of take good health for granted.

You can make your good health even better by paying more attention to the following parts of the body:

- lungs, arms and shoulders (arms and shoulders should be regularly massaged)
- heart (especially from April 8th to August 14th).

Since these are your most vulnerable organs, keeping them healthy and fit is good preventative medicine.

Your health planet, Mercury, is a very fast-moving planet, as our steady readers know. During the course of a year he will move through all the signs and houses of your horo-scope. Thus there are many short-term health trends – these will be covered in the month-by-month forecasts.

Your health planet will go retrograde four times this year, which is highly unusual. Generally he retrogrades only three times in a given year. This indicates a need to do more homework in health matters and not to rush into any new kinds of diets or therapies without doing the appropriate research first.

Pluto in your own sign is indicating a detox of the physical body. And that you benefit from detox regimes. It is a wonderful transit for those of you who want to lose weight. The symbolism of Pluto in your 1st house is the shedding of excess. So you will have a lot of cosmic support in streamlin-ing projects in the year ahead. As mentioned earlier, this is an excellent time for getting involved with things like personal transformation and personal reinvention. There are many

Reflexology

Try to massage the whole foot on a regular basis, but pay extra attention to the points highlighted on the chart. When you massage, be aware of 'sore spots', as these need special attention. It's also a good idea to massage the ankles and top side (as well as the soles) of the feet.

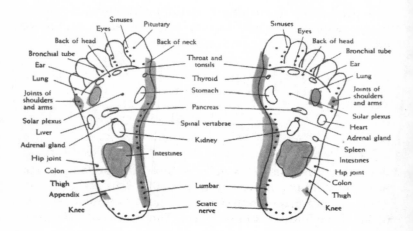

systems, Eastern and Western, that deal with this. But basically it's about shaping and sculpting your body as you wish. Some people like yoga and diet for this. Some people prefer to do it through cosmetic kinds of surgery. Some people like to do it through meditation and other spiritual techniques. All these activities are interesting in the year ahead. Cosmetic surgery is sometimes called for when dealing with structural issues. But in other cases you are probably better off in the long term with spiritual techniques, diet or yoga.

As our steady readers know by now, disease ends up in the body but never begins there. Always it has its origins in other, more subtle realms. By the time a disease actually manifests in the physical body, it has had a long history on the inner planes. In your chart, if health problems arise, look at your thinking and speech. For this is Mercury's domain. Are you thinking too much? Are you thinking the wrong kinds of thoughts? Are your thoughts based on truth? Are you reading blogs or magazines that are giving you incorrect information? Do you talk too much? Is your speech destructive or constructive? These are the questions that need to be answered very honestly if health problems arise. For the misuse of thought and speech can actually have an impact on your physical health in many, many ways. If you correct these issues, chances are that your health problem will just fall away on its own. And, even if you should still need a health professional, the healing will go faster and more easily.

Home and Family

The situation with the home and family has been relatively stable these past few years, Capricorn, and you've been enjoying a basically status-quo situation. But all of this is about to change. As we have mentioned, two powerful planets, Uranus and Jupiter, make a brief foray into your 4th house from May 28th to September 10th. This brings major, dramatic, powerful change – and it seems to me that it is happy – but sudden and dramatic. Those of you born early

344   YOUR PERSONAL HOROSCOPE 2010

in the sign of Capricorn (December 21st–25th) will feel this the most. But all of you will feel this in coming years.

Uranus' move into Aries, your 4th house, is merely an announcement of things to come. The whole family and home situation is going to be different. There are all kinds of scenarios as to how this takes shape. In some cases there will be breakups of the family unit. In other cases there will be moves – multiple moves. Also, many of you will be living in different places for long periods of time. Your home becomes a 'work in progress' – a place of experimentation – something that is always upgraded. It becomes a place where you express your originality and innovation.

I can easily envision you Capricorns building or installing home laboratories or observatories. The home will become a high-tech haven, filled with all kinds of gadgets. I can see Capricorns living in avant-garde kinds of homes – green homes, energy-efficient homes, homes that are powered by alternative (and very innovative) energies. Some of these energies and technologies might not even be invented yet – but when they are, you will be on the cutting edge.

Since Uranus is your financial planet, you will be spending more on the home and on family members. But the converse is also true – you can be earning from the home, too – from property, family-type businesses, or through family connections.

I can see Capricorns installing home offices and working from home. Home-based businesses are becoming ever more interesting – and with the advent of technology, ever more practical.

Your spouse, partner or current love is not looking to move – you are the one who wants to.

Parents or parent figures also seem more restless this year – and in coming years. This person wants to explore personal freedom and seems to resent any kind of obligation or commitment. This person will also be living in different places for long periods of time – wandering around. This person is very prosperous these days – and next year seems more prosperous than this. So this person has the financial wherewithal to explore personal freedom.

The other parent or parent figure seems to be just the opposite: He or she likes the status quo. This person believes that real freedom comes only through self-discipline. You seem personally more attached and devoted to this parent figure than the other one in coming years.

Siblings are having a status-quo family year. Children of appropriate age are making major repairs or renovations in the home – perhaps even building a home from scratch (or planning one). Grandchildren of appropriate age are also making major repairs in the home.

Finance and Career

The year ahead is most definitely about finance and career. This seems the dominant interest and focus.

As we mentioned, last year was a very profitable year for most of you. Whatever your stage or status in life, wealth should have increased. We see the same phenomenon in the year ahead.

Jupiter, the planet of abundance, spent last year in your money house bringing financial opportunity and increasing the value of the assets that you already own. If you own property, stocks or bonds, or even physical assets, they should have increased in value.

In the past few years you went more deeply into the spiritual dimensions of wealth. (Last year especially so.) This was probably a difficult lesson for you, as no one is more hard-headed, down to earth, practical than you are. Yet you discern that there is something deeper to this thing called wealth than mere materialism. There have been times when you've worked hard, followed the rules, saved, watched your costs – and yet saw few results. And then there were other times last year, and perhaps in your life, where an idea, an intuition or a hunch, or the performance of something joyful, led to a bonanza. Most people put this kind of thing down to luck. But there is no such thing as luck in the universe. Somehow or other you have, consciously or unconsciously, invoked a spiritual law – and your abundance has come to you.

This year, we see you going more deeply into the spiritual dimensions of wealth, as Jupiter (your spiritual planet) travels with your financial planet for many months in the year ahead – from approximately May through October. This will open the doors of spiritual wealth for you.

Jupiter travelling with the money planet is a classic symbol of big financial success. And this is likely to happen suddenly and unexpectedly. Intuition is always important – and during this period, even more so. Intuition is your shortcut to wealth.

You are earning big in the year ahead – and also spending big. You are a free spender these days – very unlike your normal Capricorn itself. Communication, teaching, sales, marketing and PR – intellectual pursuits – all seem like viable paths to profits. As always, it's very important that you stay up to date with the latest technology. Your technological savvy and expertise seem to play a huge role in your earnings.

You also have the aspects of someone who has an online kind of business. The use of the internet, or actually setting up an online business, is very important in your financial life. I also like industries that are involved with new inventions, new and cutting-edge technology. You have a very strong inner feeling and intuition about these kinds of fields – either as a job or business or from an investment perspective.

As mentioned earlier, your financial planet will move into your 4th house on May 28th and stay there until August 14th. (Those of you born early in the sign will feel this most.) While this transit is brief, it is an announcement of things to come in future years – you are going to be more aggressive in finance. You are ready to be more independent, ready to get involved with startup businesses or to start your own independent company. Unlike your typical self, you seem more interested in a quick buck – fast-growing wealth. While this has some good points, there are some dangers here as well. There are people who will exploit this urge for their own benefit. But you are a savvy business head and no doubt will see through these kinds of things.

The main headline of Uranus in Aries is that you will start to learn to be fearless in financial affairs. You are, by nature, a very conservative person. Perhaps you are overly cautious. Perhaps you mistake fear for caution. So you are entering a period – for many years to come – of learning to overcome your financial fear and to develop faith, confidence and courage.

As mentioned earlier, your financial planet in the 4th house indicates spending on the family and family members, and money from property (always good for you and even better in the year ahead) – residential property seems better than commercial. As you tally your earnings for 2010 you will undoubtedly find that you'll have earned more this year than last year. And this is the important thing.

Career is also very important in the year ahead as Saturn, your ruling planet, spends most of the year in your 10th house of career. Since Saturn is your ruling planet, this position is telling us that you are on top, calling the shots, above everyone else in your world including your parents, family and spouse. You are in command. You are honoured in the year ahead, not so much for your financial or career achievements but more for who you are as a person. This is a long-term trend and will go on next year as well.

This kind of aspect shows pay rises and promotions at work, promotions within your industry (if you are running your own business) and a more 'public profile'. Many of you will attain 'name and fame' in the year ahead. The degree of this depends on your stage and status in life. Whatever your stage, you will be more well known this year than in previous years.

Love and Social Life

Your 7th house of love and marriage is not a House of Power this year, Capricorn, and as our steady readers know, this tends towards the status quo. Marrieds will tend to stay married and singles will tend to say single. The cosmos is giving you freedom in this area, freedom to shape this area as you will. The problem with freedom is that you have little interest, so many of you will not exercise this freedom. This is what tends to happen when an astrological house is not strong.

Having said this, we need to make note that there are two (and perhaps three) eclipses in your 7th house of marriage. This is a lot of eclipse activity in one house in any given year. Thus your marriage or current love relationship, *and* business partnerships, will get tested in the year ahead – at least three times.

These testings need not break up your relationship. But they will bring up long-festering impurities, conflicts and dissatisfaction, so that you can correct them.

Perhaps you've swept these things under the carpet. More likely you've not even been aware that they existed or that they were as big a deal as they now seem to be. And so the cosmos brings you revelation – and an opportunity to make relationships even stronger than before. Good marriages and partnerships, good friendships, will certainly survive. Not only survive but they will become even better. It is the flawed relationships that are endangered.

Your 5th house of love affairs is not particularly strong, either. Of course, singles will date and go out, but it doesn't seem that big a deal to you this year. Even your 11th house of friendships is not strong in the year ahead. Social matters are taking a back seat to other, more important issues – your physical body, your career, your finances and your home.

Those working towards their second marriage, or in their second marriage, are having an easier time in the year ahead as compared to last year. However there is still three months of testing from April 8th to July 22nd. Though your social life is improved, I don't think there will be a second marriage for those of you who are seeking that. Those working on or in their third marriage are also having a status-quo year.

Parents or parent figures are having their marriages tested. This begins in 2010 but will continue for many years in the future. Children of marrying age are having a status-quo year. Siblings have had their marriages tested for the past 2½ years. Some of this testing continues this year, but the worst is over – if their marriage has survived the past 2½ years, it is likely it will survive this year as well. Grandchildren of marrying age are likely to marry or be involved in a very serious relationship. Love is definitely in the air for them.

Your most active love periods in the year ahead will be from May 20th to June 14th and from June 21st to July 23rd.

Since the Moon – the fastest-moving planet in the horoscope – is your love planet, there are many short-term trends in love that we will discuss in the monthly reports.

Self-improvement

For many years, as we have mentioned, you have been learning about the nature of true wealth. True wealth, as opposed to the side-effects of wealth, is always spiritual. Wealth is an actual light-substance – energy from the spirit world – and can be seen in someone's aura. This later materializes, takes on the form, of the images and desires held in the mind. Thus it becomes tangible and physical wealth. So you have been learning to access the *spirit* of wealth and have been less concerned with the material objects of wealth. You've understood that if you have the spirit of wealth, the material kind soon follows. But now, with your financial planet changing signs, you are learning another financial lesson. As we've mentioned, it's time to learn fearlessness in finance.

While you explored the spiritual dimensions of wealth, you no doubt saw that one of the main blockages in accessing spiritual wealth is fear: fear of poverty, failure and loss. Though there is no loss in the spiritual world (a total impossibility), our conditioned consciousness, our mortal mind, has all kinds of fears. So when intuition counselled a certain path, as a purchase or an investment, this fear could have raised its ugly head and blocked you. Only later did you realize your mistake. So vanquishing fear will help you in your spiritual consciousness of wealth. It doesn't mean that you get rash and do stupid things just to overcome fear. No.

You exercise your best judgement, you trust your intuition and learn to become indifferent to loss. As you lose the fear, losses will stop happening (or be very minimized). You will be able to take bold and courageous action when necessary. You will be able to follow the intuition of the moment in a bold and courageous way. This will increase your bottom line many fold.

With Saturn in your 10th house you are now in a position of power and authority. Basically this is a wonderful thing. We were created to be powerful. No way we can escape. The question is, how do we use the power we have? Many people think – and perhaps you are one of them – that being in power is just a lark and you do whatever you want: you have people obey your every whim, regardless of its validity. But you will find, especially in the year ahead, that this is not so. The people beneath the one in authority have minds of their own, and would like nothing better than to go their own way. They will analyse your every move, they will categorize you. You will be held accountable for how you use your power. So your job is to be fair and equitable. Power must be exercised from a higher place in yourself – and not in an emotional or arbitrary way. With every use or misuse of power, there will be a consequence – either pleasant or painful. Leadership, and the power that comes with it, is just another form of service to the world at large and to those beneath you.

We're seeing important changes in your spiritual life in the year ahead, Capricorn. Your spiritual planet will actually move three signs and houses of your horoscope in the coming year – highly unusual. This indicates that you will be getting results from different paths and styles as the year progresses. Early in the year, as Jupiter is in your 2nd house and in the sign of Aquarius, your intuition will be trained in financial matters. Your spiritual path will be more rational and scientific. When Jupiter moves into Pisces, from January 18th to June 6th and from September 10th to December 31st, you will be more mystical in your approach. You will get results from paths that exalt the emotions and that stress unconditional love. During these periods, intellectual understanding does not seem so important – it is the emotional, feeling experience of higher states of consciousness that are important.

From June 6th to September 10th, with your spiritual planet in Aries, neither emotion nor intellectualism will be important. You will want to express your spiritual ideals and understanding in physical activity. You will become more of an activist. You will get involved in charities or altruistic causes in a physical way. It will not be enough for you to understand or just feel the divine – you will want to express it through the physical body – through altruistic service. Each of these paths is valid. And just because you shift from one to the other does not discredit any of them. It is just about what is right for an appropriate time.

Month-by-month Forecasts

January

  Best Days Overall: 4, 5, 13, 14, 23, 24
  Most Stressful Days Overall: 1, 6, 7, 21, 22, 28
  Best Days for Love: 1, 4, 5, 13, 14, 15, 25, 26, 28
  Best Days for Money: 1, 6, 7, 9, 10, 16, 17, 18, 19, 20, 27, 28, 29
  Best Days for Career: 4, 5, 6, 7, 13, 14, 15, 25, 26

You begin your year with 80 (and sometimes 90) per cent of the planets in the independent, Eastern sector of your horoscope. This is a time to exercise your personal initiative in life – to create conditions as you desire them to be. It is a time for letting the world adapt to you rather than vice versa. Right now it's easy to create conditions; later on in the year, as the planets move to the West, it will be more difficult. So take initiative now. Other people are to be respected, but as far as your personal happiness is concerned they are more or less irrelevant.

You begin your year in the midst of a yearly personal pleasure peak. It's a time to enjoy all the sensual delights and fulfil the fantasies of the body. A time for good food, good wine and good love. A time to get your body and image in shape – the way you want them to be.

A solar eclipse on the 15th occurs in your own sign and is strong on you. It is especially strong for those of you born later in the sign – from January 13th to 20th. And most strong on those of you born January 13th–16th. Definitely take a reduced schedule a few days before and after. Avoid risky activities. Spend more quiet time at home. Those on the path should spend more time in prayer and meditation – as the best way to get through these kinds of periods is by staying in your 'highest' possible vibration.

You are still under the effect of the last lunar eclipse on December 31, 2009 (this affected those of you born earlier in the sign). The last eclipse tested marriages, business partnerships and a current love relationship. This one forces you to redefine your image, personality and self-concept. As you change your opinion of yourself, you will change your image. Generally this leads to wardrobe changes. If you haven't been careful in dietary matters, it can bring a detox of the body – not to be confused with sickness, though sometimes the symptoms are similar. The cosmos will make you aware of your mortality in various ways. It is not trying to take you out, only to deliver a message.

In spite of the eclipses, health is good. Avoid making dramatic changes to your health regime until after the 15th. You can enhance your health even further in the ways described in the yearly report.

Early in the month Jupiter is travelling with Neptune. This brings spiritual breakthroughs – interior revelations, enhanced intuition and ESP abilities – and encounters with ministers, gurus and spiritual people (some in the body and some not in the body).

Your financial intuition is especially sharp early in the month.

February

Best Days Overall: 1, 9, 10, 11, 19, 20, 21, 28
Most Stressful Days Overall: 2, 3, 17, 18, 24, 25
Best Days for Love: 2, 3, 13, 14, 15, 24, 25
Best Days for Money: 4, 5, 6, 12, 13, 14, 15, 16, 24, 25
Best Days for Career: 2, 3, 14, 15, 24, 25

This is a year of great ambition and great career success. But these days, most of the planets are below the horizon of your horoscope – so you need to focus more on your emotional life, your inner state, your family and domestic situation. You will not be ignoring your career, but pursuing it in different sorts of ways – by the ways of the night rather than the ways of the day. The ways of the day are overt, physical and logical. You make the calls and appointments, execute your plans in a physical way. The ways of the night are different. Your body is still. You visualize what you want to happen, where you want to be. You dream. You enter (in a psychological way) the 'feeling' of what you want to happen. You set goals and make plans. It is all an interior process. No less powerful than the ways of the day – in fact it is these processes that 'set up' – support – the overt actions of the day. So you are setting up, on an internal level, the career success that will happen later in the year.

Last month, on the 20th, you entered a yearly financial peak. And this continues until the 18th of this month. You are very prosperous, money comes easily and financial goals are attained quickly and relatively easily. With many planets in your money house, money will come to you in a variety of ways – through your intuition, through borrowing or outside investors, through good sales and marketing, through foreigners or foreign companies, through pay rises and promotions, through the good graces of bosses, parents, parent figures and, last but not least, through old-fashioned hard work.

A good month to pay off debt – or refinance old debt on better terms. Good to cut expenses and waste now – also to consolidate bank accounts.

Last month, on the 18th, Jupiter moved into your 3rd house of communication and intellectual interests. This month the Sun joins him (on the 18th). Your mind will be sharp this period. Learning will proceed more easily – it's a good month for students. Sales and marketing projects will go well. Your innate communication skills are enhanced. Good to expand the mind – take courses or attend lectures in subjects that interest you.

Venus travels with Jupiter from the 15th to the 17th and this brings romantic opportunities for singles. For marrieds it will tend to bring more romance in an existing relationship. The New Moon of the 15th brings new communication equipment to you and clarifies many financial matters. New cars or communication equipment can also come on the 27th and 28th. Siblings are prospering during this period, too – there are windfalls or opportunities happening. Very good financial ideas or trading ideas come to you then.

Health is good this month. You can enhance it further by paying more attention to your spine, knees, teeth, bones, gall-bladder and overall skeletal alignment until the 10th (regular back and knee massage will be good) and to your ankles and calves afterwards (regular ankle and calf massage will be powerful). Also refer to our discussion in the yearly report.

March

Best Days Overall: 1, 9, 10, 19, 20, 27, 28
Most Stressful Days Overall: 2, 3, 16, 17, 23, 24, 29, 30
Best Days for Love: 4, 5, 6, 14, 15, 16, 17, 23, 24, 25, 26
Best Days for Money: 4, 5, 11, 12, 14, 15, 23, 24, 31
Best Days for Career: 2, 3, 5, 6, 16, 17, 25, 26, 29, 30

A bit of a complicated month. There are many forces pulling you in different directions. Many contradictions in your desires and goals. Resolving all these contradictions is the main spiritual lesson of the month ahead.

For example, career is very important, but so is home and family. Each pulls you in a different direction. You can't completely abandon either of these things, so you need to juggle between one and the other. Mars, your family planet, has been retrograde since the beginning of the year – yet after the 20th your 4th house is very powerful. In fact, family is your mission this month (after the 7th) – your job is to be there for them. Yet long-term decisions can't be made – and it's difficult to take decisive actions about a family situation. You do what is possible in the short term, and then review the situation to see where things can be improved in the future.

Love is volatile and still being tested. Be especially patient with your beloved during the New Moon of the 15th – he or she seems very temperamental. Mood changes in love are swift and abrupt. If you maintain your composure, this New Moon can bring happiness in love. For singles it brings sudden (but unstable) romantic meetings.

Job-seekers have great opportunities from the 7th to the 9th. Job-seekers should look in the neighbourhood for opportunities. Spiritual-type organizations seem like interesting opportunities.

The family unit or family pattern seems threatened this period. This doesn't mean that there will be a breakup – but the threat of it is there. Seems that there are renovations going on in the home as well (though it is best to wait until Mars moves forward after the 10th). After the 20th you can make great and deep psychological progress – a good period for delving into your emotional nature either meditatively or with a professional therapist.

Health is good until the 20th but needs more watching afterwards. There are no long-term health problems here, but in the short term your energy and vitality are not what they should be. Listen to your body, rest and relax more and pace yourself. When energy is low you become more vulnerable to the various ills in the environment around you. A strong aura (spiritual immune system) will repel every negative thing – whether it be a virus or destructive type of bacteria. It also protects against discordant vibrations from others (a secret spiritual cause of many diseases). But when this aura weakens (through lack of energy) then you are more susceptible.

Enhance your health by paying more attention to your heart (after the 20th), your feet (until the 17th – foot massage will be wonderful) and to your head, face, skull and adrenal glands (after the 17th – regular scalp and face massage will be powerful then).

The New Moon of the 15th will clarify relations with siblings, neighbours and sales and marketing projects. Anything involving communication will get clarified this month. The New Moon will also bring sudden and happy financial opportunities – windfalls and the like – out of the blue.

April

Best Days Overall: 5, 6, 15, 16, 24, 25
Most Stressful Days Overall: 13, 14, 19, 20, 26, 27
Best Days for Love: 3, 4, 5, 13, 14, 15, 16, 19, 20, 24, 25
Best Days for Money: 1, 2, 8, 9, 10, 11, 12, 19, 20, 21, 28, 29
Best Days for Career: 5, 15, 16, 25, 26, 27

Saturn, your ruler, has been retrograde since January 13th. He moves back into Virgo on the 3rd. This is a plus for health. Overall energy should improve. But health still needs watching until the 20th. Refer to last month's discussion. This month you can also enhance your health by paying more attention to your neck, throat and lower jaw (from the 2nd onwards). Regular neck massage is good. Much stress and tension tends to collect there and the massage will release it. There are spots in the centre of the shoulders, which if massaged and squeezed, will also release the tension in the neck. Health and energy improves dramatically after the 20th. Your personal appearance will also start to shine – start to reflect more of the perfection of the Divine.

Your health planet goes retrograde on the 18th, so avoid making major changes to your health regime or diet. This is a time for study and research not for actual actions.

Avoid risky activities from the 14th to the 16th. Your spouse, partner or current love has a financial disturbance then – something unexpected. Changes need to be made.

On the 20th you enter a yearly personal pleasure peak – one of the happiest periods of your year. The difference between this personal pleasure peak and the one in January is mainly of focus. In January it was the physical pleasures that were highlighted – the pleasures of the physical body. But now you are exploring these, as well as other kinds of pleasures – the pleasures of the theatre, concerts, sports and of creativity – mental and emotional pleasures are also important. In fact, it is your mission to explore the happy side of life – your mission to be happy now. For singles this means more love affairs – flings – romance as a form of entertainment, but nothing more. Job-seekers need work that they love – that is fun. It is time to be more like a child – not childish, but childlike – innocent and happy.

Last month, the planetary power shifted from the East to the West – and this condition will last for another 6 months – and get even stronger. Thus, by now you have created conditions as you desired them to be (at least in the short term). You have had life, more or less, on your terms. Now it is time to live with the consequences of your creations. If you have created well, this is a time of happiness – of enjoying and resting in your creation. But if you made mistakes, it is a time for living with those mistakes. More difficult to change them now. It is time to adapt yourself as best you can. Personal initiative was important since January. Now, likeability and being able to get on with others is important. You are honing your social skills now. Your social life will start becoming more active as well.

Finances are super right now – major things are developing. And next month will be even better. Follow the intuition now. On the down side, there are many non disclosures in prospective deals – so get as many facts as you can. There are behind the scenes shenanigans that need to be looked at.

May

Best Days Overall: 2, 3, 4, 12, 13, 21, 22, 30, 31
Most Stressful Days Overall: 10, 11, 17, 18, 23, 24
Best Days for Love: 2, 3, 5, 6, 12, 13, 15, 16, 17, 18, 23,
    25, 26
Best Days for Money: 5, 6, 8, 9, 18, 25, 26
Best Days for Career: 5, 6, 15, 16, 23, 24, 25, 26

There are many interesting things going on this month, but
the main headline is Jupiter's conjunction (exact) with your
financial planet, Uranus. This only happens every 14 to 15
years. This shows huge – substantial – financial increases.
Big wealth that happens suddenly. We see these kinds of
aspects under 'bubble' situations – such as the dot com
bubble some years ago. There is a wild enthusiasm for something that perhaps has some merit, but it gets overdone. Big
wealth happens quickly – prices go sky high. But as with all
bubbles, one needs to have one's feet on the ground – be
ready to take one's profits and run. Wealth is big – enthusiasm is tremendous – but wealth is also unstable. Happily,
you Capricorns are a conservative breed and your innate
caution will help you navigate here.

The other major headline is Uranus' move into Aries on
the 28th – he has been in the sign of Pisces for about 8 years
– this too is a major cosmic happening. Again this feeds into
the 'bubble' mentality that we mentioned above. It can
make you much more risk-taking than normal.

You are earning big and spending big as well. Spending
plans can be grandiose these days. You are also very philanthropic and this will protect you from many ills.

As we mentioned in the yearly report you are accessing
the supernatural – the spiritual – dimensions of wealth these
days – not the natural ones. And, in the spiritual world,
wealth is unlimited. Your spiritual intuition – so long as it
isn't clouded by passion – will lead you to big wealth now.

You seem very lucky in speculations as well. Your 5th
house is still strong until the 21st.

Health is good this month and you are paying attention. Your 6th house of health becomes strong on the 21st. Getting your health the way you want it to be is actually your spiritual mission this month. Healing others – being involved in other people's health – is also important spiritually.

You can enhance your already good health by paying more attention to your heart (after 21st), to your kidneys and hips (until the 20th) and to your neck, throat and lower jaw (all month – refer to our discussion of health last month). Detox regimes are powerful after the 21st.

Job-seekers have better success after the 11th than before – the work planet is retrograde until the 11th. There are at least two interesting job opportunities this month.

Love is still being tested but there are some improvements this month. Your love planet spends an unusual amount of time in your own sign – it spends more than double the usual time. Thus love opportunities are pursuing you these days. You are getting your way in love – more than usual. Also romantic Venus enters your 7th house on the 20th putting you more in the 'mood' for romance. Singles seem to prefer flings rather than serious romance.

June

Best Days Overall: 9, 10, 17, 18, 26, 27
Most Stressful Days Overall: 6, 7, 13, 14, 19, 20
Best Days for Love: 1, 2, 4, 5, 11, 12, 13, 14, 21, 24, 25
Best Days for Money: 1, 2, 5, 6, 15, 24, 29, 30
Best Days for Career: 4, 5, 13, 14, 19, 20, 24, 25

On the 21st the planetary power shifts from the lower (night side) of your horoscope to the upper (day side). Yet (in another contradictory move) Jupiter moves into your 4th house making it very powerful. Yes, career is becoming ever more dominant, but the demands of the home and family are also very strong. As we have been seeing for some months, you are forced to juggle between two important things and it's not so easy. Where possible, start to shift attention to your career.

Jupiter and Uranus are still travelling together. The financial life is exciting. Many of you are having lifetime highs here. Wealth comes with breathtaking speed. You are spending on the home and family – perhaps buying new homes or expanding the present one. You are lavish in your spending and overall generosity to others.

Moves could easily happen now.

A parent or parent figure is also prospering greatly, living the good life, travelling, etc. He or she seems very generous with you. You support the family but family is also supportive of you.

Health needs more watching now – all month, but especially after the 21st. Enhance your health in the ways described in the yearly report, but also pay more attention to your heart (all month), your neck, throat and lower jaw (until the 10th), arms, shoulders and lungs (from the 10th to the 25th) and to your stomach and breasts (after the 25th).

There is a strong lunar eclipse on you on the 26th. Like the eclipse in January, this one occurs in your own sign – it has an impact on your self-esteem, self-confidence, image and personality. You are again forced to redefine yourself – redefine who you are and the kind of image you want to present to the world. Pluto, your planet of friends, is affected as well – this will test friendships as well as your marriage and partnerships. The eclipsed planet, the Moon, is your love planet. The eclipse has an impact on Jupiter as well (this is a strong eclipse and you should take a reduced schedule) – thus your spiritual life changes. You change your practice, teachers and attitudes. You re-think your involvement with certain charities as well.

Love is getting tested, but your social life is strong in spite of this. On the 21st you enter a yearly social peak. The eclipse can have a positive effect on singles – making them re-think their single status – pushing them to become more serious about love. Singles have at least three important relationships this month – or opportunities with three different people.

July

Best Days Overall: 6, 7, 15, 23, 24, 25
Most Stressful Days Overall: 4, 5, 10, 11, 17, 31
Best Days for Love: 1, 2, 5, 10, 11, 14, 20, 23, 24, 31
Best Days for Money: 3, 4, 12, 21, 26, 27, 31
Best Days for Career: 5, 14, 16, 17, 23, 24

Health needs watching this month – until the 23rd. Adding to the health pressure is another strong eclipse on the 11th (you've just gone through a strong one, last month) – this month it is a solar eclipse. Take a reduced schedule until the 23rd, but especially around the eclipse period – a few days before and after. Sensitive people often feel strong eclipses as much as two weeks before the event. Every person, though, in my experience, gets a personal message about when the eclipse period begins. If you are aware, you will get the message. Something weird – out of the ordinary – happens, or you read about some strange event in the newspaper – or something happens to a friend or family member. This is the cosmos signalling that the eclipse period is in effect and that you should start taking it easy. This could happen 2 weeks, 10 days, 5 days before the eclipse – but this is when your 'personal eclipse period' begins.

This eclipse, like the last few, is testing love relationships, marriages and business partnerships. Those relationships that have survived thus far have a good chance of continued survival. But the dirty laundry of the relationship comes up. Partners and spouses are more temperamental and you will need to be more patient with them. Every solar eclipse brings intimations of mortality, and this one perhaps more than most. Later on in the month, your 8th house becomes powerful. Thus you are forced to come to a deeper understanding of death – to come to terms with it, to confront it and get beyond it.

Your spouse or partner is making dramatic financial changes – and they seem good, for the month ahead is prosperous for them. If you are involved in insurance, property or royalty issues – they take a dramatic turn one way or the other now, and stuck issues start moving forward. If you are involved (and many of you are these days) in personal transformation and reinvention – there are important changes in your approach and techniques.

Wealth is still excellent – exciting and dramatic. But your financial planet goes retrograde on the 5th, so things might be slowing down a bit. A time to review your financial life in general and do more homework on major purchases and investments. Uranus will be retrograde for months to come, so this doesn't mean that you stop your financial life, only that you are more cautious about it. (This is easier said than done – Uranus and Jupiter are both in hot-headed, rash Aries.)

Enhance your health this month by resting and relaxing more, by avoiding risky or highly stressful activities and by paying more attention to your stomach and breasts (until the 9th) and your heart (all month). Also review our health discussion in the yearly report. Diet is more of a health issue until the 9th. If you feel under the weather it could be that you need a dietary change. Detox is powerful after the 9th.

August

Best Days Overall: 2, 3, 11, 12, 20, 21, 30, 31
Most Stressful Days Overall: 1, 7, 8, 13, 14, 27, 28
Best Days for Love: 1, 3, 4, 7, 8, 13, 17, 18, 22, 23, 29, 30
Best Days for Money: 8, 9, 16, 17, 22, 23, 24, 26, 27
Best Days for Career: 3, 4, 13, 14, 22, 23

Uranus retrogrades back into Pisces on the 15th. There are some good points here – it once again makes you more reliant on intuition and it helps you to slow your financial judgement. The challenge now is to verify your intuition. Once again – as has been the case for many years now – you are applying the spiritual laws of affluence rather than the natural ones. Finances are good, like last month, but still under review. You might feel that you are going backwards, but sometimes we go backwards in order to go forwards.

Your 8th house has been powerful since the 23rd of last month, and is strong until the 23rd of this month. Thus your spouse or partner is prospering (into a yearly high). Your focus now is to make other people rich; this, by karmic law, will enhance your own wealth. Use excess cash (and there seems to be a lot of it now) to pay off debt. Refinancing or employing techniques of creative financing are good under these aspects.

When the 8th house is strong, sexual activity – and libido – increase. Too much of a good thing can be the problem.

People attend more funerals or are more involved with death when the 8th house is strong. There is a need to understand death better. Occult interests become stronger as well.

Avoid risky activities from the 26th to 31st as Saturn is re-stimulating an eclipse point (June 26th). Family members should take it more easy – avoid risky or stressful activities – from the 25th to the 28th.

A love opportunity comes to you from the 7th to the 10th, but gets some severe testing from the 11th to the 14th and from the 25th to the 28th. There are probably dramas in the lives of parents or parent figures during this period as well – and they should take it more easy too. Career changes or challenges arise during this period.

Now that Uranus has left your 4th house (and Jupiter will leave next month) you can start to be more 'one-pointed' – more focused on your career. Until now your attention has been divided – you were doing a juggling act. This increased focus is going to bring more success. The good news is that the family as a whole and parent figures seem supportive of your career goals. They themselves seem more career-focused – and this is a help. The family as a whole will be elevated – enhanced in public esteem – during this period.

Health is much improved over last month. You can enhance it further by paying more attention to the parts of the body mentioned in the yearly report and to your small intestine.

September

Best Days Overall: 7, 8, 16, 17, 26, 27
Most Stressful Days Overall: 3, 4, 9, 10, 23, 24, 25
Best Days for Love: 2, 3, 4, 7, 8, 11, 17, 21, 28
Best Days for Money: 4, 5, 12, 18, 19, 20, 22
Best Days for Career: 2, 9, 10, 11, 21

Health again needs more watching after the 23rd. Enhance your health by maintaining high energy levels and keeping your focus on the important things in your life. Let the lesser things go. Continue to pay attention to the parts of the body mentioned in the yearly report, and to your heart (from the 23rd onwards) and the small intestine (all month). Diet, again, seems like a health issue. With energy low, it is perhaps better to eat foods that are easier to digest.

Saturn, your ruler, will be on an eclipse point all month (June 26th lunar eclipse). Avoid risky activities. Do what you need to do, of course, but re-schedule highly stressful things where possible. Drive more carefully. Most likely you will be redefining yourself – your image and your personality. You will change the way that you think about yourself and the way that you want others to perceive you. Often, this leads to wardrobe changes. You adopt a new look.

Your 9th house became powerful on the 23rd of last month, and is powerful until the 23rd of this month. Generally this brings an interest in foreign travel and travel opportunities. But with *both* Mercury and Jupiter retrograde (both planets that relate to travel) it might be better to re-schedule all but the most important journeys at least until after the 12th when Mercury moves forward. If you must travel, allow more time for getting to and from your destination. Avoid scheduling connecting flights too tightly. Get to the airport earlier than usual, as queues may be longer. It is often a good idea to make sure your travel insurance covers your ticket, so that you can make changes if necessary.

For students this is a good period, as their studies will meet with more success. There is a greater interest in religion, philosophy and theology these days – and this is as it should be. Those who are interested have the potential for important religious breakthroughs now. Legal issues are complicated and perhaps delayed – but they proceed better after the 12th than before. Legal decisions that are made are more subject to being overturned, appealed or over-ruled.

By the 10th, your 4th house is empty and your 10th house of career is powerful. Most of the planets are still above the horizon – so focus on your career. Family objectives (at least in the short term) have been fulfilled. Focus on your outer success. On the 23rd you enter a yearly career peak. Career has been good all year – your status has been elevated – but now even more so.

Love has been more or less status quo these past few months. Your social magnetism is stronger from the 8th to the 23rd – as this is when the Moon waxes. You can have good love days outside of this period – but your personal interest is not as strong as it could be. Singles have love opportunities (but not serious ones) with bosses and friends this month – with people involved in their careers or with people they meet at group activities or organizations. Online romances are interesting, too – after the 8th – but none of it seems serious or lasting. Just entertainment.

October

    Best Days Overall: 5, 6, 13, 14, 23, 24
    Most Stressful Days Overall: 1, 2, 7, 8, 21, 22, 28, 29
    Best Days for Love: 1, 2, 7, 9, 17, 18, 19, 27, 28, 29
    Best Days for Money: 2, 10, 16, 17, 19, 20, 29
    Best Days for Career: 1, 7, 8, 9, 18, 19, 28

Though health still needs watching there is much improvement this month. Saturn, your ruler, has moved away from the eclipse point. Life is less turbulent now. You are still in a yearly career peak and making great progress this month. You are marching, slowly, steadily and inexorably, towards your goals. You are still at the top, calling the shots –

elevated above everyone in your world. The place where you always believed you should be (and many of you will go even higher still). You have been learning lessons in the correct use of power and authority all year, but this month and last month have been more intense in this department. Continue to de-emphasize family and focus on your outer goals. The right action – outer success – will lead to right feeling.

Continue to enhance your health by maximizing energy levels and getting enough rest until the 23rd. Pay more attention to your heart (until the 23rd), small intestine (until the 3rd), kidneys and hips (from the 3rd to the 21st) and colon, bladder and sexual organs (from the 21st onwards). Detox is powerful after the 21st.

The New Moon of the 14th is interesting in various ways. On one level it brings clarity to your career and career moves. It will also clarify relations with parents, parent figures or bosses. Friends and social connections are helping your career. It is wise to attend a business-related party or gathering. But this New Moon also brings interesting romantic opportunities for singles – and it seems to happen at work, as you pursue your career goals, or with people involved in your career. Love seems to seek you out, rather than vice versa. The Full Moon of the 23rd brings love opportunities through family connections or through the introduction of family members. You seem very nostalgic in love matters – looking to the past – perhaps reconnecting with old flames. The 23rd might not be one of your best love days, but your interest and desire are certainly strong. You just have to work harder at love than usual.

Finances are still under review – but still very good. The pace of earnings may have slowed, but you are still sitting pretty. Continue to do more homework and study. This is a time for 'number-crunching' – working out the maths of different strategies or ideas – weighing the pros and the cons, the risks and rewards. Many of you will be planning your retirement these days. (Capricorn is always thinking of these things – even the young ones.)

Venus will start to retrograde on the 8th. Venus does double duty in your chart: she is your career planet and 'love affair' planet – the planet of fun and creativity. Thus, though your career is going great guns, certain long-term decisions shouldn't be made – give them more thought. There are many career opportunities – perhaps from other companies – coming to you, and you need time to evaluate these things. Don't rush into anything.

This retrograde will bring a love affair (not a marriage) under review. Children lack direction these days. Important decisions involving the children should be delayed – until after the 18th of next month.

November

Best Days Overall: 1, 2, 10, 11, 19, 20, 21, 28, 29
Most Stressful Days Overall: 3, 4, 17, 18, 24, 25
Best Days for Love: 5, 6, 13, 15, 16, 23, 24, 25, 26
Best Days for Money: 6, 12, 13, 15, 16, 25
Best Days for Career: 3, 4, 5, 13, 23

A child or child figure temporarily backtracks from a former course of action. He or she seems ambitious this month and is succeeding. There is a strong work ethic there now. There is a happy job opportunity for this child.

Health is much improved this month. You can enhance it further by paying more attention to your colon, bladder and sexual organs (until the 8th) and to your liver and thighs afterwards.

Pluto has been camped out on an eclipse point for many months. Friendships have been tested – they have been volatile. Some of these tests have been of a 'relationship' nature – that is, they've had to do with your actual relationship – and some came about because of dramas in the lives of friends. This is still going on. With your 11th house powerful this month (it became powerful on the 23rd of last month) you have a great opportunity to resolve many of these issues. Your focus is on friends during this period.

Until the 8th (and from the 21st of last month) relations with friends – discord with them – was a factor in health and could have been one of the spiritual root causes of health problems. Thus there is another incentive for resolving these things and bringing them into harmony.

This is a month for weeding out the good from the less good. You are in a social period, but still you can't attend every event or gathering. So you need to make some tough choices – keep the good and let the 'less good' go. Better to have a few good friends than many lukewarm ones. Better to attend a few good events than hordes of so-so events. It's time to exercise your discrimination.

Love and romance have also been tested by the various eclipses – almost all year. If your relationship or business partnership has survived by now, it is likely to continue. (Though there is another eclipse next month which will test these things.) This month, love seems status quo. Your 7th house is basically empty – only the Moon will visit there on the 24th and 25th. Most of the planets are now in the independent East. And you are approaching the point of maximum independence, which will happen next month. Your romantic life is not that important right now. (Friendships are important, but not romance.) It's time to take matters into your own hands – to once again create conditions as you like them and to have life on your terms. The cosmos desires your happiness and will support you. Your personal initiative, rather than the good graces of others, is important now. In the past 6 months you've had to live with the conditions you created earlier in the year – so you have 'road tested' your creations and know what needs to be corrected.

Sales and marketing – trading – have been a road to riches this past year – but major marketing programs are better delayed until next month.

December

Best Days Overall: 7, 8, 17, 18, 26, 27
Most Stressful Days Overall: 1, 14, 15, 16, 21, 22, 28, 29
Best Days for Love: 2, 5, 12, 16, 21, 22, 26, 31
Best Days for Money: 4, 9, 10, 11, 13, 22, 23, 31
Best Days for Career: 1, 2, 12, 22, 28, 29, 31

On the 22nd of last month you entered a highly spiritual period. This trend continues until the 21st of this month. It is a period for delving more deeply into your spiritual life, for getting more in tune – more connected – with the Higher Power within you. We are here in the world to do worldly kinds of work – to perform a certain mission right here in the 3D world. Being in the world is not the problem. But often this focus on the world – this attention on worldly matters – creates a disconnection with the Higher Power – we tend to get caught up with the life of the five senses and with its values – often without meaning to. Thus it is good that periodically we are given time to 'reconnect' and 'realign'. This is the kind of period you are in now. Those on the spiritual path will make many spiritual breakthroughs. Those not yet on the path might embark on it, or express a greater interest in spiritual or supernatural matters. All will tend to have more supernatural kinds of experiences these days – those on the path will understand them – those not on the path will just scratch their heads in puzzlement.

With the ruler of your 8th house in the 12th house of spirituality this month, those on the path will be confronted with their 'blockages' to meditation and higher understanding – and this revelation will enable them to clear these things away and proceed. Often these are subconscious fears, anger or discord. You will be given the power to clear them now. There will be interior revelations on sex and its true functions. Many will go more deeply into the spiritual dimensions of sex – which is a radically different perspective than the worldly one.

Personal transformation and reinvention have been important since last year, when Pluto entered your sign. After the 21st they will become even more important. Some of you could opt for cosmetic types of surgery – this is one of the ways that this interest pictures itself. But many of you will go more deeply into the spiritual ways to 'remake' the body – through meditation, diet and yoga (just to name a few ways).

On the 21st you enter a yearly personal pleasure peak – you've enjoyed the pleasures of the spiritual world, now it is time to give the body its due.

A lunar eclipse on the 21st is strong on Capricorns born early in the sign – from December 21st to 24th. If you are one of these, take a reduced schedule this period. This eclipse will once again test marriages, business partnerships and current love relationships – friendships of your heart will also get tested. As we mentioned earlier, you have been subjected to eclipses in this area for a whole year – the worst is over. If your relationship has survived thus far, it is likely to survive this eclipse as well. Since this eclipse occurs right on the border (the cusp) of the 6th and 7th houses, it is also having an impact on the affairs of the 6th house – thus there are job changes or disturbances at the workplace. Perhaps the rules of the workplace change in a dramatic way. Employers experience instability in the work force – employee turnover would not be a surprise now.

Finances are super and will get even better next month. Health is good. Spiritual healing techniques are powerful after the 18th.

Aquarius

~~~

THE WATER-BEARER
Birthdays from
20th January to
18th February

Personality Profile

AQUARIUS AT A GLANCE

Element – Air

Ruling Planet – Uranus
  Career Planet – Pluto
  Love Planet – Venus
  Money Planet – Neptune
  Planet of Health and Work – Moon
  Planet of Home and Family Life – Venus
  Planet of Spirituality – Saturn

Colours – electric blue, grey, ultramarine blue

Colours that promote love, romance and social
  harmony – gold, orange

Colour that promotes earning power – aqua

Gems – black pearl, obsidian, opal, sapphire

Metal – lead

Scents – azalea, gardenia

Quality – fixed (= stability)

Qualities most needed for balance – warmth, feeling and emotion

Strongest virtues – great intellectual power, the ability to communicate and to form and understand abstract concepts, love for the new and avant-garde

Deepest needs – to know and to bring in the new

Characteristics to avoid – coldness, rebelliousness for its own sake, fixed ideas

Signs of greatest overall compatibility – Gemini, Libra

Signs of greatest overall incompatibility – Taurus, Leo, Scorpio

Sign most helpful to career – Scorpio

Sign most helpful for emotional support – Taurus

Sign most helpful financially – Pisces

Sign best for marriage and/or partnerships – Leo

Sign most helpful for creative projects – Gemini

Best Sign to have fun with – Gemini

Signs most helpful in spiritual matters – Libra, Capricorn

Best day of the week – Saturday

Understanding an Aquarius

In the Aquarius-born, intellectual faculties are perhaps the most highly developed of any sign in the zodiac. Aquarians are clear, scientific thinkers. They have the ability to think abstractly and to formulate laws, theories and clear concepts from masses of observed facts. Geminis might be very good at gathering information, but Aquarians take this a step further, excelling at interpreting the information gathered.

Practical people – men and women of the world – mistakenly consider abstract thinking as impractical. It is true that the realm of abstract thought takes us out of the physical world, but the discoveries made in this realm generally end up having tremendous practical consequences. All real scientific inventions and breakthroughs come from this abstract realm.

Aquarians, more so than most, are ideally suited to explore these abstract dimensions. Those who have explored these regions know that there is little feeling or emotion there. In fact, emotions are a hindrance to functioning in these dimensions; thus Aquarians seem – at times – cold and emotionless to others. It is not that Aquarians haven't got feelings and deep emotions, it is just that too much feeling clouds their ability to think and invent. The concept of 'too much feeling' cannot be tolerated or even understood by some of the other signs. Nevertheless, this Aquarian objectivity is ideal for science, communication and friendship.

Aquarians are very friendly people, but they do not make a big show about it. They do the right thing by their friends, even if sometimes they do it without passion or excitement.

Aquarians have a deep passion for clear thinking. Second in importance, but related, is their passion for breaking with the establishment and traditional authority. Aquarians delight in this, because for them rebellion is like a great game or challenge. Very often they will rebel strictly for the fun of rebelling, regardless of whether the authority they defy is right or wrong. Right or wrong has little to do with the rebellious actions of an Aquarian, because to a true Aquarian authority and power must be challenged as a matter of principle.

Where Capricorn or Taurus will err on the side of tradition and the status quo, an Aquarian will err on the side of the new. Without this virtue it is doubtful whether any progress would be made in the world. The conservative-minded would obstruct progress. Originality and invention imply an ability to break barriers; every new discovery represents the toppling of an impediment to thought. Aquarians are very interested in breaking barriers and making walls tumble – scientifically, socially and politically. Other zodiac signs, such as Capricorn, also have scientific talents. But Aquarians are particularly excellent in the social sciences and humanities.

Finance

In financial matters Aquarians tend to be idealistic and humanitarian – to the point of self-sacrifice. They are usually generous contributors to social and political causes. When they contribute it differs from when a Capricorn or Taurus contributes. A Capricorn or Taurus may expect some favour or return for a gift; an Aquarian contributes selflessly.

Aquarians tend to be as cool and rational about money as they are about most things in life. Money is something they need and they set about acquiring it scientifically. No need for fuss; they get on with it in the most rational and scientific ways available.

Money to the Aquarian is especially nice for what it can do, not for the status it may bring (as is the case for other signs). Aquarians are neither big spenders nor penny-pinchers and use their finances in practical ways, for example to facilitate progress for themselves, their families or even strangers.

However, if Aquarians want to reach their fullest financial potential they will have to explore their intuitive nature. If they follow only their financial theories – or what they believe to be theoretically correct – they may suffer some losses and disappointments. Instead, Aquarians should call on their intuition, which knows without thinking. For Aquarians, intuition is the short-cut to financial success.

Career and Public Image

Aquarians like to be perceived not only as the breakers of barriers but also as the transformers of society and the world. They long to be seen in this light and to play this role. They also look up to and respect other people in this position and even expect their superiors to act this way.

Aquarians prefer jobs that have a bit of idealism attached to them – careers with a philosophical basis. Aquarians need to be creative at work, to have access to new techniques and methods. They like to keep busy and enjoy getting down to business straightaway, without wasting any time. They are often the quickest workers and usually have suggestions for improvements that will benefit their employers. Aquarians are also very helpful with their co-workers and welcome responsibility, preferring this to having to take orders from others.

If Aquarians want to reach their highest career goals they have to develop more emotional sensitivity, depth of feeling and passion. They need to learn to narrow their focus on the essentials and concentrate more on the job in hand. Aquarians need 'a fire in the belly' – a consuming passion and desire – in order to rise to the very top. Once this passion exists they will succeed easily in whatever they attempt.

Love and Relationships

Aquarians are good at friendships, but a bit weak when it comes to love. Of course they fall in love, but their lovers always get the impression that they are more best friends than paramours.

Like Capricorns, they are cool customers. They are not prone to displays of passion or to outward demonstrations of their affections. In fact, they feel uncomfortable when their mate hugs and touches them too much. This does not mean that they do not love their partners. They do, only they show it in other ways. Curiously enough, in relationships they tend to attract the very things that they feel uncomfortable with. They seem to attract hot, passionate, romantic, demonstrative people. Perhaps they know instinctively that these people have qualities they lack and so seek them out. In any event, these relationships do seem to work, Aquarius' coolness calming the more passionate partner while the fires of passion warm the cold-blooded Aquarius.

The qualities Aquarians need to develop in their love life are warmth, generosity, passion and fun. Aquarians love relationships of the mind. Here they excel. If the intellectual factor is missing in a relationship an Aquarian will soon become bored or feel unfulfilled.

Home and Domestic Life

In family and domestic matters Aquarians can have a tendency to be too non-conformist, changeable and unstable. They are as willing to break the barriers of family constraints as they are those of other areas of life.

Even so, Aquarians are very sociable people. They like to have a nice home where they can entertain family and friends. Their house is usually decorated in a modern style and full of state-of-the-art appliances and gadgets – an environment Aquarians find absolutely necessary.

If their home life is to be healthy and fulfilling Aquarians need to inject it with a quality of stability – yes, even some conservatism. They need at least one area of life to be enduring and steady; this area is usually their home and family life.

Venus, the planet of love, rules the Aquarian's 4th solar house of home and family as well, which means that when it comes to the family and child-rearing, theories, cool thinking and intellect are not always enough. Aquarians need to bring love into the equation in order to have a great domestic life.

Horoscope for 2010

Major Trends

Last year was Aquarius heaven. Jupiter was in your 1st house and you were living the high life. You were jovial and optimistic and the universe smiled on you. You travelled, you prospered, you were generous and the universe was generous with you. This trend will continue in the year ahead – but in a slightly different way.

This year finances become even more important than they have been for many years. And the year ahead is shaping up to be very prosperous. More on this later.

Aquarians are gifted communicators and intellectuals. However, over the last year you probably were not indulging these interests too much. This will change in the year ahead, as you are taking classes in subjects that interest you, writing, teaching, giving speeches and using your communication skills.

Mars will spend an unusual amount of time in your 7th house in the year ahead, Aquarius. He will spend over 5 months in that house. This will test existing relationships, but bring other kinds of benefits. We will discuss this further in your love forecast.

Spirituality has been important for many years, and most especially in a financial way. But since last year, as Pluto made a major move in your 12th house of spirituality, there has been a major detox going on in your spiritual practice, your spiritual ideals and attitudes. All kinds of false notions about the spiritual life are being washed out of you, and that trend will continue in the year ahead.

Health has been good for some years now and it seems good in the year ahead.

Your major interests in the year ahead are the body, the image, personal appearance and personal pleasure, and finance (from January 1st to June 6th and from August 14th to December 31st), communication and intellectual interests (from May 28th to September 10th), love, romance and social activities (January 1st to June 7th), sex, birth and death, occult studies, reincarnation, debt and the payment of debt, taxes and estates (April 8th to July 22nd), religion, philosophy, higher education and foreign travel (from January 1st to April 8th and July 22nd to December 31st), and spirituality.

Your paths of greatest fulfilment in the year ahead are spirituality, the body, image, personal appearance and personal pleasures (until January 18th), finance (from January 1st to June 6th and from August 14th to December 31st), and communication and intellectual interests (from May 28th to September 10th).

Health

(Please note that this is an astrological perspective on health and not a medical one. In days gone by there was no difference; these perspectives were identical. But nowadays there can be quite a difference. For the medical perspective, please consult your doctor or health practitioner.)

Your 6th house of health is not a House of Power this year, Aquarius, so health and health issues are not a major priority these days. Nor should they be. Health is good. The major long-term planets are either making good aspects to you or they are leaving you alone. Sure, there will be periods in the year where health and energy are not up to their usual standards – but these things come from the transits – they are temporary. When the stressful transits pass, your normal good health returns.

You can make your already good health even better by paying more attention to your stomach and breasts (diet is an important issue for you – both by birth and in the year ahead). Since the Moon is your health planet and she rules the stomach and the breasts, keeping these parts of the body healthy and sound is good preventative medicine. The Moon rules the diet, and so for you diet tends to be a major issue. This is not so for everybody – contrary to much of the popular literature on this subject – but for you it is.

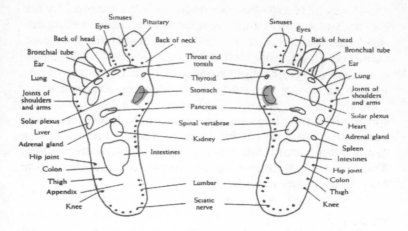

Reflexology

Try to massage the whole foot on a regular basis, but pay extra attention to the points highlighted on the chart. When you massage, be aware of 'sore spots', as these need special attention. It's also a good idea to massage the ankles and top side (as well as the soles) of the feet.

As we have written for many years, *how* you eat is just as important as what you eat. Meals should be taken in peace. Eat slowly and savour your food. (Not so easy to do with our rushed lifestyles.) The act of eating should be elevated from a mere animal function to an act of worship. This not only elevates the vibrations of the food, but elevates the vibrations of the digestive system and changes the whole chemistry of the body. (Masaru Emoto demonstrates this in his book *The Hidden Messages in Water*.) Thus it is a very healthy practice to say grace (in your own words) before eating. Bless your food, say nice things to it, give thanks and appreciation as you eat.

Diet is a very personal issue. No two people and no two Aquarians have exactly the same needs. So this is something to check with a professional.

As our steady readers know, a pathology in the physical body always has a spiritual root cause. In your horoscope, the causes of physical problems lie in the emotions, in the family situation or in a family relationship. Thus, if problems arise, examine these areas. Bring your family life back into harmony. Chances are that doing just this will restore your health. If not, your whole emotional nature will need to be looked at. Do you indulge in negative, unconstructive moods?

The feeling body is very powerful. Some esoteric philosophers compare it to nuclear power. Thus, its abuse brings strong karmic consequences. Are you being manipulative? Are you using feelings to do harm? To control? These are some of the issues to look at if problems arise.

The next area to look at is the past – the memory body. This is the domain of the Moon. In your chart, many physical problems have their root causes in traumas of the past that are not yet 'digested'. These traumas could be from early life – childhood – or even from past lives. When the trauma occurred you unconsciously formed some opinion about the world, about life, about members of a certain sex, about certain situations. Because these opinions or statements were made under trauma, they are most likely incorrect – but they are still active in your feeling body. They need to be uncovered and looked at from a conscious and calm perspective. There are meditative techniques that can assist you here. Also there are professionals who specialize in these kinds of therapies.

The main medicine for you is the maintenance of a happy, harmonious emotional life. All people need to maintain harmony in the feeling body, but for you this has dramatic health consequences. The sages assert that the main reason that a prayer goes unanswered is discord in the emotional body.

As our steady readers know, the Moon is a very fast-moving planet and in any given month moves through all 12 signs and houses of your chart. Thus there are many short-term trends that we will discuss in the monthly reports.

Home and Family

Your 4th house of home and family is not a House of Power this year, Aquarius, nor has it been one for a few years. As our steady readers know, this means that you have much freedom and latitude to shape this area as you like – generally this indicates a status-quo kind of year. There will not be too much change in your home, family and emotional situation in the year ahead. You seem content with things as they are and have little need to make dramatic changes.

Of course, as the year progresses there will be periods in the year where home and family become more important than usual and you will be spending more time and energy in that direction. This year this happens from April 1st to May 21st.

This shows that you will be entertaining more from the home, and beautifying it. The planets that move through your 4th house during this period, Venus and the Sun, both relate to love and beauty. Thus, many of you will redecorate or buy objects of beauty for the home.

If you have plans for major renovations, April 20th to May 21st is probably the best time in the year ahead.

One parent or parent figure seems to be doing major renovations in the home from January 1st to June 7th. Another parent figure seems to have moved in 2009, and could still move early in 2010.

Children of appropriate age probably should not move in the year ahead, but instead should make better use of the space they have. Siblings will see a family relationship tested as three eclipses are in effect in their 4th house of home and family. If there are hidden flaws in their home they will learn about these in the year ahead so that they can make the appropriate corrections. Grandchildren of appropriate age also seem to be making major renovations in the year ahead.

Your family planet, Venus, makes one of her rare retrogrades this year – from October 8th to November 18th. This will be a good time to review your domestic situation and see where improvements can be made. Venus will also spend a lot of time (3 months on and off) in Scorpio, your 10th house, in the year ahead. This indicates that you will be working to integrate home and career – working to have emotional harmony – a 'homely feeling' – in your office or job. The office will become more homelike, and the home more like an office.

Finance and Career

Finances have been important for many, many years now and you have been making very good progress. You are in a long-term cycle of prosperity. Your 2nd house has been strong for many years, and continues to be strong in the year ahead. Jupiter, the planet of abundance, moves into your money house on January 18th and stays there until June 6th, and then moves back in from September 10th to the end of the year. This is a classic signal of financial prosperity and abundance. Not only will there be many new and happy financial opportunities, but things that you already own and perhaps did not value suddenly increase in value. You will discover wealth that you never knew you had.

Jupiter is your planet of friends, thus the obvious message here is that friends will be instrumental in bringing you prosperity. Either they actually come to work for you, or they provide financial opportunity. Your friends are prospering and seem eager to share their prosperity with you. Your social connections are like money in the bank. Wealth of friendships is also a form of wealth, though it may not appear on any balance sheet.

You are always a technologically advanced kind of person, and this is even stronger in the year ahead. I like everything high-tech for you when it comes to finances and in the handling of your finances. All the latest financial software and electronic tools are excellent for you. I not only like technology for managing your money but as a means of making money. Online businesses such as websites, web advertising, startup companies involved in new inventions and makers of new and high-tech gadgetry are all interesting and viable paths to profits. This has been so for many years and is even more so in the year ahead. I like high-tech even from an investment perspective. You have a special intuition for the stocks and bonds of the high-tech and media industry. Involvement in professional or trade organizations will also boost your bottom line.

As we have seen for many years, you are investing in yourself. You consider yourself to be the best investment there is. Thus you dress very expensively and for success. You do not scrimp on yourself. You are creating a personal image of affluence. You have been doing this for many years, and you will be doing it even more in the year ahead.

Jupiter rules foreign travel, publishing, universities and long-distance telecommunications. Investors will want to study these industries for profit opportunities in the year ahead.

Jupiter rules your house of fondest hopes and wishes. So this is a year where your fondest financial hopes and wishes come to pass. A very happy financial year.

Your 10th house of career is not a House of Power this year, Aquarius. Normally this would show a status-quo kind of year. This year I am not so sure. Pluto, your career planet, gets eclipsed on June 26th and camps out on this eclipse point for many months. This would indicate long-term career changes. These changes are not only personal, but involve your corporate hierarchy and your overall industry. Major figures are leaving. There are shakeups in the industry, in the leadership and in the overall rules of the game.

Many of you are so financially successful that your focus is going to shift from finances to communication and intellectual interests. It is as if you have mastered a very difficult subject and now it's time to turn your attention to other things. The pursuit of wealth is not as interesting as it has been for many years. Now you want intellectual challenges. You want to develop mentally. I consider this shift a signal of success. Those of you born early in the sign of Aquarius will feel this shift this year. Those of you born later in the sign will feel this shift in future years. But the shift is coming.

Love and Social Life

Mars, as we mentioned, spends many months in your 7th house of love and marriage. Consider that a typical Mars transit lasts between 1½ and 2 months. This year Mars will spend over 5 months in one sign and house. This shows that a current marriage or serious love relationship is getting tested. The tendency here is towards a power struggle in the relationship. Power struggles are never good for either love or romance. If it is possible to avoid this – and it will be difficult – you should.

On the other hand, Mars in your 7th house indicates that you are more aggressive in love, more proactive. You go after the person you like. You make no bones about it. If you like someone, that person knows it. You're not playing coy or hard to get. Mars in the 7th house also shows someone who is quick to fall in love, someone who jumps into relationships very quickly. It is a love-at-first-sight kind of aspect. The problem with this aspect is being able to maintain this love and this intensity over the long haul. Mars is good at beginning things but has trouble maintaining things.

When your intuition is strong, these love-at-first-sight leaps will tend to be happy and harmonious. And you find that you can get directly to the essence of the relationship – the sharing of love and intimacy without having to go through weeks and perhaps months of courtship and side issues. However, if your intuition is off, these leaps of love can be quite hurtful. But, no matter. Mars in the 7th house for all these months is teaching you to have courage when it comes to love and social relationships. Sure, there will be a few rejections. Sure, not everything will work out as you hope. You pick yourself up and jump back into the fray.

Singles are unlikely to marry this year. Those of you who are into their first or second marriage are having the marriages tested. Those of you who are working towards their third marriage have very wonderful aspects from May to October.

Aquarians will have love opportunities in educational settings – at lectures or seminars – and in the neighbourhood, perhaps even with neighbours. The gym, football pitch, tennis court, exercise studio are also likely venues of romance. Siblings and neighbours play Cupid in the year ahead – especially until June 7th.

Singles are allured to athletic types. But merely being athletic is not enough. The person has to have a good mind in a good body – both the mind and the body are important.

Parents or parent figures are having a status-quo love year. Siblings are having their marriage tested. If the sibling is single, marriage is not likely in the year ahead. Children of appropriate age are having a status-quo kind of year. Singles will most likely remain single, marrieds will remain married. Grandchildren of appropriate age have a very exciting, but highly unstable, love life – marriage is not advisable, though there will be opportunities.

Self-improvement

We talked earlier about overcoming social and romantic fear. This was the lesson in the past few months of last year, and this lesson continues until June 7th of this year. The reason why so many people are not experiencing the love life of their dreams – of fulfilling romance that the heart craves – is due to fear. Fear is manifold. Perhaps the main one is fear of rejection. But there are fears related to inadequacy and unworthiness as well.

Sometimes the best way to overcome fear is to do the things that you fear. Do them and experience the consequences. They will not be anywhere near what you have imagined. True, you might experience some rejection. True, you might have some short-term pain. But you will find that the actual experience is nowhere near as dire as you had imagined it to be. In fact, it can be fun. And in many cases, although you fear rejection, it will not happen. And if it happens, it will not be as dire as you thought. Why deprive yourself of your rightful happiness?

Aquarians are intellectuals. From the astrological perspective, Aquarius represents the highest development of the mind. So it is not surprising that in their spiritual life they will approach things from a rational, scientific and intellectual perspective. You are comfortable with this approach, and there is much to be said in its favour. However, your spiritual planet has recently moved into the sign of Libra and will spend most of the year ahead there. It will retrograde briefly into Virgo from April 8th to July 22nd. But for most of the year it is in Libra. This suggests a shift in your spiritual practice and attitudes. Yes, reason, science and intellectual understanding are very important on the spiritual path, and you rightly discern that there is a science to all of this. But in the year ahead you will be developing a more love-based approach. Your heart will receive more development. It's not enough for you to have a rational understanding of the divine; you need actually to feel it in your heart. This is a year for cultivating unconditional love. When you are in love, in a state of love, you easily experience the divine. The path of beauty is also a viable spiritual path in the year ahead. For when we contemplate beauty, love naturally arises. The creative arts will also be a viable path. For as you create, whether it be a painting, a poem, a sculpture or other work of art, you will be employing the same laws as go into creating a universe. There is no better way to understand a great creator than by being a creator yourself.

Spiritual healing has been a major interest for a few years and will continue to be so from April 8th to July 22nd as your spiritual planet moves into Virgo. Many of you will be involved in prayer circles or other spiritual healing projects. Many of you will use the techniques of spiritual healing for yourself and for other people. Your spiritual planet in the 9th house also gives us other messages about your spirituality. The most important message is that Saturn will start to test all your religious and metaphysical beliefs. These will be tested by your personal spiritual experiences. This will be the ultimate test for you. All religions were based on the mystical experiences of their founders. Your mystical experience must define your religious path and beliefs. So for the next year or two, many of your religious beliefs are going to be tested, revised, reorganized and reformed. This will have a profound impact on your whole life, because your belief system, your personal religion, shapes your world view and your psychological reactions. Thus it affects your day-to-day life and behaviour in a very powerful way.

Month-by-month Forecasts

January

Best Days Overall: 6, 7, 16, 17, 25, 26
Most Stressful Days Overall: 2, 3, 8, 9, 23, 24, 30
Best Days for Love: 2, 3, 4, 5, 13, 14, 15, 25, 26, 30
Best Days for Money: 6, 7, 16, 17, 18, 19, 26, 27
Best Days for Career: 8, 9, 13, 23

You begin your year with 70 to 80 per cent of the planets in the independent East. This is a time when success and happiness come from your personal initiative. You are to be the creator of your conditions for happiness. Thus, if there is some condition that displeases you, change it or create something new. You have the power now. The world will adapt to you. If others don't go along (highly unlikely), then you can go on your own. You are having life on your terms now.

This month (on the 20th) the planetary power shifts from the upper to the lower half of your horoscope. By now career objectives (in the short term) have been achieved. You are entering the 'night-time' of your year. Time to focus on your emotional life – on being in the 'right inner state', in emotional harmony. You need to 'feel right' these days – and when this happens, doing right will follow naturally. It's time to get family relations and the daily domestic life in order as well.

Spirituality has been important for many years now, but it has been increasing in importance over the past few years. It is actually your spiritual mission now. As you progress inwardly, spiritually, all the other affairs of your life will just fall into place – very naturally – and this includes your career and finances. You have seen this last year and will see it again in the year ahead. Spirit, whose law is always beauty and harmony, will make your life like a 'ballet' – there will be movement, but events will flow with beauty and grace.

Until the 20th it is good to review the past year in a sober and honest way. Be ruthlessly honest with yourself. Where have you succeeded? Where have you failed? Where have you been just so-so? What can be done to improve things? What should be eliminated? What mistakes have been made? Where do you want to go in the year ahead? This kind of review will be helpful in starting your personal new year (your birthday) with a clean slate.

On the 20th you enter a yearly personal pleasure peak. Spirituality is not just about enjoying the abstract pleasures of the spiritual world – it is also tangible and physical. It brings to the body everything it needs for perfect harmony – and this is a period when you see it.

Love has been stressful of late – and there are still challenges – but your lover or spouse seems devoted to you – going out of his or her way to please you. Love opportunities – and good ones – are pursuing you these days. You look good, too. Venus enters your sign on the 18th giving glamour, beauty and grace to the physical image. And the Sun, your love planet, enters Aquarius on the 20th – adding a double dose of the same. But power struggles in love are the main problem – not the way you look.

A financial bonanza happened last month, but could still happen early this month.

February

Best Days Overall: 2, 3, 12, 13, 22, 23
Most Stressful Days Overall: 5, 6, 19, 20, 21, 26, 27
Best Days for Love: 2, 3, 13, 14, 15, 24, 25, 26, 27
Best Days for Money: 3, 4, 5, 13, 14, 15, 16, 23, 24
Best Days for Career: 1, 5, 6, 9, 19, 28

You have just come off a very prosperous year, and last month (on the 18th), as Jupiter moved into your money house, prosperity increased. It increases even further this month as, on the 18th, you enter a yearly financial peak.

You are a natural communicator and intellectual person. A mind person. But these days communication seems even more important than usual. Mars, your communication planet, has been the 'handle' of a 'bucket'-type chart since the beginning of the year – and it is still so now. So communication is the way you lift up your life (the bucket) – communication and your intellectual prowess. But with Mars retrograde since the beginning of the year all these kinds of projects – speeches, sales and marketing projects, mass mailings, teaching ventures – need more review and study. There are many ways that these things can be improved; this is the time to search for them.

Another reason why I feel prosperity is strong is that you are coming from your strength and power – from your natural interests and natural abilities. Jupiter is your planet of friends and networking – one of your main strengths and loves. Nobody does this better than you – and where is Jupiter? In your money house. Uranus, your ruler (and a very benefic influence) also rules these things – networking, friends, technology, electronic communication – and is also in your money house. So you are making money from your natural, innate abilities – and thus success is happening. Money-making is pleasurable to you. Another big plus. This month, on the 18th, the Sun will enter your money house, initiating a yearly financial peak. Don't spend all your money in one place!

This month, after the 18th, the love planets in your horoscope – Venus, the generic love planet, and the Sun, the actual love planet in your chart – are in your money house. This adds another dimension to finances. It indicates that your spouse or current love is supporting your financial goals and working actively on your financial behalf. It shows that your social connections – always important – are even more important financially now. A business partnership or joint venture seems in the works. You manage to combine finance and your social life in one neat package. Many of the parties you are attending are about business, or have financial undercurrents. You tend to pal around with the wealthy.

For singles, love opportunities are still pursuing them until the 18th. Nothing special needs to be done. Love finds you. After the 18th, love opportunities will come as you pursue your normal financial goals – or with people involved in your finances. You are torn in love matters this month. A part of you is very idealistic about love – the feeling of love, the chemistry is very important – but another part of you is practical and bottom-line orientated as well. You want the good provider. If you can find both in one person, that would be the ideal. Not so easy, though.

Though love opportunities are plentiful, marriage is not advisable now. Give things time.

March

Best Days Overall: 2, 3, 11, 12, 21, 22, 29, 30
Most Stressful Days Overall: 4, 5, 19, 20, 25, 26, 31
Best Days for Love: 4, 5, 6, 14, 15, 16, 17, 25, 26
Best Days for Money: 3, 4, 5, 12, 14, 15, 22, 23, 24, 30, 31
Best Days for Career: 4, 5, 9, 18, 19, 27, 31

Your communication planet, Mars, starts to move forward on the 10th. Mercury, the generic communication planet, is moving forward all month. Thus this is an excellent time to release ad campaigns, mass mailings or marketing projects. After the 20th, as the Sun enters Aries and moves into your 3rd house of communication, would be best. (Mercury will be in your 3rd house from the 17th onwards.) Aries energy is always good for starting new things, and the Moon will be waxing.

Health has been good these past few months and looks good this month as well. Except for Mars – which has been making a stressful aspect to you since the beginning of the year – all the major long-term planets are either helping you or leaving you alone. You can enhance your already good health even further in the ways described in the yearly report.

The New Moon of the 15th boosts finances, and also clarifies them in the month ahead. All the information that you need for making good financial decisions is on its way to you – very naturally and effortlessly. This New Moon also brings a happy job opportunity for job-seekers. You are in a mood to handle the minutiae – the details – of life then and should take advantage of it. (Minutiae seem a part of life and we all have to deal with them, but best when we are in the mood for them – otherwise they're just dull and boring.)

You are still in the midst of a yearly financial peak until the 20th. After that you enter Aquarius heaven: the focus is on communication and intellectual interests. Your normally sharp mind becomes even sharper – communication skills, always good, get even better. You are inspired and eloquent.

Like Gemini, you see 'learning' as fun – interesting – sometimes better than a night out on the town. A good writer will intrigue you more than the hot rock star of the moment. So what fun when the cosmos pushes you into what you love anyway?

Though relationships are still being tested and marriage is probably not advisable during this period, there are still many love opportunities for singles. Until the 20th love happens as you pursue your financial goals or with people involved in your finances. Material gifts turn you on. But wealth alone is not enough – you want that feeling of romantic passion. Yes, you love the good provider, but there's a part of you that loves the penniless poet, yogi or musician – the person who disdains mere wealth and seeks fulfilment in the spirit. The wealthy person satisfies your worldly longings, but the other type satisfies your higher longings. Oh, to be able to have both in the same person!

After the 20th both of the love planets in your chart are in the 3rd house. Love attitudes shift again. Now good communication is important in love. You are allured by the writer, teacher and intellectual. You need to enjoy the mental pleasures with your beloved. You want someone you can discuss intellectual ideas with. Intellectual compatibility becomes important in love. Singles will start to find love opportunities in educational settings – at school, lectures or seminars. Love is close to home – in the neighbourhood, perhaps with neighbours. The danger now is that you will leap rashly into relationships – you are very much a love-at-first-sight person these days.

April

Best Days Overall: 8, 9, 17, 18, 26, 27
Most Stressful Days Overall: 1, 15, 16, 22, 23, 28, 29
Best Days for Love: 3, 4, 5, 13, 14, 15, 16, 22, 23, 24, 25
Best Days for Money: 1, 9, 10, 11, 18, 19, 20, 27, 28, 29
Best Days for Career: 1, 5, 15, 24, 28, 29

Your spiritual planet, Saturn, has been retrograde since January 13th and is retrograde all month now as well. Pluto in your 12th house of spirituality – also an important factor in your spiritual life – starts to retrograde on the 7th. Avoid making major changes to your spiritual regime and practice. Progress might be slower now, or not as satisfactory as usual, but it is time to learn patience and persistence. Visions, intuitions and revelations will need more verification these days.

Your spiritual planet will change signs on the 3rd – it moves from Libra back into Virgo. This would suggest a need to focus more on spiritual healing, both for yourself and for others. Also it suggests a need for understanding the spiritual perspective on death and sex in a deeper way. There are subconscious obstructions to meditation that need to be cleared.

Your 4th house of home and family becomes very powerful after the 20th. Most of the planets are still below the horizon. (You are in the midnight of your year – the midnight hour, where the powers of the night are strongest.) Your career planet goes retrograde on the 7th and your 10th house of career is basically empty – only the Moon moves through there on the 1st, 28th and 29th. A very clear message: Let go of your career – de-emphasize it temporarily – and focus on the home, family and emotional issues. This is a good time (all month) to redecorate or beautify the home. Also wonderful for entertaining from home, attending family gatherings and doing things to foster harmony in the family unit. With your spiritual life also powerful these days, you will be able to make much psychological progress now – there is good insight into why you feel as you do, and why your moods are the way they are.

There are career opportunities happening for you after the 20th, but with Pluto retrograde give them more thought and study. Don't rush into anything. Get all the facts – these things might not be as they seem.

Health has been good so far this year, but after the 20th rest and relax more. Pace yourself. Get a good night's sleep. Energy and vitality are not what they should be. These problems are short term – not trends for the year. Enhance your health in the ways mentioned in the yearly report, but also pay more attention to your heart from the 20th onwards.

Finances are excellent now as well. You might have to work harder after the 20th, but the payoffs are there.

Until the 20th you are in a strong intellectual and communication period; after that the focus is on the home and family.

The love trends are pretty much as we described last month, until the 20th. You need mental/intellectual compatibility. After the 20th you seem more nostalgic about love – there is a tendency to look backwards – to old love experiences and old flames. This is especially so if the issues between you and these people have not been resolved. Often old flames come back into your life precisely for this reason – to clear the decks and resolve old issues – to put the old to bed or to renew things to their ultimate conclusion. After the 20th, emotional compatibility becomes important. Intellectual intimacy was nice, but now you want emotional intimacy as well.

May

Best Days Overall: 5, 6, 15, 23, 24
Most Stressful Days Overall: 12, 13, 19, 20, 25, 26
Best Days for Love: 2, 3, 5, 6, 12, 13, 15, 16, 19, 20, 23, 25, 26
Best Days for Money: 6, 7, 8, 9, 16, 18, 24, 25, 26
Best Days for Career: 2, 3, 12, 21, 25, 26, 29, 30

Many important – and for the most part, happy – changes this month. The first is the planetary shift from the East to the West that began on the 20th of last month. Your period of personal independence is mostly over with (you will not be completely dependent, of course – everything is relative) and now you need the good graces of others to achieve your goals. Personal abilities are always important, but not enough right now – you need the grace and favour others. So, start practising your social skills now.

The second important change – and this is monumental – is Jupiter's conjunction with Uranus – your ruling planet. This conjunction happens in your money house, and so it brings big and sudden wealth to you. New and important friends are coming into the picture. A very strong friendship is developing – you seem very close. You are travelling more. Earnings are sky-high. Your awesome networking abilities are very much expanded. You are leading the good life these days – good food, good wine, good clothing and good sex. You are experiencing your 'fondest hopes and wishes' on a personal, physical level.

The third major change is Uranus' move into your 3rd house of communication on the 28th. Finance (as we mentioned in the yearly report) has been important for many years, and it is still important – but for now you have achieved some cherished financial goals and can focus elsewhere: on expanding your mind, teaching and learning, writing and the like. You are travelling more this month – both domestic and foreign. New and expensive high-tech equipment is coming to you, so it will be more easy to achieve your intellectual goals – probably online.

Probably you will change your wardrobe and your look. For the past 8 or so years you have been cultivating the image of wealth. Now you will cultivate a more 'brainy' image.

Family and emotional issues are still important until the 20th. The trends of last month are still very much in effect. You can de-emphasize your career now. In a few months it will start becoming important again, but right now, symbolically speaking, you are getting a good night's rest.

On the 21st, as the Sun enters your 5th house, you enter another yearly personal pleasure period. And you have the money to enjoy it to the full.

Health still needs watching until the 20th, but afterwards health and energy return to your normal levels. Enhance your health by paying more attention to your stomach, breasts and the diet – all month – to your heart until the 20th, and to your kidneys and hips after the 20th. Emotional health and well-being is always important to you, but especially after the 20th. Your focus on emotional harmony this month will have a positive impact on your health. Spiritual healing techniques are especially powerful from the 2nd–4th, 21st–22nd and 30th–31st.

June

Best Days Overall: 1, 2, 11, 12, 19, 20, 29, 30
Most Stressful Days Overall: 9, 10, 15, 16, 21, 22
Best Days for Love: 1, 2, 4, 5, 11, 12, 13, 14, 15, 16, 21, 24, 25
Best Days for Money: 2, 4, 5, 6, 12, 15, 20, 24, 30
Best Days for Career: 9, 18, 21, 22, 26

On the 21st of last month you entered a yearly personal pleasure peak. A time to explore the fun of life – to make happiness itself your goal. Many people think that happiness is due to 'outer things' or 'outer circumstances' – but that kind of happiness is transitory. From the spiritual perspective it is just the opposite – happiness – the inner state –

produces all the outer things and conditions that we thought produced it. A good month to prove this for yourself.

Love is happy this period, but not serious. Romance is just another form of entertainment – like going to the cinema or to a resort. Perhaps this is a good thing. Mars in your 7th house has been stressing serious relationships. The person who can show you a good time is the one that allures you. Love is about fun and not about responsibility. There is a feeling that it has to be 'honeymoonish' all the time. When the tough times come – and they inevitably do – either you or your lover 'wants out'. 'I didn't sign up for this,' etc. The aspects for serious romance improve after the 10th as Mars leaves your 7th house. There is no need for you or your lover to show 'dominance' in your relationship. There is a greater chance for harmony now. Romantic Venus enters your 7th house on the 14th and this is also a help.

Venus' move into your 7th house once again produces nostalgia in love – and perhaps again brings an old flame into the romantic picture. Sometimes it is the actual old flame and sometimes merely someone who is 'similar' to that person – who has the same patterns as that person. This helps to resolve old issues. Family can play Cupid this period. There are more family gatherings and more entertaining from home.

On the 21st your love planet moves into the 6th house. For singles this brings a more serious attitude to love. Love is not just about fun and games – though this is part of it – but also about family and about service to your beloved. If you love someone, you work on their behalf and serve their interests in practical and perhaps unglamorous ways. Singles find love opportunities at the workplace or as they pursue their health goals – at the gym, yoga studio or doctor's surgery. Healers and health professionals are more alluring now. Love is close to home these days. No need to travel to exotic places, it is close by.

Health is much improved this month and you are focused here after the 21st. You are into healthy lifestyles, diet and health regimes.

Mars entering your 8th house on the 7th indicates a more sexually active period. Libido is strong. But Saturn is also in this house. Mars says 'more is better'. Saturn, says 'hold on, focus on quality not quantity'. Another good month to go more deeply into the spiritual aspects of sex.

A lunar eclipse on the 26th is announcing job changes, changes in your health regime and spiritual changes. Job-seekers need not worry. Jobs and job opportunities seem plentiful. This eclipse is basically benign to you.

July

Best Days Overall: 8, 9, 17, 26, 27
Most Stressful Days Overall: 6, 7, 13, 19, 20
Best Days for Love: 1, 2, 5, 10, 11, 12, 13, 14, 20, 23, 24, 31
Best Days for Money: 1, 2, 3, 9, 12, 18, 21, 27, 28, 29, 30, 31
Best Days for Career: 6, 14, 19, 20, 23

Last month's lunar eclipse on the 26th affected your work situation, the rules of the workplace and relations with co-workers. On the 11th we have a bit of a repeat performance. This is a solar eclipse that occurs in your 6th house of health and work. Health looks good overall, so the eclipse is proba-bly only showing changes in your health regime and not serious health problems. (Your personal horoscope, cast especially for the date and time of your birth, could modify what we say here.) This eclipse – as with every solar eclipse – tests marriages and current love relationships. The dirty laundry comes up for cleansing. Long pent-up feelings get discharged. Good relationships survive and get even better. But the flimsy ones are threatened. Be more patient with your beloved these days. He or she is much more tempera-mental than usual. Business partnerships also get tested now. Likely that your beloved will start to redefine his or her image and personality – entire self-concept – now.

On the 23rd, two important things happen. First, the Sun enters your 7th house of love – initiating a yearly social and romantic peak. Your social life is activated now. A magic button has been pushed and you are more in the mood for love. Serious opportunities are more likely now – especially from the 22nd to the 26th. Weddings in the family could have happened last month, but they can happen this month as well.

Your financial planet, Neptune, went retrograde on the 28th of last month and will be retrograde for many more months. Finances are still excellent and exciting, and this retrograde won't stop earnings, but it brings a bit of a 'breather' to finances – a slowing down. You understand that many important deals or projects can't happen immediately but will require time. This is a good opportunity to review your finances and work out the various strategies – e.g. this investment gives x amount for x amount of years, while the other gives y amount. This path leads to my goal in x amount of years, while the other paths takes y amount of years. Hope you see what we're driving at here. Work out the various financial scenarios that are before you. It takes time to do these things, but now is the time. This is a time for intellectual and emotional clarity in finances.

Retrograde activity is increasing this month. By the end of the month 40 per cent of the planets are retrograde. Most areas of your life – finance, career and your personal life – are under review. Only your love life seems to be moving forward.

Health needs more watching after the 23rd, but the stress is only temporary. Overall, health is good. This is just not one of your best periods. Pay attention to your stomach, breasts and diet all month, and to your heart after the 23rd.

August

   Best Days Overall: 5, 6, 13, 14, 22, 23
   Most Stressful Days Overall: 2, 3, 9, 10, 15, 16, 30, 31
   Best Days for Love: 1, 3, 4, 9, 10, 13, 17, 18, 22, 23, 29, 30
   Best Days for Money: 6, 9, 14, 17, 24, 25, 26, 27
   Best Days for Career: 2, 11, 15, 16, 20, 29

Ever since Uranus started to retrograde last month, self-confidence and self-esteem have not been what they should be. There is nothing wrong with you *per se*, only you are questioning yourself more, reviewing your personal goals. A little self-doubt (so long as you don't overdo it) is sometimes healthy – if done honestly it leads to self-improvement and to greater confidence and self-esteem later on. But this doesn't seem to have an impact on love, which is going strong – you are in the midst of a yearly social peak until the 23rd. In fact, a little humility is often attractive to others and enhances your appeal.

Uranus retrogrades back into Pisces this month, and so you are returning your focus to finances again. Your spirituality and intuition again become important in your life – especially in finances.

Last month, on the 23rd, the planetary power shifted from the lower half to the upper half of your horoscope. You entered the 'dawn' period of your year. You are refreshed after a good night's sleep and ready to face the day with new energy, zeal and enthusiasm. Time now to make all those dreams and visualizations tangible realities. Let go of family issues for a while and focus on your career. There are still many changes going on there – much instability – you need to tread slowly and carefully – but give your focus here. Your career planet is still retrograde, but many interesting things are happening behind the scenes.

Love is romantic and fun until the 23rd. Love is more honeymoonish – fun. Even longtime relationships are more romantic these days. For singles, love is about fun. Marriage should be fun. But this attitude changes after the 23rd as your love planet enters Virgo. Venus is in Virgo until the 7th. Your love planet will be there from the 23rd onwards. You want perfection in love and in your social life. You are like the doctor searching for pathologies in your relationship so that you can 'correct' them. Only keep in mind that your focus on pathology can actually do more damage than you thought. For if you seek, you will find. Little things can be magnified out of all proportion. By all means, perfect your relationship, but also keep the good (and not just the problems) in mind. You will need to work harder to indicate love and warmth to others this month. Your tendency will be to come from the head rather than the heart. Give more conscious attention to this.

Health needs watching until the 23rd. Rest and relax more and maintain high energy levels. There is nothing seriously wrong, just lowered energy. Enhance your health in the ways mentioned in the yearly report. Your enthusiasm for health regimes will be strongest from the 10th to the 24th.

September

   Best Days Overall: 1, 2, 9, 10, 18, 19, 20, 28, 29
   Most Stressful Days Overall: 5, 6, 11, 12, 26, 27
   Best Days for Love: 2, 5, 6, 7, 8, 11, 17, 21, 28
   Best Days for Money: 2, 5, 10, 12, 19, 20, 21, 22, 29, 30
   Best Days for Career: 7, 11, 12, 16, 26

Mars re-stimulates an eclipse point on the 1st, so drive more carefully, mind your temper and avoid arguments, confrontations and risky behaviour. This is not a day to be a daredevil. Cars and communication equipment can behave erratically, too.

The Sun will re-stimulate an eclipse point from the 27th to the 29th and this can produce disruptions or upheavals in love – short term. It can test a current relationship or produce dramas in the life of your beloved. Be more patient with your beloved and with friends during this period.

Your spiritual planet, Saturn, will re-stimulate an eclipse point all month. Dreams, intuitions and spiritual teachings need more verification. You are making changes in your spiritual practice and attitudes. Spiritual mentors or gurus are experiencing dramatic events in their lives. There is much upheaval in a spiritual organization or charity that you are involved with.

Your 8th house got strong on the 23rd of last month and will remain strong until the 23rd of this month. A time for getting rid of excess in your life. Happiness and success are not so much about 'adding' things to your life, but about getting rid of the things that don't belong there. When this is done, happiness and success just sort of naturally happen. So, this is a good time to detox the body, the home, the mental and emotional life. Get rid of possessions that you no longer need. Get rid of the clutter in your home and in your mind. Simply, simplify. Those on the spiritual path will be more involved with spiritual detox as well – exorcisms, the cleansing of the home and environment from discarnate entities or negative geo-pathological fields. Psychic cords, connections and rapports that are no longer useful – or discordant – should be broken. The spiritual atmosphere about you needs a good cleansing.

When the 8th house is strong, sexual activity tends to increase. Libido increases. All in proportion to your age and stage in life.

These detoxes will improve your love life dramatically. After the 23rd love will be more romantic, more idyllic, more idealistic. Sexual chemistry will be important, but other things will also become important – philosophical and spiritual compatibility. You will come more from your heart than from your head, and this will be a help. You will gravitate to mentor types – gurus and professors – people you can learn from. Singles find love in educational and religious-type settings. Perhaps in a foreign land or with a foreigner. Marital problems can be eased by a foreign journey or by taking courses together as a couple – by worshipping together. Professors and ministers – the priests in your life – are more apt to play Cupid these days. There is a love meeting with a spiritual, creative person – perhaps a guru type – later in the month.

October

Best Days Overall: 7, 8, 16, 17, 25, 26, 27
Most Stressful Days Overall: 3, 4, 9, 10, 23, 24, 30, 31
Best Days for Love: 1, 3, 4, 7, 9, 17, 18, 19, 27, 28, 30, 31
Best Days for Money: 2, 8, 10, 17, 18, 19, 27, 29
Best Days for Career: 5, 9, 10, 13, 23

A love encounter with a guru or spiritual person – someone involved in your spiritual life – is still likely on the 1st and 2nd. But this can also manifest as a romantic meeting in a spiritual-type setting – a spiritual lecture, retreat or meditation seminar.

You are basically an intellectual type. Too much feeling – too much emotion – is not comfortable for you – it interferes with your thought process. Also, you tend to express yourself in a logical way – more through the mind than through the heart. Yet these sterling qualities can be a problem this month. There is a lot of water in your horoscope. At times as much as 70 per cent. Thus people in general are more emotional, more feeling-orientated these days. Your matter-of-fact, logical approach – the way you speak – can be devastating to more sensitive types. So be more aware – especially with loved ones. It will be harder to 'think straight' this month as well – especially after the 23rd, as the energy is more emotional. You can do it, but you have to work harder at it.

Foreign travel is important this month, as your 9th house is powerful, but with Venus (your 9th house ruler) going retrograde on the 8th, best to do your travelling before then. If this is not possible, protect yourself – allow more time to get to your destination, make sure you have travel insurance on the ticket, and don't schedule connecting flights too tightly.

Career is powerful and successful this month. Pluto, your career planet, started moving forward last month – and by now you have greater clarity as to what you have to do and where you have to go. Your 10th house of career is powerful all month, but especially after the 23rd. You enter a yearly career peak then. With your 4th house basically empty (only the Moon visits there on the 23rd and 24th) and the ruler of the 4th retrograde – not much you can do at home anyway. Long-term decisions need more time and thought. You might as well focus on your career. Family seems supportive of your career as well – you don't seem to be alienating them. The family as a whole is elevated in status. Family members – parents or parent figures – are also succeeding in their careers. You have a lot of help in your career this month – from family, your spouse, friends or a current love, siblings and neighbours – and even children.

All this focus on your career – and it is demanding – puts more stress on your health after the 23rd. So rest and relax more. There's no way you can avoid the demands of your career, but you can focus on the important things and let the less important go. Organize your day so that more gets done with less energy. Make sure to get a good night's sleep. Pay more attention to your heart after the 23rd as well.

Love seems happy this month. You put your beloved on a pedestal and he or she loves it. You seem to give your beloved due honour and glory. You make your relationship a priority in your life – in spite of all the career demands. The problem is that your beloved – your spouse or partner – seems to be calling the shots. Right now you don't seem to mind, but that can change in future months.

November

Best Days Overall: 3, 4, 12, 13, 22, 23
Most Stressful Days Overall: 5, 6, 19, 20, 21, 26, 27
Best Days for Love: 5, 6, 13, 15, 16, 23, 26, 27
Best Days for Money: 4, 6, 13, 14, 15, 16, 23, 25
Best Days for Career: 1, 5, 6, 10, 19, 28

Career is important and successful. You are still in the midst of a yearly career peak until the 22nd. The whole family seems successful – like last month – and they seem basically supportive of your goals. You are adept at meeting just the right people who can help your career. Your likeability is a big factor in your success. Sure, there are some career challenges – you had them last month as well – but your drive, your zeal to succeed (plus all the help you're getting) easily enables you to overcome.

Love is still happy and much of what we discussed last month still applies. You give priority to your relationship – it is important in your life – you give your beloved his or her just due. You are not taking love for granted. For singles, two things seem important in love these days (last month as well): good sexual chemistry, and high position and status. For marrieds, good sex will cover many sins in the marriage. Problems in the marriage can also be helped by pursuing career ventures as a team. Make your spouse your career partner, even if you don't actually work together. Confide in each other. Seek advice and counsel.

After the 22nd, your love attitudes change somewhat. Friendship – equality – is important. Good philosophical compatibility is also important. No matter how good the sexual chemistry is, if there is not a basic friendship between you and a basically similar world view, the relationship will have problems.

Though equality seems important, your partner or spouse still seems to be calling the shots – and this can create some tension.

Your career planet retrogrades back into Libra, your 9th house, before going direct on the 18th. This suggests many things. First off, new career opportunities need more study – especially if the changes are major. Second, your willingness to travel and go further in your education seem to play important roles in success. Third, you need to be a good mentor to those below you and a good disciple to those above you.

Last month the planetary power shifted from the West to the East. You have entered a period of greater independence, which will get stronger day by day and month by month – personal independence will reach its maximum around your birthday in 2011. Thus, you need not adapt to difficult conditions. Change them or create new ones. Other people are important and it is nice to be popular, but personal ability – who you are – is more important for success than whom you know or how popular you are. Personal initiative and drive will bring you success.

Finances have been good all year and are especially good this month. The trends we wrote of in the yearly report are still very much in effect now. Networking, online activities, friendships and organizations are not only important on a financial level, but in general as well. Your 11th house, which rules these things, is very powerful after the 22nd.

December

Best Days Overall: 1, 9, 10, 11, 19, 20, 28, 29
Most Stressful Days Overall: 3, 4, 17, 18, 23, 24, 30, 31
Best Days for Love: 2, 5, 12, 16, 22, 23, 24, 26, 31
Best Days for Money: 2, 4, 11, 12, 13, 20, 23, 29, 31
Best Days for Career: 3, 4, 7, 17, 25, 26, 30, 31

Spirituality has been important to you for many years. Last year, when Pluto moved into your 12th house, it actually became your mission in life – the most important thing in your life. We have discussed this in the yearly report. But this month, as your 12th house gets powerful, it becomes even more important. It is the centrepiece of the whole month ahead.

Some 50 per cent of the planets will either be in your 12th house or move through there this month. Thus, you are seeing the fruits of your spiritual efforts. Perhaps you had some 'dry spells' in your practice. Perhaps you wondered whether your practice was 'working' or having any impact. This month you see that it had.

When the 12th house is strong, most people start having super normal experiences, enhanced ESP, intuition and prophetic types of experience. But your experiences will be particularly remarkable. It's the kind of a month (especially from the 23rd onwards) where you want to leave the world and sit at the feet of the guru in some mountaintop retreat (and many of you will be doing this). The material world loses all interest for you. You disconnect from it and connect closer to the Spirit. Some sages affirm that one second of spiritual bliss surpasses a lifetime of pleasures in the material world. And you will be experiencing a lot of this – especially those of you on the path.

This is a period when you socialize with spiritual types – fellow followers of the path. Singles (and perhaps marrieds too) will make friends with angels, masters and cosmic beings. This will be your social life – and it is quite adequate.

Those not yet deeply into the path will have love opportunities in spiritual organizations, spiritual groups, meditation seminars and spiritual retreats. The hot spots in town are not where love is for you these days.

Your financial well-being is also very dependent on your spiritual connection – your intuition – your high vibration. So all these spiritual activities will help in a very bottom-line, practical way.

Your dream life becomes so active and vivid, that many would prefer to stay asleep than to wake up – sleeping is much more entertaining.

A lunar eclipse on the 21st occurs right on the cusp of the 5th and 6th houses and will have an impact on both these houses. Thus there are job changes coming up – changes in the workplace and in the conditions of work. The dreams you are having during this period should be taken with many grains of salt. In general, your dreams will be prophetic and accurate this month – but during the eclipse period you might just be seeing flotsam and jetsam stirred up by the eclipse.

There will be changes in your health regime or diet. Those who employ others will have some employee turnover – or weird behaviour by employees. Those of you in the creative arts will make important changes in your creativity. Children, or those who are like children to you, can have dramatic experiences. Also they will be redefining their image and personality. This eclipse is basically benign to you, but children, aunts and uncles (who also might be having dramatic experiences) should take a reduced schedule.

Pisces

Ӿ

THE FISH
*Birthdays from
19th February to
20th March*

Personality Profile

PISCES AT A GLANCE

Element – Water

Ruling Planet – Neptune
  Career Planet – Pluto
  Love Planet – Mercury
  Money Planet – Mars
  Planet of Health and Work – Sun
  Planet of Home and Family Life – Mercury
  Planet of Love Affairs, Creativity and Children
    – Moon

Colours – aqua, blue-green

*Colours that promote love, romance and social
  harmony* – earth tones, yellow, yellow-
  orange

Colours that promote earning power – red,
  scarlet

Gem – white diamond

Metal – tin

Scent – lotus

Quality – mutable (= flexibility)

Qualities most needed for balance – structure and the ability to handle form

Strongest virtues – psychic power, sensitivity, self-sacrifice, altruism

Deepest needs – spiritual illumination, liberation

Characteristics to avoid – escapism, keeping bad company, negative moods

Signs of greatest overall compatibility – Cancer, Scorpio

Signs of greatest overall incompatibility – Gemini, Virgo, Sagittarius

Sign most helpful to career – Sagittarius

Sign most helpful for emotional support – Gemini

Sign most helpful financially – Aries

Sign best for marriage and/or partnerships – Virgo

Sign most helpful for creative projects – Cancer

Best Sign to have fun with – Cancer

Signs most helpful in spiritual matters – Scorpio, Aquarius

Best day of the week – Thursday

Understanding a Pisces

If Pisces have one outstanding quality it is their belief in the invisible, spiritual and psychic side of things. This side of things is as real to them as the hard earth beneath their feet – so real, in fact, that they will often ignore the visible, tangible aspects of reality in order to focus on the invisible and so-called intangible ones.

Of all the signs of the zodiac, the intuitive and emotional faculties of the Pisces are the most highly developed. They are committed to living by their intuition and this can at times be infuriating to other people – especially those who are materially, scientifically or technically orientated. If you think that money or status or worldly success are the only goals in life, then you will never understand a Pisces.

Pisces have intellect, but to them intellect is only a means by which they can rationalize what they know intuitively. To an Aquarius or a Gemini the intellect is a tool with which to gain knowledge. To a well-developed Pisces it is a tool by which to express knowledge.

Pisces feel like fish in an infinite ocean of thought and feeling. This ocean has many depths, currents and undercurrents. They long for purer waters where the denizens are good, true and beautiful, but they are sometimes pulled to the lower, murkier depths. Pisces know that they do not generate thoughts but only tune in to thoughts that already exist; this is why they seek the purer waters. This ability to tune in to higher thoughts inspires them artistically and musically.

Since Pisces is so spiritually orientated – though many Pisces in the corporate world may hide this fact – we will deal with this aspect in greater detail, for otherwise it is difficult to understand the true Pisces personality.

There are four basic attitudes of the spirit. One is outright scepticism – the attitude of secular humanists. The second is an intellectual or emotional belief, where one worships a far-distant God figure – the attitude of most modern church-going people. The third is not only belief but direct personal spiritual experience – this is the attitude of some 'born-again' religious people. The fourth is actual unity with the divinity, an intermingling with the spiritual world – this is the attitude of yoga. This fourth attitude is the deepest urge of a Pisces, and a Pisces is uniquely qualified to pursue and perform this work.

Consciously or unconsciously, Pisces seek this union with the spiritual world. The belief in a greater reality makes Pisces very tolerant and understanding of others – perhaps even too tolerant. There are instances in their lives when they should say 'enough is enough' and be ready to defend their position and put up a fight. However, because of their qualities it takes a good deal of doing to get them into that frame of mind.

Pisces basically want and aspire to be 'saints'. They do so in their own way and according to their own rules. Others should not try to impose their concept of saintliness on a Pisces, because he or she always tries to find it for him- or herself.

Finance

Money is generally not that important to Pisces. Of course they need it as much as anyone else, and many of them attain great wealth. But money is not generally a primary objective. Doing good, feeling good about oneself, peace of mind, the relief of pain and suffering – these are the things that matter most to a Pisces.

Pisces earn money intuitively and instinctively. They follow their hunches rather than their logic. They tend to be generous and perhaps overly charitable. Almost any kind of misfortune is enough to move a Pisces to give. Although this is one of their greatest virtues, Pisces should be more careful with their finances. They should try to be more choosy about the people to whom they lend money, so that they are not being taken advantage of. If they give money to charities they should follow it up to see that their contributions are put to good use. Even when Pisces are not rich, they still like to spend money on helping others. In this case they should

really be careful, however: they must learn to say no sometimes and help themselves first.

Perhaps the biggest financial stumbling block for the Pisces
is general passivity – a *laissez faire* attitude. In general Pisces
like to go with the flow of events. When it comes to financial
matters, especially, they need to be more aggressive. They
need to make things happen, to create their own wealth. A
passive attitude will only cause loss and missed opportunity.
Worrying about financial security will not provide that security. Pisces need to go after what they want tenaciously.

Career and Public Image

Pisces like to be perceived by the public as people of spiritual
or material wealth, of generosity and philanthropy. They
look up to big-hearted, philanthropic types. They admire
people engaged in large-scale undertakings and eventually
would like to head up these big enterprises themselves. In
short, they like to be connected with big organizations that
are doing things in a big way.

If Pisces are to realize their full career and professional
potential they need to travel more, educate themselves more
and learn more about the actual world. In other words, they
need some of the unflagging optimism of the Sagittarius in
order to reach the top.

Because of all their caring and generous characteristics,
Pisces often choose professions through which they can help
and touch the lives of other people. That is why many Pisces
become   doctors,   nurses,   social   workers   or   teachers.
Sometimes it takes a while before Pisces realize what they
really want to do in their professional lives, but once they
find a career that lets them manifest their interests and
virtues they will excel at it.

Love and Relationships

It is not surprising that someone as 'otherworldly' as the
Pisces would like a partner who is practical and down to

earth. Pisces prefer a partner who is on top of all the details of life, because they dislike details. Pisces seek this quality in both their romantic and professional partners. More than anything else this gives Pisces a feeling of being grounded, of being in touch with reality.

As expected, these kinds of relationships – though necessary – are sure to have many ups and downs. Misunderstandings will take place because the two attitudes are poles apart. If you are in love with a Pisces you will experience these fluctuations and will need a lot of patience to see things stabilize. Pisces are moody, intuitive, affectionate and difficult to get to know. Only time and the right attitude will yield Pisces' deepest secrets. However, when in love with a Pisces you will find that riding the waves is worth it because they are good, sensitive people who need and like to give love and affection.

When in love, Pisces like to fantasize. For them fantasy is 90 per cent of the fun of a relationship. They tend to idealize their partner, which can be good and bad at the same time. It is bad in that it is difficult for anyone to live up to the high ideals their Pisces lover sets.

Home and Domestic Life

In their family and domestic life Pisces have to resist the tendency to relate only by feelings and moods. It is unrealistic to expect that your partner and other family members will be as intuitive as you are. There is a need for more verbal communication between a Pisces and his or her family. A cool, unemotional exchange of ideas and opinions will benefit everyone.

Some Pisces tend to like mobility and moving around. For them too much stability feels like a restriction on their freedom. They hate to be locked in one location for ever.

The sign of Gemini sits on Pisces' 4th solar house (of home and family) cusp. This shows that the Pisces likes and needs a home environment that promotes intellectual and mental interests. They tend to treat their neighbours as family – or extended family. Some Pisces can have a dual attitude towards the home and family – on the one hand they like the emotional support of the family, but on the other they dislike the obligations, restrictions and duties involved with it. For Pisces, finding a balance is the key to a happy family life.

Horoscope for 2010

Major Trends

The past 7 or so years have certainly been exciting, Pisces. They have been filled with sudden and dramatic change in many areas of life. Your life has been unstable to say the least. However, life has been exciting. You have been on the fast track. The cosmos has been liberating you to follow your true path in life. Barriers had to come down, and come down they did. Sometimes very dramatically. For many years you have been exploring personal freedom, and this trend is continuing in the year ahead.

Spirituality is always important to you. This is your basic nature. However, in the past 7 to 10 years it has become even more important. And last year even more important. For Jupiter and Neptune, two of the most spiritual planets in the horoscope, were travelling together in your 12th house of spirituality. Most of you were having supernatural experiences. Many of you were actually leading a supernatural life. This trend will ease off a little this year.

The main headline in the year ahead is Jupiter's move into your 1st house. This is a most fortunate transit which brings optimism, personal pleasure, the good life, travel and, in your case, very happy career opportunities. More on this later.

Pluto's move into your 11th house last year began a long-term cycle of purification in your friendships. A cosmic detox started to happen in your friendships. This trend continues even stronger in the year ahead.

Love has been difficult for many of you for the past 2½ years, but the good news is that most of the difficulty is over with. Saturn, which has been causing the problem, will spend most of the year ahead in your 8th house rather than your 7th house. Except for a few months as Saturn retrogrades back into your 7th house, the love situation should be much improved. More on this later.

Your most important interests in the year ahead are spirituality, the body, the image, the personal appearance and personal pleasures, finance (from May 28th to September 10th), health and work (January 1st to June 7th), love, romance and social activities (April 8th to July 22nd), sex, birth and death, reincarnation, occult studies, debt and repayment of debt, taxes and estates (January 1st to April 8th and July 22nd to December 31st), friendships, group activities and organizations, and spirituality.

Your paths of greatest fulfilment in the year ahead will be friendships, group activities and organizations, spirituality (until January 18th), the body, the image, personal appearance and personal pleasure (from January 18th to June 6th and from September 10th to December 31st), and finance (from June 6th to September 10th).

Health

(Please note that this is an astrological perspective on health and not a medical one. In days gone by there was no difference; these perspectives were identical. But nowadays there can be quite a difference. For the medical perspective, please consult your doctor or health practitioner.)

Health is much improved over the past 2½ years, Pisces. If you got through the past 2½ years with your health intact, you've done very well. Health and overall energy began to improve last October as Saturn left Virgo and his stressful aspect to you. This year Saturn will return to Virgo for a few months but will spend most of the year leaving you alone. The good news is that your 6th house of health is strong for the first part of the year. This shows a great focus on health, diet, exercise and healthy lifestyles.

You can make your already good health even better by paying more attention to the following parts of the body:

- heart (all year but especially from April 8th to July 22nd)
- feet
- head, skull, face and adrenal gland (from January 1 to June 7).

Since these are your most vulnerable parts, and because problems, should they happen, would tend to begin there, keeping these parts of the body healthy and fit is sound preventative medicine.

The Sun is your health planet. In the physical body the Sun rules the heart. Hence the importance of the heart in your overall health.

Reflexology

Try to massage the whole foot on a regular basis, but pay extra attention to the points highlighted on the chart. When you massage, be aware of 'sore spots', as these need special attention. It's also a good idea to massage the ankles and top side (as well as the soles) of the feet.

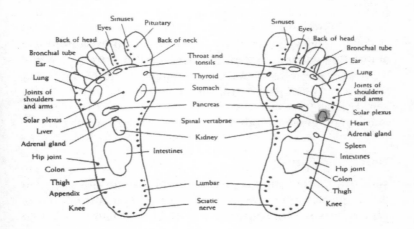

Mars will spend the first 5 months of the year in your 6th house of health. In the physical body Mars rules the head, face, scalp and the musculature. Hence the importance of these parts of the body in your overall health. Physical exercise seems very important for the first part of the year – the muscles need to be kept in tone. In many cases a day at the gym or an extended jog will do more for you than a visit to a health professional. You need to stay more active.

Since the Sun, your health planet, is a relatively fast-moving planet, moving through all the signs and houses of your horoscope in any given year, there are many short-term health trends that we will cover in the monthly reports. These trends will depend on where the Sun is and the kind of aspects it is receiving.

Saturn's return to Virgo (April 8th to July 22nd) is a stressful aspect for you. However, by itself it is not enough to cause serious problems. Nonetheless it will be a good idea to rest and relax more during this period and conserve your energy. The tendency will be to lower-than-usual vitality. Listen to your body, rest when tired, work smarter and not harder, and delegate tasks whenever possible – and you'll get through during this period with flying colours.

Regular foot massage is an excellent therapy for you and you respond beautifully to it. Pisces should always wear sensible shoes, shoes that fit right, and keep your feet warm during the winter.

On a long-term basis health is going to be improving dramatically after July 22nd. Saturn leaves his stressful aspect on you for many years. Also, beginning May 28th Uranus will leave your sign, which will also help you healthwise. This year Uranus flirts with the sign of Aries, but next year he will move in for good – another long-term positive for health.

Home and Family

Your 4th house of home and family is not a House of Power this year, Pisces, thus we would expect a status-quo kind of year. You seem satisfied with the home and family situation as it is, and seem to have no need to make any dramatic changes. I consider this a positive. The status quo tends to equate with satisfaction, contentment and comfort. It's about time, too – the past few years have been fraught with much change and dislocation. A breather is in order.

There will be a lunar eclipse in your 4th house of home and family on December 21st. Those of you born later in the sign will feel it more than those born early in the sign. This eclipse will bring some family shakeups, dramatic experiences with family members, and generally bring up the flaws in the physical home so that you can correct them. But these things don't seem too serious and they soon pass.

A parent or parent figure is having major career changes in the year ahead and these seem sudden and dramatic – this parent or parent figure seems to have had a rough two years and was perhaps suffering from depression. The worst of it is over and they should start feeling better after July 22nd. A move is not advisable for this person. Another parent figure will move in the year ahead, or if not actually move will buy additional properties, renovate the home, buy expensive items or make other kinds of investments in the home. This parent or parent figure could have moved many times in recent years but this move seems to be the final one as his or her wanderlust seems to have played itself out.

Children of appropriate age should not move in the year ahead though they probably want to. Siblings are making major renovations in the home in the year ahead and could even be building a home from scratch. Grandchildren of appropriate age probably moved last year and could still move this year until January 18th.

Family and family interests will be most powerful from April 25th to June 21st this year. This will be a good time for renovations, re-modelling, redecorating or entertaining from home. A good period for strengthening family ties as well.

Mercury, your family planet, is a fast-moving planet – the fastest next to the Moon. So there are many short-term trends in the family situation that will be discussed in the monthly reports.

The marriage of your parents (or people like parents to you) will get severely tested beginning in May. It seems highly unstable. This could apply to their business partnerships as well. Siblings and children of marrying age are having their marriages tested as well – and this will be a long-term process. The marriage will either terminate or become so different – so changed – that it is 'like' a new marriage.

Finance and Career

Finances have not been a major interest for some years now, Pisces. But, this is about to change. On January 18th, Jupiter, the planet of abundance, moves into your own sign. A very fortunate transit financially and in many other ways. It brings a sense of overall optimism and confidence. You can do and achieve anything. Your horizons, personal and financial, are greatly expanded.

As mentioned, this transit brings you the good life. You eat the best foods, drink the best wines, travel to the finest places (and travel in style). It is a year of personal pleasure, of exploring the pleasures of the body. You live a sort of jet-setter life this year.

But there is even more happening. Uranus will move into your money house from May 28th to August 14th. This shows – especially for those of you born early in the sign – major and dramatic financial changes. When Uranus is involved in finances, people change their investments, change their financial planners or advisers, change their brokers and bankers and, more importantly, change their whole financial thinking and strategy. This year you will only feel the first stirrings of this transit. In future years you will feel it more and more. Along with this, on June 6th Jupiter will make a brief visit to your money house, bringing tangible and actual financial prosperity. Jupiter expands your financial horizon. He brings financial opportunity. He shows you wealth that you didn't know you had. Things that you own – physical things, properties, stocks or bonds – start to increase in value.

High-tech items and the latest in financial software and hardware seem to be very important in your financial life. You are, and should be, applying the latest scientific high-tech techniques to financial management. Also it's very important for you to stay up to date on the latest technological advancements in your field. Your technological expertise seems to be a major factor in your earnings.

I like high-tech industries from an investment perspective as well.

Jupiter's move into your sign is showing much more than just prosperity. Jupiter is your career planet. He is your planet of success, fame and recognition. Thus happy career opportunities are seeking you out in the year ahead. Not much you need to do – you just have to be you and go about your daily business. People of power and position, elders, parent figures, all seem very devoted to you and your welfare in the year ahead. And this is a great plus. You are the image of success in the year ahead. You dress that way and create this kind of image.

Whatever your age or stage in life, you have more fame and renown this year.

Keep in mind that Uranus is also your spiritual planet. Jupiter is the planet of religion and metaphysics. So the transit of these two planets into your money house is showing the importance of intuition, prayer and the deeper understanding of spiritual wealth. As we have mentioned you are very spiritual by nature; now you need to apply this to your financial affairs. And you will. You seem very personality exalted and elevated in the year ahead. Your career achievements are recognized and honoured. Your success is not behind the scenes but out front for all to see.

Your financial planet, Mars, spends an unusual amount of time in your 6th house of health this year. This also gives us many messages. Although Dame Fortune is solidly behind you, you will be earning your money mostly from your work. Your work will create your luck. Your financial planet in the 6th house also shows earnings from the health field. You spend more on health but you also earn from this field.

Mars is a relatively fast-moving planet and will be in many signs and houses of your horoscope during the year. Thus there are many short-term trends in finance that will depend on where Mars is and the kind of aspects he receives at any given time. We will discuss these in the monthly reports.

Mars in Leo for 5 months shows that you are more speculative in the year ahead. And it seems that you are successful. Of course, never speculate blindly, but only under intuition. Your financial planet in Leo until June 7th also shows 'happy' money – money earned in joyful and creative ways. You will be spending more on leisure activities but also earning from these kinds of things. Perhaps you go to the theatre and meet an important client. Or you go to a party and someone gives you an important financial tip which turns out to be profitable. You are very concerned, especially until June 7th, with enjoying the act of money-making.

Love and Social Life

Your love life has been difficult for some years, Pisces. Saturn has been in your 7th house for over two years and will spend a few more months in your 7th house in the year ahead. This has severely tested your marriage, your current love relationships, business partnerships and even friendships. Many of you have divorced in recent years. Many of you have considered divorce even though you have not actually gone through with it. If your current relationship has survived the past two years it will probably survive the year ahead. For Saturn will spend most of the time in your 8th house. By July 22nd, as Saturn leaves your 7th house for good, you have got through the worst.

Those of you working on your first marriage, or still single, are not likely to marry this year but your social life should be easier. Probably you will date more and attend more parties. Those of you in or working on a second marriage will have tests in that marriage, too. Good relationships will of course survive and get even better. Inherently flawed relationships will probably not survive. Those of you working on or in your third marriage are having a status-quo kind of year. Those working towards their fourth marriage have very wonderful opportunities. You may or may not marry, but you will enjoy a significant relationship.

By now (after 2 years of Saturn in your 7th house) you have learned to value quality over quantity. One or two quality relationships are worth more than hordes of luke-warm or false ones. These latter only sap your attention and energy. They tend to bring unpleasant karmic consequences as well. Your love and social life are now 'streamlined' – the wheat has been separated from the chaff.

For those whose marriages have survived, there is more self-knowledge. More understanding of the strength of your mutual commitment. Many issues between you and your beloved have been resolved. We rarely know if love is real (and not just mere convenience) during the good times. It is in the tough times that we learn this distinction.

Since your love planet, Mercury, is such a fast-moving planet (only the Moon moves faster than Mercury), there are many short-term trends in your love life. Love and social opportunities tend to come to you in many ways and through many kinds of people. This depends on where Mercury is and the kind of aspects that he receives. These short-term trends are dealt with in the monthly reports.

We should mention that your love planet will be retro-grade four times this year. Usually he only retrogrades three times in a given year. So there is more retrograde activity happening in your love life. The good part of this is that you get more opportunity to review and improve your love and social life. The uncomfortable part of this is that relation-ships will seem to be going backwards rather than forwards more times in the year ahead. There will tend to be more glitches in your love and social life than usual. But, after 2 years of a Saturn transit in your 7th house, this should not be too much of a problem.

Self-improvement

Your spiritual planet, Uranus, which has been in your own sign for many years, makes a huge move from Pisces into Aries from May 28th to August 14th. The full transit will really happen next year, but right now you are getting a foretaste of things to come. This move shows that there are big changes happening in your spirituality. Until now perhaps you have been growing in your rational, scientific and emotional spiritual development. It was enough for you to read the spiritual books or sit in meditation and experience the higher energies in your heart. But as your spiritual planet changes signs, these activities will not be enough. It is as if the divine is saying to you, enough of nirvana, of exploring higher spiritual states, now it is time to apply what you know in the world and in action. Your physical body needs to be involved in your spirituality. Your spiritual understanding will express itself in action. Perhaps it will be involvement in altruistic activities or charities, or things of that nature. Your spirituality must be of some benefit to the world around you. Probably you will be doing less meditation and more altruistic service. The path of karma yoga seems very interesting this year and for many years in the future. There are many fine books on karma yoga and you should read as much as you can about it. Karma yoga is about disinterested action. Egoless action, where the ego is sort of set aside and only the divine is the doer. This is easier said than done. When the divine is the doer, there is no thought of results or consequences. There is no fear of failure nor desire for success. For every action will be naturally and normally successful.

I also like hatha yoga, eurhythmics and tai chi during this period (and in future years). In meditation, one sort of leaves the body behind. But now you are called on to 'bring the body' with you in your exploration of higher states – to refine the body and spiritualize it.

As mentioned earlier, you will be applying your spiritual understanding to your financial life. You are always charitable and generous, and in future years probably even more so.

You are always in tune with your intuition, but now it will be trained in financial matters. It is as if you are throwing out every rulebook of finance and just following the intuition of the moment. Financial strategies that have never worked for you may now, in a given instance, work. Financial strategies that have always worked for you in the past may now not work. It is the intuition of the moment that will matter.

As mentioned, Saturn will still spend a few more months in your 7th house of love, marriage and social activities. There have been many disappointments in love. These were not punitive. Only educational. The main spiritual lesson of this transit is to learn the art of forgiveness. But not just forgiveness with your mouth, more organic forgiveness, where there is no trace of hard feelings or negativity left in the body. This kind of deep forgiveness comes only through understanding. When we understand the other's perspective and all the pressures and causes that produced their disappointing actions, forgiveness becomes very easy. For, given the same circumstances we might have acted the same way.

Saturn will spend most of the year in your 8th house. This suggests a re-ordering of your sex life and sex attitudes. This does not mean that you will stop having sex. Only that you will focus more on quality and less on quantity. Fewer sexual experiences but of higher quality are to be preferred over many sexual experiences of inferior quality. This is something that is probably hard for many of you to understand, but it is true. And you will no doubt learn this in the next 2 years.

Month-by-month Forecasts

January

Best Days Overall: 1, 3, 4, 18, 19, 28
Most Stressful Days Overall: 4, 5, 11, 12, 25, 26
Best Days for Love: 4, 5, 13, 14, 15, 23, 24, 25, 26
Best Days for Money: 2, 3, 6, 7, 11, 12, 16, 17, 18, 21, 22, 27
Best Days for Career: 6, 7, 10, 11, 12, 16, 17, 18, 27

You begin your year with most of the planets above the horizon – in the 'day' side of your chart. Thus career and 'outer' success are very important. Home, family and psychological issues can be downplayed. Though your yearly career peak will happen many months from now, you are still in a very powerful career period. Jupiter, your career planet, crosses your Ascendant and moves into Pisces on the 18th. Happy career opportunities are seeking you out. Nothing you need to do. These are coming – you either accept or reject them. The offers seem plentiful.

Jupiter's move into your sign initiates a cycle of prosperity that will be strong for the next 2 years. You are living the high life – the good life. You are in the fast lane. Even those of you who don't have a lot of money will be living 'as if' you have. Above your income level.

Most of the planets are in the independent Eastern sector as the year begins. Thus you have the power (and the support) to create conditions as you desire them to be. If present conditions don't suit you then either change them or create new ones. Your happiness is not up to others, but up to you.

Health is good this month, but with Jupiter moving through your 1st house you will have to watch your weight. Female Pisceans are more fertile these days. You can enhance your already good health by paying more attention to your heart (all month), your spine, knees, teeth, bones, gallbladder and skeletal alignment (until the 20th), and your ankles and calves (after the 20th). Regular back massage is powerful until the 20th. Calf and ankle massage is powerful afterwards. Foot massage is always good for you.

Your 11th house is powerful until the 20th. You are in a strong social period – but more with friends, groups and organizations. There is much socializing online and through social networks as well. The online world and social networking sites are good for romance as well – singles should explore these. Your love planet is retrograde until the 15th; this means your love life is under review. After the 15th your social judgement should be much improved. Friends like to play Cupid, and in some cases friends want to be more than that to you. You seem more conservative in love this month. Perhaps you experiment, but within traditional bounds.

A solar eclipse on the 15th is basically benign to you and seems to affect your friends more than you. Friends have dramatic types of experiences. Friendships can be tested as well. Since the eclipsed planet, the Sun, is your work planet, this eclipse is announcing job changes and perhaps changes in the conditions of the workplace – the rules, etc. A parent or parent figure is forced to make dramatic – and long-term – financial changes.

You are still very much under the effects of the last lunar eclipse of December 31, 2007. This tested love affairs and brought dramatic events in the lives of children (or children figures).

February

Best Days Overall: 5, 6, 15, 16, 24, 25
Most Stressful Days Overall: 1, 7, 8, 22, 23, 28
Best Days for Love: 1, 2, 3, 11, 12, 14, 15, 22, 23, 24, 25, 28
Best Days for Money: 4, 5, 7, 14, 15, 17, 18, 24, 26
Best Days for Career: 4, 5, 7, 8, 14, 15, 24

Finances will be outstanding in the year ahead. But now, and last month, we see some complications. First off, your financial planet is retrograde (and was retrograde last month as well). Second, Mars is the 'handle' of a 'bucket type' chart – most of this month (and last month as well). Thus finance is extremely important these days. It is the 'handle' with which you will lift up your entire life. Yet, you seem to lack direction here. There is much uncertainty as to where you should go and what moves need to be made. Your financial life is basically under review now. The good news is that you *will* do this review – and often this interior process is as important as the external moves you make – it lays the groundwork for these things. You *will* work out the numbers – play out the different financial scenarios – calculate what move produces what result, etc.

The other good news here is that these financial conundrums are the actual doorways of financial success. The problem contains the solution within itself. As you go within and see where improvements can be made in your product, service or earnings – the solutions will start to come. The cosmos, in its own mysterious way, is opening the doors of abundance through this uncertainty.

Last month on the 20th you entered one of the most spiritual periods of your year. This continues until the 18th of this month. Thus, you hardly touch the ground these days. You live in another world – the world of the supernatural. You love it. You smile tolerantly when more materialist types of people ask you to 'come down to earth' or say that you live in 'cloud cuckoo land' – perhaps, but you wouldn't trade this for all the diamonds in Africa. You will have many spiritual breakthroughs and meet people (socially and romantically) who share your perspective on life – spiritual-type people.

The interest in spirituality will continue even after the Sun moves into your 1st house on the 18th. For the Sun in Pisces is naturally spiritual and other-worldly. But now you will be using spiritual methods and techniques to reinvent your personality and transform your body. You will also see that the spirit takes very good care of the body. Spirituality is not a denial of physical pleasure.

This is an excellent month – from the 15th onwards – for job-seekers. If there was a job change due to last month's eclipses, you will see why they happened. Dream job opportunities are coming – and there is also elevation and promotion involved. The 13th to the 16th and the 27th and 28th seem especially good for jobs. (Also for your career in general.)

Health is good, but you can enhance it further by paying more attention to your heart and feet (all month) and to your ankles and calves until the 18th.

Love is improved over last month. There are love opportunities online, or with groups and organizations – all month – and in spiritual settings after the 10th. If you are going to the bars and clubs looking for love, you're just wasting time.

March

Best Days Overall: 1, 3, 4, 18, 19, 28
Most Stressful Days Overall: 1, 6, 7, 21, 22, 27, 28
Best Days for Love: 1, 4, 5, 6, 14, 15, 16, 17, 25, 26, 27, 28
Best Days for Money: 4, 5, 6, 14, 15, 16, 17, 23, 24, 25, 31
Best Days for Career: 4, 5, 6, 7, 14, 15, 23, 24, 31

A happy month ahead. You are still in the midst of a yearly personal pleasure period, exploring and fulfilling all the sensual fantasies of the body – living the good life – the high life – the jet-set kind of life (each according to their status and position in life). You look great of late, too. Venus was in your sign last month and will be there until the 7th of this month – this brings beauty, grace and glamour to your image. A sense of style. You know just how to dress and accessorize. The Sun in your sign gives energy and 'star power' to your image. There is more self-confidence and self-esteem. Jupiter in your sign not only brings the good life, as mentioned, but career opportunity and an 'image of success'. The world sees you as a successful person.

Others are certainly taking notice and it is easy to understand why they are pursuing you these days – especially until the 17th. There are very happy romantic meetings for singles from the 7th to the 9th – perhaps with people involved in your career, or as you pursue your career goals.

Health is good as well. When the Sun entered your sign last month (on the 18th) good health was much more than just 'no symptoms' – it meant looking good as well. This 'vanity factor' makes you more focused on health issues – if only for cosmetic reasons. When you are healthy you look good. When you are under the weather, your appearance suffers. You can enhance health further by paying attention to your heart and feet (foot massage) all month, and to your head, face and skull from the 20th onwards. Head and face massage is powerful after the 20th.

When personal appearance and health are so connected, if you feel under the weather you should buy a new outfit or have your hair or nails done. Do something that improves your image and you will actually start to feel physically better.

There are many happy financial developments going on as well. Your financial planet, Mars, has been retrograde since the beginning of the year. This month on the 10th it starts to move forward. There is more forward momentum, more forward progress in your financial life now. You are more clear as to what you want to do and where you want to go. On the 20th (and the timing here is perfect) the Sun enters your money house (and makes fabulous aspects to your financial planet as well) and initiates a yearly financial peak. Job-seekers were successful last month and the month ahead also looks good. Friends, family, your spouse or partners are all financially supportive. But earnings seem to mostly come the old-fashioned way – through work.

The New Moon of the 15th is most interesting. Yes, it will clarify issues involving the body and the image, but it also brings sudden – lightning-like – creative inspiration and revelation. It's as if you have been in a dark room and suddenly someone turns on the lights – now you see reality.

April

Best Days Overall: 1, 10, 11, 19, 20, 28, 29
Most Stressful Days Overall: 3, 4, 17, 18, 24, 25, 30
Best Days for Love: 5, 15, 16, 24, 25
Best Days for Money: 1, 3, 10, 11, 13, 14, 19, 20, 22, 28, 29, 30
Best Days for Career: 1, 3, 4, 10, 11, 19, 20, 28, 29, 30

You experienced some brief flashes of inspiration last month, and this month you will receive even more (next month even more than this month). These things are important in that they are enough to change your whole life – your whole direction in life. In some cases these flashes will bring a book, an article, a painting or piece of music – in other cases it will reveal a new or different direction in life. Reality

– your circumstances – are not what you thought or believed – and thus you will adjust your actions to the new truth that has been revealed.

You are still in the midst of a yearly financial peak until the 20th. A very prosperous period – you are focused on finance – it is important to you and thus you are willing to overcome the natural challenges that arise in these matters. This focus – this drive – is 90 per cent of success. Money comes, but you are earning it. Job-seekers still seem successful. (There is a happy job opportunity in a foreign land, foreign company or involved with travel on the 25th and 26th.) There is luck in speculation until the 20th (last month was also good for this) but the bulk of your earnings are from your work. Probably you will have opportunities for second jobs, side jobs or overtime. Investors should look at the health field for profit opportunities. Gaming, entertainment, sport, electric utilities and energy also seem like interesting industries to explore.

Health is basically good, but Saturn retrogrades back into Virgo on the 3rd and makes a stressful aspect to you. By itself Saturn is not enough to cause any major illness, but you might feel low in energy. You need to rest and relax more, pace yourself and work smarter, not harder. Organize your day so that more gets done with less energy.

Saturn's move back into your 7th house once again tests a current relationship – and in fact will test your social circle in general. Your love planet, Mercury, goes retrograde on the 18th. Your love life is under review. Singles will date and have fun, but go slow in love – let it develop as it will – don't make major decisions one way or the other. This testing of love will be brief – it will only last a few months. Use this period – from the 18th onwards – to see where improvements in love can be made. Clarify your needs for yourself. Clarify for yourself what you want.

Singles find love opportunities in the neighbourhood, with neighbours or in educational settings – at lectures and seminars and the like. No need to travel far and wide for love.

Until the 7th, 90 per cent of the planets are moving forward. The Sun will be in Aries – the best 'starting energy' in the zodiac. Try to launch those new projects before the 7th.

May

Best Days Overall: 7, 8, 9, 17, 18, 25, 26
Most Stressful Days Overall: 1, 15, 21, 22, 27, 28
Best Days for Love: 2, 5, 6, 12, 15, 16, 21, 22, 25, 26, 30
Best Days for Money: 1, 8, 9, 10, 11, 18, 19, 20, 25, 26, 27, 28
Best Days for Career: 1, 8, 9, 18, 25, 26, 27, 28

Most of the planets are still below the horizon – you are in the 'midnight' of your year – and so your focus should be on the family and your emotional life – getting into your emotional comfort zone. Having said this, there are amazing career developments happening this month – so keeping your focus on the family might not be so easy. These career demands will be difficult to deny. Handle them as best you can, but keep as much focus on the family as possible. These are dream opportunities that happen suddenly, out of the blue. But if they disturb your emotional harmony or family situation, you might have to either negotiate better terms or pass.

Jupiter, your career planet, travels with Uranus this month – the conjunction is exact. This shows dramatic career changes. You reach the stratosphere. In many cases you will be more of a 'star' these days – involved with radio, TV, the electronic media and the like. But the online world could be calling to you as well.

These career changes are naturally bringing financial change – experimentation. For Uranus makes a rare move – a foray – into your money house on the 28th. It also comes into more harmonious aspects with Mars, your financial planet. So your career and financial life are getting shaken up – but in a very good way. You are being liberated to follow your true spiritual mission in life – your true work. There is a financial liberation happening as well. (Those of you born early in the sign of Pisces will feel it now, but all of you will feel this in coming years – you will know what it means to be 'financially free'.)

Last month, on the 3rd, Saturn moved into a stressful aspect with you. Now on the 21st the Sun joins him. So health needs more watching – especially after the 21st. Pay more attention to your heart (reduce stress, refuse to worry or fret), your head, face and skull (regular scalp and face massage is wonderful – exercise more), to your neck, throat and lower jaw (until the 21st) and to your lungs, arms and shoulders (from the 21st onwards). The main thing, as our steady readers know, is to maintain high energy levels. Never allow yourself to get overtired – for that is when you become vulnerable.

Love is still under review and still being tested. Your love planet starts moving forward on the 11th, bringing more clarity and confidence to your love life. But you need still to take things slow and steady in love. No need to rush into anything. Love is still in the neighbourhood or in educational settings this month. Good communication and mental compatibility are always important in love, but this month even more so.

June

Best Days Overall: 4, 5, 13, 14, 21, 22
Most Stressful Days Overall: 11, 12, 17, 18, 24, 25
Best Days for Love: 4, 5, 10, 11, 13, 14, 17, 18, 19, 20, 24, 25
Best Days for Money: 5, 6, 7, 8, 15, 17, 24, 26, 27
Best Days for Career: 5, 6, 15, 23, 24, 25

Last month's Jupiter–Uranus conjunction (still in effect now) brought more than just career change. It brought spiritual revelation. Many of you met your spiritual teachers last month – your guru – and it could happen this month as well. This conjunction revealed your 'spiritual career' – your spiritual mission – pretty specifically. It was more than just about your 'worldly affairs'. No question that the cosmos is calling you to great things – things that seem 'beyond you'. But these revelations also reveal that the cosmos believes more in you than perhaps you believe in yourself.

For a Pisces there is no more joyous thing in the universe than the knowledge that they are on their path and fulfilling their mission.

These things are going on this month as well.

Uranus' move into your money house has other meanings, too. Uranus is your spiritual planet. Thus intuition – inner guidance – is important in your financial life. But more than that, you must be intuitive and willing to *act* – take quick and immediate action on these intuitions. He who hesitates is lost. You are starting to approach finances in a whole new way – all the rule books are no longer valid. You have the aspects for 'quick and sudden' wealth. Only keep in mind that this kind of wealth tends to be unstable. You need to take steps to guard it.

On the 6th, Jupiter, the planet of luck and abundance, enters your money house – so there is great prosperity now. You are working hard (your financial planet moves into Virgo on the 7th) but there is luck in speculations, too. A business partnership or joint venture could be forming after the 7th. Bosses, elders, parents or parent figures – even the government – seem supportive of your financial goals. If you have issues with the government this is a good year – and a good month – to deal with them. (These issues have been favourable since the beginning of the year – the government is on your side and very supportive.)

A lunar eclipse on the 26th is basically benign to you, but children, children figures in your life and friends might be advised to take a reduced schedule. The eclipse seems stronger on them than on you. This eclipse brings dramas in the lives of children and friends – and will test friendships as well. Good friendships will survive – but there is a lot of dirty laundry that needs to be dealt with. Be more patient with children and friends during this period – they are apt to be more temperamental.

Health still needs watching until the 21st. After that you will see great improvement. Enhance health by paying more attention to your heart (all month), your head, face and skull (until the 7th), your kidneys and hips (after the 14th), your lungs, arms and shoulders (until the 21st), and your stomach and breasts (after the 21st). Intense physical exercise is less important after the 7th than it has been all year. You can de-emphasize this now.

July

> Best Days Overall: 1, 2, 10, 11, 19, 20, 28, 29, 30
> Most Stressful Days Overall: 8, 9, 15, 21, 22
> Best Days for Love: 1, 2, 5, 12, 14, 15, 21, 22, 23, 24
> Best Days for Money: 3, 4, 5, 6, 7, 12, 15, 16, 21, 24, 25, 31
> Best Days for Career: 3, 12, 21, 22, 31

Last month on the 21st you entered another one of your yearly personal pleasure peaks – you are into a party period, a period of leisure, a period to explore the things that give happiness. Your 1st personal pleasure period – from February 18th to March 20th – was mostly about physical and sensual pleasure. This one is a bit broader – it includes the aesthetic pleasures of life as well as the bodily pleasures.

Joy is not only good in itself, but in your chart this period you will see its bottom-line, practical health benefits. Just being happy will cure many a so-called physical malaise. And even if the sickness is so dire that it is incurable (though often this is misdiagnosed), joy will help you handle it better. In many cases these days, a night out on the town will do more good than a visit to a health professional. Personal creativity will also improve your health. This is one of the great joys of life which, unfortunately, few ever experience. There is something euphoric and rapturous when one is caught up in a creative flow. A good period to take up a creative hobby – or spend more time with one of your hobbies – it is fun and therapeutic.

Health is vastly improved this month. Not just on a temporary level, but on a long-term basis. On the 21st Saturn moves away from his stressful aspect to you. It is like a huge weight being lifted off your shoulders. On the 30th Mars will move away from his recent (though short-term) stressful aspect too. You will have short-term periods in the year ahead where your energy is not up to par, but your overall health is good – these are short-term trends and not trends for the year ahead.

A solar eclipse on the 11th is basically benign to you. It affects children, uncles and aunts more than you. They are advised to take a reduced schedule. Since the eclipsed planet, the Sun, is your work planet, this eclipse is showing job changes (but no need to worry – job-seekers are having great success – if a present job ends there are better ones coming into the picture). There are dramatic experiences in the lives of children, uncles and aunts (or people who play these roles in your life). Children are making (or experiencing – depending on their age and stage of life) important financial changes – dramatic ones. Aunts and uncles are redefining their image and personality and can experience detoxes in the body. Those of you in the entertainment business or the creative arts make important changes to your creativity.

On the 23rd you enter a serious, work-orientated period – and as mentioned this is good for job-seekers (also for people who employ others).

Love is getting easier. Saturn in your 7th house was testing a current relationship. Mars, too, was there. This could have produced power struggles in your relationship. Now both these planets (by the end of the month) will be out of the 7th house and presumably these tests are over with. Singles find love in the usual places until the 9th and after the 27th – at parties, places of entertainment, sports activities and the like. Family connections also play a role in love. Until the 9th love is about a good time – not serious. After the 9th love is about service to your beloved. Love opportunities happen at work or as you pursue your health goals. After the 27th, love is more romantic.

August

Best Days Overall: 7, 8, 15, 16, 25, 26
Most Stressful Days Overall: 5, 6, 11, 12, 17, 18
Best Days for Love: 2, 3, 4, 11, 12, 13, 20, 21, 22, 23, 30, 31
Best Days for Money: 1, 4, 5, 9, 13, 17, 22, 23, 27, 28
Best Days for Career: 9, 17, 18, 27

On June 21st the planetary power shifted from the independent East to the social West. Personal independence has been greatly reduced – and perhaps is not that necessary. You entered a period where you needed to develop your social skills, your ability to gain the co-operation of others. Personal independence, professional competence or personal initiative is not the path to success these days – it is the good graces of others that are important now. This period continues this month – and even gets stronger. On the 23rd you enter a yearly social peak. Your love life takes dominance.

In a way it is good that love is so important these days – for there are some challenges and complications here – and only your strong interest and your social drive will enable you to overcome these things.

The two love planets in your horoscope are in the sign of Virgo (not the best places for them). Venus entered Virgo on the 10th of last month. Mercury, your actual love planet, entered Virgo on the 27th of last month. Thus you are looking for perfection in love. Nothing wrong with that, but you will have to work harder to show your natural warmth and love to others. Your passion for perfection – your tendency to over-analyse and to come from the head rather than the heart – can create coldness and distance between you and your beloved. Also, with these aspects there is a tendency to attract these kinds of people as partners.

The other complication is Mercury's retrograde on the 20th. This, as we have mentioned, puts your love life under review. Actions in love should be more internal – for singles, it might be better to plan your future love life (by gaining clarity on what you want and how to go about getting it) than to actually engage in love relationships haphazardly and out of boredom, or because it is the 'thing to do'. Marrieds can do internal work to see where things can be improved.

Finances are still great this month, but the pace is a bit slower. Overall 40 per cent of the planets are retrograde – and after the 20th, 50 per cent of them will be retrograde. Two out of the three planets involved in your finances are retrograde as well. Earnings are still strong and there are many, many positive things happening – but there needs to be some development time. A business partnership or joint venture still seems in the works. Whatever the love problems might be, your spouse, partner or current love seems supportive – though he or she needs to start managing money better. Spare cash is probably better off used to pay off debt rather than to make new investments. Make sure to set aside money for taxes. Those of you of appropriate age should focus more on estate planning now.

Job-seekers still have good success all month, but especially until the 23rd.

Health needs watching after the 23rd, but as mentioned this is a short-term issue. Just rest and relax more and don't panic over every little ache or pain or symptom. There is probably nothing seriously wrong – just low energy.

September

Best Days Overall: 3, 4, 11, 12, 21, 22
Most Stressful Days Overall: 1, 2, 7, 8, 13, 14, 15, 28, 29
Best Days for Love: 2, 7, 8, 11, 16, 21, 27
Best Days for Money: 2, 5, 10, 11, 12, 20, 21, 22, 23, 24, 25
Best Days for Career: 5, 11, 12, 22

The lunar eclipse of June 26th was testing friendships, and this process seems to be intensified in the month ahead. Saturn, your planet of friends, is camping out on an eclipse point (that same eclipse of June 26th) all month. It actually started to re-stimulate this point on the 26th of last month. So friends are having dramatic and perhaps shocking kinds of experiences. Many are redefining their images and personalities – and usually this is not a voluntary process – they are forced into it by slander or malicious gossip. So some of the problems in your relationships are not about you, but about what is going on in their lives. Only in certain cases is it about you. Good friendships will survive.

Uranus retrograded out of your money house on the 15th of last month. Jupiter follows suit on the 10th. You are still in a prosperous year but the pace of finance is slowed down – there is a breather happening – probably a good thing. No one can take so much intensity – even of a positive nature – for too long.

Last month the planetary power shifted from the night side (the lower half) of your horoscope to the day side (the upper half). So career is becoming ever more important. However, Jupiter, your career planet, has been retrograde since July 23rd, so many happy career developments need time to manifest. Give new offers more study – and rest assured there are many offers coming to you. But they might not be all that they claim to be. Put your career under review now.

This is another month of intense spiritual revelation, as Jupiter and Uranus are once again in exact conjunction. (They have been in conjunction from a practical perspective since May – but now the conjunction is very exact.) The doors of heaven are opening up to you and revealing new secrets. Your spiritual mission is being further clarified. However, as mentioned, give more time for these revelations to digest – and it would be good to get verification from other sources.

Your normal life tends to be supernatural, Pisces. This is just your nature. But this month it is even more so than usual. There are more dreams, visions, prophecies, involvement with gurus and invisible beings than usual.

Health still needs watching until the 23rd. Pay more attention to your heart, lungs, small intestine, arms and shoulders all month, and to your kidneys and hips after the 23rd.

Love is getting more clear after the 12th as Mercury moves forward. But still make more effort to show your natural love and warmth to others. Be more careful of destructive criticism. Love challenges don't seem to affect your sex life – it's a sexually active time all month, but especially after the 23rd.

October

Best Days Overall: 1, 2, 9, 10, 18, 19, 28, 29
Most Stressful Days Overall: 5, 6, 11, 12, 25, 26, 27
Best Days for Love: 1, 5, 6, 7, 9, 17, 18, 19, 28
Best Days for Money: 1, 2, 9, 10, 19, 20, 21, 22, 29, 30
Best Days for Career: 2, 10, 11, 12, 19, 29

Saturn has left its stressful aspect with you and this month there's a lot of water in your horoscope. Sometimes as much as 70 per cent of the planets will be in water signs. Some people are uncomfortable with this – it creates much emotionalism and excess sensitivity – but fishes love water – it is their native element. So health is good and you shine. You have abundant energy to achieve your goals.

Your 8th house became strong on the 23rd of last month and is strong until the 22nd of October. Thus your interest is in 8th house matters – occult studies, life after death, reincarnation, personal transformation and reinvention, ascension and resurrection. The only problem with this is that the ruler of the 8th house, Venus, makes one of her rare retrogrades on the 8th. This doesn't stop your interest, but counsels a more interior approach to these things – planning these kinds of activities, doing homework, studying them is better than actually doing them right now.

Those on the path often have dreams of past life events or memories of them – some are made aware of them through past life regressions and things of that nature. All well and good, but withhold judgement on what you learn. Take more time to digest this knowledge. And it might be a good idea to get verification of what you learn.

The 8th house gives an ability to pay off or incur debt – to profit from outside money. So these things should be done before the 8th – and afterwards be more cautious about them or plan future activities.

Many of you will be involved in estates and tax issues – there can be delays and changes of the mind in these activities – a lot of forward-backward motion. If you must indulge in these things, make sure all the details are perfect.

In your horoscope the retrograde of Venus also behaves a lot like a Mercury retrograde. So be more careful in your communications. Avoid signing contracts or making major purchases. Avoid mass-mailings or major advertising campaigns. Hold off until Venus starts moving forward on the 18th of next month.

Your 9th house becomes strong after the 23rd. A happy time. Foreign lands call to you and you will probably answer the call. A good month to further your higher education and your philosophical knowledge. This is a month for religious and spiritual breakthroughs for those who want them.

Health is good and can be made even better in the ways mentioned in the yearly report. But this month also pay attention to your kidneys and hips (until the 23rd) and to your colon, bladder and sexual organs from the 23rd onwards.

November

Best Days Overall: 5, 6, 14, 15, 16, 24, 25
Most Stressful Days Overall: 1, 2, 7, 8, 22, 23, 28, 29
Best Days for Love: 1, 2, 5, 6, 13, 17, 23, 27, 28, 29
Best Days for Money: 6, 7, 15, 16, 17, 18, 25, 27
Best Days for Career: 6, 7, 8, 15, 16, 25

On the 28th of last month Mars, your financial planet, crossed the Midheaven and entered your 10th house. Mars will be in your 10th house all of this month. Money is high on your agenda now. This can create some 'sticking points' in your career as you and superiors might not agree on financial terms – but give these things time – a compromise will be found. Basically, elders, bosses, parents and parent figures are supportive financially and want your prosperity – the problem seems to be in how far they want to go to help.

Career is very strong and successful this month – more so than all year. Jupiter, your career planet, starts to move forward on the 18th – and this more or less coincides with your yearly career peak, which begins on the 22nd. You are succeeding the old-fashioned way – through sheer hard work. You just outwork your competitors. Your work ethic is noticed by the powers that be. Even family seems supportive of your career goals during this period, so you need not overly focus on the family now. They seem to understand. The family as a whole is raised in status. Family members are elevated, too.

All this extra work is a stress on your health. Keep in mind that overall health is good. But temporarily you may need to rest and relax more – especially after the 22nd. As always try to maintain high energy levels. Don't let yourself get overtired. Focus only on the essentials in your life and let the lesser things go. Pay more attention to your heart (all month), colon, bladder and sexual organs (until the 22nd) and your liver and thighs after the 22nd. Safe sex and sexual moderation are important until the 22nd. Detox regimes go well. After the 22nd regular thigh massage is good.

Love seems happier these days. We don't see a marriage here, but happy love and social experiences. Until the 9th, the sexual chemistry is the allurement. But philosophical compatibility is also very important. Singles are allured to foreigners and highly educated people. Mentor types – professors and ministers – are attractive. You like people you can learn from. After the 9th it is power and position that allures you. And you seem to be meeting them. These people are helping your career. You are succeeding through hard work, but social contacts – or your spouse or partner – are also a big factor. Career success is a combination of whom you know (they open the doors) and your hard work – your performance. Singles find love opportunities as they pursue their normal career goals or with people involved in their career.

December

Best Days Overall: 3, 4, 12, 13, 21, 22, 30, 31
Most Stressful Days Overall: 5, 6, 19, 20, 26, 27
Best Days for Love: 2, 7, 12, 16, 22, 25, 26, 27, 31
Best Days for Money: 4, 6, 13, 14, 15, 16, 17, 23, 26, 31
Best Days for Career: 4, 5, 6, 13, 23, 31

Last month, on the 22nd, the planetary power shifted from the social West to the independent East. It is not fully there yet – but day by day, month by month, you are becoming ever more independent and more able to create circumstances and conditions that suit you. The period of compromise and consensus is over with. No need to adapt too much to others or to conditions. You can have life on your terms. Your personal abilities – who you are and what you can do – are more important than whom you know or your personal popularity. This doesn't mean that you are rude or disrespectful to others – only that you rely on yourself.

As the Sun enters Capricorn at the time of the winter solstice, the Sun – the most important planet in the solar system – is said to be having its 'birthday'. (This is the inner meaning of Christmas – the birth of the 'Sun of God'.) From that point onwards the days will start (here in the northern hemisphere) getting longer and longer. The Sun could be said to be in its 'waxing' phase. Thus this period has excellent 'starting energy'. Couple this with the fact that 90 per cent of the planets will be moving forward then (only Mercury, your love and family planet, will be retrograde) – and the starting energy is even stronger. So this is a time to launch those new projects into the world.

A lunar eclipse on the 21st is strong on you – especially if you are born later in the sign of Pisces (March 14th to 20th). If you are one of these, take a reduced schedule during this period. This eclipse occurs right on the border (the cusp) of the 4th and 5th houses and will have an impact on the affairs of both these houses. This eclipse brings dramatic experiences in the lives of children and family members – perhaps in the life of a parent or parent figure. Sometimes there are repairs in the home. Family members are more volatile and temperamental during this period, so be more patient. Your dream life will be more active but shouldn't be taken too seriously. Those of you in the creative arts will make important changes in your creativity. Speculations should be avoided during this period.

Health still needs watching until the 21st. After that you will see great improvement. Enhance your health in the ways mentioned in the yearly report, but also pay more attention to your liver and thighs (until the 21st) and your spine, knees, teeth, bones, gallbladder and overall skeletal alignment (after the 21st).

There is travel related to your job after the 21st. Looks like foreign travel. Job-seekers have opportunities in foreign lands. Prosperity is good. This month (after the 8th) it seems to come through friends and through your involvement in organizations. Probably you will invest in high-tech equipment. You need to stay up to date. Prosperity is only going to get stronger next year.

Love is under review from the 10th to the 30th. Don't despise these occasional reviews – they are just as important, in their own way, as overt social action. They are the pause that refreshes. If a relationship is troubled, getting stale or not the way you want it, a pause, a holiday can rekindle the relationship. Oftentimes we don't appreciate what we have until there is some separation.